ACROSS THE SABBATH RIVER

Also by Hillel Halkin

Letters to an American Jewish Friend

Across the Sabbath River

IN SEARCH OF A
LOST TRIBE OF ISRAEL

Hillel Halkin

Houghton Mifflin Company

BOSTON   NEW YORK

2002

For information about permission to reproduce selections from
this book, write to Permissions, Houghton Mifflin Company,
215 Park Avenue South, New York, New York 10003.

Visit our Web site: www.houghtonmifflinbooks.com.

Library of Congress Cataloging-in-Publication Data is available.
ISBN 0-618-02998-2

Printed in the United States of America

Book design by Victoria Hartman

QUM 10 9 8 7 6 5 4 3 2 1

The author is grateful to Yosi Hualngo, Dr. Khuplam M.
Lenthang, and Shlomo Gangte for permission to reproduce
materials used in this book.

Maps by Orna Tsafrir-Re'uven

∴ ∴ ∴
_____

CONTENTS

✻ 1 ✻

Siyata Di-Shmaya

"HILLERH, I HAVE BAD NEWS," said Chen-Hua, waking me from my nap in our fourth-floor room in the Wenchuan County Teachers Center Guest House. The news must have been bad, because he usually pronounced all the *l*'s in my name without difficulty.

"The police are here," Chen-Hua said. "They say we must move immediately. They say this is not a hotel for tourists. They say we broke the law by going to the Chiang village today. It is in a restricted area."

"Restricted for whom?"

"For foreigners. We are close to Tibet."

"Tibet is hundreds of miles from here. Who told them we went to the village?"

"I don't know. Perhaps our driver."

Of course. The man had driven like a maniac, using his horn instead of his brakes. An hour ago he had been in our room, demanding the two hundred yen promised him for the day. The day had ended for him in midmorning at the bottom of a pitted jeep trail he had refused to drive his jeep up, leaving us to climb to the village on foot. In the end he had settled for fifty — and the satisfaction of snitching.

My watch said five-thirty. Although it was the week of the summer solstice, the sun had already dropped behind the high mountains across the river. The river's roar pounded through the open window like a trucking route.

"Have you told Rabbi Avichail?"

"No," Chen-Hua said.

"Well, he's not going to move now," I said. "It's too close to the Sabbath. Go tell the police it's against our religion to change hotels before tomorrow night."

Chen-Hua stood in the doorway beside the earthenware spittoon that the Wenchuan County Teachers Center Guest House provided for its guests. He was wearing the green shorts and cream-colored polo shirt with black squiggles that were the only clothing he had brought with him and holding the transistor radio he took everywhere. He was wondering how to explain our religion to the police.

"Go tell them," I repeated.

Chen-Hua must have stopped on his way down to the lobby at Avichail's room on the second floor, because when I knocked on the door, Avichail already knew. Dressed in his trousers, a large knitted skullcap, and a *tallit katan*, the fringed undershirt worn by Orthodox Jews, he was steering a head of cabbage through a hand-turned grinder on the dresser. The hotel table was covered by a white cloth set with four paper plates and cups, an open can of Israeli gefilte fish, a bottle of Carmel-Mizrachi grape juice in lieu of wine, and two crackers standing in for the traditional challah. Avichail's traveling companion, Micha Gross, sat on a bed, slicing the main course for our Sabbath meal, thick slabs of Israeli baloney.

"When will you pray?" I asked. There was no pressing need to decide on a course of action. Chen-Hua was still talking to the police, a conversation Avichail deemed it best to keep out of. Whatever came of it, he and Micha would stay put unless dragged off bodily.

"Six-thirty," he said.

I glanced down at the courtyard on my way back to the fourth floor. Two soldiers with rifles were standing beside a pickup truck. Its tailgate down, it was waiting for our bags.

The Teachers Center Guest House was the only hotel that had seemed livable to us when we arrived the night before in Wenchuan, a city of fifty thousand in the Min River Valley of western Szechwan Province. It had toilets that actually flushed, faucets that yielded hot water, electric fixtures that did not dangle from the walls with copper wires extruding from their casings like the tongues of poisonous snakes. No one had told us it was reserved for teachers. The manager, Mrs. Li, a carefully groomed woman with a smile of hot lipstick and cool amusement, appeared happy to take our money. The place looked empty. It would be a blow to have to leave it, even though Wenchuan was a drab town that attracted few travelers, except for those on their way to Juizhai Gou, a famed nature reserve a day's drive past the valley's head to the north.

I showered and stepped out of the bathroom to find Chen-Hua jumping on his bed. He leaped three or four times, straining to touch the ceiling, fell back on the mattress, reached for his radio on the night table, and switched it on.

"Chen-Hua, what are you doing?"

"Exercising." He held the radio close to his ear, playing with the dial. "It is good for the leg muscles. Soon President Clinton will give a press conference."

The president was in Beijing. Chen-Hua did not have much in the way of muscles. He was twenty-one years old, an interpreter we had picked up in Chengdu, Szechwan's capital, and weighed perhaps a hundred pounds with his transistor. Yet on our ascent to the village he not only had carried all our packs, he had run ahead with them like a gazelle.

"What happened with the police?"

"The police." Chen-Hua had a Chinese habit of thoughtfully repeating the last part of one's question. "They are considering letting us stay until tomorrow night. Mrs. Li spoke to someone on the telephone. I think he was the local party boss."

The radio glued to his ear, he leaned over the edge of the bed to switch on the television while opening a book. Presently he asked, "There is an English sentence — 'That was quite an accomplishment.' Is it also correct to say, 'The man paid the woman an accomplishment'?"

"No," I said. "What he paid was a compliment."

He looked again at his dictionary and asked, "Then what exactly is the meaning of the phrase 'A left-handed compliment'?"

I was becoming fond of Chen-Hua. "Suppose I told you," I said, "that for a Chinese you were extremely intelligent. That would be pretty left-handed."

He went back to his book. Troubled, he glanced up from it. "So you think I am intelligent only for a Chinese?"

By the time I had extricated myself it was time for the Sabbath prayer. "It will take half an hour," I told Chen-Hua. "Then I'll come for you and we'll eat."

"Oh, good," he said. Having never before tasted Western cuisine, he had developed a liking for canned Israeli hummus and cucumber-and-tomato salad smeared with mayonnaise. His face fell each time I insisted, desperate to get away from such fare, that he accompany me to a local restaurant instead of partaking of Avichail's kosher food.

I returned to the second floor. The soldiers and the pickup truck were gone from the courtyard. Avichail and Micha, in clean white shirts, were already swaying back and forth, facing west toward the river and Jerusalem. Unlike them, I had to use a little prayer book I'd brought from Israel, because I no longer remembered what I'd known by heart as a boy. Only now did I notice that, by an odd coincidence, the book's silver-plated cover was stamped with the names and symbols of the biblical tribes: Reuben, Simon, Judah, Dan, Naphtali, Gad, Asher, Issachar, Zebulun, Benjamin, Ephraim, and Manasseh.

Avichail's prayer was pleasant. It had a droning sadness like my father's, a melancholy that asked for nothing but its own bittersweet longing. Only his melody for "Come, My Love, to Meet the Bride" was different, importuning. It had a faster, more urgent tempo:

> Shake off the dust from thee and arise,
> My people, and don thy glorious clothes;
> The son of Jesse soon arrives;
> My soul's redemption draweth nigh.

When the prayer was over I went to get Chen-Hua, and the four of us sat down at the table. Avichail recited the Kiddush, the blessing for the fruit of the vine, over the grape juice and rose to go to the bathroom, followed by Micha and me. "Oh, wash hands," Chen-Hua said happily, coming after us. It was the one Jewish ritual that made sense to him. Hands washed, he asked Avichail, "What will we do about a hotel tomorrow night?"

"Mmmmm!" Avichail said, putting a finger to his lips and shaking his head. "Mmm-mmmmmm!" Unable to explain that one was prohibited from talking between hand washing and bread blessing, he waited for Micha to take his seat. "Blessed art thou, O God, our Lord, King of the Universe, who bringeth forth bread from the earth," he intoned, breaking the crackers and giving each of us a half. "You may speak now," he told Chen-Hua.

But when Chen-Hua repeated the question, Arichail still refused to answer it. It was the Sabbath; vexing and worrisome topics were forbidden. "Eat," he said, passing the cole slaw.

Chen-Hua took the bowl but not the hint. "My opinion is that we should leave Wenchuan," he said. "It is boring here anyway. We can go to Jiuzhai Gou. There is much to see there."

Avichail and Micha exchanged glances. I said, in Hebrew, "I think it's time to tell our friend what we're up to. We can't go on hiding it from him."

"I'm not so sure," Micha said. "If the police question him, he may talk. What do you think, Eliahu?"

Avichail said, "I don't think it makes much difference at this point. You can tell him after dinner. Have some potato salad." The potatoes had been boiled in an electric kettle and drenched in mayonnaise too. *"Ya ribon o-o-lam ve'olmaya, ve'olma-a-a-aya,"* Avichail sang, breaking into a Sabbath hymn. Micha joined him. They both had good voices. We sang some more hymns and recited the Grace After Meals.

When the table was cleared, we went for a walk by the river. Micha and Avichail fell behind, and I strolled ahead with Chen-Hua. "So you've had enough of Wenchuan," I said.

"Yes. Jiuzhai Gou is beautiful."

"So is the Min River Valley."

In a way, once you got past the industry in its lower stretches, it was, with its gray, angrily foaming water bordered by a narrow strip of farmed land on each bank and towered over by green peaks, heavily terraced below and shooting up to heights of nine and ten thousand feet.

"There is nothing in it but Chiang villages."

"Look, Chen-Hua," I said, "there's something you should know. The Chiang are the purpose of this trip."

"The Chiang?" We had turned onto a bridge that crossed the Min slightly below its confluence with its tributary, the To.

"They're a people found nowhere else in China."

"But what is interesting about them?"

"Rabbi Avichail suspects they are lost Jews."

Chen-Hua consulted a mental dictionary. "I think lost means misplaced," he said in puzzlement.

Since he knew no more about the Bible than most Chinese, it took a long walk up the To's right bank for me to explain. We were out of the center of town now, and the low current of the Chinese street lamps left the buildings in dingy obscurity. A few families still sat at their dinners at the sidewalk restaurants, where the day's dirty pots and pans had been piled on the outdoor stoves for washing in the street.

Long ago, I told Chen-Hua, when the Jewish people first lived in their land, they were divided into twelve tribes: two in the southern kingdom of Judah and the others in the northern kingdom of Israel. The tribes were small, surrounded by powerful enemies, and in 720 B.C.E. the northern capital of Samaria was conquered by one of them, the Assyrians. According to the Bible, they carried away the northern tribes into exile and replaced them with people uprooted from elsewhere. The exiles were never heard from again.

"What happened to them?"

"No one knows. Some think they assimilated into their new environment and disappeared. Others say that only the ruling class was carried off and that the peasantry stayed behind and mixed with the newcomers to form a people called the Samaritans. Their religion was similiar to that of the Judeans, who became the ancestors of today's Jews. Most of the Samaritans eventually converted to Christianity and Islam, and today their descendants are Palestinian Moslems. Less than a thousand of them still practice the old Samaritan religion."

"You still have not said who was lost."

"For thousands of years there have been legends about the northern tribes still existing somewhere in remote and inaccessible regions. People have searched for them all over."

"Has anyone found them?"

"Many have claimed to. The scholars don't take them seriously."

"Then Rabbi Avichail is not a scholar."

"No. He's a rabbi from Jerusalem who believes some of the legends are true and has traveled widely trying to prove that. He's come to China to investigate the Chiang."

"But the Chiang don't look like you Jews," Chen-Hua said. "They look like us Han."

"That's true." When they weren't wearing their traditional clothing, I couldn't tell them apart from Chinese. "Rabbi Avichail believes they may be lost Jews because of some books written by a man named Thomas Torrance."

It began to drizzle, the first rain we had seen in China. Chen-Hua and I passed the last bridge across the To and headed toward the toll gate at the road to Songpan and Jiuzhai Gou. Trucks loaded with big logs were parked near the barrier. All the way from Chengdu they had kept rolling by, the logging trucks, carting away whole forests from up north.

"Torrance was a Scots missionary who lived among the Chiang after World War One. They still spoke their old language and practiced their old religion then, not like the villagers we met today. He wanted to make Christians of them. But the more he came to know them, the more he believed they were descended from an ancient tribe of Israel. Rabbi Avichail wants to see if the customs and beliefs he described in his books still exist."

"But we saw today that they didn't."

"That was only in one village. Rabbi Avichail hopes to find Chiang who are more knowledgeable. The problem is that the authorities mustn't know what we're doing. We didn't ask for a research permit, because it could have been denied us or taken too long to be issued."

We reached the barrier and turned back. The blurry lights of Wenchuan were now ahead of us.

"Does that mean we will stay in this place?"

"If we can."

"We will not go to Jiuzhai Gou?"

"I'm afraid not."

"Do *you* think the Chiang are lost Jews?"

"I doubt it."

Chen-Hua mulled this over while we retraced our steps along the To. He said, "Hillerh, I am very disappointed."

ᴪ

I couldn't say I was. My expectations had been low from the start.

I first met Eliahu Avichail the year before, in the summer of 1997. For some time I had heard of him as a Lost Tribes hunter, one of the last of a nearly extinct breed that had once roamed the earth more prolifically. Scholars and academics considered him a crackpot. "You've got to be kidding," one said when I told him that I planned to join the rabbi on an expedition.

Yet in the living room of his small Jerusalem apartment, through which his grandchildren wandered freely in search of chocolates and crayons, he had seemed level-headed enough as he described his travels to Moslems in Kashmir, Tatars in Dagestan, Knanites in Kerala, the Karens in Burma, and other peoples whose customs supposedly resembled those described in the Bible. The Kashmir trip, made in 1982 in the hope of meeting Pashtuns from across the border in Pakistan, a country for which his Israeli passport was invalid, was the first. The Pashtuns had caught his attention when, while teaching in a religious high school, he came across literature linking them with ancient Israel. In 1975 he had given a lecture on the subject at the Rabbi Kook Yeshiva in Jerusalem, the intellectual bastion of modern Israeli Orthodoxy where he had studied. Tsvi Yehuda Kook, the yeshiva's head and the son of its founder, sent for him and said, "If this is true, you can't just lecture about it. Do something!"

It took him a while. For several years he tried to contact Pashtun informants through intermediaries. Then he decided to look for them himself. As his interest in lost Jews widened, so did his travels. They yielded more than mere knowledge. In Portugal he reached communities of Marranos, descendants of Jews forceably converted to Christianity at the time of the Inquisition, and kindled in them an interest in Judaism. From the northeast Indian states of Mizoram and Manipur he brought to Israel several hundred men and women who called themselves B'nei Menashe, or Sons of Menashe, and claimed descent from the Israelite tribe of Manasseh. Mestizos living as Jews in the Peruvian Andes were also encouraged by him to come to Israel. The Indians and Peruvians underwent Orthodox conversions and applied for Israeli citizenship. Neither the country's rabbinate nor its interior ministry were happy with the development.

"You mustn't confuse the two things," Avichail told me. "The Peruvians, like the Portuguese, have nothing to do with the Lost Tribes. Some of their ancestors were Marranos from Spain who fled the Inquisition to South America. It followed them there, and they went underground. All the stories about biblical tribes in the Americas are nonsense."

A white-bearded, mild-mannered man in his sixties, he had an obsession that sounded rational once you accepted the initial premise. "If the Bible says the tribes were carried away and will return," he maintained, "they were carried away and will return. But you have to look for them in the right places. That means starting with the Assyrian empire, which was expanded northward and eastward by the Babylonians who conquered it and by the Persians who conquered the Babylonians. The exiled tribes could have moved in the same directions, migrating along trade and caravan routes until they lost contact with their southern brothers. The Caucasus, central Asia, even the Far East — that's where you would expect to find traces of them. And that's where you do find many traditions and practices reminiscent of Jewish ones — the growing of ear locks, for example, or the lighting of Sabbath candles, or the Pashtun *joi nemaz*, which is like a Jewish prayer shawl. Today, the people who do or remember these things are Christians and Moslems, but their ancestors must have been Jews."

The fax phone rang in his study. He went to check it and came back with a sheet of paper bearing news from Manipur. An outbreak of ethnic hostilities in the area had forced many B'nei Menashe to flee their rural homes for the capital of Imphal. "The situation is difficult," said the message. "Please help and advise."

"What help can you give?" I asked.

Avichail, who ran a minuscule organization called Amishav, My People Returneth, looked worried. "I don't know," he said. "We don't have much money. There's not even enough for the next expedition."

"Where would you go if there was?"

"China. There are people there known as the Chiang. They have Semitic features, believe they are descendants of Abraham — they call him Biran or Bilan — and worship a single God named Abba-Malakh. In times of danger they call out to Him, 'Ya-Weh!'" Abba-Malakh meant Father-Angel in Hebrew, and Ya-Weh, or Yahweh, was how Bible scholars believed the sacred four-consonant name of the biblical God, once commonly transcribed as Jehovah, was pronounced. "Their religion forbids graven images and has a hereditary priesthood that offers sacrifices like those in the Bible. The B'nei Menashe and the Karens have traditions of coming from China, too. I suspect all three groups are related."

"Well," I said, "if you ever do go to China, perhaps you'll take me along as a journalist. Maybe I could help with the financing."

"Why not?" said Eliahu Avichail.

It was a deal — and one that, several months before our planned departure, I nearly backed out of. Avichail's knowledge of the Chiang had been gleaned from a single author, and one day, while on a visit in New York, I ventured into the East Asian department of the Columbia University library to see what else I could find. The catalog listed several works in Chinese, as well as an article in English, "The Chiang People of Western Szechuan: The Miscalled 'West China Jews,'" written by Professor V. R. Schuyler Cammann. It began:

> The Chiang people were an ancient tribe of non-Chinese aborigines who lived in the mountains of west China bordering on Tibet until they were annihilated or dispersed in recent years. Aside from brief mention of them by occasional travelers, the only relatively complete accounts of them in English were written by two missionaries who lived in Szechuan during the first half of the present century. The first of these writers was a devout Scotsman with a highly developed imagination, named Thomas Torrance, who gradually became convinced that the Chiang were descended from ancient Israelites, and discussed them with this bias. The other was David Crockett Graham, Ph.D., an American missionary-anthropologist, who gave straightforward factual reports on Chiang religion and culture, inevitably exposing the lack of foundation in Torrance's theory.

Drawing on Graham, Cammann proceeded to demolish Torrance. The Chiang, he wrote, had been shamanistic animists, not monotheists. They had also had the bad luck during the Chinese civil war to be in the way of the Red Army's Long March and to oppose it, in consequence of which they were treated badly by the Communists. "Even if survivors might still be found in the former Chiang territory," Cammann concluded, "it seems most unlikely that they would retain any traces of their traditional religion."

I phoned Avichail and told him to cancel our trip.

"Why?"

I recounted the gist of Cammann's article.

"So what?" he said. "If I believed what every professor wrote, I'd never get past my front door."

He thought as much of the professors as they did of him. A deal was a deal: we flew to Hong Kong and then to Chengdu. Nevertheless, we did meet there with Professor Shi Ying Pin of Szechwan University. A specialist in the province's ethnic minorities, he caused a vindicated look to be sent in my direction when he assured Avichail that the Chiang, though reduced in numbers to a mere 80,000, still existed and practiced their old faith. "In one God?" Avichail asked eagerly. "One God, they believe in Him?" "Ummm," answered the professor. It was not quite clear what he meant by that. He unfolded a map on his desk and drew a circle around Wenchuan to show us where the Chiang could be found. "Ah! Must ask proper authorities," he replied when pressed for further details.

⚜

Although the village we had visited without police permission was not far from Wenchuan, it seemed remote by the time we reached it. In fact, it had seemed remote from the road below: a cluster of gray houses high up on the terraced flank of a steep mountain, with a tall stone tower looming above them. Such structures, Torrance had written, were characteristic of the Chiang, built as early warning systems and defensive bastions against the Chinese armies that repeatedly marched into their secluded valleys.

The To River foamed behind us. It looked as treacherous as the Min, though neither had anything on our driver. Chen-Hua had found him on a street corner during our first morning in Wenchuan. Before that, stepping out of the Wenchuan County Teachers Center Guest House, we had passed a group of elderly people sitting on some steps. The women wore the blue tunics and black turbans that were a Chiang trademark, according to my guidebook. "Chiang!" I sang out. Avichail said to Chen-Hua. "Go. Go ask them where their wise men are."

But the old people did not know where their wise men were and we walked to the corner to hire a four-by-four. Despite our rations of kosher food that were doled out as carefully as water in a lifeboat, I was beginning to realize that we were going to rely heavily on improvisation. If not for me, we wouldn't even have had a guidebook, a map, or malaria pills. "Is this Eliahu's usual method?" I asked Micha as we watched Chen-Hua negotiate with drivers.

"His method is *siyata di-shmaya*," Micha answered, using the rabbinic term for "the help of Heaven." He had been with Avichail on many trips.

If it was *siyata di-shmaya*, however, that made the next driver agree to take us to a Chiang village, *siyata di-shmaya* was out for lunch when he dumped us at the foot of the mountain. "Just head up that trail," he said to Chen-Hua, not wanting to stress his new tires. It would take us half an hour, he promised.

It was more like two and a half. We soon left the trail, which looped around the mountain's far side, and hiked straight up, following paths and steppingstones that zigzagged from terrace to terrace and stopping often to catch our breath. Corn, peppers, eggplants, and pole beans grew in plots so small that some had only a single plump plant. Barefoot men and women coming down the mountain with baskets on their backs or water buckets balanced on their shoulders glanced wonderingly at us without breaking stride. For part of the way we were joined by some Tibetan boys looking for farm work.

"Ask them, Chen-Hua," Avichail said, "if they know about a river that spits rocks."

The Tibetan boys, though, did not actually come from Tibet, where a nineteenth-century Jewish traveler had reported the existence of the Sambatyon, the legendary river beyond which the Lost Tribes were to be found. They came from north of Songpan and were ignorant of Tibetan geography.

The Chiang village looked empty when we reached it. Most of its inhabitants were presumably in the fields. The houses, built of chinked stone and stacked on the mountainside so that the flat roof of one formed the patio of the one above it, did not look Chinese. They bore the resemblance, remarked upon by Torrance, to peasant houses in the Middle East.

"Keep your eyes out for white stones," Avichail said. Torrance had written at length about these stones, describing them as the Chiang's most important cult objects. Placed on the rooftops, where the Chiang sacrificed to the one God, their simple purity symbolized the "effulgence of His glory." We had seen such a stone in a museum in Chengdu, a rough sphere of quartz, about a foot in diameter, that looked like a big lump of frozen dough. Yet while we had passed shiny outcrops of quartz on our climb, no specimens were visible on the village roofs. The only signs of religion were Buddhist posters of guardian spirits glued to some of the front doors. From afar came the chant of children at their lessons.

We headed for the tower along a passageway of roofs strewn with farm implements, firewood, heavy logs, and bales of wattling. Lying cracked in an open shed, like a deposed idol, was a stone bust of Mao Tse-tung. Avichail raced ahead, pointing his video camera like a gun, sprinting up ladders and across parapets like the paratrooper he had been before his rabbinical ordination.

All at once, in the fortress-like window of the last house beneath the tower, appeared two small faces. Another peered out from behind the parapet of the roof, and a fully visible child was perched on a bare rafter. A woman looked down, too, from a window above the first.

No one waved or smiled. No one seemed frightened or amused, not even when Avichail stumbled and nearly went flying with his camera. The grave curiosity that tracked us seemed entirely intent on our next step. Perhaps the natives had peered this way from the trees at the men stepping out of Columbus's ships. Indeed, once we were all assembled face to face, the explorers and three generations of the explored, Chen-Hua established that the village had never before seen foreigners.

"Ask them," Avichail told him, waving off a grimy thermos of red tea offered by a spiky-haired man, the head of the household, "ask where are the white stones. Ask about sacrifice."

Chen-Hua looked like someone who, having been sent to knock on a strange door for directions, is now told to demand the family Bible.

Avichail's brusqueness startled me too. It had the same tempo with which he had made for the stone tower and was no way to approach total strangers. "Chen-Hua," I said, "tell these people that we saw their village from the road. Say it looked like a good place to visit. Ask how many of them live here."

There were, the spiky-haired man replied, forty families.

All farmers?

Chen-Hua translated. All.

Did they often get to Wenchuan?

Often. They shopped and sold their produce there. They had frequent contact with the Chinese. There was no difference between them. They spoke the same language and lived the same way.

"Ask if they speak the Chiang language among themselves."

Chen-Hua asked. "No," he said. "Only Han. A terrible dialect."

He sounded indignant at having been brought all the way from Chengdu to hear such terrible Chinese.

"Not even the old man and woman?"

The children's grandparents stood to one side, the old woman in the Chiang tunic and turban, the old man with a long-stemmed pipe on which a high plug of tobacco balanced like an inch of ash on a cigarette.

"No. All the speakers of the old language are dead."

"What is their religion?"

"It is Buddhism."

"Only Buddhism?"

"Only."

"But before Buddhism," persisted Avichail. "There was a religion before Buddhism? Ask the old people. The religion before Buddhism, what was it?"

Chen-Hua gave us their answer. "There was no religion before Buddhism."

"All right," Avichail said impatiently, "let's go. These people know nothing. We'll talk to the teacher at the school."

The teacher, however, was gone. It was Friday, and the school, from which we'd heard the chanting children, had let out early. We walked back down to the road in less time than it took to climb up and paid the driver of a passing car to take us to Wenchuan.

"Well," I said that evening, "it looks as if Cammann was right and Professor Shi was wrong. The Chiang have lost their old culture. We'll never know if Torrance imagined it all or not."

We had come a long way just to learn that.

"Professor Shi!" scoffed Avichail. "We need educated Chiang, not Chinese professors. If this is a teachers' center guest house, there must be a teachers' center. We'll look for it in the morning."

Chen-Hua was asleep when I went upstairs. The score of *Titanic*, his sleepy-time music, was still playing on his tape.

⚹

In the morning Mrs. Li informed us that the police had agreed to extend our stay at the Wenchuan County Teachers Center Guest House. She also confirmed Avichail's hunch. At the south end of town, across the river, was the District National Normal College for Teachers.

Micha and Avichail said their Sabbath morning prayers, and we set out. Within the confines of a city, walking on the day of rest was permitted.

Wenchuan was livelier by day. Fruit and vegetable vendors lined the sidewalks. Han, Chiang, and Tibetan women wove in and out of the traffic with baskets and babies on their backs. At the little restaurants, the big noodle vats blew off clouds of steam. The bells of the bicycles and rickshaws backed the piping of the sparrows in a brisk, atonal music. The sparrows, suspended from lampposts in their bamboo cages, were the only animals in town. For pets and beasts of burden the Wenchuanese made do with themselves.

The District National Normal College started off well. The first person we stopped — *siyata di-shmaya!* — was an English teacher named Frank. All his students, he told us proudly, had English names too. Though knowing nothing about the Chiang, Frank invited us to his campus apartment, made a few phone calls, and informed us that a librarian who was an expert on the Chiang — *siyata di-shmaya* again! — lived on the floor above. But the librarian was out of town, and none of the scattering of Chiang students sprawled on the lawns with their Han friends were of any help. "Hello, hello!" they called, waving their chopsticks above their lunchtime noodle bowls, eager to practice their English. When asked about the old Chiang religion, they made insouciant gestures of ignorance.

That evening, after Avichail had recited over the last of the grape juice the Blessing of Separation between the Sabbath and the week, we went for a ramble in the streets. Chen-Hua strode ahead. Suddenly he stopped by a sign at the foot of a dim alley and said, "There's another school here. It is the District Normal College for Teachers."

If the District National Normal College had been a flop, what, at nine o'clock on a Saturday night, could we expect from a mere District Normal College? Yet when we walked up the alley to the college gate, this reasoning proved unfounded. The student body of the District National Normal College, of which the Chiang were a small minority, came from all over China; the District Normal College, its lawless compound shabby by comparison, accepted students from the Wenchuan area alone, among them a high proportion of Chiang. There were Chiang everywhere: hanging out loudly in the square by the gate, watching a Saturday night movie in a ground-floor lecture room, dancing to loud rock music in a hall that smelled of beer and cigarettes. A group gathered around us, and some of their friends went to look for a Chiang teacher.

They returned with Mr. Yu, a tall, handsome man with a nose like a scimitar, our first case of the supposedly Semitic features ascribed to the Chiang by Torrance. A chemistry teacher, he invited us to his office, where two other Chiang faculty members joined us. One, Mr. Wen, had a blinking, rumpled face; the other, Mr. Hsiao, a beery breath and some command of English. Even so, there being seven of us in the room, all sometimes talking at once, more was said than understood.

Enough got across, however, to earn me another of Avichail's I-told-you-so looks. Schuyler Cammann, we were informed by the Chiang teachers, was wrong after all. The Chiang village we had been to was not typical. Being so close to Wenchuan, it had assimilated Chinese ways. If we ranged farther afield, we would find villages in which the old language and customs still prevailed. We could even see as many white stones as we wanted.

"Just what are the white stones?"

Chen-Hua translated Mr. Wen's answer. "They are a symbol of the white stone god."

"The white stone god, he is the only God?" Avichail asked.

As Mr. Wen was answering Chen-Hua, who was being prompted by Micha and Avichail, Mr. Yu was speaking to Mr. Wen; Mr. Hsiao was addressing us in broken English; and the Hebrew speakers were arguing among themselves.

"He is the powerful god."

"The *most* powerful god?"

"His name, it is Abba-Malakh?"

"White stone bring good luck."

"They say there is also the mountain and the sky god."

"Ask, ask if it is Abba-Malakh."

"They do not know the name of the white stone god. Long ago the Chiang lived in the mountains of Tibet. They had a big war with their enemies. When their enemies were winning, the great Chiang chief had a dream. In his dream he was told to take stones and roll them in snow. Then throw them at the enemy."

"This big chief, he was Abraham?"

"Bilan. Ask if they know Bilan."

"All house have white stone for protect it."

"The enemy thought the stones were snowballs. The stones killed the enemy. That is why the Chiang sacrifice to them."

"To them or on them? Ask, Chen-Hua!"

Mr. Yu screwed up his face in pain. He was describing a Chiang cheek piercing ceremony to Mr. Hsiao.

"On them. No. To them."

"You can see for yourself, the white stone is just a household god."

"He never said that. You're putting words in his mouth."

Avichail leaned over and whispered in Mr. Hsiao's ear.

Mr. Hsiao shook his head. Mr. Wen spoke to Chen-Hua. Chen-Hua said, "The sacrifice is made before the stone. The blood is poured over it."

Avichail whispered again.

"No understand," Mr. Hsiao said.

It went on like that: white stones, sacrifice, rooftops, blood, snowballs, Abraham. Finally, Micha seized a moment of silence to ask, "Chen-Hua, is there a traditional Chiang village we could visit where someone might explain these things to us better?"

Chen-Hua asked Mr. Yu. Mr. Yu spoke to Mr. Hsiao. Mr. Hsiao turned to Mr. Wen. "Chongfung," Mr. Wen said.

Chen-Hua knew where that was. He had seen the road sign on the way from Chengdu.

Mr. Wen spoke again. Chen-Hua said:

"Mr. Wen has a friend in Chongfung. He will write him a letter. We can take a bus there."

Chen-Hua translated what Mr. Wen wrote:

"Dear Teacher Wang: There are some foreigners wanting to know and have a meet with the priest. Please arrange for them. Thank you."

Siyata di-shmaya!

⚜

The next day I asked Avichail what he had whispered to Mr. Hsiao the night before.

"'Ya-Weh,'" he said. "I thought it might get a reaction."

He went off to buy fruit and vegetables with Micha and Chen-Hua before taking the bus to Chongfung. I stayed behind to catch up on my notes, lingering on the stairs to listen to the wild mountain harmonies of the Chiang chambermaids singing in the kitchen.

Chen-Hua looked flustered when he returned to our room. "Is anything wrong?" I inquired.

"Anything wrong. No, Hillerh."

But on our way to the bus station Micha asked, "Did Chen-Hua tell you what happened?"

"No. What?"

"Eliahu saved his life. We were buying peaches from a Chiang. Chen-Hua was bargaining, and the Chiang began to shout and knocked him down. A dozen more of them piled on, punching and kicking him. Eliahu pulled them off and crouched over him to protect him until they calmed down."

On the bus to Chongfung I asked Chen-Hua about it.

"They were asking for too much money," he said. "They hate me because I am a Han."

"Look at it their way," I told him. "Here's a chance for them to earn a few more yen from some rich foreigners, and you keep them from doing it."

"It's not right to charge foreigners more," Chen-Hua said. "I would not be doing my duty if I permitted that." He put his transistor radio back to his ear. "There is a discussion of the Paula Jones case," he reported.

The bus let us off at the side of the road. Next to it, gray and scaly, tumbled the Min. Chongfung was on the far bank, which was reached by crossing a rickety wood suspension bridge. A banner was strung above the road. Chen-Hua translated its large red characters: "It says Chongfung, Number One Visiting Place."

A few yards beyond the banner was a ticket window.

Had we found ourselves by the entrance to the District National Sparrow Reserve, it could hardly have been more absurd. An official traditional Chiang village! We had been duped. Last night's teachers were government touts.

"Your number one tourist stop in a place without tourists!" Micha said. "Well, let's pay up and get the tour."

But there was no tour. There was only a little grocery store that sold soft drinks and ice cream, a cluster of houses, and a road running through a valley to a larger cluster on a low hill about a mile away. A Chiang watchtower rose above them. Having neglected to bring a tour bus, we walked.

The road passed through corn fields and small orchards of plums and pomegranates. In the main village we asked for the school, and at the school, for Teacher Wang. Soon he came. Grunting unhappily as he read Mr. Wen's letter, he agreed to take us to the priest.

This entailed another long hike to the highest house on the hill. There were no theme parks or native jewelry stands on the way. Actually, Teacher Wang told us as we climbed the hill, Chongfung had been designated a tourist site only three years before because of its accessibility and adherence to the old traditions. Its inhabitants had not yet decided what to do about that.

There were indeed white stones in the corners of all the roofs, ranging in size from tennis balls to basketballs. Avichail asked Teacher Wang about them. Then he asked about other things. Did the villagers perform sacrifices? Where? How did they bury their dead? Was the corpse placed in a coffin? Was it washed first? How did the people mourn? What were the marriage customs? Did the groom give the bride gifts? How was a couple divorced? Each answer led to more questions exploring possible points of resemblance to biblical rites.

A cow came down the stone steps leading up to the priest's house and we stepped aside to let it pass. At the top of the steps was a courtyard of mucky earth, from which a short ladder led to the priest's shrine. Or was it his office? Or his kitchen? Once our eyes grew accustomed to the dark, windowless room, it appeared to be an equal part of each. A side of bacon and some strings of sausage hung from a rafter beside a weak electric bulb. From a second beam a kettle was suspended by a metal chain over an open hearth. In the middle of the room stood a center post on which was draped something furry. A pile of onions lay beside some farm tools on a bench; behind the bench was a wall with framed photographs; above the photographs, a shelf was curtained by rice-paper screens. The photographs showed the priest, in his priestly regalia, with smiling Chinese officials.

His name was Wang Tsu Tsin and he welcomed us in a Mao cap and a plain shirt tucked into a black skirt. A short, grizzled man with a shrewdly good-natured face, he had his first question put to him by me. How long had he been a priest?

Chen-Hua translated the reply with a grimace of concentration, condensing long sentences into short ones.

"His language is hard to understand. He says he became a priest as a teenager. His father gave him the knowledge. Only a priest's son can become a priest."

"Ask if he has sons himself."

"Yes. Four."

"Will any of them become priests?"

"No. None."

"Why?"

"There is not enough money in it."

Avichail stirred restlessly. "What does any of this matter?" he said. "Ask him, Chen-Hua, to show us what a priest does."

The priest went to the shelf and lifted a rice-paper screen. He took three objects from the shelf. The first was a highly burnished wooden staff. A wooden snake was coiled around it. The snake had a head like a weasel's.

"The bronze serpent of Moses!" Avichail exclaimed. "Torrance mentioned it."

The priest thumped the staff on the floor and spoke to Chen-Hua. "It protects him when he comes to the sacrifice," Chen-Hua said. "The sacrifice takes place on the roof."

The second object was a pair of silver bells. The priest shook them rhythmically.

"With these he chants."

"To whom?"

Wang Tsu Tsin pointed to the raised screen. "Apimala."

Avichail excitedly corrected him:

"Abba-Malakh!"

The third object consisted of two lacquered wooden tablets joined by a leather thong. Each was about a foot and a half high and had a column of Chinese-looking characters.

"Ask what it says, Chen-Hua."

The priest did not know.

"He can't read?"

"He can read Chinese. But this is in an old language. No one understands it anymore."

"Ask if his father did."

"No. It is very old."

"Try to read it, Chen-Hua."

Chen-Hua took the tablets outside into the sunlight. "This is not old Chinese," he said. "I don't know what it is."

According to Torrance, the Chiang had once had a written language and a holy book that was lost. Cammann dismissed this conjecture. I counted the characters on each tablet. Five. Two tablets, ten characters.

Or commandments? It was a wild thought.

The priest took the fur from the center post and pulled it over his head. It was a monkey skin with a head and two eye holes, through which he looked out. He fetched a drum and slipped his arm through its shoulder strap. It sounded like a slow heartbeat when he beat it. He shut his eyes and chanted, shaking the bells. The chant was slow and halting, like footsteps groping in the dark.

It should have been demeaning, this peep show for strangers who might leave behind a few yen. But Wang Tsu Tsin did not look demeaned. He was paid by the villagers for his services, too; perhaps to his mind there was no great difference. "What did he chant?" Micha asked.

Chen-Hua said, "He told the god he is coming. He asked the god not to harm him."

"When does he do this?"

"When someone is sick. Or needs help from the gods."

"Gods," I said to Avichail.

"No," Avichail said. "He said the God."

"Gods. Didn't he, Chen-Hua?"

"Chen-Hua," Avichail commanded, "ask him. Ask if there is one God. Ask who created the world."

Chen-Hua asked. Wang Tsu Tsin wrinkled his brow. He pointed to two rice-paper screens and gave a lengthy reply. Chen-Hua said:

"He says something about two gods. They are called Moh-chi-tsu and Zer-pir-wah. Moh-chi-tsu is a girl and Zer-pir-wah is a boy. They created people."

"How, Chen-Hua?" I asked. "How did they create them?"

"That doesn't matter," Avichail said. "They are all Abba-Malakh."

"Of course they're not," I said. "Each screen stands for a different god."

Avichail turned to Chen-Hua. "Ask him!" he said. "Paper is God? If I burn paper, no more God? Ask!"

Chen-Hua looked horrified. He appeared to believe that Avichail was threatening to burn down Wang Tsu Tsin's shrine.

"Ask, Chen-Hua! Burn paper, no God?"

"I . . . I don't want to ask," Chen-Hua said. "I don't understand this. I don't understand this old man's language."

"Ask!"

Chen-Hua was on the verge of tears.

Micha came to the rescue. "We were told that the sacrifices take place on the roof. Perhaps the priest will show it to us."

Wang Tsu Tsin led us up another ladder to the flat roof. With a sweep of his arm, he indicated where he sacrificed the animals brought to him. Once again Avichail had a list of questions. Was the animal sacrificed on an altar or on the ground? How was it killed? Was its throat slit? What was done with the blood? Was it sprinkled on the white stone? Was the sacrifice cooked and eaten? Did the priest get a special part of it? Were there purification rites beforehand? Were there holidays on which the entire village sacrificed together?

Yes, the priest said. On the harvest festival the whole village climbed a mountain. He pointed to a peak behind the village. There was singing and dancing and sacrificing.

"To Abba-Malakh?"

Wang Tsu Tsin nodded.

"Abba-Malakh," Avichail said, "he is the same as the white stone god?"

Chen-Hua asked and said:

"No. The white stone god is different."

"But he has a name, the white stone god?"

The priest answered briefly. Chen-Hua said, "He has no name."

"Then he is Abba-Malakh! Ask, ask, Chen-Hua."

Chen-Hua did not know what to ask.

"Ask if there is one God or many."

Chen-Hua asked. Wang Tsu Tsin answered. Chen-Hua asked again. The priest answered a second time. Chen-Hua clasped his head in his hands. "There are many gods. There are several gods. There are many several. He says it would take a month to explain it all. I want to go back to Chengdu."

He started down the ladder.

I caught him by the squiggles of his shirt. "You can't quit on us," I told him. "We'll get you back to Chengdu as soon as we can. Now act your age and translate."

Chen-Hua bit his lip. His thin back trembled beneath my rebuke.

"Ask the priest, Chen-Hua," Avichail said, "what happens to him when he dies."

"When he dies," repeated Chen-Hua. He spoke to the priest. The priest smiled as if asked something funny. Chen-Hua said, "His body will be burned."

"And his soul? He has a soul? What will happen to it?"

But the priest did not have a soul. "There will be nothing left," Chen-Hua said.

"All right," Avichail declared. "We can go."

"Just a minute!" I couldn't part with Wang Tsu Tsin like that. "Chen-Hua," I said, "ask him what will happen when he dies to the old religion in Chongfung."

Chen-Hua asked. "It will die too," he said.

"But what about the gods? What will they do?"

The priest shrugged. The gods would manage.

"Chen-Hua," I said, "ask if they are the gods just of the Chiang."

The old man pushed back his Mao cap. "Some are also for the Han," he told Chen-Hua.

"Let's go," Avichail urged.

"Wait!" I pointed to us three foreigners. "Ask. Are some also for us?"

The priest said a few words. "Some are also for you," Chen-Hua said.

There was a bit of comfort in that. "Tell the priest," I said, "that I wish we had a month to give him." The loneliness of a god with no one left to look after him was more terrible than any I could imagine.

☙

We spent the rest of the week farther up the Min River Valley, ranging as far north as Songpan. We visited more Chiang villages and received more answers to more questions, none of which altered the basic picture. In the village of Chaochung we met some young high school teachers. One said to Avichail: "You are from Jerusalem. I have heard that many tribes lived there and that one was lost and is the Chiang. What do you know about this?"

An electric current ran through us. But it turned out that the young teacher was merely repeating the notions of Torrance that he had read about in a Chinese book. He and his colleagues seemed pleased by the thought of being a lost Jewish tribe. The Jews were powerful and smart.

Avichail was pleased, too. He left some literature and his address. "They seemed interested," he said. "Perhaps they'll write. I can only sow the seed. The rest is up to them."

By Friday afternoon we were back in Chengdu.

We viewed our week among the Chiang differently. Although Schuyler Cammann had been mistaken about the Chiang's physical and cultural survival, I thought his criticisms of Torrance had stood up. I couldn't see the remotest connection between the Chiang religion and the Bible.

Avichail disagreed. To him, the important thing was that Torrance's descriptions had proved reliable. It was true that we had found evidence of ordinary paganism in Chiang religion. But Torrance himself had observed that, whereas the Chiang once lived in isolation, their modern contact with the Chinese had introduced impurities into their faith. These could only have multipled since the 1920s. The crucial question was what the Chiang religion had been like in Torrance's day — and to that, Torrance remained the best witness.

This struck me as wishful thinking. The one puzzling thing was those strange tablets.

In Chengdu we shared a triple room. Watching Avichail and Micha set the Sabbath eve table, I noticed that there were only three plates. "Set another place," I said. "Chen-Hua said he's joining us."

Avichail unscrewed the cap from our last bottle of grape juice. "No, he isn't."

"Why not?"

"He has a mother in Chengdu. Let her feed him."

"What does that mean?"

"We want to have a proper Sabbath meal."

"For Jews only?"

"The Sabbath was given to Jews."

"I don't get it," I said. "In Chaochung you were beaming because some Chiang asked you a few polite questions about Judaism. You said you were sowing the seed. And here's a young man you saved from a mob who would rather spend a Jewish Sabbath with us than with the mother he hasn't seen in a week — and you don't want him."

"He's only interested in our food."

"It's not just your awful food. It's —"

There was a knock on the door.

I fled to the bathroom to avoid seeing what came next. When I finally stepped out, the Sabbath candles were lit and Avichail and Micha were praying. A dirty plate with smearings of potato salad was on the dresser. Avichail had fed Chen-Hua supper before turning him out. I didn't know if that made it better or worse. I sat through the meal, picking at my food. After the final Grace I rose from the table and said, "I'm going for a walk."

"Sit," Avichail told me. "We'll have a lesson. You'll take your walk afterward."

A "lesson" was yeshiva parlance for a religious homily. He delivered it, propped on one elbow on his bed, by the flickering light of the candles. Micha lay on his back on a pillow. I sat in the armchair by the window.

Avichail chose for his text the verses in Zachariah:

> And I will pour upon the house of David and upon the inhabitants of Jerusalem the spirit of grace . . . and they shall look upon him whom they have pierced and they shall mourn for him as one mourneth for his only son . . . the land shall mourn, every family apart: the family of the house of David apart and the family of the house of Levi apart.

"This passage is knotty," he said. "Who was pierced and why is he mourned for as an only son?"

He began to unravel the knots. According to the Aramaic targum of Yonatan ben Uziel, the only son was the Messiah son of Joseph — the herald, destined to die in battle, of the Messiah son of David. Although it was the Messiah son of David and the Priest of Righteousness from the house of Levi who would bring the final redemption, each of the three figures symbolized a different sphere of deliverance. They formed a circle within a circle within a circle, all three needing to be entire for the redemption to be complete. The son of Joseph stood for the material sphere, the regaining of Jewish independence. The son of David stood for the religious sphere, the spiritual perfecting of Israel. The Priest of Righteousness stood for the universal sphere, the acceptance of Judaism by all mankind.

"And so," Avichail said, "Zachariah speaks of the first Messiah, who will come from the house of Joseph. But Joseph, Jacob's most beloved son, was the one son who did not have a tribe named after him. His own two sons, Jacob's grandsons, Ephraim and Menashe, received that honor in his place. And just as the southern tribes of Judah and Benjamin were together known as Judah, from which came David, son of Jesse, so the northern tribes were known as Ephraim, or the house of Joseph.

"He who has eyes to see knows that the process of redemption is already under way. But even its first circle, the regaining of our independence in the state of Israel, cannot be complete until the house of Joseph returns. And herein lies hidden a great truth."

A candle guttered and went out.

"For as the house of David represents our people's spirit, the house of Joseph is the body. All know that the body cannot exist without the spirit. But not all know that the opposite is also true. The exile of the ten tribes was a great blow to our people, not because of the loss of numbers or of land, but because of the exile of matter from spirit. This is the true exile that we have lived in for thousands of years. Such was the teaching of my master, Tsvi Yehuda Kook of blessed memory, and of his father and master, Rabbi Avraham Yitzhak Hacohen Kook. At the redemption's completion, matter and spirit will be reunited. We are told —"

The second candle sputtered.

"We are told the Messiah will come riding on a donkey. Why a donkey?"

He answered his own question.

"Because a donkey is the essence of materiality. Rabbi Yosef said, 'May I see the Messiah even from a donkey's dung heap.' He meant that at the end of days all matter will be as holy as spirit, even the dung of a donkey. All mankind will be holy too."

Avichail's eyes rested on me. He said softly, "But that is not our task. The third circle of redemption is not given to us to complete. We are not sent to make Jews of the Gentiles. That is for the Priest of Righteousness. Our mission is to restore lost Jewish souls. Every member of the ten tribes is a Jewish soul that stood at Sinai. This is what the rabbis taught. The soul that was not at Sinai does not concern us. We have the same obligations to its possessor that we have to all men, but no more."

The second candle went out. A moment later the telephone rang.

No one picked it up. Observant Jews do not use telephones on the Sabbath. But by the second or third ring it struck me that, in all of China, there was no one who could be phoning us. Nor could it be Avichail's or Micha's families in Israel. They would not call on the Sabbath either. Even in an emergency this was permitted only if it was necessary to save a life.

That left my family.

The ringing stopped. Avichail continued his lesson in darkness streaked by the weak light of the lamps by the river.

Damn him and his donkey dung! And his religion, with its three circles of redemption and its obligations to all men who could be made sick with worry because the flow of electrons from a telephone was comparable to the forbidden act of lighting a fire on the Sabbath.

Someone knocked. Avichail broke off. Micha went to open the door.

It was a chambermaid. She said something in Chinese and switched on the overhead light. Then she went to the phone, picked up the receiver, and listened for a tone. Getting one, she shrugged at our failure to respond to the switchboard, replaced the receiver, said something else in Chinese, and left the room.

Avichail sat up on the bed. "Micha!" he exclaimed. "We'll have to sleep with the light on all night. Get her back here."

Micha hurried into the corridor and returned with the chambermaid. "You shouldn't have left this on," he said, pointing to the light. He was not permitted to tell her to turn it off.

She stared at him blankly.

"This light. It bothers us."

She regarded the light. "No good?"

"No good."

"Ah!"

The chambermaid understood. She went to the lamp on the table and switched that on too.

"What am I supposed to do now?" Micha asked.

"Learn Chinese," I said. "I'm going for my walk."

࿔

The caller turned out to have been Chen-Hua, who had wanted to know what time he was to come in the morning. It was our next-to-last day in

China, and he had agreed to accompany me to the market and help me shop for gifts.

It was raining again. Soon the daily monsoons would begin. We walked along the Jinjiang River, into which the Min emptied in the plains above Chengdu. A sluggish channel when first we saw it, it now coursed swiftly with a flotilla of refuse.

Gray China grew bright in the rain. Colorful umbrellas opened like flowers, and the bicycle riders donned plastic capes of lilac and magenta. We tramped through the mud of Chengdu's big market while Chen-Hua told me of his dream of studying computers in America. A man tried selling me a large turtle. If I ate it, he said, I would live to be a hundred.

I lingered by the antique stalls. In one I fingered a necklace made of little hand-carved wooden skulls, no two of them alike. It was exquisite work, but I wasn't sure my wife or daughters would wear skulls.

"Chen-Hua, look!"

Siyata di-shmaya!

From under some bric-a-brac I pulled out two wooden tablets like the ones we had seen in Chongfung. Each had five characters.

Chen-Hua took them from me. "These are in ordinary Chinese," he said.

"What do they say?"

"They're a pair. This one says, *Shu zhong qian kun da*, there is much knowledge in books. And this one, *Bi xia tian di kuan*, there is much to write about."

He asked the stall owner about them and told me, "They're late Ching dynasty. People hung them as decorations in their homes."

So much for the Ten Commandments.

"People do the same in the West," I said. "Well, that's one mystery less."

"Not really," Chen-Hua said. "We still don't know the language of that writing in Chongfung."

That was true.

"There's something else that's mysterious," he added. "How do you explain the fact that both you Jews and the Chiang worship the same white stone god?"

Could he be serious? "Chen-Hua," I said, "what makes you think we Jews worship the white stone god?"

"Don't you?"

"Of course not."

"But I thought . . ." Embarrassed by his blunder, he felt deceived. "Why did Rabbi Avichail make me ask all those questions if the white stone god isn't part of your religion?"

I had to laugh. It was the strangest moment of a strange trip. Avichail was right about that. Chen-Hua's soul had been nowhere near Sinai.

⚚ 2 ⚚

Mu Kaw Lee and Mu Lee Kaw

FROM CHENGDU we flew to Bangkok. We had a connecting flight the next day to Chiang Mai, the hub of a district in northwest Thailand heavily populated by non-Thai hill peoples like the Yaos, Hmongs, Lahus, Akhas, Lisus, and Karens.

It was the Karens who interested Avichail, which was why he had decided to add them to our itinerary. They were an estimated four million of them, most living across the border in Burma, in areas barred to foreign travelers by the Burmese military regime. They had been in on-and-off rebellion against that regime for years. Like most of the region's ethnic minorities, of which they were the largest, they spoke various dialects of a Tibeto-Burmese language and at some point in the past had migrated to their present home from southwest China, driven by Han expansion. Some of the groups displaced by the Chinese, such as the Chiang, had retreated westward into the mountain fastnesses near Tibet. Others had moved southward, keeping to altitudes that the plains-dwelling Thais and Burmese did not contest.

Although Avichail had once met some Karens in Rangoon, most of what he knew about them came from a book written by an American Baptist named Harry Ignatius Marshall. Marshall was of the David Crockett Graham rather than the Thomas Torrance mold of missionary, a member of the American Oriental Society whose book, *The Karen People of Burma: A Study in Anthropology and Ethnology*, published in 1922, was the product of meticulous work. Yet there were some curious things in it. These had to do with certain oral traditions, found in old poetry and folktales, that had striking parallels with the Bible. The Karens, Marshall wrote, believed in a God named Y'wa, who, while not involved in the world's daily affairs, was its eternal creator. It was Y'wa who fashioned the first man, and from his rib the first woman, Naw Ee Oo; who placed them in a garden to serve him; who cast them out and doomed them to mortality when a serpent persuaded them to eat forbidden fruit. Karen legends also told of a great flood and of a tower whose collapse had scattered the families of man. Since there were no allusions in these legends to "the life or teachings of Christ," it seemed reasonable to Marshall to assume a "Hebraic source" for them, perhaps "some wandering storyteller or unknown missionary."

Marshall was not the first to arrive at this conclusion, a cautious one that made no claim for the Karens being a biblical tribe of Israel. He was preceded in it by an earlier Baptist missionary, Francis Mason, who had been in Burma in the first half of the nineteenth century. Mason was even convinced that, although the Karens were illiterate when he encountered them, they had once possessed the Hebrew Bible, since they told stories about a lost book or scroll that had contained all the wisdom of their ancestors.

Avichail, naturally, made a great deal of this, all the more so because Marshall believed the Karens to be ethnically related to the Chiang. On the face of it, the case for a Karen connection with ancient Jewish or Israelite sources was the stronger of the two. Our two weeks among the Chiang had been comical not only because no one could learn anything substantial about a people in so short a time and unprepared a fashion, but because, like many Lost Tribe hunters before him, Avichail was unable to distinguish significant fact from trivial coincidence. Things like a staff carved with a snake or the resemblance of "Apimala" to "Abba-Malakh" were meaningless. The caduceus had been a religious symbol in ancient Greece, too, and any two languages had words that sounded alike. But a man and woman banished by a creator-God from a garden for eating forbidden fruit at the instigation of a serpent could hardly be coincidental. The parallel was too intricate and exact.

You could explain it in different ways, of course. Perhaps Christian contacts *had* been responsible for bringing "Old Testament material" to the Karens; New Testament stories about Jesus may have made less of an impression and been forgotten. Or perhaps the transmitting religion was Islam, which reached southeast Asia long before Christianity and had many biblical tales in its Koran. Moreover, the Bible too had its sources, ancient Middle Eastern myths and beliefs that could have spread independently. And who was to say that a missionary like Mason had not himself disseminated biblical stories and failed to recognize them as his own when they were retold to him in native garb?

These questions did not overly exercise Avichail, though he was eager to ascertain whether such tales still existed among the Karens. He had his own questions, which he lectured about on the night of our stopover in Bangkok at the local Jewish watering hole, a small kosher restaurant run by a Lubavitcher Hasid. Facing an afterdinner audience of Israeli backpackers, a Jewish magazine photographer from London, an ultra-Orthodox alms gatherer bound for Singapore, and a smooth specimen of driftwood whose bored Thai girlfriend eyed the gold chain on his bare chest as if wondering what she could get for it, Avichail asked:

1. Do the Lost Tribes still exist?
2. If they do, are they living as Jews or as Gentiles?
3. What is our responsibility for them?

He replied:

1. The ancient sages did not agree on this matter. Rabbi Akiva, in commenting on the verse in Deuteronomy "And the Lord will root them out of their land in anger . . . and cast them into another land, as it is *this day*," said, "The ten tribes will not return, since just as *this day* passes and does not come back, neither will they." But Rabbi Eliezer held that "Just as *this day* grows dark and tomorrow grows light again, so the tribes will emerge from the darkness shrouding them." Most of the sages believed the tribes existed and would one day return.
2. The Lost Tribes are living as Gentiles, for the prophet Hosea declared, "Ephraim, he hath mixed himself among the nations." Nevertheless, we are assured by the rabbis that the tribes will have special signs, remnants of their former status, by which it will be possible to identify them.

3. The great Gaon of Vilna has told us that as the coming of the Messiah draws nigh, there will be "an awakening in the lower spheres to match the awakening in the upper spheres." It is not enough, therefore, to expect the Lost Tribes to return by themselves. We in the lower spheres must awaken them. However, it is not our task to bring them all to the land of Israel — not when there are said to be thirty million Pashtuns with special signs in Afghanistan and Pakistan alone. We are charged with bringing a symbolic number of them to stimulate the upper spheres.

Three backpackers came up to Avichail after the lecture. I had noticed one of them at a table while we were eating. A lanky, copper-haired boy with a rope belt in his jeans, he had passed several times from a state of apathy to an agitated activity that alone seemed capable of rousing him from his lower-sphere somnolence. Now, fully awake, he asked to join our expedition. Two girls, like stranded hitchhikers sticking out their thumbs at a passing car, also requested to come along. While Avichail explained that we were full up and jotted down the name of a travel agency in Chiang Mai recommended by the boy with the rope belt, it occurred to me that if he was looking for lost Jews, he need go no farther than Bangkok. And perhaps it was he himself who was lost, like the comic hero of the Yiddish novel *The Brief Travels of Benjamin the Third*, unaware, as he wanders through Czarist Russia in search of the biblical tribes, that he is more outlandish than any of them could possibly be.

Micha, who had slipped outside, came back with the good news that he had sighted the moon. "I'll be right there," Avichail said, as if an important guest had arrived — and, in a manner of speaking, one had. We were well into the Hebrew month of Tammuz and had not yet blessed the new moon, for which he had vainly scanned the gray skies for nearly a week. Quickly gathering some prayer books, he hurried outside with the Lubavitcher and some others. Though he did not jump up and down three times as do some Jews when intoning, "As I dance before thee and cannot touch thee, so may none of my enemies touch or harm me," but merely rose on the balls of his feet as if on toeshoes, the mumbling men with their little books in the Bangkok street still made a strange sight. High above them great tatters of cloud streamed across the quarter moon like Buddhist prayer flags.

We returned to our hotel room to discover that Avichail's video camera had been stolen while we were out. With it had gone our inner-line permits to the Indian border state of Mizoram, the final planned stop of our trip. "He'll drive me crazy," Micha said after Avichail went off to report the loss to the police. "Of all places to stick our permits, in his camera case!"

⚱

It was because of the stolen video camera that we found ourselves standing, at a few minutes past six the next evening, before the locked door of the North Star Travel Agency in Chiang Mai. A signboard on the sidewalk said:

NON TOURISTIC
NEW REMOTE AREA

MONEY BACK GUARANTEE! IF YOU WOULD LIKE A TREK DIFFERENT THAN USUAL TREKS AROUND CHIANG MAI WE CAN GUARANTEE YOU AN AREA WHERE YOU WILL NOT SEE ANOTHER TREKKING GROUP WHILE YOU ARE WALKING RAFTING ELEPHANT RIDING OR STAYING IN HILLTRIBE VILLAGES. IF YOU SEE OTHER TREKKING GROUPS WE WILL REFUND YOUR MONEY.

Already closed, too, were most of the tourist shops lining the city's main street. Taking me aside, Micha explained why he and Avichail were late. "I spent all day with him looking for a camera. He didn't like anything he saw. Finally, after we've been to every store in Chiang Mai, he spots what he wants in a window. But it's a demonstration model, and he won't pay the full price, and even though the storeowner is ready to knock it down a thousand baht, he holds out for two. 'One.' 'Two.' 'One!' 'Two!' 'Eliahu,' I say, 'Buy the damn thing. You're arguing over small change.' 'It's a matter of principle,' he says. As a matter of principle, he has no camera."

They were like Sancho Panza and Don Quixote. For the most part, they got along well. Although Micha grumbled like a housewife at an absent-minded husband, he deferred to Avichail unquestioningly in spiritual matters.

In the end we found an open door at the V-Sign Trekking Agency and booked a jeep and driver-guide for the morning. Avichail's mood, however, failed to improve. Chiang Mai was swarming with tourists. What could be left of the old ways described by Mason and Marshall in Karen villages trampled by elephant-riding trekkers? "I don't imagine we'll learn any more than we did from the Chiang," he said. "We'll have to depend on books."

Despite all his travels, it was books that made him most comfortable. Places as such did not interest him; neither, apart from their possible Israelite origins, did the people living in them. More than once in China his lack of curiosity had exasperated me. Any suggestion that we stray from our route to take in some scenic vista, the briefest conversation unrelated to his investigations, left him pouting. Even when his mood was expansive, there was no room in it for his surroundings. Once, near Songpan, we found ourselves at twelve thousand feet, high on a ladder leaned against the Himalayas. Our driver had stopped to let a herd of yaks cross the road, driven by Tibetan women with the red-flecked cheeks of ripening apricots. From somewhere came a warble like a blackbird's. It made you want to sing too — and Avichail did, starting in his pleasant tenor with "By the shores of Galilee/ A castle stands in majesty," and on through every Hebrew song he could think of. For the next hour, until the clouds rolled in, the Tibetan landscape passed by to the soundtrack of an Israeli campfire.

The road from Chiang Mai was more pedestrian. It traversed a thickly settled valley and passed neat towns and shopping centers that looked like Suburban Anywhere. Even the traffic was sedate. Unlike the Chinese, the Thai motorists could have passed a driving test in Connecticut. E Tien, our chubby guide, who had promised to take us to Karen villages unspoiled by trekkers, even used his rearview mirror and his signal lights.

Not that driving couldn't be hazardous in Thailand, too. After a while we asked E Tien why, the few times he honked his horn, it seemed to be at nothing in particular. He replied that he was greeting the spirits.

"What spirits?"

The ones that caused accidents. Take that curve up ahead. Right after it, on the right side of the road, we would see a little house. It was a spirit house. There had been a bad collision there several years ago. Collisions were the work of angry spirits. Mostly the spirits were angry because they had no place to live. If you built them a house, the accidents stopped. Even then, it was a good practice to give them a friendly greeting as you drove by. The spirits liked that.

A moment later we passed a dollhouse on a post, and E Tien tooted a salute.

"But you can't really believe that!" we said. He had told us he was college-educated and "not religious."

He did, though. From beneath the dashboard he pulled out a little Buddha on a chain that was even stronger magic against spirits. It had been given to him by an uncle who had a method for testing store-bought Buddhas. E Tien's uncle tied the Buddha to a chicken and fired a pistol at the chicken's head. If the chicken lived, the Buddha was a good one.

Who were we to scoff? Avichail had his own magic, a Prayer for the Road said each time we set out for anywhere, a rapid burst of sentences that began: "May it be acceptable to Thee, our Lord our God and God of our fathers, that you bring us forth in peace and guard our steps in peace and stand by us in peace and bring us to our destination alive, joyful, and in peace." He never traveled without it.

Yet Thai religion had its own peculiar logic. It wasn't so much its is-and-isn'ts, which were perhaps no odder than those of Western faiths, as the way these meshed with its do's-and-don'ts. One day we were in the Karen village of A Gai Nei, watching a local priest named La Aa perform an exorcism. La Aa was treating a woman, a mother of two small girls, for fever and aches. The woman had been to the doctor but had not been helped, and now she knelt on the floor of her hut beside La Aa, who was carefully winding a purple ribbon around a small bamboo platform as though roping off a miniature boxing ring. The ribbon ran around four posts, each topped with a white paper flag. One end of it was tied to a flat wooden doll standing in the middle of the ring. The doll had a diamond-shaped head and stubby arms. When La Aa finished circling the posts, he took a banana stalk, split it lengthwise, and passed the ribbon through it. Then he pressed the split halves together and tied the ribbon's other end to the woman's neck.

A second platform with a doll, a facsimile of the first, lay on the floor behind him. The woman's two daughters were playing at the rear of the hut. Near them, her husband, a tall man with glasses, was placing wooden sticks on the fire of a cooking hearth. "The woman has a bad spirit," E Tien explained. "It comes from the jungle. It lured away her soul and came to live in its place. Now the priest will make it leave and go back to the jungle. Then her soul will return."

He was translating the commentary of a villager with a limp who had joined us by the doorway of the hut, from which La Aa had agreed we could watch. Two scrawny black chickens were tied to the doorpost. "Everyone gets better after seeing the priest," the man with the limp told E Tien.

La Aa came to the doorway. He wore Western clothes; a green towel wrapped around his head like a turban was his only badge of office. The man with the limp put La Aa's Karen into Thai, and E Tien put it into English. "Now comes a part you must not watch. Afterward you may watch again."

La Aa shut the door of the hut. There came a sound of low chanting.

"He is calling to the spirit," the man with the limp said.

I asked if he had ever seen a spirit.

The man squirted a red jet of betel juice from the wad in his cheek. No one could see a spirit, he replied. You could only hear them.

"What do they sound like?"

He shut his eyes and frowned. Then he made a sound like *eeeeee — eeee — yiiiiiii*. It was a high-pitched whimper, like a sleeper's in the worst part of a nightmare.

Whooooooshhh!

A large ball of fire, visible through the slats of the bamboo wall, flared in a corner of the hut. I jumped back, afraid that the hut had caught fire from the cooking hearth.

Whooooshhhh! A second corner went up in flames.

The man with the limp spoke calmly to E Tien. E Tien said, "The spirit has left the woman's body. Now it is inside the house. It wants to stay. The priest is using the fire to drive it out."

Whooooshhh!

Whooooshhh!

The fireball danced around the hut. Then it stopped.

After a while La Aa opened the door and stepped outside. He held a curved knife and a little platform with a doll. The spirit was now in the doll and had agreed to go back to the jungle. La Aa would bring it there. He would make the spirit promise never to return, and then he would release it.

La Aa started slowly up a dirt path that ran through the village to the jungle. With its flags and ribbons, the little platform looked like a birthday cake. The jungle was several hundred yards away, a green wall beyond the last house. La Aa grew smaller as he neared it, his turban blending with the foliage until he was a headless figure with baggy pants.

I asked, "What was all that fire?"

"The priest was spitting rice whiskey on a torch of burning sticks. It's a trick to frighten the spirit."

Tricking a spirit was fair play. Now it was intermission time. The man with the limp turned to go, grunting crossly.

"What's the matter with him?" Micha asked.

"His knee hurts," E Tien said. "He says the priest could cure it."

"Then why doesn't he go to him?"

"He says he can't because he's a Christian. The minister doesn't allow it. The minister makes him go to the doctor. The doctor is no damn good."

It seemed an odd way of doing things, following one religion and its rules though convinced that another knew better. But it was a calculated gamble. Raised in the old Karen faith and then baptized, the man with the limp believed in jungle spirits *and* Jesus while acknowledging the latter to be more powerful. Jesus could consign you to everlasting heaven or hell, whereas a jungle spirit might make you sick or, at the worst, kill you. That made Jesus a better bet. It was just annoying that he had to be so inflexible. Why should he mind the priest's curing anyone's knee?

Had the man with a limp been a Buddhist, thus belonging to the third religion practiced in A Gai Nei, he would have had no problem. The Buddhists and La Aa got along. Buddhism and native religions had co-existed for centuries in southeast Asia, for inasmuch as the one taught that all things were illusion, the good and bad spirits of the others were no more illusory than anything else. But Christianity had no such tolerance. If jungle spirits existed, they were creatures of the Devil with whom only the Devil's helpers would consort. And yet evangelical Christianity was gaining ground in every Karen village we had been in. The Christian churches were aggressive. Besides the promise of personal immortality, a childish fantasy from the Buddhist point of view, they offered a concerned God, free education and health care, the excitement of revivals, the uplift of hymn singing, and the prestige of Western culture. The Buddhists were hard pressed to compete.

The man with the limp came back as La Aa was returning from the jungle, carrying only his knife. The sick woman still knelt on the floor where he had left her, tied to the first doll with her arms clasped around her knees. Her husband came out of the hut, freed the chickens, and brought them inside.

La Aa lifted a basket with Thai money and recited a prayer. As though about to slaughter the chickens, he took a cutting board and whetted his knife. Instead, though, he put the knife down and picked up a folded square of banana leaf. He opened the leaf and emptied loose rice grains from it into a bowl. Then, taking a bamboo tube, he chanted over it while pouring its contents into the bowl, too.

"Rice whiskey," said E Tien.

La Aa chanted over the bowl. He picked it up and tapped its bottom. He tapped and tapped, chanting faster. He scooped some rice from the bowl, cast it onto a cloth, and bent over the grains to study them. The man with the limp explained, "He is looking for the woman's soul. The rice will tell him where it is."

La Aa shook his head. The rice had not spoken clearly. He tapped the bowl again, scattered more rice, and studied the grains. This time he was satisfied. He rose and walked behind the woman. Chanting, he took a swig of whiskey and spat it over her. It sprayed from his mouth in a fine cloud as though from an aerosol can. He swigged and spat, swigged and spat, until the woman was thoroughly wet. Whiskey ran down her dark hair like rain.

La Aa placed the banana stalk with the ribbon on the cutting board. He took his knife, and held it over the stalk. He chanted again. Then, with a whack, he brought the knife down. The banana stalk flew apart. The snapped ribbon twitched like a cut worm.

La Aa removed the severed half of the ribbon from the woman's neck. He knotted its ends, slipped it back over her like a necklace, and sent her husband to look for her soul.

The woman's husband took the doll with its platform of flags. He left the hut and circled behind it. He passed through a vegetable garden, climbed partway up a hill, halted, and glanced around as if searching for something. Then he placed the doll on the ground and left it there. His wife's soul was shy. It would not enter the doll in his presence.

The husband returned to the hut. La Aa was chanting over the chickens. With the blunt side of his knife he slapped each one on its head, and handed them to the woman's two daughters. The daughters put down their toys and killed the chickens. One held their legs while the other pressed gently on their throats, bearing down and easing up and bearing down again. The chickens died without protest, as if submitting to an anesthetic procedure.

The ceremony was over. The woman rose from the floor and went outside to fill a pot with water from a pump. The daughters plucked the chickens. La Aa would share the meal with the family when it was cooked. Meanwhile, he stood in the doorway and chatted with us. He performed such ceremonies, he said, four or five times a week. His fee was a hundred baht. He would have more work if not for the Christians. But the old religion was not doing badly. His oldest son would follow in his footsteps.

I asked La Aa how he knew the woman had had a jungle spirit. He said he could tell by her pulse; a quick heartbeat was a sure sign. Avichail wanted to know why he hadn't cut the chickens' throats. That, La Aa answered, would not have been a good idea. Spirits were attracted to blood. The blood from a chicken's throat would make it harder to get rid of them.

La Aa spoke to E Tien. E Tien said:

"The priest wants to shake your hands for good luck."

Micha and I shook La Aa's hand. Avichail backed away. "Goodbye, goodbye," he said from a safe distance.

Judaism had its peculiar logic, too. Avichail would have shaken La Aa's hand gladly if E Tien hadn't said it would bring him luck. That made it like a blessing. He wasn't about to be blessed by an idolater who practiced black magic.

He was sorry to see that such practices existed. "Not that I didn't know about them before," he said as we drove back to Chiang Mai. "Marshall wrote of them. Still, I'm disappointed."

He had hoped that a Lost Tribe would have higher standards. Yet a minute later he was relating how his beloved Rabbi Kook had exorcised a haunt talking from a woman's throat. "Such haunts used to be more common," he said. "That's because we now live in the land of Israel. Its holiness makes it hard for them to operate."

᭞

La Aa was a medicine man, or shaman, a representative of the oldest religion on earth. Long before Judaism, Buddhism, Christianity, and Islam;

before the great pagan creeds of the ancient world with their temples, bureaucratized priesthoods, ceremonial cults, and sacred literatures; even before the communal rituals of so-called primitive cultures, the shaman was the intercessor between man and the supernatural. It was he who ventured to the spirit world to look for lost souls, appease angry ghosts, and uncover the meanings of dreams; who in eras the names of which fall on our ears like the slow plunk of water in caves — the Cro-Magnon, the Aurignacian, the Solutrean, the Magdalenian, the Capsian-Microlithic — summoned the beasts to the hunt and saw the dead safely home. Professionally speaking, the old Chiang priest in his tatty monkey skin in Chongfung was a colleague of the man known as "the buffalo dancer," the earliest known depiction of a shaman, dressed in a bison hide, drawn some thirty thousand years ago in the French grotto of Trois Frères.

Shamanism was the indigenous religion of the Tibeto-Burmese hill tribes of southeast Asia. Although the tribesmen were rice farmers with a material culture far advanced from that of prehistoric times, hunting for meat and raiding for slaves was still a way of life for them when Western colonialism encroached on their jungle territories in the nineteenth century. Until then they had maintained a degree of contact with the Asian civilizations in the lowlands — with the Chinese to the north, the Hindus and Moslems of Assam and Bengal to the west, the Buddhist kingdoms of Burma and Thailand to the south and east. But those were relations of trade and sometimes of war; cultural influences were slight. Groups like the Karens, Lisus, Akhais, and Yaos had continued to observe their traditions while absorbing relatively little from the more sophisticated faiths around them.

These traditions centered on village priests, who often inherited their roles from their fathers. Their functions were varied. They treated illness; propitiated the spirits that caused it; presided over the feasts and ceremonies of the year; blessed the farmers, hunters, and fighters on whom each village depended; performed, with the correct chants, the sacrifices that accompanied these rites; divined propitious times and places for new undertakings; ushered souls into and out of the world; and were the repository of the oral wisdom of their people, with its stories of gods and spirits, human origins, fabled heroes and warriors, animals and men, good and bad actions and their consequences, the afterlife, and other things. In a world without books, a priest like La Aa had once been the village library.

Finding him had not been easy. Although E Tien kept his promise and soon headed off the main road and away from the popular tourist spots, the Karen villages we came to had nothing in the way of traditional priests. The first village, Sap Na, reached by a dirt track that followed a brook upstream through thick jungle, had a Protestant church. There were Karen words in Latin characters over the doorway. One of them was *Yoha*.

"That could be Y'wa," Avichail said, telling E Tien to ask about it.

The man E Tien asked was named Chu Hum. Chu Hum agreed that Yoha was God.

"Yoha created the world?" asked Avichail.

No, Chu Hum said. Jesus created the world. That was why he was sacrificed to on Christmas. Three pigs were killed in his honor in front of the church.

"But when you are sick, you pray to Yoha?"

No, Chu Hum said. When he was sick he went to the hospital.

The dogs in Sap Na were all asleep, sprawled on the village paths as if they had fallen while staggering home from an all-night revel. Collared pigs and tethered buffaloes shared the space beneath the bamboo huts with chickens and motorcycles. Corn, beans, and cabbages grew in gardens. Below, at the base of the hill, paddies gleamed in the morning sun. Villagers were at work in them, transplanting tufts of new rice. The church pastor, Chu Hum said, was down there, too. He was the one we should ask about such things.

We drove on to Sap Hot, where someone had a book about Yoha and went to fetch it. It was a Protestant hymnal. We drove on to Pa Mon. Pa Mon had two churches, one Kristian and one Kristang.

"What's the difference?"

The Kristian church was Protestant. The Kristang church was Catholic. Hpu Poi, the man who explained this, had been a Buddhist and was now a Kristian.

"Why not a Kristang?"

The Kristians' rice, Hpu Poi explained, grew better. But most of the inhabitants of Pa Mon were Buddhists.

Avichail was getting discouraged. "Maybe we should go back to Chiang Mai and look for a scholar," he said.

Hpu Poi told E Tien that in the next village, Pan Ton, there was a Kristian schoolteacher who might know more. His name was Su Lei Dei and his father had been a priest in the old religion.

We drove to Pan Ton. Su Lei Dei was wearing a T-shirt that said HAL-LELUJAH. One arm was bound at the wrist with a piece of string. This, Marshall had written, was the traditional Karen method of keeping the soul from leaving the body. Souls were notorious for wandering off if left untended.

Yes, Su Lei Dei said, his father had been a *mal khak*, an old-style priest. That was back in the days when people prayed to spirits and sacrificed pigs and chickens to them. They turned to many gods because they did not know the truth about the One God. This was the work of Mu Kaw Lee, who was Lucifer. The truth was written in a book the Karens had lost.

Avichail came alive. "You know about the lost book?"

The lost book, Su Lei Dei said, was the Bible. Now that the Karens had it again, they believed in Jesus.

Avichail trotted out his questions. Birth customs. Marriage customs. Funeral customs. Sacrificial customs. "If your father touched a dead man, he could make sacrifice?"

"Yes," Su Lei Dei said.

"If he was with his wife the night before, then too?"

"Yes."

Avichail put away his notebook. A biblical priest was forbidden to do such things.

Su Lei Dei's other answers did not call to mind biblical religion either. But if we wanted to speak to a real priest, he said, there was one in Ah Gai Nei, half an hour's drive away. He and some friends would soon be setting out with a film projector and a Christian movie for a revival meeting there. We could follow their car.

That was how we first met La Aa. His home, like all Karen houses, stood on stilts and was reached by a ladder that widened toward the top. Seated on the floor with two sons who were nursing bottles of beer, he was smoking a long-stemmed pipe. He showed no surprise at three Israelis barging in on him. Perhaps he'd been expecting us. I had read in a book by the wife of Francis Mason — "Mrs. Mason of Burmah," as she called herself — of a Karen belief in an ancient contact, one day to be renewed, with *falang*, white foreigners. The Karens, Mrs. Mason wrote, believed the *falang* were their younger brothers, separated from them when men took to speaking different languages. One day they would return, bringing the Karens' lost book.

La Aa knew this story. Long ago, he said, God had sent the Karens a book of gold. He gave it to a messenger on horseback and told him to deliver it. But on his way the messenger met a *falang*. "What do you have there?" the *falang* asked. "It's a book," said the messenger, "that I'm bringing to the Karens." "Do you mind if I have a look?" the *falang* asked. The messenger did not mind, and the *falang* read the book and wanted it for himself, so he said, "Look here, gold is not as shiny as silver. Why don't I copy this book for you on silver?" The messenger agreed and the *falang* copied the book. He gave the messenger the silver one, and went on his way, keeping the gold book for himself.

The messenger rode on with the silver book. After a while he left the land of the *falang* and came to the land of the yellow man. The yellow man asked to see the book and wanted it, too. "Look here," he said, "silver is not as strong as buffalo hide. Why don't I copy the book for you on hide?" The messenger agreed, and the yellow man copied the book on buffalo hide, gave the copy to the messenger, and kept the silver book for himself.

The messenger rode on with the buffalo hide. After a while he came to the land of the Karens, who were working in their paddies. "I have a gift for you from God," he said, handing them the buffalo hide. "It's a book." The Karens did not know what a book was. Since they were too busy planting their rice to ask, they thanked the messenger, hung the buffalo hide on a tree, and went back to work. While they were working a dog came and ate the hide. At the end of the day, when they remembered their gift, it was gone.

"This book, what was in it?" Avichail asked.

La Aa did not think it was the Christian Bible. "It was about the education of the Karen people," he said. "It was about how to survive. It had stories."

"About what?"

"Olden times."

"How God created man?"

"Yes. God made Saw Ah Dee and Naw Ee Oo. Then came a big flood."

"Wait," Avichail said. "Before the flood. What happened before the flood?"

La Aa didn't know.

"Something about a garden?"

La Aa knew nothing about a garden. Perhaps the old priests had known. Much had been forgotten.

"But what happened to the man and woman God created?" Avichail asked.

La Aa couldn't say. He knew only that their children and grandchildren, and all the generations that came after them, had lived as one family for a long time. The whole world spoke one language: the Karens, the Thais, the Chinese, the *falang* — everyone. They had one religion. Then Mu Kaw Lee built his tower.

"Mister Mu Kaw Lee wanted to get to the sky. That was where God lived. Mu Kaw Lee wanted to fight with God, so God knocked down his tower with thunder."

"The name of God, it was Y'wa?" Avichail asked.

No, La Aa answered. That god was not Y'wa. It was La Ma Su. La Ma Su threw a thunder ax at Mu Kaw Lee's tower.

But Y'wa, La Aa had heard of him?

Yes, La Aa said. His father had told him about Y'wa. Y'wa was a big god. No one was bigger in the whole world. All life began with Y'wa. La Ma Su and Y'wa were different gods.

"What happened to Mu Kaw Lee?"

"He wanted a wife, so he returned to earth and married there and became the father of twelve tribes."

One of La Aa's sons interrupted him. The second son joined in. After a while they reached an agreement.

"The priest wishes to make a correction," E Tien said. "Mu Kaw Lee was not the father of these tribes. He fought against them. Some were lost. They were scattered to China, Burma, Tibet, even Japan."

I said in Hebrew, "That doesn't sound like an old legend to me."

Avichail agreed. There was, he said, an organization in Tokyo that claimed the Japanese were a Lost Tribe too; it had sent a mission to the Karens several years ago, and the idea must have come from that. "Ask the priest," he directed E Tien, "if he has heard of Abraham."

The question went from English to Thai to Karen. Then the answer came back the other way. "Yes. He has heard of Abraham. But that's a Christian story. The priest doesn't know Christian stories. He only knows Karen stories. They are very long. It would take three days and three nights for him to tell them all."

We didn't have three days and three nights, but we were free the next day, when La Aa would be performing a ceremony. There was a woman he was going to heal. We were welcome to come back and watch.

We discussed our visit with La Aa on the ride back to Chiang Mai. Avichail was content with it. "We've confirmed the story of the lost book," he said. "We've heard it was written on parchment like a Torah scroll and had the stories of Genesis."

"Just a minute," I objected. "We heard a total of three such stories. One was about the flood. That means nothing. There are flood stories all over the world. A second was about the creation of man and woman, and that's universal, too. The most you can say for it is that La Aa's name for the woman, Naw Ee Oo, was the same as Marshall's. That leaves the Tower of Babel. You can't base a theory just on that."

"What about the Yud-Kay-Vav-Kay?" Micha asked, using the Orthodox way of referring to the sacred four-letter name of God.

"All right, so the Karens had a god named Y'wa, or Yoha, or whatever," I said. "What does that prove? He's not even the God of the Mu Kaw Lee story."

"The priest said he was above all other gods," Avichail countered. "And he told us that Mu Kaw Lee then descended from heaven to take a wife. That's exactly what we find in Genesis where it says, 'And the sons of God came unto the daughters of men, and they bore children to them.'"

"All I can say," I said, "is that if the Karens are a Lost Tribe, they were lost before the twelve tribes existed, because every one of their stories with a biblical parallel refers to a time prior to the biblical Patriarchs. There's nothing about Abraham, Isaac, or Jacob, nothing about being slaves in Egypt, nothing about Moses, nothing about Joshua, nothing about the judges, Samuel, Saul, David, Solomon, the kings of Israel and Judah. How do you explain that?"

Avichail turned around in the front seat. "You know, you may have something there! 'But unto the sons of the concubines which Abraham had, Abraham gave gifts, and sent them away from Isaac his son, while he yet lived, eastward, unto the east country.' This is the east country! We're in it."

So now the Karens were descended from Abraham's concubines. Why hadn't anyone thought of that before?

The day after the exorcism in Ah Gai Nei was a Friday. Avichail and Micha decided to fly back to Bangkok for the Sabbath. There was a synagogue there, and the Lubavitcher's kosher restaurant was more attractive than our dwindling stock of cans. I opted to stay in the north and meet them on Sunday at the Bangkok airport for our flight to Calcutta, giving me two tribeless days to tour with E Tien. I felt paroled.

By now, though, E Tien had been bitten by the bug. "Is everyone in Israel looking for the Lost Tribes?" he asked me.

"No," I told him. "Most Israelis couldn't care less."

"Well, I care," he said. "I want to know if the Karens are or aren't."

Although I managed in the next two days to ride an elephant, eat fried crickets in the home of E Tien's friend Phon, and fall off the slippery levee of Phon's rice paddies into three feet of muddy water, E Tien made sure we kept up the quest. He even infected Phon, who drove us around one day in his pickup truck.

But the quest was too late. In the half dozen additional Karen villages we visited, no one knew any more than La Aa. Of all the stories mentioned by Marshall, we kept encountering the same two, in different versions: the lost book and the toppled tower. Over and over we heard the refrain "Our fathers knew more than we do." "And my children won't know what I know," a man named Tu Hkaw said in the Buddhist village of Mai Sai Puk. "They don't want to listen. They'd rather hear Western music."

Tu Hkaw did not think of his children as part of a worldwide trend. Yet from his porch in Mai Sai Puk, with its view of women at outdoor looms weaving gaudy shirts and blouses for the tourists E Tien would bring, globalization was happening under his nose. Like every Karen village in Thailand, Mai Sai Puk was in transition. While a young man chugged past Tu Hkaw's porch with a primitive contraption strapped to his chest, a motorized paddy cultivator of which he was the human chassis, a woman smoking a homemade cigar hulled rice with a log pestle, a device as old as the hills, that her foot raised and lowered like a seesaw. Little children hitched rides on it and scooted in and out of the low spaces beneath the houses.

Tu Hkaw thought the tower to heaven had been a joint venture of the Karens, the *falang*, and other people. It was built "to meet God" — that is, Buddha — and it went up, up, up — Tu Hkaw's hands climbed an imaginary rope — until Buddha poisoned its stones, and everyone forgot how to talk. It was Buddha, too, who sent the Karens the lost book, which they put aside and forgot. He kept sending them messengers to ask whether his book had arrived, and they kept saying that it hadn't.

In the village of Mei Kong Pei, the tower's builder was a single man. He was halfway to the sky when his mother called to him to stop, making him so angry that he knocked the tower down. Everyone scattered in different directions to keep from being hit by the stones, the Karens to one land, the *falang* to another, the Asians to a third.

The man who told us this, Nu Bu, had just returned from the village of Hue Paw, where he was treated for a cough by a priest named Daw. Nu Bu had never heard of Y'wa and believed the world was created by Buddha's dog, which killed a deer and ate it so quickly that pieces of meat fell from its mouth and turned to earth. The lost book, he said, was written by Buddha in a cave. When it was time for Buddha to depart from the world, he invited everyone to a party, at which the book was his farewell gift. The Moslems, hurrying to get there first, did not bother to wash, and they are dark to this day. The Christians took their time and washed thoroughly, which is why the *falang* are so light. The Karens were busy in their rice fields. *Yang awn, yang awn,* they said, meaning "later, later," and never went to the party at all. And so the Thais call the Karens "Yang."

In Hue Paw we found Daw at the home of the Kiao family, whose wrists he had just finished restringing for another year. The Kiaos were eating the sacrificial meal, kneeling around it and using their fingers. Daw told us that the tower to heaven was built not by a man named Mu Kaw Lee but by a girl named Mu Lee Kaw. Mu Lee Kaw quarreled with her mother and built the tower to run away from home. She reached the sun and asked, "Can I stay with you?" "Oh, no," the sun said. "I'm much too hot. Go ask the moon." So Mu Lee Kaw climbed higher and asked the moon. "Oh, no," the moon said. "You can't count on me. You see, I keep changing my shape. Go ask the sky." The sky said to Mu Lee Kaw,

"Yes, you can stay with me, but first I have to test you by thunder." So the sky cast three thunderbolts to the left of Mu Lee Kaw and three thunderbolts to her right, and when she wasn't frightened, the sky married her to its son. One day she decided to visit her mother and climbed down to earth with her husband. Since he did not like the taste of dog, Mu Lee Kaw told her sister Mu Kaw Lee, "Whatever you do, do not cook dog for my husband." But Mu Kaw Lee, jealous of her sister, cooked a pot of rice with a dog's head and served it to the sky's son, who angrily darkened the world for seven days and seven nights and destroyed Mu Lee Kaw's tower. All the animals ran for cover and were separated. All the people were separated, too. They were so frightened, they forgot how to talk.

"Did that really happen?" I asked.

"It really did," Daw said. "But a very long time ago, at the time of the first men."

Daw wasn't sure where the first men came from. He should have listened more to his father's stories, he said. But he believed everything had started with a single man and a single woman. All else came from them.

"Saw Ah Dee and Naw Ee Oo?"

The Kiaos buzzed with excitement at my knowledge. Naw Ee Oo, one Kiao said, became pregnant and gave birth to a pumpkin. She and Saw Ah Dee chopped it up and from the pumpkin seeds came all the people of the world.

An argument broke out. Not all the Kiaos thought mankind came from a pumpkin. Some thought people had come from a hole in the ground. Others insisted the hole people were not the first. There were people before them, who were killed by a great fire. A man and a woman survived the fire in the hole, and it was they who repopulated the world.

Daw had an idea. In Mei Ta Loo lived an old priest named Pah Maw. Why not ask him what was in the beginning?

We piled into Phon's pickup — Daw, E Tien, myself, and six or seven Kiaos in the back — and headed for Mei Ta Loo. Rain was falling, streaking the dirt road with orange rivulets. The Kiaos had a fine time getting wet. They laughed and joked each time we hit a bump.

The teak leaves tiling Pah Maw's roof had a wet, coppery sheen. Pah Maw was leaning against a post inside the entrance. A frail-looking man, he wore only a pair of shorts. He was mostly a rib cage and two ears. The ears were remarkable. They hung like fallen breasts and had large holes for the heavy plug earrings that Karen men wore in olden times. Pah Maw's earrings had been lost or discarded. You could stick a finger through his ear lobes.

The two priests greeted each other warmly. They took out their pipes and leaned back to back against the post, like a pair of bookends. Each time one spoke, he let out a puff of smoke and filled it with words, like a cartoon character.

The Kiaos gathered around, waiting for the polite talk to end so that Daw could ask Pah Maw where people came from. After a while he did, and Pah Maw said, "In the beginning, in the *very* beginning, before Saw A Dee and Naw Ee Oo, there was only water. That was all there was. There was nothing to eat but fish. One day the Karen people went fishing. A fisherman looked into the water and saw something he had never seen before. He reached down to pull it out, but he couldn't because it was the earth. And so he took off his shirt and laid it down to claim the earth for the Karens and then went off to look for fish. But a Thai fisherman had been watching. As soon as the Karen paddled off, the Thai picked up the shirt and saw the earth beneath it; he took off his own shirt, put it beneath the Karen's, and went off to look for fish. He did not know that a *falang* fisherman was watching him. The minute the Thai was gone, the *falang* took off *his* shirt and put it beneath the other two. Then a tree grew from the earth and the water receded. That is why to this day the best land belongs to the *falang*. The next best went to the Thais. We Karens have the poorest land of all because we didn't watch over our shirt."

The Kiaos laughed at the way their ancestors had been short-changed. They didn't seem bothered by the existence, in Pah Maw's story, of a human race before humans were created. One of Pah Maw's sons brought in a tray with betel nuts, a plate of green areca leaves, and a bowl of wet lime. He snipped the nuts with what looked like a manicurist's scissors, helped himself to a sliver, smeared a leaf with lime, rolled the betel in it, popped it in his mouth, and passed the tray around. The Kiao next to me did the honors for me. I hurriedly spat out the bitter leaf, causing another peal of laughter.

After we dropped the Kiaos back in Hue Paw, I remarked how jolly they were. "Yes," E Tien said, "they were very pleased."

"With Pah Maw's story?"

"No. With you."

I was the first *falang* to have visited Hue Paw and Mei Ta Loo. "They think it is a good sign," E Tien said. "They hope that now the tourists will come."

He himself thought both villages had potential. "They have jungle. They have elephants. They have everything we need for good trekking." The V-Sign Agency had to keep its competitive edge. These two days had been good for him, too.

⚜

On our return trip to Chiang Mai, E Tien turned off the main road and headed for a place called Nang Den. He had heard of a Karen priest there named Hpu Poi. It was not much out of our way.

Nang Den turned out to be a Thai rather than a Karen village. You could tell from the more orderly layout of the streets and the larger, wood-frame dwellings. A boy directed us to Hpu Poi's house, which stood behind a hedge of rose bushes. The priest was at home with two Thai men, who lay on the floor like lounging mastiffs. He sat in a far corner with his back to the door, facing a table placed against a wall. On it were some bowls, a basket of money, a liter Coca-Cola bottle filled with water, and a candle. On a shelf in a corner stood a television set. A teenager watched a program while doing her homework in an exercise book.

Hpu Poi was chanting. After a while he stopped and turned around, his glance curiously taking in the *falang*. He wore a long white jacket like a druggist's smock. On a tray before him were the roots of some plants, over which he began to chant again.

E Tien chatted with the two Thais while Hpu Poi chanted. One had stomach problems. The priest's medicines were good, he told E Tien. They were genuine Karen remedies. You didn't have to go through a lot of mumbo-jumbo for them. You paid 320 baht to have them blessed and took them home.

Hpu Poi filled two smaller bottles from the Coke bottle and chanted over them. He stopped to stare at the television. The screen showed a Thai village like Nang Den. Hpu Poi regarded it with interest, as if hoping to see someone he knew. Then he went back to blessing the water and slicing some pieces of root. He wrapped them in paper, handed each man his package with a bottle, and gave him instructions for its use. Meanwhile, a woman had arrived and taken a seat by the back wall, which served as Hpu Poi's waiting room.

Back in the car, E Tien commented, "He wasn't a real priest. He's more like a Thai healer."

I wondered which was greater: the distance between Hpu Poi and La Aa or between La Aa and the buffalo dancer of Trois Frères. Hpu Poi and La Aa were both Karens and lived within a hundred kilometers of each other. La Aa and the buffalo dancer were eons apart. But they shared the same dealings with the spirit world. Hpu Poi was running a succesful clinic.

Of course, that was only one way of looking at it. La Aa did not live in the Stone Age. He lived in a village with televisions and motor vehicles and contending ways and ideas. And the modern ways were winning. His religion was not yet on the endangered list, as was Wang Tsu Tsin's. It might survive for another generation or two. Yet many traditions had already been lost or jumbled. A complex language had changed structure and been reduced to a cruder creole or pidgin.

I did not believe that the biblical parallels in Karen mythology could be dismissed out of hand; it was improbable that observers like Marshall or the Masons had simply made them up. But what they actually heard and merely summarized in their books was no longer knowable. The story of the tower built by Mu Kaw Lee (according to Marshall, a devil figure in Karen lore), inverted by others to a female Mu Lee Kaw, was too small a piece of the puzzle to permit a guess at the rest of it. Yet even it gave one pause. While two legends about a tower built to reach the sky could originate independently in different parts of the world, this was unlikely with two legends about a tower's collapse causing the linguistic and geographic dispersion of mankind. That wasn't the kind of imaginative lightning that strikes twice. If it was found in different places, one had to assume some connection between them.

Perhaps, then, the Karens did encounter or know of parts of the Bible in a more distant past. Their story of a lost scroll could be interpreted as such a memory. It could explain lines of old Karen poetry, such as the ones quoted by Marshall:

> The book of the ages was rooted by the pigs.
> At first the women neglected it.

The men also did not look at it.
If both men and women had studied it,
All the world would have been happy.
Our book of old that Y'wa gave,
Our book of silver that he gave,
Our elders did not obey.
Lost, it wandered to the foreigner.

"But there are other explanations," I told E Tien. "After all, the Karen were an illiterate people surrounded by literate cultures — the Thais, the Burmese, the Chinese, the Indians. It would have been natural to account for this by a story. In all the versions we've heard, they lost their book while working in the fields. That sounds like a way of saying that, as a society of subsistence farmers, they lacked the leisure time for reading. The Chiang in China believed they once had a holy book too. That doesn't make it the Bible. And even Mu Kaw Lee's tower, however woven into the fabric of native folklore, could have started with early nineteenth-century missionaries. Look at the way that business of the twelve tribes was picked up from the Japanese. Within a few years it was part of a Karen legend."

"So we'll never know," E Tien said.

"Not unless we find Karen hideaways deep in Burma where the old stories and songs are still sung and told."

It would take the overthrow of the Burmese regime to allow anyone to find that out. Meanwhile, there was not a shred of evidence linking the Karens with the Israelites exiled by the Assyrians. Their religion was typically southeast Asian. If they had picked up biblical narratives from "a Hebraic source," as Marshall put it, this source could have been Christian or Islamic or even a single traveler straying from the highways of antiquity or blown off course by a monsoon. Perhaps this was why, if Mrs. Mason was to be believed, the Karens thought their lost book would be brought back by their "younger brothers," who would "come by water."

But what did that mean? The Indian Ocean or the South China Sea, both far beyond present Karen territory? One of the great rivers flowing down from the foothills of the Himalayas, such as the Irawaddy or the Salween, along the valleys of which the Karens themselves may have migrated from their Sino-Tibetan borderlands long ago? The whole thing was an enigma.

⚝ 3 ⚝

Aizawl

THE INDIAN ENGINEER waiting for his flight to Lucknow was fascinated. "Did you say 720 A.D.?" he asked.

"B.C."

"Incredible. And if you decide these chaps are a Lost Tribe, you'll bring airplanes and whisk them all away?"

He was thinking of the Ethiopian Jews, airlifted to Israel in the 1980s. But the Ethiopians had a long history of living as Jews, even if it was pure fantasy to believe they were descended from the biblical tribe of Dan, as Israel's chief rabbi had ruled in 1973. The B'nei Menashe of northeast India were a recent development. "To qualify as immigrants to Israel," I told the engineer, "they would have to convert to Judaism. That means rabbis to convert them. There aren't any in India."

"What about your friend over there?"

"It takes a rabbinical court of three to convert. And months of study. You have to convince the court that you've learned the rules of Judaism and intend to observe them."

"Suppose you pretend to intend?" The idea of a country to which admission depended on convincing three bearded men that you were going to practice their religion intrigued him.

"It's not like cheating on your income tax," I assured him. "No one audits you."

The intricacies of Judaism were too much to explain in the July heat of Calcutta Airport, especially when I had one ear tuned to the conversation that, a few seats away, Avichail was having with Jeremiah Hnamte. Jeremiah, identified by the calling card he had given me (blue Star of David in one corner, red menorah in the other) as "General Secretary, B'nei Menashe Council, Aizawl, Mizoram," had come to Calcutta with new inner-line permits to replace the ones stolen in Bangkok. Now he was telling Avichail that his community had just split in two. Some of its members had reverted to "Christian ways" and started a new congregation. They had rented a building and put up a sign saying, HA-RAV ELIAHU AVICHAIL SYNAGOGUE. Worse yet, they confused the prayers and even bowed the wrong way. Ha-Rav must put an end to it.

Avichail was noncommittal. "They'll have to take the sign down" was all he would say.

The big ceiling fans flogged the dead air. Our seven A.M. flight to Aizawl had been delayed. At six-thirty, we were told that the weather there was bad; at eight, that it had improved but there were only two seats available for the four of us; at nine, that there were seats but our luggage was too heavy to take off with; at a quarter to ten, that the plane could take off but would lack fuel for the return trip; at ten-fifteen, that fuel might be available in Aizawl; at eleven, that Aizawl was not answering the telephone; at twelve, that it had fuel but the weather was bad again. Now we were scheduled for two. Micha went to fetch more paper cups of Indian coffee that tasted like tea while Avichail discussed with Jeremiah Hnamte the possibility of a joint Israel-Mizoram commercial venture. "What does Mizoram produce?" he asked.

Jeremiah took off his baseball cap and stared, with heavy-lidded eyes, into the space his head had left behind. After a while he said, "Dzindzer."

"Ginger! Very good!" Avichail declared. "We will send you agronomes to help you grow ginger and then buy it from you." Seeing me point to the departures board, which had just moved our flight back again, he called cheerfully, "Oh, that I had wings like a dove, for then would I fly and be at rest!"

It was his sixth trip to the area. In 1979 some "Jews of northeast India," as they then referred to themselves, had written to the head librarian of the Hebrew University in Jerusalem, asking for information about Judaism. The letter reached Avichail, who wrote back and received an answer. Three years later he flew to Calcutta, only to discover that

Mizoram and Manipur had been through an armed insurgency. All foreigners were barred from them. The following year he returned to Calcutta, having been assured that a permit would be granted him. Once again it was not. This time, however, a delegation of "northeast Jews" came to meet him.

On first telling, their story had to strike even a Lost Tribes enthusiast like himself as dubious. In the early 1950s, they said, in a village in northern Mizoram, a man named Chala had a vision. An angel revealed to him that the Mizo people were the descendants of Israelites and should return to their ancestral land. For a while, knowledge of his revelation remained confined to his fellow villagers, some of whom adopted Old Testament ways while continuing to profess Christianity. Gradually, however, word spread north to Manipur. By the 1970s a group had formed there around the belief that the descendants of Israelites should live by Israel's faith. Attempts were made to contact Jews in Calcutta and Bombay and to put into practice what could be gleaned from them about Judaism. But Eliahu Avichail was the first truly knowledgeable Jew his visitors had encountered. In his Calcutta hotel room they begged him to teach them all they needed to know about their new religion.

Avichail was perplexed. "They had an ancient ancestor named Manasia and Jewish tradition on their side," he had told me in his Jerusalem apartment the day we met. "The rabbis say that Menashe will be the first of the Lost Tribes to return. This will be the reward for their ancestors having risked their lives to bury King Saul when he was slain by the Philistines. But I would have felt better if it hadn't all started with a vision. If only there had been something before Chala . . . How could I believe it just because a man dreamed it?" And yet there was more to it than Chala's vision. "The more we talked, the more I saw they had *signs*. They had priestly sacrifices, like those in the Bible, which they offered to a God named Yah. They had once practiced circumcision. They had an ancient song about crossing the Red Sea. They had a story like the Karens' about a sacred scroll that was lost. It was burned by the Chinese. It was the same scroll; that was obvious."

It wasn't obvious to me. As I saw it, two different peoples telling the same story about themselves increased the likelihood of its being fictional; for Avichail, it confirmed that it was true. Convinced, he agreed to be the group's mentor. Once the travel ban was relaxed, he obtained the elusive permit, returned to India several times, and taught the rudiments of modern Israeli-style Orthodoxy in Aizawl and in Imphal, the capital of Manipur. In 1990 he began bringing groups of B'nei Menashe, as the "northeast Jews" were now called, to Israel and arranging for their temporary housing, religious studies, and conversion, following which they were granted full citizenship under the country's Law of Return. At present there were four hundred of them in Israel and an estimated ten times that number in India. Three-quarters of these lived in Manipur.

Avichail had hoped to include Manipur in our trip, but the ethnic warfare there had grown worse. It was between the Kukis, the ethnic group most of the Manipuri B'nei Menashe belonged to, and a people called the Nagas, and it made a visit inadvisable. "There's been shooting along the road from the airport to Imphal," he told me. "It isn't worth the risk."

⚶

In the end the departures board said CANCELED, and we left for Aizawl the next day. The flight took us over Bangladesh and the Ganges-Brahmaputra delta. Great rivers snaked over a vast flood plain on which land and water tilted inconclusively. It was like looking down on the second day of Creation, before the two were separated. Then we climbed above the clouds.

When we broke through them an hour later, the landscape had changed. We were flying over green hills. Scattered villages sat on hilltop clearings, tin roofs glinting on red earth. From above, the jungle pressed against them, they had the look of provisional encampments.

The jungle came into focus as we descended. Its solid canopy dissolved into dimensions. It was tiered, pocketed, spongiform. It had depths and cavities and upright spars. It had not one shade of green but a hundred. It was spiked and studded like a coral reef.

The green, jewel-like reef was moving. Leafy fans waved in the gray air. Tall stalks tossed finny branches. Our sixteen-seater cruised the tops of them. Then it was swimming alongside them in a winding canyon. The hills shot up on either side. It chuted the curves, cleared the pommel of a saddlebacked ridge, and hit the tarmac with a hard bounce. It was like landing on the bottom of an ocean.

The plane taxied to the end of the runway; from there we walked to a shack-like terminal, where Indian soldiers and men and women holding signs of welcome were waiting for us. There was an Israeli flag. The men wore skullcaps and looked Chinese or Tibetan. The browner ones looked Burmese. They had a two-handed handshake, pressing your hand between both of theirs. *Salom, salom,* they said. *Chibai, chibai.* Avichail appeared to know them all.

Jeremiah Hnamte relinquished us to the care of a brown-skinned woman. She wore a blouse buttoned at the neck, a long cotton-print skirt, and a prim English bonnet. Her face was long and thin like her body, and she held an umbrella in one hand. She resembled a Burmese Mary Poppins.

The woman showed our permits to a soldier and led us, with our luggage, to a car. Her named sounded like "Zaitantsungee." She giggled when she said, "Call me Zai." She giggled often, as if her throat had a staircase down which she kept nervously falling. She had the Mizos' problem with palatals. "The Dzoos community expects you in synagogue at four o'clock," she told Avichail. "Eats person has been informed." She was, it seemed, the organizer of our visit, a fact Avichail accepted with reluctance. "She's not one of ours," he told us in Hebrew as we began the drive into Aizawl. "She's a Christian, but supportive. She runs an insurance agency and has a husband in the state legislature. We couldn't have gotten our permits without her."

He broke off to say the Prayer for the Road. It was a timely notion, because the Mizos did not drive like Thais. They ignored the English road signs with their admonitions like NO HURRY, NO WORRY, took the turns of the narrow road at full throttle, and gave passing vehicles just enough clearance to avoid rubbing off their paint.

Zai apologized for the length of the ride. A new airport, she said, was under construction. Meanwhile, the present one, forty kilometers from Aizawl, was on the nearest piece of level land to the capital. "We are a much mountain country," she apologized.

Her voice tumbled down more steps, regained its footing, and said, "I have something important to discuss with you, rabbi. It is the Jewish community. I am distressed by it."

Avichail maintained a discreet silence.

He must have heard, Zai continued, of the recent rupture. Until a year ago the B'nei Menashe of Aizawl had lived in harmony, but now there was much dissension. The new congregation was having a bad effect. It was headed by a man named Peter Tlau. He was not the brains behind it, though. The brains were Zomaya's. Zomaya was a Christian pastor and not circumcised.

"Not circumcised," Avichail said, "is bad."

"Not circumcised," Zai affirmed. "You must make peace between them."

Avichail sighed. "Peace," he said, "is a great commandment of Judaism."

The English speed warnings were mixed with signs in Mizo. This was a language written in exotic combinations of Latin characters in which "Zaitantsungee" was spelled Zaithanchhungi and "Zomaya" as Zohmengaiha. The only words I could identify were "Jesus" and "Bible."

"Forgive me for asking," I said to Zai, "but why does this matter to a Christian like yourself?"

Zai said, "Because we Mizos are Israel. We are from the tribe of Manasia."

She had written a book about this, based on research. "We Mizos come from a place called Chhinlung. This has been identified in southwest China. We had a Torah scroll that was burned by Shi Huang Ti, China's first emperor. Then he enslavéd us to work on his Great Wall. He did this because we have built the Pyramids in Egypt. We ran away and hid in caves. Then we left China to come here."

I let the Torah scroll and the Pyramids pass. "What does that have to do with the tribe of Manasseh?"

"Manasia was our first ancestor. His name is uttered in the prayers of our old religion. When we sacrificed to God we said, 'We, the children of Manasia, offer you the blood of this animal.' When a priest chased a devil from someone he told it, 'Release this man; he is not in your power. We are the children of Manasia.' When we cut the jungle for a new village we asked forgiveness for the sake of our grandfather Manasia."

"But Manasia could have been anyone. He could have been a southeast Asian like you."

Zai did not think Manasia was a southeast Asian. The old Mizo religion was too much like the Bible. It worshiped a single supreme God. It had the same laws. The first British missionaries had encountered these. "They told our grandparents, 'Since you observe all the customs of the Bible, you must believe in Jesus, because he too is in the Bible.'"

I observed that if that were so, it was strange that the missionaries themselves hadn't declared the Mizos a lost tribe. Why did that have to wait for Chala?

Zai did not know the answer. She knew only that the Mizos felt a mysterious kinship with Israel. They followed the news from there all the time. It meant more to them than the news from India. After the Israeli commando raid on Entebbe, all the people of Aizawl had celebrated in the streets. You would have thought the rescued hostages were Mizos. And when Prime Minister Rabin was killed, the streets were empty. Aizawl was in mourning.

It was now visible, Aizawl, through the scarves of mist that intermittently wrapped the green hills, its houses flung over them in picturesque disorder. There was no pattern or discernible axis for the eye to arrange these on. They appeared to have slipped or tumbled down the hillsides to the clusters they now formed, the larger ones stopping farther up while the smaller ones continued to roll. You couldn't tell where the slide had started or where it was bound for.

It took a long time to reach its edges. The shortest distance between two points in this land of nothing flat was a meander that swung away from its destination each time it seemed headed for it. And once we were in its streets, Aizawl was not as pretty as the revolving postcard views from afar. The more we neared its center, the more cluttered it grew. The bright colors were coming off the houses. Squeezed together like furniture in an overcrowded room, these were bricolages of whatever material — brick, glass, tin, cinderblock, fiberboard, iron, aluminum, wood, plasterboard, asbestos — had been weldable, nailable, or gluable to something else. Telephone and electric wires streamed wildly. The traffic was unruly and the city's sidewalks were too narrow to walk on. Their backs turned to the vehicles that missed goring them by inches, the pedestrians would have been safer with the bulls in Pamplona. The policemen alone were out of harm's way. High on their stands in white gloves, they blew unheeded whistles while gesturing gracefully, like orchestra conductors.

But I saw Zai's point. After the second or third sign I began counting them. Israel Appliances. Israel Bazaar. Israel Grocery. Israel Authorized Retail Shop. Israel Agency. I had never been in such an Israelite town.

Israel Metal Fabrication. Israel Store. Zion Hardware. Israel Millennial Enterprise. Hotel Ritz.

"This is where you are staying," Zai said. "I've reserved two rooms, a double and a single. I'll come for you this evening." She was holding a reception for us.

⚜

Minchah is the shortest of the three daily Jewish prayers. Although religious law permits it to be said at any hour of the afternoon, it is usually coupled in synagogue with Ma'ariv, the evening prayer. Minchah precedes sunset, and Ma'ariv follows. If there is congregational business, it can be sandwiched between them.

But though it's over in ten minutes, you can tell an observant Jew, or someone raised as one, by his Minchah as much as by anything. He knows when to stand and when to sit, when to pray softly and when out loud, when to say "amen" and when "blessed be He and blessed be His name." Such things are elementary. You pick them up as a child, as you do the sway of the body and the tone of the voice. For Minchah has its own tone, a dry murmur different from the brisk chant of the morning prayer or the wistful crooning of the evening one.

You can learn all this. Plenty of born-again Jews do. In the end you can't tell them from the born-and-breds. But they have their daily models, other Jews to pray and study with. The astounding thing about the members of the Shalom Zion Synagogue of Aizawl, now saying a last "amen" at the end of the mourner's Kaddish, was that they had accomplished it on their own. I had just seen them say Minchah as if they had been doing it all their lives. When the prayer leader put on his prayer shawl and called in Hebrew, "Happy are they that dwell in Thy house, they will ever praise Thee," they had responded without pause, "Happy are the people who thus fare, happy are the people whose God is the Lord." Commencing the Eighteen Benedictions, they had bent their knees and bowed in unison as each whispered, "Blessed art Thou, O Lord our God and God of our fathers, God of Abraham, God of Isaac, and God of Jacob." Concluding with "Thou who makest peace in the heavens, grant peace unto us and unto all Israel," each took three steps backward and bowed with knees straight — to the left with the first step, to the right with the second, straight ahead with the third. It was a flawless performance.

Directed by Avichail, of course. But how often, over the years, had they rehearsed with him? A week here, a week there — if that much.

Some of the synagogue's founders were now in Israel, and some of those present were meeting him today for the first time. Many could not read Hebrew; they used prayer books with the words spelled phonetically in Mizo and had no idea what they meant. And yet, with an inspired mimicry, they had learned their parts perfectly. They had even mastered the Minchah murmur. Close your eyes and you could have been, if not for those slipped palatals, in a synagogue in Jerusalem.

The men put away their prayer books. I recognized some of them from the airport. The prayer leader, Eliezer Sela, was one. Jeremiah Hnamte was there, too, in his baseball cap. And seated with his followers on a back bench was the breakaway Peter Tlau. Peter had been to see Avichail in the Hotel Ritz an hour ago. "It's all a matter of face," Avichail had told us on the short walk from the hotel to the synagogue. "They'll have to patch things up between them."

The curtain screening off the women's section at the rear was now slid open on its clothesline. The women's section was as crowded as the men's. Some of the occupants were holding small children or carrying babies in cloth shoulder slings. There was an air of expectancy. Avichail was going to give a lesson.

He took a seat on the podium. Eliezer Sela's daughter Rivka sat beside him. She had been in Israel and knew some Hebrew.

He began with a rabbinic maxim. "On three things," he quoted, "the world rests: on truth, on justice, and on peace." *On truth, justice, and peace,* he repeated. Each needed the other two. There could be no truth without peace, for truth fled when men fought. There could be no justice without truth, for justice was perverted by lies. There could be no peace without justice, for injustice led to war. Truth, justice, and peace were like the three primary colors. All else was made from them.

Rivka Sela translated into Mizo. It was a twittering language, full of chirps and hiccuppy high notes. Often she resorted to English for words that seemed to have no Mizo equivalents. "Community." "Synagogue." "Judaism." "Tolerance." "Standards." Avichail helped her when she got stuck.

Solemn eyes regarded him. He was appealing for peace in the community. Yet he was not asking the warring congregations to re-unite. He would not force them to pray together. There was room in Aizawl for more than one synagogue. There was room for more than two. "May we

see the day when there are five, ten, twenty synagogues in this city!"
That, too, was but a fraction of the number of synagogues in Jerusalem.
Judaism was a religion of tolerance.

His eyes swept the room, brushing Peter Tlau and Jeremiah Hnamte.
Peter was the Burmese type of Mizo. Jeremiah was the Tibetan. Avichail
said, "But tolerance does not mean lack of standards. Many synagogues
cannot be many Judaisms. There is only one Judaism, the Judaism of the
Torah. And Judaism has its truth."

He expounded. "One God. The Sabbath. The dietary laws. The Ten
Commandments. Circumcision. These are the truths of our religion. If
you deny them, you are unjust. If you are unjust, there can be no peace. I
ask you to live in truth, so that you may live in justice and peace."

It was a carefully phrased verdict. The breakaway synagogue was a
fact. So was the need for circumcision. Jeremiah and Peter could work
out the rest for themselves.

Avichail asked if there were any questions. Eliezer Sela raised his
hand.

"I have something to say," he said. It concerned "Come, my love, to
meet the bride," the Sabbath hymn I had learned Avichail's melody for in
the Wenchuan County Teachers Center Guest House. "When we welcome the Sabbath bride on Friday nights, we bow twice to her on the
words 'Come, O bride, Come, O bride.' In this synagogue we have always made our first bow to the rear" — Eliezer Sela pointed toward the
women's section — "and our second bow to the front." He pointed to the
door, positioned to the right of the Holy Ark. "This is what Ha-Rav
taught us. But now there are people who say they have heard otherwise.
They have changed Ha-Rav's teachings and bow twice to the rear. My
question is: which is the proper way to bow?"

You could feel the room suck in its breath. Peter Tlau leaned forward
on his bench. Jeremiah Hnamte regarded his hands, whose fingers met in
a delicate arch. Avichail said, "To answer your question, we must first ask,
who is the Sabbath bride? Is she a real bride with a wreath of flowers on
her head and a long white gown? Of course not! To bow to such a bride
would be idol worship. We would be no different from the Christians,
who worship idols and images. The Sabbath bride is a figure of speech
for the Shekhinah."

There was laughter at the thought of the Sabbath bride decked out

with flowers. Rivka Sela had trouble with "Shekhinah." Avichail helped
her. "This is God's holy presence in the world. When our Temple was
destroyed, God left its western wall standing so that the Shekhinah,
whose abode was the Temple, would not leave us. For this reason we
are told that the Shekhinah abides in the west. And since Jews pray by
facing Jerusalem, which for most of them is to the east, the west is at their
rear. They therefore bow twice to the rear to welcome the Sabbath
bride."

Peter Tlau beamed. Jeremiah Hnamte stared through the arch of his
hands.

Avichail continued. "You in Mizoram, however, live to the east of Jerusalem and pray by facing west, so the direction of the Shekhinah is in
front of you. And since there are places where it is customary for Jews to
welcome the Sabbath bride by bowing once to the rear and once to the
front door, this is how I taught you to bow. Eliezer Sela is right."

Peter Tlau's face fell.

"However," Avichail added, "it is important to understand that these
are only customs. A custom is not a sacred truth. It is not written in the
Torah. Some Jews bow to the rear and some also bow to the front. Both
are acceptable."

The solemn eyes waited for more. But there was no more. Avichail
folded his arms on his chest to indicate that he had answered Eliezer
Sela's question.

No one stirred. Peter Tlau and Jeremiah Hnamte glanced about as
if to read the name of the winner in the faces around them. Nothing
was written there. No one knew who had won. Disappointment spread
through the synagogue like a slow stain. The distinction between truth
and custom was too subtle. How could it not matter in which direction
you bowed to the Sabbath bride? Why observe a custom that wasn't true?
Ha-Rav had said there was only one Judaism — and now he was saying
there were two, one that bowed to the front and one that bowed to the
rear. If the world rested on justice, where was the justice in this?

And yet when Avichail asked for more questions, none was forthcoming. It was unthinkable to challenge his authority. This was not like the
Jerusalem yeshiva where he taught, whose students did not fear to dispute with him. He was about to call for the evening prayer when a man
rose and said, "I have something to say. We have heard that our brothers

in Manipur have received more visas to Israel than we have. Why should that be?"

There was a murmur of assent.

Avichail said, "I will answer you. But first let me ask, who here wants to go to Israel?"

Everyone in the synagogue raised a hand.

"You see, that's the problem," he said. "The government of Israel is now granting one hundred visas a year to Mizoram and Manipur together. We have had to struggle to obtain even that number, because Israel does not recognize your Jewish descent. There are nearly a hundred of you in this synagogue right now. To whom shall I give these visas? In Manipur the situation is more urgent. Your brothers there are caught in a civil war. That is why they are given priority."

Someone said, "Ha-Rav says we are not recognized as Jews. But we have heard that many of the Ethiopians now coming to Israel are Christians. Why does Judaism recognize them and not us?"

He pronounced it "Dzudáyzm."

Avichail nodded. The complaint was not new to him. "The ancestors of these Christians," he explained, "lived as Jews. They became Christians only recently because of great threats or enticements. Jewish law is clear on this point. A Jew abandoning his religion under duress remains a Jew. But your case is different. I believe you are of the tribe of Menashe. But I am only Eliahu Avichail. When I go to the chief rabbi of Israel and tell him this, he asks, 'How do I know?' I cannot say, 'Because Chala had a dream.' I must present evidence. The chief rabbi is hard to please. If I speak of your ancient sacrifices, he says, 'Show me such a sacrifice today.' If I tell him about Manasia, he asks, 'How do I know this is Menashe?' I need your help to bring me more proof. Yes, Ezra."

The young man called upon had already risen and was waiting to be recognized. He spoke in a painfully determined English, forming the words one by one like a stutterer.

"You tell your chief rabbi — this. It is true. When there be a log on the road — our fathers say — 'Come, sons of Manasia, let us move it!' So! They move the log. But my granddaddy pray not only to God of Manasia. Also — to God of Terah, Abraham, and Moriah."

Avichail laughed good-naturedly. There was no God of Terah, Abraham, and Moriah. "Believe me," he said, "it's easier to move a log than the chief rabbi." He gave the lectern a thump. "Ma'ariv!" he announced.

ⵣ

There was thunder and lightning all night. Before falling asleep I glanced at Zai's little book about Mizo-Israel identity.

She had given me a copy at her reception. Most of its comparisons between the Bible and the old Mizo religion were not to be taken seriously. Many were on the order of "Among Mizos, each of the opposing parties in a battle traditionally selected a champion. These two champions met on a single bridge and fought. Likewise, we see in the Bible that David, the champion of the Israelites, defeated the giant Goliath."

This was out-Torrancing Torrance.

More useful was Zai's geographical and historical introduction. I learned from it that Mizoram had been known to the British colonial administration of India as the Lushai Hills. That these had an average height of 900 meters, and ran in a north-south direction, interspersed by deep gorges in which rivers flowed toward the Bay of Bengal. That traditionally the Lushais had been organized in independent village-states led by local kings or warrior chiefs. That their territory was first invaded by the British in 1844, when troops entered it on a punitive expedition. That it was conquered and declared a district of British India in 1892 and the first English missionaries arrived two years later. That they found a native animist religion in which, as the Reverend Enoch Lewis Mendus wrote in his *Diary of a Jungle Missionary*, "There is a consciousness of a supreme spirit or Deity whom the Lushais call 'Pathian,' the Giver and Preserver of life. They believe him to be by nature or disposition . . . good-natured, amiable, and humble, but somewhat inactive, particularly as regards controlling the evil spirits." That by the time of Indian independence, in 1947, the Lushais, now known as the Mizos, had been Christianized almost entirely. That, consequently, "the literacy rate is very high among the Mizos, which is surpassed in India only by Chandigarh, Kerala, and Delhi." That Mizoram, formerly part of Assam, was declared the twenty-third state of the Indian union in 1986 as part of a peace settlement formally ending a separatist insurgency led by the Mizo National Front. That as of 1991 its population was 700,000, nearly all of it ethnically homogeneous.

In the morning it was still raining heavily. I stayed in my room to write while Avichail went with Micha to teach a Hebrew class in the synagogue. In Aizawl he had little time for his historical investigations. He had a flock to tend to, and its needs were numerous.

I filled the last page of my notebook, looked for a new one, and saw I had run out. Despite the rain, I decided to go out and buy one.

The Ritz was on Aizawl's main shopping street, which ran along the knife edge of a hill. Steep flights of stairs descended to the parallel streets below. I passed the lane leading down to the synagogue and headed toward a fork several hundred meters ahead. If I bore right there, I had been told by the Indian staff at the hotel desk, I would come to several bookstalls that sold writing materials.

I had not yet reached the fork and was regretting venturing out without even a hat when an umbrella appeared magically over me. Holding it was Ezra, the young man from the synagogue. Laboriously, as if he had carried the word a long way and did not want to drop it carelessly now, he said, "Sir!"

And thrust a calling card into my hand.

I stood reading it under the dripping umbrella. It was decorated, like Jeremiah Hnamte's, with blue Stars of David and said:

EZRA CHHAKCHHUAK (HUALNGO)

LEADER

BAKHURIM KULANU

B'NEI MENASHE

AIZAWL

MIZORAM

"Come," said the leader of Bakhurim Kulanu, Hebrew for All We Young Men, an organization that, it would take me some days to discover, did not exist. "A man wants to see you."

He had an intense stare. Though he had no way of knowing that I would pass this way, he had apparently been lying in wait for me.

"What man?"

"Aw," Ezra said. That was Mizo for "yes."

He held his umbrella over my head and let the rain come down on him.

I followed him up the street. At the fork, we bore left. A bit after that, he halted by some steps. A faded sign said: CHHINLUNG ISRAEL PEOPLE CONVENTION, GENERAL HEADQUARTERS.

A small waterfall ran down the steps, making them hazardous. At the bottom was a grimy courtyard. Ezra pushed open a wooden door and began to climb more steps. At the top he opened another door, and we entered a large room furnished with chairs, benches, and a shabby couch. Several loungers stopped their chatting to regard us. The walls were covered with posters and a large hanging cloth on which were printed in red the same words as the faded sign's. These formed a circle around a second circle made, once again, of blue Jewish stars. Inside that was a red star.

The place had the air of a political clubhouse. It reminded me of the civil rights workers' offices I had seen in the American South in the 1960s. A tall woman rose from the couch. Her long skirt was a rich loom weave that would have cost a lot in an ethnic crafts' store in New York. "I'm so glad you could come," she said. "I'll tell my husband you're here."

She was gone before I could ask who her husband was. Presently he appeared from a back room and greeted me. "So you are the journalist traveling with the rabbi."

I asked, "And whom do I have the pleasure of interviewing?"

"Sorry! I thought Ezra had told you." Out came another card. This one had Jewish stars, too, and the words:

LALCHHANHIMA SAILO

PRESIDENT

CHHINLUNG ISRAEL PEOPLE CONVENTION

Lalchhanhima Sailo watched me slip the card into my wallet. "I founded the CIPC four years ago," he said. "We're the fastest-growing organization in Mizoram. We now have one lakh supporters and chapters in two hundred and eighty villages." A lakh was Indian for a hundred thousand. "That's the number that signed our petition to the United Nations. Not all are from Mizoram side. Many are from Manipur side, Burma side, Bangladesh side, Tripura side. We sent the petition to the Secretary General, Mr. Kofi Annan. You'll want to see it, of course."

He sent his wife to bring it.

His Indian English with its quick, eager syllables was the best I'd heard since my engineer's in Calcutta Airport. It came, he said, from Delhi. He had a bachelor of general law degree from JNU. "That's Jawarhalal Nehru University. In the end I came back to Aizawl, though. I had to. We're not Indians, you see. That's what this is all about."

"This" was the document his wife now placed before me.

A "Memorandum Submitted by the Chhinlung Israel People Convention to the United Nations Organisation," it got right to the point.

This memorandum seeks to represent the case of the Chhinlung Israel people, presently known as Mizo, in India for our right to unity, re-unification and solidarity, and for the realisation of our true identity as the Lost Tribe of Israel in India, for which a fervent appeal is submitted to the United Nations Organisation to proclaim to the world, fulfill, and uphold our true identity as the Lost Tribe of Israel.

Traditionally the Chhinlung people claims to come out of a mythical rock called "Chhinlung" near the Great Wall of China, and before that claims descent from Joseph's sons Manasseh and Ephraim. This is proven by our verbal stories passed down to us by our ancestors and so by the migration of our ancestors about 750 B.C. from Canaan to China, then about the middle of the 12th century from China to our present land. In the migration process they halted at several places, some for long periods and some for short, cutting through Shan State of present Burma (Myanmar) to Arakan, the Chindwin Valley, the present Chin Hills of Myanmar, and the present Mizoram State of India . . .

The land of the Chhinlung spreads over a wide area, extending into the present Manipur State, North Cachar of present Assam State, Zampui ranges of present Tripura State, Chittagong Hill Tracts of present Bangladesh, Chin Hills area, Matupui area, Khumi area, Mire area, and Arakan of present Burma. The present Mizoram State was carved out arbitrarily for administrative convenience purposes against the will of its people, the Chhinlung, by the British rulers. Therefore, looking into this population break-up it is a great injustice that the Chhinlung/ Mizo, having the same culture, speaking the same language, professing the same religions, and knit together by common custom and traditions, should have been called and known by different

names and scattered among different people with their homeland
sliced out and given to others.

"Allow me to read you our concluding appeal," Sailo said.
He had a clear, ringing voice that seemed aimed at an invisible microphone.

> So for this end, it is in good will, faith, and understanding that
> the Chhinlung people voices its rightful and legitimate claim
> of being the Lost Tribe of Israel through this memorandum.
> So let the Governments of India, Myanmar, and Bangladesh in
> their turn and in conformity with the unchallengeable truths ex-
> pressed in the charter of Human Rights give us the recognition
> of the Lost Tribe of Israel and not call us by the Gentile names
> given to us wrongly. We also appeal to the United Nations Or-
> ganisation for the restoration of our basic human rights in con-
> formity with the spirit of the Atlantic Charter, so that we can
> identify ourselves as belonging to one ethnic group.

He laid down the document and said, "We have sent copies to the
presidents and governments of India, the United States, Great Britain,
Russia, France, China, Israel, Bangladesh, and Myanmar. A response has
been received from the United Nations. It is most encouraging."
He took from a file a letter sent by an undersecretary of the United
Nations Commission on Human Rights:

> Dear Mr. Sailo,
> We wish to acknowledge receipt of your letter. We regret that
> we have many such applications to process and will inform you of
> the status of your request at the earliest opportunity.

Lalchhanima Sailo said, "Now that we have been acknowledged by
the United Nations, we are awaiting final status clarification. Then we
will proceed with a national referendum to declare our true identity."
Was he deranged or merely far more naïve than his polished Delhi ex-
terior suggested? "You surely don't expect," I said, "that India, Bangladesh, and Burma will cede you territory for a Lost Tribe state."
"Indeed not. We are a purely educational movement, operating in full
accordance with Articles 51-E and 73-C of the Indian constitution. Our

aim is to declare who we are. There are over two million of us living in three different countries and going by half a dozen different names. In Mizoram we are the Mizos. In Manipur we are the Kukis, the Paites, the Hmar. In Burma we are the Chin or Lai. Everywhere we are limbs of the same body. We propose to call that body by a single name. The right to change a state's name is granted by the constitution of India."

"To a biblical tribe's?"

"To anything."

"But what makes you think you are such a tribe?" I asked. "I keep hearing the same vague things. This memorandum is no different. Here, for example. 'The migration of our ancestors from Canaan to China.' What migration is that? How do you know about it? What are these 'stories passed down'? I haven't heard a single one. And this Chhinlung you're named for — I've been told it's a town in China, and here you say it's a mythical rock. What does either have to do with the Great Wall? And in addition to descending from the tribe of Manasseh, you now descend from Ephraim, too. You're a lawyer. You know what rules of evidence are."

"Evidence," Lalchhanima Sailo said, "is hard to come by in Mizoram. There are few people with firsthand knowledge of our old religion. One hundred years of Christianity have wiped that out. Even elderly Mizos alive today were raised as Christians. Burma side is different. The old ways are still kept up there, especially down south, in the Arakan Hills. But you couldn't possibly go there. I'll see whom I can find for you to talk to."

It was agreed that I would return in two days. That would give him time to round up his witnesses.

I wasn't sure what he was up to. Although he had asked Ezra to bring me to him, he wasn't a B'nei Menashe. Nor, however, did he consider himself a Christian. "My father wasn't one either," he said. "He was baptized but never believed in it. We Sailos are a family of chiefs. My grandfather, Saikulara Sailo, was the chief of Kawnpui. He hated the Christians and their missionaries. Christianity is the reason we Mizos no longer know who we are."

"But it is who you are," I said. "You're a Christian society."

"It may seem so. But every Mizo knows something is missing. He just doesn't know what it is. He sees no alternative to Christianity. And your rabbi's people aren't helping. People think their Judaism is only a way to get to Israel. But Israel doesn't recognize us, isn't it? Besides, we couldn't all go there if it did."

We stood in the doorway. He had a broad, handsome face, its forehead slashed by an ax blade of black hair. With sudden, hard candor he said, "Look here. I don't care what my religion is. I want to know who I am. Show me I was once a Christian, and I'll be a Christian. Show me I was a Jew, and I'll be a Jew. Show me I was an idol worshiper, and I'll worship idols. *But show me who I am.*"

He was a pan-Mizo nationalist looking for a unifying myth. Had he been born a generation earlier, he would have fought in the jungle with the Mizo National Front. But the MNF had lost its war for independence — had been sold out, Sailo said, by its leader Laldenga, who had settled for mere Indian statehood. And Mizoram, though it had its own legislature and elected officials, was effectively ruled by an Indian governor appointed by Delhi and backed by a garrison of the Assam Rifles based conspicuously in the center of the capital. I had passed its walled compound with its rifle-bearing sentries and heard the barking of troops on parade.

It wasn't a police state. Someone like Sailo couldn't have operated if it were. But the police were around, and they weren't just waving on the traffic. They let me know it that afternoon when, sitting in on one of Avichail's Hebrew classes, I was informed that the Central Intelligence Division wished to see me. Jeremiah Hnamte would take me there in his car. It was nothing to worry about, I was assured. A routine check.

That was all it was. I was registered in a blotter and chatted up over tea by a friendly inspector, who returned my passport with the declaration that all Mizos and Israelis were brothers. "Salom, salom," he said as I departed.

Yet Sailo had to assume that he was being watched. Was the Lost Tribe claim a mere tactic, a biblical varnish for his Mizo identity politics? Although it wouldn't fool anyone keeping tabs on him, it might be enough to keep him within the law.

On our way back from the CID, Jeremiah complained about Peter Tlau. Despite his promise to remove it, Peter had not taken down the sign with Ha-Rav Avichail's name. This was deception. Anyone could see that Ha-Rav preferred the Shalom Zion Synagogue. He gave his lessons and said his prayers there. He would never pray with Christians.

⁂

That night we had a visit from Peter. I was sitting with Avichail and Micha in their room when he knocked. With him was Zohmengaiha, the uncircumcised Christian pastor. Zohmengaiha wore a suit and tie and carried a leather briefcase. A small, mild-mannered man, he placed the briefcase on a table and let Peter introduce him in English.

Peter looked nervous. They had come, he said, on a serious matter. People were spreading bad stories about them. "Very, very bad stories! They say Mr. Zohmengaiha does not wish to circumcise. They say he wish to remain a Christian. This is not so. Mr. Zohmengaiha wish to circumcise. He know it is the will of Hasem."

Peter used the Hebrew circumlocution for God that means "the Name." He frowned angrily on "very bad" and "not so," his face miming the words like a storyteller's. "Mr. Zohmengaiha," he said, "has a medical problem. He has come to tell Ha-Rav about it."

Zohmengaiha took a sheaf of papers from his briefcase. His problem, he explained, was diabetes. He had brought his medical records. This was his albumen count. And here was his blood sugar: 450 mgs after fasting. The doctors had told him that circumcision was dangerous for a man in his condition. Even minor surgery could lead to complications. He knew Judaism forbade endangering one's health even to perform a commandment. He had come to ask the rabbi whether he could be a Jew and attend synagogue without being circumcised.

Avichail glanced at Zohmengaiha's blood sugar count. He spoke gently, like a doctor with bad news. "I'm sorry, but this is not possible," he said. "Since the time of our father Abraham every Jew must be circumcised." The prohibition on endangering health did not apply to Zohmengaiha, because Zohmengaiha was not a Jew. He would have to be circumcised to become one. But there were new medical procedures. "I have heard that circumcision can be done by electricity," Avichail told him. Perhaps not in Aizawl. But there were certainly doctors in Bombay or Calcutta who knew about such things.

Zohmengaiha bowed his head. He had the stoic air of having expected as much. He knew the God of Sinai did not give discounts. This was what had attracted him to Judaism in the first place. He had been a Church of God minister and had fallen ill. While in bed he had read the Bible day and night. With each book he had seen more clearly how the New Testament cheated on the rigors of the Old. He would take Ha-Rav's advice and go to Calcutta.

The matter of Zohmengaiha's circumcision disposed of, Avichail turned to Peter. He wished to summon him and Jeremiah to the Hotel Ritz the following evening for a *din Torah*, a rabbinical trial. Despite his lesson in the synagogue, he had heard their bickering had not stopped. They had refused to bury the hatchet as he had asked them to. "Since you cannot do it by yourselves, you will do it with me," he said.

"Yes, Ha-Rav," Peter answered. "Tomorrow evening." He joined his palms in front of him and moved them back and forth, Burmese-style, to signify compliance.

Peter was a Chin from Burma. Perhaps this accounted for his emotional temperament, unlike that of the stolider Mizos. "Oh, Mr. Hillel," he said, following me back to my room with Zohmengaiha when we left Avichail's. "I am afraid of this meeting with Mr. Jeremiah."

"You needn't be, Peter," I said. "The rabbi only wants to make peace."

"Peace. Yes. Of course." Peter wrung his hands unhappily.

"Then what is it?"

He grimaced as if at a dreadful truth. "You do not know Mr. Jeremiah. Mr. Jeremiah is very cunning. Mr. Jeremiah has tell my people the wrong time you land at the airport. So! My people are not there to welcome you."

Peter's group had been about to set out for the airport when news reached them that we were already in Aizawl. That was how treacherous Mr. Jeremiah was. Their quarrel had begun with last year's elections for the B'nei Menashe Council. Peter and Jeremiah had run against each other for general secretary. Although the results were narrowly in Jeremiah's favor, Peter's faction checked the voting list and discovered that many of Jeremiah's voters had never been to the polls. "I said to him, 'Mr. Jeremiah, how can this be? These people do not come to vote.' 'Peter,' he say, 'you are best keep silent. You are new in this community. Who you think you are to say all this?'"

Peter's eyes widened with surprise on "how can this be" and narrowed to heavy-lidded slits on "best keep silent." Mr. Jeremiah had threatened him. Mr. Jeremiah was guilty of bad things. Peter mimed putting money in his shirt pocket. He patted the pocket and made smug Tibetan eyes.

I asked why, if there were financial irregularities, Rabbi Avichail had not been informed of them.

"Everyone is afraid. Mr. Jeremiah is the one to make up the list for Israel. Whoever protest him is not on the list."

"Well," I said. "here's your opportunity to have it out with him in front of the rabbi."

Peter clapped his mouth in horror. "Oh, no, Mr. Hillel! I cannot tell Ha-Rav. Ha-Rav will not believe me. Ha-Rav does not come to my synagogue. Why he go only to Mr. Jeremiah? My synagogue is name in his honor." He looked for confirmation to Zohmengaiha, who nodded sympathetically. "I have tell everyone he will come. They are expect him. If he does not come, they will say, 'That Peter, he is a very bad man. Why that Peter lie to us?'"

I tried to calm him. "Peter, you heard what Rabbi Avichail said. He gave your synagogue his blessing."

"Then why he does not come? Mr. Jeremiah has put ideas into his head. He has tell him we follow Christian ways. This is not true. We only say, we are in Mizoram, we are not yet in Israel. In Mizoram let us teach Judaism to the Christians. We will not tell a Christian, 'No, you are not welcome.' But of course he must circumcise. This is the will of Hasem."

Peter had been a Christian lay leader in Burma before coming to Aizawl, where he ran a computer agency. Besides reading the Bible like Zohmengaiha, he was influenced in his adoption of Judaism by his grandfather. His grandfather had been angry at Peter's father, an NCO in the British army, for becoming a Christian. He had told Peter many times that the Chin people were the children of Manasia. Years later, hearing of Chala's vision, Peter understood who Manasia was.

His grandfather had taught him a song. He sang it for me:

> *Saion alut ten ten.*
> *Saion alut ten ten.*

> We are entering Zion.
> We are entering Zion.

It sounded like a children's jingle. "Your grandfather must have learned that from the missionaries," I said.

"Oh, no, Mr. Hillel. It is very old."

Peter was childlike himself. He had the old colonial awe of the White Man. Perhaps others in Aizawl did too, but none was so demonstrative of it.

⚶

I heard Peter's grandfather's song again the next day at the Chhinlung Israel People Convention's office. The Mizo words differed but slightly from the Chin ones:

> *Lut theng theng,*
> *Lut theng theng,*
> *Saiona alut theng theng.*

They had the same jingly tune. There was a dance that went with it. Lalchhanhima Sailo and a man pointed out to me as Ezra Chhakchhuak (Hualngo)'s father demonstrated. Ezra's father put his hands on Sailo's hips and they did a conga line around the room.*

Sailo had gathered about twenty people for me to talk to. It didn't take me long to realize that he was right about Mizo memory. Apart from himself, only four of those present knew anything appreciable about the

---

* A word should be said at this point about the Mizo names in this chapter, the different forms of which may bewilder the reader. Traditionally, a Mizo had only one name, given at birth. Usually, a male name ended with *a* and a female name with *i*, as in Zohmengaiha and Zaithanchhungi. Under British and Indian rule, however, some Mizos chose last names, which they usually based on clan or tribal affiliation. Thus, a man named Lalchhanhima who came from the Sailo clan might call himself Lalchhanhima Sailo. Yet all Mizos did not do this, and the growth of Mizo nationalism, which viewed the old clan and tribal divisions as hindrances to a common identity, produced the counter-trend of dropping last names again. As a result, some Mizos today have last names and some do not. Since wives do not commonly take their husband's name in marriage, both practices may exist in the same family. Single-named Zaithanchhungi, for example, was married to triple-named L. N. Tluanga.

The confusion went beyond that. The B'nei Menashe developed the custom of taking a Hebrew or biblical first name upon entering the "Jewish" community and adding to it (if it did not already exist) a last name; e.g., Jeremiah Hnamte. Moreover, one's previous Mizo first name might continue to be used outside B'nei Menashe circles. Yosi Hualngo, for instance, grew up as Biakenga, took a Hebrew first name and his clan name when he joined the B'nei Menashe, and continued being known as Biakenga by his Christian friends. His son, given the Hebrew name Ezra, took his mother's clan name in addition to his father's, as seen in "Ezra Chhakchhuak (Hualngo)" on his calling card. And there were B'nei Menashe who Hebraized their last names, too, such as Eliezer Sela, a Sailo by clan. There were no hard-and-fast rules about any of this.

pre-Christian past, and this, too, was spotty and based heavily on hearsay. As described by my notes, the four were:

> Yosi Hualngo. Was in the synagogue with Ezra. A gaunt man with hollow cheeks and an intense manner like his son's. Born in 1941 to a family of old religion priests in a village near the Mizoram-Burma border.
>
> Sapchhunga. An eighty-year-old retired police officer, a dignified gentleman. Speaks English. Likes to preface his sentences with, "It is only my presumption, of course."
>
> Sapliana. A former Salvation Army brigadier. Seventy-six and hard of hearing.
>
> Lalthuari. A striking woman in her forties from Burma. Ironic seen-it-all eyes, a let's-not-kid-each-other smile. She gives me one when I ask what she is doing in Aizawl, and answers that she is in "the import-export business." I take this to mean smuggling, a common occupation. She is a *pawd chuan*, as she puts it, a Christian dropout, now with no religion.

The questions I asked them were taken from Avichail's list. As first probes, these were reasonable. The problem lay in evaluating the responses. It was like trying to decide whether the blips on a radar screen were mere fuzz or represented something real. So far, in our travels, we had seen all or mostly fuzz.

Now, though, something odd was happening. Despite the small number of informants, the blips were coming very fast. Take my first question, for example, which concerned circumcision. Avichail had been vague when I asked him why he thought the Mizos once practiced it. Yet, as he told Zohmengaiha, a more basic Jewish rite did not exist. From their earliest beginnings, the Israelites had circumcised and named their sons on the eighth day after birth. To be uncircumcised was by definition to be an alien. If there was a single custom that members of a "lost" biblical tribe might be expected to have retained, this was it.

Of course, Jews were not the only ones to circumcise. Moslems did too. And Moslems were concentrated in the Bengali plains not far from the Lushai and Chin Hills. But Moslems did not circumcise on the eighth day or in infancy, while not a single non-Moslem people in southeast Asia was known to have practiced circumcision at all. All questions about it asked of the Chiang and Karens had drawn a blank. Yet here, translated by Sailo, was what I was hearing:

Yosi Hualngo: As a boy he was told by his father's elder brother, Hualkhaia, that "in olden times," on the eighth day after birth, the father pulled back the child's foreskin and the priest severed it with two heated stones held with banana peels. This was no longer practiced when Yosi's father, Piangriangchhunga, was born in 1900. Instead, the priest passed the baby through a coiled vine, rubbed its foreskin without removing it, and declared, "Long ago this is how our forefathers cut our children." Such a ceremony was known as *bawrh keu*.

Sapchhunga: Although he had not been circumcised himself, an older brother had been. In some villages where circumcision was no longer practiced, a wild grape vine was twisted into a coil, and the child was passed through it on the eighth day. It is only his presumption, but he assumes this was in place of circumcision.

Lalchhanhima Sailo: This was practiced in his father's village, too. A male child was named eight days after birth. He himself had been circumcised by his father. He never knew this until, one day, he was bathing with an older, uncircumcised brother who said, "Hey, brother, what a funny wee-wee you have!"

Lalthuari: Although she was raised as a Christian, many people in her village in Burma were still practicing the old religion when she was small. Circumcision was never talked about. That is, the women didn't discuss it. She believed some of the men practiced it, though.

I wrote all this down with a sense of bafflement. I had no way of knowing how accurate any of it was. Zaithanchhungi, although describing the coiled vine ceremony in her book, called it by a different name, placed it on the seventh day after birth, and did not connect it with circumcision. I could only say that if the Mizos *had* once circumcised on the eighth day before substituting a symbolic ceremony that also lapsed, they had followed a ritual practiced by no one but Jews.

None of the other material that came up that day, or at another session the next day, was as dramatic. Often the conversations went nowhere. It was hard to keep everyone focused. People drifted in and out; subjects were raised, dropped, and returned to. Yet the number of blips kept growing. More and more customs with biblical parallels kept turning up. A seven-day period of mourning for the dead (Lalthuari, Yosi

Hualngo). Priest-administered laws of purification or quarantine after physical contact with a corpse (Yosi Hualngo), or after menstruation, skin disease, and leprosy (Lalthuari). Levirate marriage (Sapchhunga). A seven-year limit to enslavement, followed by manumission (Lalchhanhima Sailo). Rules of sanctuary for unintentional murderers (Lalchhanhima Sailo). Priestly garments like those described in the Book of Exodus (Yosi Hualngo, Lalchhanhima Sailo). A four-cornered altar on whose posts was sprinkled the blood of sacrificed animals (Yosi Hualngo, Lalchhanhima Sailo). A single supreme God known as Pathian, Khuahnu, Khuahpa, or Khuahvang. (Sapliana, Yosi Hualngo, Lalchhanhima Sailo). A custom called *ram dai* in which the corners of harvested fields were left unpicked, so that the poor could gather food (Yosi Hualngo). A prohibition against taking eggs from a bird's nest (Yosi Hualngo). It was hard to know what to make of such things. Even if true, none was particularly significant in itself. They could even be fuzz if taken all together. But could they be fuzz alongside eighth-day circumcision?

There were also blank spaces on the screen. Nothing blipped for the Jewish Sabbath day. Nor for the biblical dietary restrictions. Not even that most deeply rooted of Jewish food taboos, the ban on pork, evoked any echo. The Mizos ate pork freely, nor could anyone recall a time when they didn't. Like all southeast Asians — Moslems again excluded — pork was a staple in their diet. I had seen people carrying live pigs around the streets of Aizawl in sacks and baskets like packages of groceries.

But wait. We were talking about sacrifice in the old religion.

> YOSI HUALNGO: Some parts of the sacrifice were eaten and some were not. The part not eaten was given to "the Creator, who has no beginning nor end." The blood of the animal was emptied into a skin bag or cup while the priest chanted, "Ho, Za, Ho, Za, take your blessing." There was also a pig sacrifice made to Ram Huai, the Devil or king of the jungle spirits. When such a pig was sacrificed, it was carried in a cloth to the gate post of the village. The pig was hung on the gate post and no one ate any part of it.
>
> LALCHHANHIMA SAILO: There were two different kinds of priests, the *sadawt* or "priest for the entire people and chief," and the *bawlpu* or "priest for individuals." The *bawlpu* sacrificed pigs to Ram Huai but did not eat them.

SAPLIANA: "After a pig sacrifice in our village all the footprints around the altar were immediately erased."

A VOICE FROM A BENCH: "In our village pigs were never sacrificed!"

LALTHUARI: In Burma the king of the jungle spirits is called Ram Huilal. To this day a pig is sacrificed to him when a new section of jungle is burned. It is then taken outside the village and hung on a tree trunk. The priest never eats of any pig sacrifice.

This was curious. It indicated not just a partial aversion to pigs but the association of them with the powers of evil. Where could such an attitude have come from? Certainly not from the culture of the Tibeto-Burmese hill tribes.

And what about Za, who was, according to Yosi Hualngo, the "Creator without beginning or end"? The Mizos' difficulty with palatal consonants extended to *y*. I had heard Yosi himself called "Zosi." Za could be Yah, a shortened form of Yahweh commonly used in the Bible. The English word "hallelujah" was the biblical *hallelu Yah*, "praise Yah."

And who was Manasia? Nearly everyone at the CIPC office had heard of him. Sapliana recalled his grandfather asking Manasia to bless his new gun. Yosi Hualngo remembered that when a path was cleared in the hilly jungle near his village, the evil spirits were warned, "We the sons of Manasia are coming. You above the road, you below the road, keep away!" Lalchhanhima Sailo knew that when a tree was axed in a field, it first was told, "O tree, we do not cut you down because you are our enemy, but because you are in the way of Manasia."

Could this be the biblical Manasseh? It seemed absurd. How could Israelites exiled by the Assyrians have reached an area thousands of miles beyond the Assyrian empire and survived there for millennia without leaving any historical record? I had to caution myself against being carried away. None of my informants had actually practiced the old religion. All had been raised as Christians and taught the Bible as children. How did I know they weren't projecting their knowledge of it onto an imagined past? In the language of the laboratory, they were contaminated samples. Moreover, Sailo had his own agenda; he made no bones about it. How trustworthy was he?

He was eager to win me over. At one point, taking out a pocket knife, he whittled three small sticks to make a *langlap*. In the old religion, he explained, this was a religious symbol suspended over the sacrificial altar. Lalthuari knelt at his feet and tied the sticks into a six-pointed frame while he held them. With colored thread she wove on them three concentric hexagrams, the inner one red, the middle one white, the outer one black.

"What do you see?" Sailo asked me.

"A Tibetan mandala."

"A Star of David!"

You couldn't blame him for not knowing that this was an ancient magical sign that became a Jewish symbol only in the Middle Ages. Sapliana, who had been watching the *langlap*'s construction, said something in Mizo.

"It's like this," Sailo translated. "When the missionaries first came to Mizoram, they made friends with the priests and debated them. They asked to be allowed to witness their sacrifices. When they saw the *langlap*, they said, 'See, your own religion teaches the truth of the Gospels! The black stands for your sins. The red is the blood of the Lamb. The white is your purified souls.' In this way they turned the hearts of the people."

Lalthuari's fingers worked deftly. She was wearing a Burmese gown of many colors and had let down her long, lustrous hair, which fell to the floor as she knelt. She could have been in a jungle clearing, preparing to worship the old gods. Sailo, seated in front of her, broad-boned, looked like a Chinese idol.

☙

The next morning Ezra appeared at my door. "Come," he said, "there is a great miracle."

"A miracle?" I had just finished my breakfast.

"Aw."

"What kind of miracle?"

"It is Joseph's *mawg*."

"Joseph's *mawg*? What's a *mawg*?"

"*Mawg*." He raised an imaginary glass to his lips.

"A mug! Joseph's mug!"

"Aw."

We took a taxi to an outlying neighborhood. Aizawl sprawled over hills of which the highest was the city's center, so that the farther you ranged from it, descending through districts of flimsy houses that looked like summer bungalow colonies, the more altitude you lost. By the time we reached our destination, we had traveled to a different climate. The chilly clouds that grazed the Ritz were far overhead, and banana trees grew by the roadside.

Ezra's father was waiting for us with three skullcapped men, L. Benjamin, Daniel Menashe, and Yosi Hnamte. We turned into an unpaved street, entered a small house, and were ushered into a room where chairs were set around a low table. An old man sat in one of them, holding a wooden staff. He was blind, and the wrinkles on his face were deep as ditches. His name was Kolkopthanga. The staff belonged to his grandfather, Chief Suakpilala (or Sookpilul, as the British called him), who led the resistance to the British military conquest of the Lushai Hills. Fighting was in Kolkopthanga's blood. He had been decorated for bravery while serving with Mountbatten's Chindits against the Japanese in World War II.

"Sir, behold!" L. Benjamin said.

A pewter bowl was on the table. It had a design of elephants around its rim.

"Count the elephants."

There were twelve.

"The very number of the tribes! It is a pot for sacrification blood. Given to Sookpilul by the English. Sookpilul has given them ivory and blankets."

But the pewter bowl was only a preliminary. A second relic was now brought. It was a silver cup with a floral pattern. Reverently admired, it stood eight inches tall in the middle of the table.

"So! It is Joseph's drinking cup from Egypt. You may read what is written."

Daniel Menashe handed me the cup. On it was the inscription:

> To Sookpilul
> A Looshai Chieftain
> The Gift of the British Government
> 20th September 1871

"What makes you think this cup was Joseph's?"

"Kolkopthanga heard it from his granddaddy."

The English, Sookpilul had told Kolkopthanga, said the cup came from Ethiopia. It had been brought there by the tribe of Dan. As a token of respect, the British government had decided to return it to Dan's cousins, the sons of Manasseh.

I turned it over. Inlaid with grime, a barely legible stamp on its bottom said *Calcutta, Cooke & Kelvey*.

I replaced the cup on the table. All eyes were on me. Ha-Rav had asked for more evidence. Here it was. "You must tell the chief rabbi," L. Benjamin said.

Perhaps the English had really told Sookpilul some such story. There would have been much merriment at regimental headquarters. *You should have seen old Sooky fall for it, harh, harh, harh!* "The chief rabbi," I said, "will of course want to know about this. But he will not rely on Kolkopthanga's word alone."

This objection had not been anticipated. Of course! Anyone could claim a cup was Joseph's. There was a hurried caucus in Mizo, and L. Benjamin said, "Sir! You can write the British government. They will have records."

All but the blind Kolkopthanga looked at me hopefully. An official letter from London would surely convince the chief rabbi. The British government would not refuse an Israeli journalist.

"All right," I promised. "I'll write to London."

Their nods of satisfaction only made my lie seem worse. But the truth would have hurt them more.

Or was I deceiving myself as much as them by believing that?

"Come!" Ezra had more evidence to show me. It was in the Aizawl museum. We took a taxi back up all the hills. Inspired by the exploits of Sookpilul and Kolkopthanga, he spoke on the way of the clash of identities within him. "I am Judaism," he said. "But I am Mizo. I love my Mizo people."

The museum looked permanently closed for disrepair. The first floor was deserted. On the second, some men were drinking tea. You could have written your name in the dust that filmed the showcases of old costumes, artifacts, blankets, baskets, weapons, traps, drums, and village gateposts. A life-size model of a Lushai warrior with a spear and ivory hair comb was encased in glass like a fly in amber. Beside it was an oil painting of a traditional Lushai village, thatched roofs peeping over a stockade. Human heads were impaled on the palisades.

Ezra led me to a large stone covered with writing. "This," he said, "can no one read."

The characters, though amateurishly gone over with white paint, looked old. Pronged and segmented like a collection of rare beetles, they belonged to some alphabet I could not identify. They bore no resemblance to Burmese or Hindi. If they reminded me of anything, it was ancient Hebrew or Phoenician. There was no explanatory caption.

"Where was this found?"

Ezra didn't know. We asked the tea drinkers. The tea drinkers did not know either. They suggested that we speak to the director. The director, they told us, had not been seen for several days.

Ezra had an idea. A friend of his was a historian. We would ask him.

We took a taxi back down all the hills.

Ezra's friend was named Ralthanga. Ralthanga was not exactly a historian. He was a grade school history teacher. But he endorsed the theory that the writing on the stone was ancient Hebrew. He was certain the Mizos came from the Middle East. On their route, they had passed through Afghanistan, Kashmir, and Tibet. The proof was that the Ladakhi people of Kashmir spoke a language like Mizo. A Ladakhi had visited Mizoram, and Ralthanga had copied down some of his words. Here was a notebook with the numbers one to ten in both languages.

They were practically identical.

"You see?" Ralthanga said. "We are Israel. Not Aryan. Not European. Semitic!"

No one could have accused him of looking Aryan or European. "But Ladakhi is a Tibeto-Burmese language," I said. "It's not surprising that its numbers are like Mizo ones. And those are not Semitic names." I pointed to a genealogical chart that hung on the wall. It spanned twenty-five generations of Ralthanga's ancestors from Khinzu, Aisa, Duhlung, and Nogui to his father, Lalnginga. Next to number ten, Galina, was written, "Came to Mizoram from Burma."

"We are Israel," Ralthanga insisted. "Our forefathers married different peoples: Afghans, Nepalis, Tibetans, Chinese. But we worshiped only Za. Then the British came and we forgot. Now we do not know who we are."

Those were the same words I had heard from Sailo. "Have you thought of becoming Jewish?" I asked.

But Ralthanga would not abandon Christianity. "For me it is not possible," he said as if speaking of an incurable addiction. Still, Judaism would spread. The next generation would embrace it.

"Hers?"

Ralthanga's daughter, a child of six or seven, with neat, straight bangs, had entered the room and was staring at my Semitic nose.

"Aw!"

"Your daughter will be Jewish?"

"Awww!"

Ralthanga's daughter stepped right up to me and scrutinized me closely as if I were a picture in a book. Her curiosity satisfied, she walked away.

�⚶

Before his rabbinical trial, Avichail had unexpected callers. Such people dropped in on him at all hours with problems, pleas, inquiries, suggestions, letters for relatives in Israel. They came with gifts, mostly clusters of small Mizo bananas that lay rotting in the corners of our rooms. They knocked shyly and entered quietly, as if intruding on the presence of a wonder worker.

These particular callers were from Manipur. They had traveled by foot, bus, and car to reach Aizawl. They were four members of the Ngaihe family and the brothers Thonzakhual and Thonzakap Tombing. Whether from excitement, worry, or a sense of decorum, Mother Ngaihe burst out crying immediately. When she was hushed, Thonzakap Tombing held out some typed pages and said, "Sir, we have come with a petition."

They were Paites, members of a large tribe that stretched from southern Manipur to northern Mizoram and Burma. It was from their village of Mualkawi that the fax had been sent to Avichail that day in Jerusalem. Many of their homes had been burned by the Kukis, who accused them of siding with the Nagas. The Kukis and Paites were now such enemies that the Kuki B'nei Menashe in Imphal refused to talk to the Paite B'nei Menashe in Mualkawi. There was no work in Mualkawi, and people feared for their lives.

Thonzakap Tombing read the petition. It concluded: "In the context of the foregoing facts of circumstances, it is our fervent hope and earnest request that your good office would consider our case in the true perspective sense and grant us immediate deportation to Israel of all brothers/sisters of Judaism in the affected area."

Avichail had been dealing with such requests all week long. All week he had patiently explained how little he could do. Now he said, "What you ask is difficult. I cannot put anyone from Manipur on the list for Israel without going through the community in Imphal, and I cannot go to Imphal to make peace between you. You must do it yourself."

"But that is impossible, sir," Thonzakhual Tombing said. "The Kukis in Imphal will kill us. They have only to hear us speak to know we are Paites."

"Then stay in Aizawl until things calm down."

"We cannot, sir. The Paite militia granted us a week's pass. They will kill our families if we do not return."

"How then can you go to Israel?"

"That is different. Deportation is not desertion."

"Perhaps you and your families could take temporary shelter in Burma."

Avichail was regarded with amazement. "Burma, sir? How can we go to Burma? We cannot even speak the language. The Burmese will put us in prison."

Despair was on their faces when they left.

Soon after, Jeremiah Hnamte and Peter Tlau arrived, each with a party of followers. Avichail told the followers they would have to wait outside and announced the rules of the engagement. "One person will speak at a time. I ask the questions. I give the judgment."

Jeremiah spoke first, staring through the arch of his fingers. He did not know what Mr. Peter had against him. The whole quarrel had started with the election. He had won it fair and square. Then Mr. Peter accused him of cheating. But he did not cheat. All his voters were circumcised. Had Mr. Peter won the election, he, Jeremiah, would have abided by the results. He would not have started another synagogue as Mr. Peter had.

Avichail said, "You may speak now, Peter."

But Peter surprised the court. Pointing to the ceiling, he declared, "Hasem knows all," and refused to say another word.

"Hashem surely knows all," Avichail agreed, "but I know only what you tell me."

Peter, however, stuck to his plea of no contest. He would not say bad things about Mr. Jeremiah. Judaism did not allow it. Judaism forbade the evil tongue. He had heard Ha-Rav say so himself. If Ha-Rav would come to pray in Peter's synagogue, he would not find the evil tongue there.

And so Avichail handed down his verdict, recorded by me as court clerk and duly signed by both parties. Peter was to recognize Jeremiah as the elected general secretary of the B'nei Menashe Council. Jeremiah was to recognize Peter's congregation, henceforth to be renamed the South Aizawl Synagogue. He was to include it in the disbursement of communal funds, inform it of events of common interest, and refrain from discriminating against it in any matter, including the lists of those chosen to go to Israel.

Jeremiah was pleased. Peter looked glum. Despite having seized the moral high ground, he had been forced to change the name of Ha-Rav Eliahu Avichail Synagogue without getting what he most wanted. Ha-Rav had not promised to pray there.

Their parties were waiting in the hallway. As Peter exited, Jeremiah extended a hand. Just then someone said something with the word "Christian" in it. Jeremiah's men laughed, and Peter angrily pushed aside the hand.

For all its pettiness, it was a textbook case of religious schism. On the face of it, the break was over a minor matter of ritual. If you dug deeper, there was personal ambition. Dig still deeper and you got to money and power. Get to the bottom of it, and there was religion after all. The Shalom Zion Synagogue was isolationist. The South Aizawl Synagogue was ecumenical. If it weren't stretching a point, you might have called them the Orthodox and Reform wings of Mizoram Jewry.

Avichail, though on the side of Orthodoxy, had been fair. That night, though, we had a bitter argument. It started with my reproaching him for not praying in Peter's synagogue. Since none of the B'nei Menashe were technically Jews anyway, why pray with one group and not with the other? And what was wrong with being open to Christians? Many Mizos were interested in Judaism. They felt Christianity had stolen their patrimony. Why not encourage them?

Micha jumped in. "We aren't missionaries," he said. "It isn't our job to teach the world Judaism."

I protested. Did Judaism have nothing to say to the world? No desire to say it?

"No! The Gentiles have the seven commandments of the sons of Noah. That's enough for them. The six hundred and thirteen commandments of the Torah are for us."

"You're turning Judaism into an exclusive club!"

"You're turning it into a public relations agency!"

"You're making it an irrelevance! This whole trip is irrelevant. Here we are, running around Asia in search of imaginary Jews when in Israel right now there are tens of thousands of underpaid Asian workers — Thais, Filipinos, Chinese — living on the fringes of society. If you want to bring Asians to Judaism, start with them."

"God forbid!" Avichail said.

It might have gone on all night if Sailo and Yosi Hualngo hadn't chosen that moment to appear.

They had brought with them a document. It contained, Sailo said, fragments of priestly chants remembered by Yosi from his childhood.

The document was typed in English. Despite its length, I read it aloud to Avichail and Micha:

> The Ritual Chantings of the Priests of the Menashe of olden days, still used in 1956 in Mizoram as heard by Yosi Hualngo, from his own father, Piangriangchhunga Hualngo, of Lianpui Village in Mizoram.
>
> 1. We did not like to say the real name of God; because it has been too precious, we were not allowed to say out the name of God; and so, the following are the equivalent names of the heavenly Father:
>
> PATUAN = Eternal Father
>
> KHUANU = KHUAPA = Care Taker Of Everything.
>
> THLAROPA = Owner Of Our Souls.
>
> CHUNGKHUANULANG = One Who Dwells Up Above.
>
> HUALHIMTU = Guardian.
>
> 2. "My son, you should never take the name of God in vain. I

am the priest of the Menashe, but even I pronounce the name of God. only when the real times comes." So, he whispered to Yosi Hualngo's ear and said, "God.'s name is YA or ZA. But never say it out in vain."

3. The following places and forefathers are recorded in a chanting form:

1. TERA = Father of Abraham.
2. APRAM = Abraham.
3. IAKSAK = Isaac
4. MURIA TLANG = Mount Moriah
5. IAKOP = Jacob.
6. AKUPTA = Egypt
7. SEN TUIPUI = Red Sea
8. SIN-AI TLANG = Mount Sinai
9. BIAHTHU MIN HLAWNA = Where He offered secret oral communion of love. (The Place of the Covenant.)
10. KAN CHUUK KAN CHHOHMA = The places where we used to go up and down.
11. LUT THENG THENG SAIONAH = Entering Zion
12. APNITAN = Afghanistan.
13. HIMALAWI = Himalaya.
14. LUNGDINGAH = At Lungding in Tibet.
15. KUNGMINGAH = At Kunming in China
16. MONGGOLAWITAH = At Mongolia
17. MOIRANG = Moirang in Manipur
18. PANGRAWN = Now Seipui (Burma, Chin Hills)
19. SANGRINGAH = Where the Parchment had been eaten by dogs, Lake of no return, between Burma & China.
20. TINGTUNAH = At Chingtungin, border of China and Burma.
21. AIRAWDUNG = Irrawady River in Burma.
22. CHINDUNGAH = At Chindwin River in Burma.
23. KHAMPATAH = At Khampat. (first town of our forefathers in Burma).
24. THAN TLANGAH = At Than Mountain range in Chin Hills
25. SUK LUIAH = At Suk river (Burma, Chin Hills).
26. RUN LUIAH = At Run river (Burma, Chin Hills).
27. MUCHHIP = Mount Muchhip, Burma.
28. TIAULUIAH = At the Tiau, river of border between India and Burma.

All these forefathers' places passed through, all these are very secret and Holy to the people who call themselves the Menashe.

4. The worship in the form of Chantings:

"Response, do response us, Ya! O Ya (Za)! O Ya! Do response you, the dweller of the Mount Moriah! The dweller of the famous Red Sea, do respond! The dweller of the Mount Sinai, do respond! The dweller of Mount Zion, respond, do respond! O Ya! Ya! Respond, do respond!"

5. Swinging-offering chanting:

The priest holds a red rooster by its two legs and swings it around saying: "O Ya! This offering is made for all the people."

6. Offering or Prayer for the sick or for suffering people:

The priest said: "Answer me, I command you to tell me who you are. Who are you inside (name of person)? Who are you to make (name of person) sick? Who are you to harm (name of person)? Get out! Get out of (name of person)! Do you ask me who I am? I am the Ya priest. I will stab you, I will cut you, get out of this man!"

7. Kawngpui Sial (making the path):

(It is meant for seeing if the year would be good, prosperous, etc.)

"Here we come, the children of Ya; the descendants of Menashe; we are coming, we are coming our way. Keep the way open for us, you who can block our way on the road, upper the road, below the road, you keep away from our way."

8. The following songs are sung in the forms of chantings:

Tera, (the father of Abraham), our enemy has been swallowed by the great sea.

Tera, we are guided by cloud by day, by fire by night.

Pharaoh and his riders have been thrown into the Red Sea.

In olden days the parchment we had has been eaten by the nasty Tuluk curs. (The Tuluk curs are Chinese dogs or the Chinese people who destroyed the parchment or the writings.)

We are longing for, longing for the land of God., we are longing for Za's city Zion.

Yosi Hualngo
Aizawl, Mizoram
India.

It was after midnight when Yosi and Sailo left. For another hour, we sat up discussing their visit.

The document was a hodgepodge. It was not clear how its parts fit together. Yet if they really were, as Yosi claimed, fragments remembered from old priestly chants, they constituted a sensation. The presence of biblical traditions in the old Lushai religion could be considered confirmed by them. They had the biblical names of Abraham, Isaac, Jacob, and even Terah. They had a reference to Egypt. They had lines of the song about crossing the Red Sea. They had the "entering Zion" jingle. They had biblical place names like Moriah and Sinai. They had still other names, indicating stages of a migration route to southeast Asia. As a young man interested in the old religion, Yosi said, he had written these things down. Then, during the Mizo insurgency, in which he had fought as an MNF officer, his village was burned by Indian troops and his notes were lost. What he had given us now were his memories of them.

But these were memories dating by his own testimony to the 1950s. Could they be trusted? How did we know they weren't partly or wholly invented? "There are details that don't seem right," I said to Avichail and Micha. "Why would descendants of ancient Israelites invoke Abraham's father, Terah, a figure of no importance in the Bible? Why would they call Egypt by its Greek name? Why would they speak of 'the Red Sea' when the Hebrew Bible calls it 'the Reed Sea,' *yam suf?* And tell me how Yosi Hualngo can know old priestly chants that no one else does. Or remember them forty years later. It smells fishy to me."

"Why make it up?" Micha asked.

"He could have been put up to it by Sailo. He could be out to promote himself. We need to talk to him some more. We need to know exactly where all this comes from. He'll be in synagogue tomorrow for the Sabbath eve prayer. Let's ask him to come again on Saturday night."

That was our last night in Aizawl. On Monday evening we had a flight from Bombay to Israel. Not wanting to risk Sunday's Aizawl-Calcutta flight being canceled by bad weather, we had decided to drive to Silchar in Assam. There was a better airport there with daily Calcutta connections.

On Friday evening, however, Yosi was not in the Shalom Zion Synagogue. The congregation watched Avichail carefully when it was time to welcome the Sabbath bride. It bowed with him to the rear on the first "Come, O Bride." Then it wheeled with him on the second "Come, O

Bride" and bowed to the front. The movements were executed with military precision.

Nor was Yosi in the South Aizawl Synagogue when I dropped by there the next morning. Neither was Zohmengaiha. Shortly before the Sabbath a messenger had brought a note to the hotel from him. It read:

"To Rabbi Eliahu Avichail,

"Ha-Rav! I, Ben Aryeh Pachuau (Zohmengaiha) Show you my Medical Certificate of Anfitness for Circamseson to be Circamsise to you. And because of this, if you do not want to visit the South Aizawl Community, may you bear the prize of my blood in front of Hashem. We know that in Torah in the book of Moses father Abraham was called before being Circamsese, Genesis 12."

A subtle theological point. Not until Chapter 19 of Genesis did Abraham remove "the flesh of his foreskin." Had the father of the Jewish people sought to pray with Avichail before then, Zohmengaiha was suggesting, he would have been sent to the doctors in Calcutta.

The South Aizawl congregation was smaller than Shalom Zion's. It was less sure of itself, too, and stumbled at times, though on the whole it performed creditably. In the Blessings of the Morn, the customary thanks to God for "not making me a Gentile" were omitted.

Soon after this, Avichail walked in. Peter, who had been sitting quietly on the front bench, jumped to his feet as if not believing his good fortune. Just when all had seemed lost! He led Avichail to a place of honor and asked him to sit.

Avichail declined. He had only come to say a few words. Although he would be happy to remain, he said, he had left his prayer book and prayer shawl in the Shalom Zion Synagogue the night before and would pray there. He wished the new congregation success. "May you prosper and go from strength to strength," he said. "And may you live in harmony with all your brothers in Aizawl. Sabbath peace be upon you."

He turned to go. Peter clutched at his sleeve and begged, "Stay just for a few prayers, Ha-Rav."

But he was in a hurry to be off.

So Peter was cheated of his full triumph. He tried to make the best of it. In the sermon he gave after the Torah reading, he made much mention of Ha-Rav Avichail while gesturing grandly, like a hunter telling of having bagged a fearsome trophy.

But his eyes were the eyes of Esau, who cried out, "Hast thou but one blessing, my father? Bless me, O my father, even me also."

ᶜᵇᶻ

It was the last calling card. It came from

P. Saidinga, M. Sc. Agr.
President
Ephraim National Conference
Aizawl, Mizoram.

He was sitting in the armchair of my hotel room, one leg beside my packed bags.

"It is a misfortune you are leaving," he was saying. "In three days we shall convene the first Ephraim National Conference. We have rented Vanapa Hall, the biggest hall in Mizoram. We shall hoist the Ephraim flag and feast the mythun, the biggest animal in Mizoram. There will be singing and dancing in the name of the Lord God Za."

P. Saidinga proclaimed:

"We have been taken across the Red Sea! In the night we are led by fire and in the day by cloud!"

He explained:

"This was mentioned by the priests in their murmurings."

He confided, tapping his head:

"I see it. I see it here. There will be two Israels, one for Palestine and one for Mizoram. Oh, I see it! We will rule the world together in the name of the great Lord Za."

Master of the science of agriculture, he laid before me a drawing of the Ephraim flag.

"So! This is the sun rising on a field of green, which represents the hills of Mizoram. These are the twelve gates of the twelve tribes. Here — the cedar tree of Ephraim. Here — the olive tree of Judah. On the right, Mizo colors of red, black, and white represent exaltation. On the left, Jesus Christ."

I was rescued by a messenger come to tell me that our transportation for Silchar had arrived.

We set out in a caravan of two cars and a bus. Avichail and Micha rode in the first car. I rode in the second with Elisabeth Zodingliani, editor of the *Ephraim Tribune*. The bus was full of B'nei Menashe accompanying us to Varengte, the last town before the Assamese border. They wished to remain with Ha-Rav until the last minute.

The trip took all day. The weather was bad and so was the road. It wound northward through dripping jungle and gradually flattening hills toward the Assamese plain. On the way we stopped in Bawlpui and Kawlasib, places with B'nei Menashe communities. In each, Avichail spoke at the local synagogue and answered the usual questions: Israel, circumcision, relations with Christian neighbors. In Bawlpui he was asked if it was permitted to travel to synagogue on the Sabbath. The questioner came from a small village lacking the ten participants needed for a prayer group. Avichail answered, "Jewish law does not permit travel on the Sabbath. However, since you are not yet Jews, you are not bound by this law. It is therefore not a sin for you to travel. Public prayer is important. But so is living as a Jew."

The Talmudic dialectic sailed over his listeners' heads and through the open window, where a wet breeze was swaying the bamboos.

We were like the traveling courts of old, stopping to hear petitioners and moving on. In Kawlasib, Avichail was approached by a woman. She had a tense, drawn face and a patch over one eye. The eye, she explained through an interpreter, had been poked by a stick and damaged so badly that the doctors wanted to remove it. Only a miracle, they said, could save it.

Avichail was not happy to be asked for a miracle. "I am not a doctor," he said. "I can only pray for you. And my prayers are worth less than your own."

The woman knew he was not a doctor. But the doctors could not help. Her only hope was for the rabbi to bless her eye.

Her other eye hopped like a cripple's good leg from Avichail to the interpreter. We were standing in front of the synagogue, a bamboo structure with an English sign over its door that said:

"There is no any place for a Jew to enjoy the pleasures of this world. For he was designed to be trustee of eternal treasure of Torah."

Avichail sighed. "Ask for her name and the name of her mother," he told the interpreter. He put his hand on the woman's head and recited mechanically: "May He who blessed our fathers Abraham, Isaac, and Jacob heal this sick woman, ——— the daughter of ———, and send her a speedy cure from heaven, together with all the ailing of Israel, health of body and health of soul, and let us say amen."

The woman waited passively for him to finish, without joy or hope. She already knew no miracle would be forthcoming.

That night in Varengte he said to me, opening up for the first time, "Do you think I know the answer? Do you? I look at these millions and I ask myself, can these dry bones live? How? Ezekiel asked the same question. 'Lord God, thou knowest,' he said.

"I feel so alone. When my master and teacher Tsvi Yehuda Kook was alive, I had someone to talk to. It was he who encouraged me to take this path. If only . . ." He looked at me almost lovingly. "If only you were a believing Jew. I don't believe that in your heart you aren't. I see how this speaks to you. You could be like a brother to me."

We left Varengte early in the morning. A few kilometers beyond it was a barrier with a sign: "Stop and Report to Police Check Gate. All Non-Mizos Will Produce Inner-line Permit."

Then we were out of the hills and on the flat Indian plain. It stretched as far as we could see. Hump-backed cows sunned on the road and let the cars slalom around them. Bare-chested men plowed with water buffalo in the paddies. The buffalo plodded a step at a time, their great bellies swinging from haunch to haunch as they sank into the mud and pulled out of it. The men plodded after them, barefoot. They had the slow, patient gait of those who know that no number of steps will bring them any closer to the horizon.

After the empty green spaces of Mizoram, the rural landscape seemed as crowded as a city. People were everywhere — men in dhotis, women in saris, naked children, working in the fields, squatting by the road, riding bicycles and rickshaws, walking in groups with bags, bundles, buckets, milk cans, water jugs, staffs, umbrellas, implements, babies, wheelbarrows, calves and goats on leashes. They were carried calmly along on the current of their own dense humanity. They did not ask themselves who they were. The earth they walked on had always been theirs. They did not seek the clarity of definition. There was a great peace in all this confusion.

⚜ 4 ⚜

A Short History of the Lost Tribes

My FIRST LOST TRIBE lived in Brooklyn.

I was seven or eight, a Manhattan boy, raised on West End Avenue. Beyond West End, toward the Hudson, was Riverside Drive, and beyond that, Riverside Park. The tall, solid buildings of both streets were predominantly Jewish; my own was heavily populated with little ladies, refugees from the Nazis, who wore net veils and brown shoes and said *danke schoen* when you held the elevator door for them. In the other direction, to the east, was Broadway, a shopping street, followed by Amsterdam and Columbus. These were Irish Catholic. They had low tenements with fire escapes and storefronts that mainly housed, or so it seemed to me, bars and funeral parlors. It was as if all the Irish did was drink and die from it.

The Irish kids were tougher than we were. They went to parochial schools with names like Tolentine and Cardinal Hayes and crossed Broadway after school to look for fights. Sometimes, cornered, we stood our ground and lost. Mostly we turned and ran.

One day a classmate told me a wondrous tale. He had heard, he said, of a place in Brooklyn called Borough Park where gangs of Jewish boys beat up Christians. I was enthralled. Brooklyn was a far country. I swore to reach it and join one of those gangs.

I never made it to Borough Park and soon afterwards the state of Israel was declared and my thoughts turned to fighting in a Jewish army. Yet when eventually I came across the old Jewish legend of descendants of biblical Israelites surviving as fearless warriors in hidden corners of the globe, I didn't need its psychological import explained. I had already dreamed of such distant brothers.

This legend is medieval. It first appeared at a time when the Jews were reduced to a scorned minority in the Christian and Moslem worlds, fifteen hundred years after the tribes of northern Israel were supposedly exiled from their homeland in ancient Palestine.* We know of this exile from four passages in the Bible: three in II Kings and one in I Chronicles. According to II Kings 15:

> In the days of Pekah king of Israel came Tiglath-Pileser king of Assyria and took Ijon, and Abel-beth-ma'achah, and Janoah, and Kedesh, and Hazor, and Gilead, and Galilee, all the land of Naphtali, and carried them captive to Assyria.

In II Kings 17–18 is an account of a slightly later event.

> In the twelfth year of Ahaz king of Judah began Hoshea the son of Elah to reign in Samaria over Israel. And he did that which was evil in the sight of the Lord . . . Against him came up Shalmaneser king of Assyria; and Hoshea became his servant and gave him presents. And the king of Assyria found conspiracy in Hoshea, for he had sent messengers to So king of Egypt. . . . Then the king of Assyria came up throughout all the land and went up to Samaria and besieged it three years. In the ninth year of Hoshea, the king of Assyria took Samaria and carried Israel away into Assyria, and placed them in Halah, and in Habor by the river of Gozan, and in the cities of the Medes . . . And the king of Assyria brought men from Babylon, and from Cuthah, and from Ava, and from Hamath, and from Sepharvaim, and placed them in the cities of Samaria instead of the children of Israel.

Finally, II Chronicles 5 has this version:

> And the God of Israel stirred up the spirit of Pul king of Assyria, and the spirit of Tilgath-Pilneser king of Assyria, and he carried

---

* Although Jewish tradition has always spoken of the "ten [lost] tribes," only nine of these belonged to the northern kingdom of Israel and could have been exiled by the Assyrians. The tenth, the tribe of Simon, was the southernmost of all the tribes and had its territory in today's Israeli Negev, from which it disappeared long before the Assyrian exile. Possibly it was assimilated, like Benjamin, by the more powerful tribe of Judah. Because of this I prefer to speak of the "Lost Tribes" rather than the "Ten Tribes," though the reader should keep in mind that the two terms are for practical purposes synonymous.

them away, even the Reubenites, and the Gadites, and the half tribe of Manasseh,* and brought them unto Halah, and Habor, and Hara, and to the river Gozan, unto this day.

What are the historical facts referred to here?

Chronicles, generally thought to date from the fifth or fourth century B.C.E., is later than Kings, which was most likely composed with the aid of older records in the early sixth century. Since Tiglath-Pileser (or "Tilgath-Pilneser," as a scribe mistakenly copied it) and Pul (Tiglath-Pileser's Babylonian name) are one and the same Assyrian king, and the tribal territories of Reuben, Gad, and the eastern half of Manasseh were in the areas listed in II Kings 15, the verse in Chronicles can be discounted as a late conflation of the two passages in Kings. Setting it aside, then, and supplementing the account in Kings with our knowledge of Israelite and Assyrian history, it is possible to arrive at the following reconstruction:

1. In 734–732 B.C.E., some two centuries after the Davidic monarchy, as narrated by the Bible, was fragmented into a northern kingdom of Israel and a southern kingdom of Judah, most of the north was overrun and annexed by the Assyrians, leaving only its capital city, Samaria, and the surrounding countryside unconquered. This happened in the reign of Israel's king Pekah ben-Remalyahu (737–732), when the Assyrian ruler Tukulti-apil-Essara III (745–727), the "Tiglath-Pileser" of the Bible, was expanding his frontiers southward and westward.

2. In 726, Tukulti-apil-Essara's son and successor, Sulman-asared V (726–722), called Shalmaneser in the Bible, marched on Samaria and reduced its king, Hoshea (730–722), to a vassal. In 722, suspecting Hoshea of conspiring with the Egyptians, he again laid siege to the city. The battle lasted three years. Shalmaneser died before it ended and was succeeded by his son Sargon II (721–705), who presided over the fall of Samaria and the final destruction of the kingdom of Israel in 720.

3. After both Tiglath-Pileser's and Sargon's conquests, the Assyrians deported Israelites to different regions of Assyria and replaced them with exiles from elsewhere.

---

* According to the Bible, the tribe of Manasseh (or, in its Hebrew form, Menashe) split in two after the exodus from Egypt, one half remaining east of the Jordan with the tribes of Reuben and Gad when the other tribes crossed the river westward into Canaan.

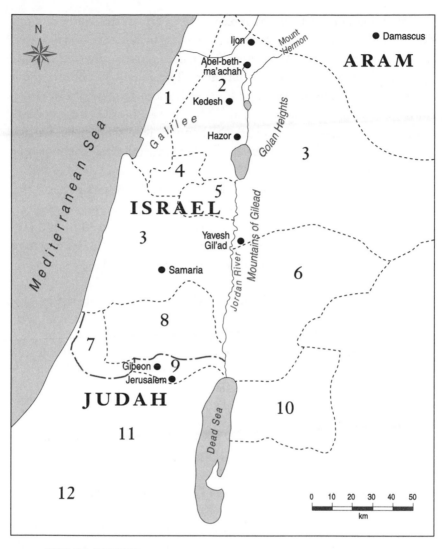

BIBLICAL PALESTINE
WITH ITS TRIBAL TERRITORIES

The remainder of Kings narrates the last years of the southern king-dom of Judah, which was ultimately destroyed by a new regional power, the Babylonians, in 586. With the fall of Samaria, the northern tribes dis-appeared. We know no more about them. The Bible says nothing about the fate of the Israelites exiled or — if such there were — of those per-mitted to remain in their native land. The next we hear of contemporary Samaria, in the Books of Ezra and Nehemiah, is in the Persian period, two hundred years later, when the region was inhabited by a people called the Samaritans.

Yet the northern tribes did not vanish from the Bible's pages. They lived on as a memory of a more glorious past and a hope for a more glori-ous future. Their eventual return was repeatedly predicted by the He-brew prophets as the climax of God's reconciliation with His chastised but still chosen people. Jeremiah wrote tenderly of this day:

> Thus, saith the Lord. The people which were left of the sword found grace in the wilderness, even Israel. . . . Again I will build thee and thou shalt be built, O virgin of Israel; thou shalt again be adorned with thy tabrets, and shalt go forth in the dances of them that make merry. Thou shalt yet plant vines upon the mountains of Samaria: the planters shall plant and shall eat them. . . . Be-hold, I will bring them from the north country, and gather them from the coasts of the earth, and with them the blind and the lame, the woman with child and her that travaileth: a great com-pany shall return thither. . . . Hear the word of the Lord, O ye na-tions, and declare it in the isles afar off, and say, He that scattered Israel will gather him, and keep him, as a shepherd doth his flock.

Although Jeremiah was prophesying less than a century and a half af-ter the fall of the northern kingdom, the exiled inhabitants had already been mythicized. They were no longer a familiar people living in an identifiable place and known through social, commercial, and religious contacts; rather, located in a vague "north country," they were removed to a hidden cloister in time and space to await, in God's safekeeping, the appointed day of their deliverance. Although we learn of one tribe of them in the apocryphal Book of Tobit, which tells the story of "Tobit, the son of Tobiel, of the tribe of Naphtali, who was led captive in the days of Shalmaneser . . . in the captivity of Nineveh in the land of Assyria," this work was composed no earlier than the fourth century B.C.E. and is almost certainly fiction. So is a passage in the Fourth Book of Ezra, a first-century C.E. story that relates how "the ten tribes which were led away from their own land into captivity . . . formed this plan for themselves, that they would leave the multitude of the heathen and go to a more distant region where mankind had never lived . . . And they went in by the narrow passages of the Euphrates River. For at that time the Most High performed signs for them, and stopped the channels of the river until they had passed over . . . a journey of a year and a half; and that country is called Arzareth." The fact that "Arzareth" is simply a garbling of the Hebrew *eretz ahereth*, "another country," shows that the author of this account had no idea where the northern exiles actually were. They had become, although the term had yet to be invented, the Lost Tribes of Israel.

☫

In early post-biblical Jewish literature — the writings of the descendants of the southern tribe of Judah, who eventually came to be known as the Jews — the Lost Tribes are mentioned sporadically. They did not greatly concern the pragmatic rabbis of the Talmudic age, conventionally dated 100–600 C.E. As illustrated by the disagreement cited by Avichail in his talk in Bangkok, some rabbinic authorities thought the exiled northerners had disappeared forever, and some did not. There is a discussion in the Babylonian Talmud about whether Gentiles coming from "Halah," "Habor," and "the cities of the Medes," the places in Assyria to which the tribes were said to have been deported, should be considered their possible descendants. The discussion locates these places in the mountains of Kurdistan while implying that the tribes are no longer there in any identifiable form. Cloaked in mystery, they are declared by the Jerusalem Talmud to be, rather, in three legendary places: "across the Sambatyon River," "enshrouded in cloud beyond the Mountains of Darkness," and "under Daphne of Antioch."

The city of Antioch, today the site of Turkish Antakya and a great metropolis of the Roman Empire, of which Daphne was a well-known quarter, was prone to devastating earthquakes; the worst of these, in 526 C.E., caused an estimated 300,000 deaths, and an earlier calamity was asserted by the ancient rabbis to have entombed some of the tribes in a state of suspended animation. The rabbis do not similarly specify the geographic location of the "Mountains of Darkness" or "the Sambatyon." The latter is, however, known to us from two non-rabbinic sources. One is the first-century C.E. Jewish historian Josephus Flavius, who related that the Roman emperor Titus, on his way back to Italy after conquering Jerusalem, passed through Syria and saw a remarkable river. "When it is in flow," Josephus wrote, "it fills its channel, and its current is torrential; then suddenly its sources fail completely and for six days the riverbed is dry; then again, as if no change had happened, the water gushes out on the seventh day just as before. And as it has always been observed to keep strictly to this timetable, it was called the Sambatyon or Sabbath River, named after the sacred seventh day of the Jews." Josephus' contemporary, the Roman historian and naturalist Pliny the Elder, situated this river in Judea, where it flowed, he wrote, six days a week and rested on the seventh. Pliny's description fits a "Sabbath river" better and is closer to that of the rabbis — who, however, knowing Judea well, did not put the Sambatyon there or anywhere in particular. Its "torrential current" was described by them as a dry one, consisting of huge, hurtling stones.

And so, buried underground, beyond fearsome peaks, or across an impassible river (for on the Sabbath, when the Sambatyon rests, so must a Jew), the tribes were inaccessible. Although the prevailing opinion was that they existed, it was pointless to look for them. In any event, their restoration was growing imminent. As the Talmudic age ended and the world order was toppled by the fall of Rome and the rise of Islam, a Hebrew genre of pseudo-prophecies, messianic oracles of the End of Days, began to appear. The earliest of these, the Book of Elijah, predicted the Lost Tribes' return in the year 614. That autumn, it promised, on the twenty-second day of the month of Tishrei, they would arrive from Babylonia; on the twenty-fifth, from beyond the Sambatyon; a month later, from even farther afield. Angelic hosts would destroy Israel's enemies in a great battle, and a new Jerusalem with a new Temple would descend from the skies. The time was nigh.

᛭

But it was not. The Messiah failed to come, a new world order replaced the old, and in or about the year 883 a man claiming to belong to a Lost Tribe turned up all by himself. He called himself by the Hebrew name Eldad Ha-Dani, Eldad the Danite, and he set the Lost Tribe legend on a new course, one that transformed it from a vague fable of no practical consequence to a hallucinatory mixture of alleged fact and wild rumor that was to send the minds of men, and in time men themselves, on a fruitless treasure hunt lasting for centuries.

Eldad appeared in Kairouan, now a city in Tunisia, with a story that he told to the local Jews in a strange Hebrew — the only language, so he said, that he knew. It was, he explained, the language still spoken by members of the biblical tribe of Dan, who had emigrated from their territory soon after the death of King Solomon, first to Egypt and then farther up the Nile, to avoid the internecine warfare between Judah and Israel. Now they lived in tents alongside the exiled tribes of Naphtali, Gad, and Asher in the fertile and gem-rich "land of Havilah" near "the seven kings of Cush" — the biblical name for Ethiopia. These four tribes were continually at war with the seven kings, each tribe fighting for three months a year while the others farmed their fields and tended their flocks; their warriors rested only on the Sabbath and charged into battle on horseback, with the cry, "Salvation is from God for all the brave tribes of Jeshurun, selah!" All booty was shared equally among them under the supervision of their ruler, King Adiel, who gave a special portion of it to "the wise men who study the Torah." This, Eldad said, meant only the Bible, nothing being known of Talmudic jurisprudence. Indeed, some of his interpretations of biblical law differed from the rabbinic ones known to the Kairouanese.

Eldad told his listeners more amazing things. Adjacent to the four tribes lived "the Sons of Moses," descendants of priests and Levites who had served in the Temple in Jerusalem. Unlike the Danites, they had not wandered to Havilah but had been transported there magically after the Babylonian sack of Jerusalem and set down beside a broad river named the Sabatyon (sic), which "hurls stones and sand without water, with a mighty sound and such force that it could smash a mountain of iron" and be heard a day's march away. On the Sabbath, when its flow subsided, God shrouded the Sons of Moses in thick cloud to render them invisible to their enemies. They dwelled in sumptuous palaces in a land without wild beasts, poisonous snakes, or even flies and fleas; had cows that calved and fields that ripened twice a year; never stole or locked their doors; never lied or took oaths; and lived in perfect health to a minimal age of one hundred. Their only communication with the four tribes was carried out by shouting across the Sabatyon, and thus it was that the Danites learned the sorrowful news of the Temple's destruction.

The Jews of Kairouan did not know what to make of Eldad. Uncertain whether he was genuine, they wrote for advice to the Babylonian exilarch Rabbi Tsemach Ga'on, the acknowledged head of North African and Middle Eastern Jewry, who responded favorably. Eldad's story about the migration of the tribe of Dan to Ethiopia, he wrote, was known to him from other sources and should therefore be considered credible. Any divergence between rabbinic law and the customs Eldad described could be attributed to the Danites' long isolation.

The correspondence between the Jews of Kairouan and Tsemach Ga'on is the primary source of what we know about Eldad. Later Hebrew versions of his story, more fantastic yet, are embellishments influenced by medieval yarns like the Sinbad the Sailor tales. They relate how, upon setting out from the Ethiopian coast, he was shipwrecked, captured by cannibals, almost eaten, rescued by fire-worshiping pirates, and finally ransomed by a Jewish merchant from the tribe of Issachar. In his further adventures he encountered the other Lost Tribes, variously located by him in the Arabian Peninsula, east of the Persian Gulf, and in and beyond the Caucasus.

The real Eldad continued his travels from North Africa to Spain, where his presence is mentioned in a Hebrew letter written to the Jewish king of Khazaria by Hasdai ibn Shaprut, a minister in the Andalusian court. Then his traces disappear. Who was he? There is no scholarly consensus to this day. Viewed by some historians as a simple imposter, a roaming freeloader making the rounds of the Jewish world in the guise of a Hebrew-speaking biblical tribesman, he is thought by others to have been in the employ of the Karaites, a Jewish sect that denied the authority of the Talmud, and by still others to have been an imaginative Falasha Jew from Ethiopia. The main difficulty with the latter theory is that, although there were Jewish- or Judaizing-dominated regions of Ethiopia in the later Middle Ages, none is known to go as far back as the ninth century. Nor is it clear how Eldad, if he did come from Ethiopia, could have acquired his Hebrew and the rabbinic lore he garnished his story with. The Falashas themselves had no Hebraic knowledge and no tradition of descent from the tribe of Dan. If they did have a pre-medieval origin, it most probably stemmed from a migration across the Red Sea by Jews from Yemen or from an earlier trek southward from Elephantine on the Nile, where a colony of Judean mercenaries guarded the Egyptian frontier in the sixth and fifth centuries B.C.E.

It is noteworthy that several of the places cited in the apocryphal stories of Eldad's travels, such as Arabia, where members of Ephraim and half of Manasseh were said to live; the Transcaucasian steppes, supposedly inhabited by Manasseh's other half and Simon; and the region east of the Persian Gulf, were in fact home to fully or semi-independent Jews in Eldad's day. The so-called Khaibar Jews, known from Arab sources, lived relatively free of Moslem control on the Nejd Plateau, north of Mecca, until the fifteenth or sixteenth century; the kingdom of Khazaria, ruled by a royal house that had converted to Judaism, held sway in the Volga basin until the late tenth century; and the Cochin and Bene Israel Jews of India had self-governing communities on the Malabar Coast. Given their remoteness, it would have been natural for such Jews to be associated with the Lost Tribes and woven into the Eldad narrative.

For the first time, the Lost Tribes had a geography. It remained to be explored.

⚶

In 1165 or 1166, three centuries after the appearance of Eldad, a Jew named Benjamin ben Jonah set out on a rare journey from his hometown of Tudela in Spain. He worked his way up the Spanish coast, across the south of France, down to the heel of Italy, and across the Adriatic to Greece and Constantinople, from where he sailed to Cyprus and Syria, visited the Holy Land, and proceeded eastward, via Damascus and Mosul, to Baghdad. He spent a while there and headed farther east into Persia before reversing course for Egypt, possibly via the port of Aden on the Arabian Sea. In 1171 he returned to Europe and wrote, in Hebrew, a slim account of his trip; it has come to be known as *The Travels of Benjamin of Tudela.*

Benjamin was no Marco Polo, neither in the ground he covered nor in his descriptive abilities, but he did leave a written record of more of the world than we have from any other Jew of his age or long after it. Moreover, this record includes not only his own observations but things he had heard from travelers along the way and brief accounts of places he never saw. A hundred years before Marco informed Europe of similar wonders,

Benjamin told his readers how pearls were dived for in the Persian Gulf; that musk came from Tibet; that there were in Asia great birds, called rocs, that lifted men in their talons and carried them vast distances (Marco merely had them lift elephants), and that in India there existed dark-skinned Jews and the custom of self-sacrificial immolation. He reported that the annual rise of the Nile was caused by rain in the mountains of Africa, described the cultivation of pepper, and mentioned the fierce storms of the South China Sea.

Mostly, though, Benjamin was interested in other Jews, and much of his account is a catalogue of the Jewish communities he came across — their geographical location, size, shrines, and customs. One can tell when he was writing from firsthand knowledge and when from hearsay not only by the amount of detail he gives, but also by the sobriety of his figures. As long as he was speaking from experience, these remain reasonable: three hundred Jews in Marseilles, three hundred in Rome, two thousand in Constantinople, two hundred in Jerusalem. Even his estimate of forty thousand for Baghdad may be accurate, given the city's great size and Jewish importance. Yet when Benjamin turned to the Jews of Arabia and wrote that there were three hundred thousand of them "in forty large towns and two hundred villages," he was obviously passing on tall tales. This number, he wrote, included fifty thousand Jews of Khaibar, "whom Shalmaneser king of Assyria led thither into captivity." They belonged to the tribes of Reuben, Gad, and Manasseh, lived in strongly fortified cities, and made "war upon all other kingdoms. No man can readily reach their territory, because it is a march of eighteen days' journey through the desert, which is altogether uninhabited, so that no one can enter the land."

Benjamin also transmitted two other reports of the Lost Tribes. One placed several of them in the same mountains of Kurdistan to which they were relegated by the Talmudic rabbis. The other concerned Dan, Naphtali, Asher, and Zebulun — the first three of which, along with Gad, were placed by Eldad in Ethiopia. Benjamin located them "in the mountains of Naisabur," a town in northeastern Iran near today's Afghan border. He wrote:

> The extent of their land is twenty days' journey, and they have cities and large villages in the mountains; the river Gozan forms the boundary on one side. They are not under the rule of the

Gentiles, but have a prince of their own, whose name is Joseph Amarkala the Levite . . . And they sow and reap and go forth to war as far as the land of Cush by way of the desert. They are in league with the Kofar el-Turak, who worship the wind and live in the wilderness, and who do not eat bread, nor drink wine, but live on raw meat. They [the Kofar al-Turak] have no noses, and in lieu thereof they have two small holes, through which they breathe. . . . Fifteen years ago they [the Kofar al-Turak] over-ran the country of Persia with a large army and took the city of Rayy; they smote it with the edge of the sword, took all the spoil thereof, and returned by way of the wilderness.

How did three of Eldad's four tribes get to Central Asia? Two points must be kept in mind. One is that "Cush" obviously did not mean Ethiopia to Benjamin. The other is that medieval European notions of geography often confused Ethiopia with India and considered the Horn of Africa and Arabia to belong to the Indian land mass. This suggests the following possibilities:

1. Either Benjamin or travelers he talked to, familiar with Eldad's story, took "Cush" to refer to the Hindu-Kush range, a southwestern spur of the Himalayas running into Afghanistan, and connected Eldad's four tribes with warlike Jews living west of it. Alternately, "Cush" may have been identified with Kushka, Kuhsan, or Khash, all towns in western Afghanistan. Benjamin also applied the name "Gozan," familiar from the biblical story of the Assyrian exile, to an unknown river in this region.

2. The opposite was the case, and it was Eldad, hearing three hundred years before Benjamin's time of Central Asian Jews in "the land of Cush," who mistook this for Ethiopia and invented a story about Lost Tribes there.

3. There is no connection between Eldad's story and Benjamin's, and the presence of the same tribes in them is pure coincidence.

The first theory is the most likely one. In any event, we know that this passage from Benjamin's *Travels* is not wholly imaginary, because what seems at first glance to be its most implausible detail, the noseless "Kofar-al-Turak," turns out to be its most demonstrably factual one. "Kofar" is the Arabic word *kafir*, "infidel"; "al-Turak" is *el-atrak*, "Turks"; and a devastating invasion of Persia by fierce Turkish-Mongol horseman, whose flat Oriental noses might be perceived by a European or Semite as little more than "two breathing holes," took place, not fifteen years before Benjamin was in the area, but closer to thirty, in 1141, when the Mongol leader Ye Lu Ta Shih routed a Moslem Seljuk army led by Sultan Sanjar on the steppes east of Samarkand. Ye Lu Ta Shih went on to found the first Mongol empire in Central Asia and took the name Gur Khan, "king of the world." He was the historical figure who first inspired the legend of Prester John, which was to haunt Europe throughout the late Middle Ages.

It is not impossible that mountain-dwelling Jews living near the Hindu-Kush range were actually allied with Gur Khan's army, especially since earlier Jewish writers, such as the tenth-century Saadia Ga'on and the eleventh-century Moses ibn Ezra, mention Afghanistan — the medieval Khorasan — as the home of Jews descending from the Lost Tribes. Yet even without them the legend of Prester John has an intimate link with the Lost Tribe story. It was, in a sense, a Christianized version of it.

⚹

The first known mention of Prester John, or Presbyter Johannes, as the name appears in medieval Latin, occurred in a twelfth-century chronicle penned by the German bishop Otto of Freising and titled *Historia de duabus civitatibus*. There Otto recounted a meeting with Hugh, the bishop of Jabala, a Crusader outpost on the Lebanese coast. This took place when Hugh came to Italy in 1145, shortly after the fall of the Crusader stronghold of Edessa to the emir of Aleppo, Nur-ed-din, and four years after Gur Khan's rout of the Seljuks. Otto wrote:

> He [Hugh] related that not many years ago, a certain Johannes, a king and a priest, living in the Far East, beyond Persia and Armenia, who like all his people was a Christian though a Nestorian, made war on . . . the kings of the Persians and Medes . . . and stormed the capital of their kingdom . . . putting the Persians to flight with most bloodthirsty slaughter.
>
> He [Hugh] said that after this victory the said Johannes had advanced to the help of the church of Jerusalem, but when he reached the Tigris, he was unable to take his army across the river in any vessel. . . . He is said to be of the ancient lineage of those Magi who are mentioned in the Gospel, and to rule over the same peoples as they did, enjoying such glory and prosperity that he is said to use only a scepter of emerald.

The Seljuks were an Islamic dynasty controlling much of the land to the east and north of Crusader territory, so reports of their defeat by a Christian king at the opposite end of their empire gave the hard-pressed Crusaders a psychological boost. In actual fact, Gur Khan was a Buddhist who had Nestorian Christians among his troops and who never approached the Tigris, much less sought to push across it toward Jerusalem; yet the news of a mysterious army marching out of Asia to attack Christendom's enemies from the rear electrified Europe. The excitement mounted when, in 1165, letters purportedly written by Prester John himself began to appear. One, in Greek, was addressed to the Byzantine emperor Manuel Commenius; a second, in Latin, to the Pope in Rome; a third, in German, to the Holy Roman emperor Frederick Barbarossa; a fourth, to the king of France. Soon more versions were circulating in Italian, Provençal, Hebrew, and other languages.

While differing in detail, all the letters had similar contents. In them Prester John introduced himself as a fervent Christian living in a fabulously rich kingdom comprising "most of India," brimming with honey, milk, silver, gold, and precious stones, and free of "venomous reptiles," "creeping serpents," scorpions, and even "noisy frog croaks." Its wealth was divided fairly among its people, who knew nothing of poverty, lying, flattery, theft, or adultery. When the king went to war against his enemies, he marched with one hundred thousand horsemen, accompanied by "servants and camels and elephants carrying provisions."

Prester John's kingdom was hard to reach. On one side of it lay a desert, beyond which lived satanic cannibals, "the people of Gog and Magog." On its other side was an "ocean of sand," from which ran a river separating it from "the tribes of Israel." This river flowed all week long and rested on the Sabbath. Ten thousand archers were needed to guard it, because, Prester John wrote, should the Lost Tribes ever get across it, "their numbers are so great, inhabiting ten cities for every one of mine, that they would vanquish the entire world." But relations with the tribes were friendly. Their merchants were allowed across the river to trade on the Christian bank, and Daniel, "the great king of Israel," paid Prester John an annual tribute of two hundred camel loads of gold, silver, and precious stones.

Clearly, the letters were fictitious. Clearly, too, whoever composed their prototype knew the story of Eldad Ha-Dani. This is apparent not only from the description of the Lost Tribes living beyond a river like the Sambatyon, but from the utopian nature of Prester John's kingdom, similar to the domain of Eldad's Sons of Moses. If — as has generally been assumed — the fabricator was a Christian seeking to bolster Europe's morale while criticizing its moral laxity by an implied comparison with a Christian utopia, he was familiar with Jewish writings. If, on the other hand — as has been proposed by the French medievalist Jacqueline Pirenne — the original version of the letter was the Hebrew one, its author was a Jew. His motive may have been to impress upon the Christian world the fact that, apart from its failure to live up to its ideals as Prester John did, the Jews, far from being a vulnerable minority that could be persecuted with impunity, were the brethren of a vast horde that might someday come to their aid.

Whoever wrote it, the letter had an effect beyond anything he might have imagined. Taken seriously yet transmogrified, the figure of Prester John soon separated from Gur Khan and became a free-floating persona attaching itself to a long series of partly or wholly imaginary Christian kings reigning behind Moslem lines. The belief that Ethiopia was part of India, and the existence in it of an actual Christian kingdom frequently at war with its Moslem neighbors, only further complicated matters. Prester John was identified with Gur Khan's contemporary, Kuchlug; with Toghril, a leader of the Christian Kereyit Turks killed in battle in 1203; with Wang or Unc Khan, a Kereyit slain by Genghis Khan in the early fourteenth century; with Unc Khan's brother; with shadowy Mongol rulers known as "King George" and "King David"; with the Ethiopian king Wedem Ra'ad (1299–1314), who sent an embassy to King James II of Aragon; with his successor, Amda-Sion; with Dawit I, who received a letter in the early fifteenth century from England's Henry IV addressed to "Prester John, the powerful and magnificent prince, King of Abyssinia"; with the Malabar Coast of India. Medieval travelers like Marco Polo, Oderic of Pordenone, William of Rubruck, and Giovanni de' Marignolli kept a sharp eye out for him. Emissaries were sent to find him; diplomatic and military strategists accepted his existence. When the Crusaders were encamped at Damietta in 1221, debating whether to withdraw from Egypt or march on Cairo (which, disastrously, they did), the hoped-for opening of a second front by Prester John was a reason broached for pressing on with the campaign. When the Portuguese commenced their maritime activities along the African coast in the early fifteenth century, they made repeated efforts to find Prester John in the continent's interior so that they could forge an anti-Moslem alliance with him. Prince Henry the Navigator, mistaking the Senegal River in West Africa for a branch of the Nile, considered sailing up it to Prester John's kingdom.

The Jewish world, too, took Prester John's existence for granted. As the king blocking the Lost Tribes from coming to its rescue, however, he was perceived as a hostile power whose fall was eagerly awaited. In 1454 missives went forth from the Jews of Jerusalem, telling of a dramatic development: word had reached them that, the Sambatyon having ceased to flow, the Lost Tribes had crossed it and were doing battle with the army of Prester John in order reach the oppressed descendants of Judah and once again conquer the land of Israel. They had already killed many thousands of Christians and overrun one of Prester John's provinces, forcing him into an alliance with the cannibals of Gog and Magog. When the Italian rabbi Ovadiah of Bartenora visited Jerusalem in 1487, he heard similar news, though by now the battle was said to be going badly, Prester John having gained the upper hand.

Prester John was a mirage flashing on the horizons of Europe for centuries. Through him the supposed existence of the Lost Tribes, hitherto a purely Jewish concern, entered Christian consciousness. Without him the baffling episode of David Ha-Re'uveni could not have taken place.

☙

Ha-Re'uveni — "the Reubenite," as Eldad was "the Danite" — appeared in Venice with an Egyptian valet in 1523. No one was much taken with him. Dressed in Oriental robes, swarthy, short, and of irritable temperament, and so destitute that he had to ask local Jews for a loan to pay his travel expenses to Rome, he told an improbable story. He had set out from his native land, he said, with a chest full of gold that had been stolen in Egypt, leaving him with only some large, handsomely embroidered tribal banners that were the diplomatic credentials given him by his brother Joseph — who, David told the Venetians, "sits on his throne in the desert of Habor and rules over three hundred thousand souls, the tribes of Gad, Reuben, and half of Manasseh."

David had not traveled directly from "the desert of Habor" to Italy.

Disguised as a Moslem, he related, he had taken a circuitous route that led first to the port of Jeddah on the Arabian Red Sea; then across the water to the Sudanese coast; from there into the mountains of Ethiopia; next — after fleeing precipitously from the Ethiopian king Lebna Dengel, who first welcomed and later sought to kill him — to the Upper Nile and down it to Cairo; thence to Palestine; and, finally, back to Alexandria and a ship for Venice. He was on an important mission from his brother, he said, which was why he was in a hurry to see the Pope in Rome.

To the surprise of the scoffers, he succeeded. Arriving at the Vatican on a rented white horse, David obtained an audience with Clement VII, the former Giulio de' Medici, from whom he sought letters of recommendation to Francis I, king of France, Charles V, the Holy Roman Emperor, and John III, king of Portugal. Why Clement agreed to receive him is uncertain. Presumably, aware of the contemporary identification of Lebna Dengel with Prester John, he was intrigued by David's tale. He was, indeed, sufficiently impressed by the interview to promise him a letter to John of Portugal, the monarch, he explained, most capable of helping him. The letter was delivered after David spent a year being kept under investigation in Rome. Clement also provided David with a papal passport, allowing him to enter Portuguese territory, from which all Jews had been banned following their expulsion in 1496.

In 1525 David set out for the Portuguese court. There, he revealed to John the mission that he had already confided to Clement — namely, to obtain European firearms, military advisers, and ships; sail them around the tip of Africa to the Red Sea; and launch a surprise attack on the Ottoman Turks from the south that would culminate in the capture of Jerusalem. The troops would be provided by the Lost Tribes. These were not limited to "the desert of Habor." As David put it (no doubt more candidly than in his talks with John) in a private conversation with a fellow Jew, recorded in a Hebrew journal that he kept:

> There are nine and a half other tribes in Ethiopia* with kings of their own, the closest to us being the two tribes of Simon and

---

* David's count of nine and a half tribes in Ethiopia and two and a half in "the desert of Habor" makes twelve Lost Tribes. Although there is no support for such a view in Jewish tradition, he apparently held that some members of the southern tribes of Benjamin and Judah were living with the other ten.

Benjamin, who live in a large, rich land between the White Nile and the Black Nile above the kingdom of Sheba, and with whom we are in league. . . . First we will capture the land of Israel and its surroundings, and then our generals will bring to it, from the west and from the east, all the scattered people of Israel . . . and all kingdoms will honor the king of Jerusalem.

Asked "Are you then a prophet or the Messiah?" he answered, "God forbid! I am a greater sinner than anyone, and I have killed many people, more than forty of my enemies in one day. I am not a wise man nor a prophet nor a son of prophets, but a general and the brother of King Joseph."

John, like Clement, did not dismiss David out of hand. The Ottomans were in a period of rapid expansion. Soon to be knocking at the gates of Vienna, they had just taken Damascus, Jerusalem, and Cairo from the Mameluks. Since further southward gains in the Red Sea, where they were already meddling, could threaten shipping routes to the new Portuguese colonies in India, any prospect of a military alliance against them was worth exploring. At that very moment, in fact, a Portuguese embassy was at Lebna Dengel's court to discuss such a possibility. David was told to wait in Portugal while his proposal was examined.

Now, however, complications set in. In Portugal were tens of thousands of Marranos — inwardly loyal Jews, their numbers swelled by refugees from the 1492 Spanish expulsion, compulsorily baptized by John's predecessor, Manuel I. Hearing of David, many flocked to him in an atmosphere of messianic hope, believing he had been sent by God to end the travail of Jewish exile. His lodgings became — not entirely to his pleasure, for he justly feared the consequences — a Marrano gathering place. Rumors spread that he was engaged in returning converted Jews to Judaism; indeed, that his entire story was a cover for such an operation. Matters came to a head when John's secretary, Diego Pires, a young Marrano who had fallen under David's influence, circumcised himself against David's advice and fled abroad. Soon after this David was summoned by the king, informed that his plan had been rejected, and ordered to leave Portugal at once. In his journal he wrote that he had been tantalizingly close to success when Pires undermined him. John had already promised him eight ships and four thousand blunderbuses and muskets, only to change his mind under pressure from the Catholic

Church. "I was happy enough when you appeared with your offer of help," David quoted John as saying, "but now you will be the ruin of my kingdom."

The journal breaks off with David's leaving Portugal, a departure made hazardous by crowds of emotional Marranos, quarreling servants, suspicious officials, menacing visits from the Inquisition, and intrigues to kill David at sea. What probably saved him from Inquisitorial arrest at this point was his Vatican passport. It was not, though, a fate he could ultimately avoid. In 1527 he returned to an Italy in which Clement was unable to help him, having been taken prisoner in May of that year when Rome was sacked by Charles V. For a while David disappears from our sight; then, in 1530, he resurfaces in the company of Pires, now a Jewish revivalist preacher who called himself Shlomo Molcho and proclaimed the imminent coming of the Messiah. Alone perhaps, Molcho still believed in David's Jerusalem campaign, and after escaping the Inquisition in Venice, he and David, carrying a banner emblazoned *Maccabee*, slipped across the Italian border to seek protection from Charles. The Holy Roman Emperor, however, had no interest in the Red Sea and no desire to become involved. He detained the two men and sent them back to Italy, where Shlomo Molcho was burned at the stake in Mantua in 1532. Not being a renegade Christian, David was spared that penalty. He was shipped to an Inquisitorial prison in Spain and died there some time after 1535.

Like Eldad Ha-Dani, David Ha-Re'uveni remains a historical mystery. Even with the help of his journal, whose preoccupation with servants and household expenses makes it read more like the diary of a harried touring country squire than of a visionary statesman, it is impossible to probe his inner consciousness. Nothing about his behavior in Italy and in Portugal suggests a mountebank or a madman. On the contrary, he ran risks that were more than self-serving, and from his own account he appears as a simple if stubborn man, devoid of megalomaniac delusions. Everything points to him as a Jewish patriot convinced that he could succeed if his requests were met.

But succeed with whom? What would he have done with four thousand weapons and eight ships had John provided them? His sailing to Africa from Jeddah may indicate that the "desert of Habor" (a place name taken from the account of the Assyrian exile in Kings), with its alleged kingdom of three hundred thousand Jews, was the Khaibar of Arabia mentioned by Benjamin of Tudela. The numbers he cites for Arabian Jewry, the same as the exaggerated ones given by Benjamin, strongly suggest the latter's *Travels* as his inspiration, as do both men's placement in Arabia of the identical three Lost Tribes. Yet although the Khaibar Jews were a reality, their numbers, nowhere near that large to begin with, had dwindled greatly by David's time. It is highly unlikely that he could have fielded, trained, and armed enough of them to sail to the head of the Gulf of Aqaba and march from there to Jerusalem.

Perhaps the clue to his thinking lies in his trip to Ethiopia, a puzzling detour if he simply wished to get to Italy. The Falasha Jews of that country, then at the height of their power, were firmly entrenched in the rugged mountains of the northwest, from where they took part, now on one side and now on the other, in the many wars between Lebna Dengel and his enemies. In 1541, just a few years after David's death, they joined a Portuguese expeditionary force fighting for Lebna Dengel's son, Galawdewos, against the Ottoman-backed Moslem general Ahmed ibn Ibrahim. It is thus probable that David visited Ethiopia with the aim of enlisting them in his cause. He may well have succeeded in making contact with them. His geographical terms are different from ours, but if by the "Black Nile" he meant the Blue Nile, and by the "White Nile" the tributary known today as the Atbara, then the area in which he located the tribes of Benjamin and Simon, with whom he claimed to be "in league," corresponds to Falasha territory. The unexplained episode of Lebna Dengel's attempt on his life while he was disguised as a Moslem makes sense if linked to such a purpose, for the Falashas were then fighting against the Christian king, who may have discovered that David was on a secret mission to them.

Where David originally came from will probably never be known. Although he spoke a passable Arabic, analyses of his quirky Hebrew have shown European, possibly German, influences. The most likely profile of him is of a dark-complexioned Ashkenazi who had lived in the Arab world and encountered warlike Arabian and Ethiopian Jews, whom he planned to marshal as an expeditionary force to the Holy Land. Whether he genuinely believed they hailed from the Lost Tribes, or said so only for effect, is difficult to determine, as is whether his plan was pure fantasy or included realistic elements. From our perspective it is tempting to view him as the first modern Jewish political strategist, a proto-Theodor Herzl who believed that a Jewish return to Palestine was achievable through a combination of *realpolitik* and military daring. If so, he was a man well ahead of his time.

ᴥ

It can be no coincidence that in 1523, the year of David Ha-Re'uveni's arrival in Venice, a Christian pamphlet appeared in Vienna entitled, *Von Ainer Grosse Meng vnd Gewalt der Juden die Lange Zeit mit Vnwonhaftigen Wuesten Beschlossen vnd Verbrochen Gewesen, Yetzunder Ausgebrochen vnd an Tag Kommen Seyn*, that is, "Of a Great Horde and Power of Ancient Jews Hitherto Hidden Away in an Uninhabitable Desert and Now Broken Out and Come This Day." The pamphlet, crediting its information to an Italian Jew visiting Trieste, announced that six hundred thousand African Jews bearing arms, the descendants of Shalmaneser's exiles, were now in Egypt, threatening to march on Jerusalem.

Trieste was a short sail from Venice, where the Jew from Italy must have met or heard of David, and henceforward Jewish and Christian Lost Tribe fever was to mount apace, in part because increased contact between the two religions in the wake of the Renaissance and Reformation encouraged mutual infection. Among Christians, the emergence of numerous chiliastic Protestant sects — some, particularly among England's Puritans, strongly oriented toward an Old Testament literalism — led to a belief in the Lost Tribes' return as a harbinger of the Second Coming. For Jews, a new tide of messianism, goaded by the disaster of the Spanish expulsion and a growing belief in the possibility of hastening the recalcitrant End of Days by kabbalistic practices, made the tribes' reappearance an anxiously awaited event. Reports of them began to multiply, one stranger than the next. One of the strangest originated in 1646 with a Jerusalem rabbi named Baruch Gad, who related that he had been attacked by bandits while on his way to Persia and left without food and drink in the desert. Close to death, he was revived by a spear-carrying, Hebrew-speaking warrior from the tribe of Naphtali. The warrior told Rabbi Baruch to wait for him beneath a tree, and returned three days later with a letter from King Ahituv of the Sons of Moses, which described the Lost Tribes beyond the Sambatyon and their longing for Jerusalem. Baruch's account and King Ahituv's letter were authenticated by leading Jerusalem rabbis and circulated widely.

The figure in whom Jewish and Christian Lost Tribism converged most fully was the Dutch rabbi and author Manasseh ben Israel (1604–1657). Born in Spain to a Marrano family that, like many others, moved to Amsterdam and returned to Judaism, Manasseh was a contemporary of Spinoza and of Rembrandt; the latter drew his portrait and illustrated his books. Amsterdam in those days was a bustling Atlantic crossroads at which Jewish rationalism and mysticism met. The Sephardic ties and culture of the Marranos; the Ashkenazi learning of Central and Eastern Europe; reports of early Jewish colonists back from the Americas; a Christian toleration for and interest in Judaism — all contributed to its distinctive milieu, and Manasseh was involved with each. His books, dealing with a variety of theological topics, were written in Latin for a Christian audience, and he regularly exchanged views with such Dutch humanists as Hugo Grotius, Johannes Buxtorf, and Gerhard Johannes Vossius. He was also ardently interested in the Lost Tribes, on which he published a work in 1650 called *Spes Israelis*. This was translated (by Moses Wall, a friend of the poet John Milton) into English in 1652 as *The Hope of Israel, Written By Manasseh ben Israel, an Hebrew Divine, and Philosopher, and Dedicated by the Author to the High Court, the Parliament of England, and to the Council of State.*

Manasseh meant this dedication seriously, since he was at the time seeking to persuade the Puritan government of Oliver Cromwell to readmit the Jews, legally barred from England since 1290. What did the Lost Tribes have to do with this? Everything, he argued in an appeal to Puritan reason. The Bible prophesied that the exiled Israelites would be brought back from "the four corners of the earth" — and now that they had been discovered, Manasseh wrote, even in North and South America, the only corner they were missing from was England. It was the English, therefore, who were holding up the Redemption, which they were now called upon to let proceed.

The Hope of Israel did more than merely state this argument. It sought to prove that the Lost Tribes had indeed been found in the Americas. To this end, Manasseh set forth all the evidence he had collected, beginning with a story told him by a Marrano and former prisoner of the Inquisition, a Jew, recently returned from South America, named Aaron Levi or Antonius Montezinus. While in the Andes, Montezinus recounted, he had met an Indian who confided that he was a "Hebrew"; moreover, this man took him to a riverbank to meet an entire group of Hebrew Indians

who told Montezinus that "our fathers are Abraham, Isaac, Jacob, and Israel." Desiring to accompany them back to their village but refused permission, Montezinus impetuously "caste himselfe into their Boat" and
"being forced out againe, fell into the River, and was in danger to be
drowned, for he could not swim; but being got out of the water, the rest
being angry, said to him; attempt not to passe the River, nor to enquire
after more than we tel you."

Montezinus' story, with its Sambatyon-like river hiding a Lost Tribe,
may have been pure fabrication. It is not impossible, however, that he did
meet Indians who, having had contact with other Marranos fleeing the
Inquisition to South America, had picked up a smattering of Jewish lore.
Manasseh, though he considered Montezinus a "vertuous" witness, did
not ask his readers to accept the tale on faith. Rather, he used it as a starting point to inquire whether the Lost Tribes *could* be in the Americas —
and answered positively by citing the Talmud, Josephus, Eldad Ha-Dani,
Benjamin of Tudela, David Ha-Re'uveni, and a wide range of other Jewish and Christian authorities to show that the tribes, who were "not in
any one place but in many," had reached China and "Tartary," that is,
northeast Asia stretching to the ends of Siberia. From there, Manasseh
posited, by continuing across the "Streight of Anian," a strip of water di-
viding Asia from America much like the Bering Strait, they could have
migrated to the New World. In fact, the two continents may have been
connected by an ancient land bridge that was later destroyed by an earthquake, so that "it doth not seeme to me such an absurdity to say that the
Israelites went out of Tartary into America by land."

The novelty of Manasseh's views, fanciful as they may seem to a modern reader, lay in a geographical rationalism and critical reading of previous literature that made *The Hope of Israel* a pioneering work of Lost
Tribe scholarship. Cromwell, in any event, was convinced, although
surely not by the book alone. In 1655 a council of ministers at Whitehall
voted in Manasseh's presence to rescind England's ban on the Jews.

Yet in Jewish circles, it was the mysticism rather than the rationalism
of the times that prevailed, triggering the greatest messianic movement
in Jewish history since the birth of Christianity. Amsterdam was one of
its main centers. This movement focused on the messianic pretender
Shabbetai Tsvi (1626–1676), who proclaimed himself the Redeemer in
Izmir, on the Aegean coast of Turkey, in June 1666; attracted hundreds

of thousands of spiritually intoxicated followers; and ended his eschato-
logical career three months later with his arrest by the Ottomans and
conversion under pain of death to Islam. Even before his proclamation,
stories of the Lost Tribes' return, periodically epidemic since the time of
David Ha-Re'uveni, had become rampant in the Jewish world. A new
wave of them began in July 1665 with the report, apparently emanating
from North Africa, that Moslem pilgrimages to Mecca had been canceled because of a huge army of biblical Israelites besieging the city; witnesses were said to have testified that its soldiers spoke only Hebrew and
were accompanied by columns of fire and smoke. Soon a second story
followed from Egypt: another Lost Tribe army, comprising one million
and one hundred thousand men, was advancing through Africa, and all
arrows and bullets fired to halt its advance were magically deflected back
at those who shot them. Dizzying rumor followed rumor. Mecca had
fallen; the general of the conquering army was named Jeroboam and already ruled seventy cities; eighty ships with a million more Jewish warriors had set out from India; the Turkish sultan was offering Jeroboam
Alexandria and Tunis in return for his withdrawal from Mecca; more
Lost Tribes were coming from Tartary and Persia; the Sons of Moses had
reached Gaza; a ship of Lost Tribesmen, blown off course by a storm, had
put into port in Aberdeen, Scotland. Its shrouds and sails were white silk,
the words *Ten Tribes of Israel* were boldly inscribed in red on its mainsail,
and its troops wore blue uniforms with black stripes and ate only rice and
honey.

Besides circulating orally, these stories saw print in a large number
of languages. Combined with the news of the Messiah's appearance in
Izmir, their effect was prodigious. In Amsterdam, Venice, Livorno, Constantinople, and many other places Jews sold their houses and properties,
liquidated businesses, packed their belongings, and even dug up the buried bones of their loved ones to take with them on their journey to the
Holy Land, where the Lost Tribes were expected any day. Although it
was Shabbetai Tsvi who set off the frenzy, some of the reported tribe
sightings preceded him and helped create the atmosphere in which he
achieved fame. Mutually reinforcing, the two phenomena were as closely
linked in their subsidence as in their eruption. Like twin cones of a vol-
cano in which pressure had long been building, their blowout covered
the terrain with sterile lava. It took the Jewish world a generation or

more to recover from the communal fissures and mass disillusion caused by Shabbetai Tsvi and his apostasy. While messianic episodes continued to occur (the most recent being that of New York's Lubavitcher Rebbe, Menachem Schneerson, in the 1990s), religious messianism as a major force in Jewish life was exhausted, its emotions transmuted into such secular forms as revolutionary socialism and modern Zionism.

Nor would the Lost Tribes again overrun the Jewish imagination. Although they continued to inhabit Jewish folklore, they no longer dwelt there as a mighty multitude who would one day march to the relief of their downtrodden co-religionists. The expansion of geographic knowledge brought about by European exploration and colonization left no room for them in their old haunts. By the end of the seventeenth century, Asia, Africa, and India had ceased to be *terrae incognitae* that could be peopled with whatever fantastical creatures one wished. Prester John was finally dead of old age. The last frontier for the Lost Tribes was now the Americas — to which, well before publication of *The Hope of Israel*, the pursuit of them had begun to shift.

⚱

Theologically, the natives of the New World posed a problem for their Christian discoverers. Once it became clear that they were not, as Columbus had thought, Indians or Asians but a previously unknown race, it had to be asked where this race came from. If it did not descend from one of the families of man mentioned in the genealogical chapters of Genesis, which traced all humanity to Adam and Eve, the Bible was falsified. If it did, to which of these families did it belong?

And at the same time, the Lost Tribes had yet to be found. What, then, could be more tempting than to solve both mysteries at once, fitting the missing peg into the pegless hole by assuming some or all of the Amerindians to be vanished Israelites? The tribes had been gone from sight for nearly twenty-five hundred years, almost half the world's age, by biblical reckoning. Surely that was enough time for them to have reached and populated even so vast a territory as North and South America.

On the face of it, therefore, it seemed entirely reasonable to look for the tribes across the Atlantic. The first to find them there were the Spanish, and the first Spaniard to make the identification in print was Francisco López de Gómara, whose 1553 *History of the Indies* pointed out the physical resemblance of the "large-nosed" Indians to the Jews. De Gómara's contemporary, Bartolomé de Las Casas, the so-called Apostle of the Indies, believed there was also linguistic proof of an Israelite-Indian connection, such as the island of Cuba deriving its name from the Hebrew word for "helmet," *kova*, because of its helmeted chiefs. And in a book written in the 1560s, the Yucatán bishop Diego de Landa observed, "Some of the old people of the Yucatán say that they have heard from their ancestors that this land was occupied by a race of people who came from the East and whom God had delivered by opening twelve paths through the sea. If this were true, it necessarily follows that all the inhabitants of the Indies are descendants of the Jews."

Gregorio García's seventeenth-century *Origin of the Indians of the New World* treated the subject more systematically. Although most of the Indians, García concluded, were probably of Chinese or Scythian origin, some might be, as "the Spaniards who reside in the Indies generally believe, the ten Jewish tribes who were lost in the captivity of Salmanezer, king of Assyria." A Spanish priest in Venezuela, Joseph Gumilla, had an explanation for the natives' ignorance of their own past. "The nations of the Orinoco River and its streams," he wrote in *Orinoco Illustrada*, "observed many Hebrew ceremonies . . . without knowing [that these] had been transmitted by traditions, handed down from father to son, [or] being able to assign any reason for the practice of them."

In North America, where English colonization started a century after its Spanish counterpart, Lost Tribe claims were soon cropping up too. In 1634, a bare fourteen years after the landing at Plymouth Rock, the New Englander William Wood was already dismissing such speculation, declaring that while "some have thought that they [the Indians] might be of the dispersed Jewes, because some of their words be neare unto the Hebrew, by the same rule they may conclude them to be of the gleanings of all Nations, because they have words which sound after the Greeke, Latine, French, and other tongues." Yet such sensible skepticism did not stem the tide. A few years later, Charles Beatty announced, in his *Journal of a Two Months Tour*, that he had found the Lost Tribes among the Delawares. In 1650 the Puritan minister Thomas Thorowgood, a foremost representative of the "Jewish Indian" theory, published *Jews in America, or, Probabilities that the Americans Are of that Race*, in which he listed not only linguistic similarities, but over fifty parallels between Indian and biblical practices. Attacked by the Englishman Sir Hamon L'Estrange, in *Americans No Jews, or, Improbabilities that the Americans are of that Race*, which argued that such parallels were common to many people, Thorowgood replied in 1660, in *Jews in America, or Probabilities that Those Indians are Judaical, Made More Probable by Some Additions on the Former Conjectures.*

Thorowgood had many supporters, among them Roger Williams, the founder of Rhode Island; the Massachussets preacher John Eliot, the first translator of the Bible into a North American Indian language; and the Salem witchcraft trial judge Samuel Sewall. William Penn agreed, too, finding Indians so Semitic-looking that, when among them, a man might think himself in the Jewish neighborhoods of London. Besides, Penn observed, "they agree in rites; they reckon by moons; they offer their first fruits; they have a kind of feast of tabernacles; they are said to lay their altar upon twelve stones." (Penn's colleague Richard Frame took light-verse issue with this, writing of the Pennsylvania Indians in 1692: "Some men did think they were the scattered Jews / But yet I cannot well believe such News; / They neither do New Moons nor Sabbath keep, / Without much Care they eat, they drink, they sleep.") The Puritan theologian Jonathan Edwards found Hebrew elements in the Muhhekaneww language, of which he published an eighteenth-century grammar. James Adair's 1775 *History of the American Indians*, a compendious volume of comparisons between ancient Israelite and Cherokee, Creek, and Chickasaw customs, made the point that a native name for God, Yohewah, was the same as the Hebrew Jehovah.

As the frontier moved westward, so did the Lost Tribes. The Methodist preacher J. B. Finlay wrote that he had found them among the Wyandottes of Ohio, while Elias Boudinot's *Star of the West* (1816) piqued the interest of his friend Thomas Jefferson, who, before rejecting the Jewish Indian theory, discussed it with John Adams. Yet by the middle of the nineteenth century, despite several alleged archeological finds of a sensational nature (such as a pair of phylacteries supposedly retrieved from an Indian burial mound in Pittsfield, Massachusetts, in 1820, and a Hebrew coin said to have been unearthed in Tennessee three years later), serious minds had lost interest in the matter. Advances in knowledge had passed the point at which it could be considered a creditable proposition. By the

1830s the American craniologist Samuel Morton was comparing Indian and Eurasian skull measurements to show that the Lost Tribe theory was physiologically impossible. Although many of his hypotheses were later proved to be wrong, the empirical methodology he represented would soon lay the whole question to rest.

For all its absurdities, the Jewish Indian debate helped move the discussion of the Lost Tribes into the scientific age. No less than its opponents, the theory's backers sought to argue on factual grounds. Although biblical prophecy was important to many of them, they turned, for the first time in the history of the subject, to extensive linguistic and ethnographic data from the field to support their argument. That this data was often mistaken and capriciously interpreted mattered less than their appeal to it, which made it possible to prove them wrong.

But only in the court of rational opinion. For as sometimes happens when reason wins a battle with religion, religion — or, rather, a sudden mutation of it — broke off all further contact with reason in its retreat. Thus it was that, paradoxically, the final defeat of Lost Tribism in America turned into its greatest triumph, that bizarrest of American faiths, Mormonism.

۩

The Mormon faith has been called white America's one genuinely home-grown revealed religion and it has been called a parody of all revealed religion, and it is both, just as it is the first major religion in history to have demonstrably started as a knowing hoax on the part of its founder. Although one can suspect other beliefs of similar origins, the suspicion cannot be documented. In the case of the Mormon "prophet" Joseph Smith the documentation is ample, beginning with Smith's composition of the *Book of Mormon* — claimed by him to have been found on "golden plates" buried in the earth near his home in Palmyra, New York in 1823 — for motives of financial gain.

The influence of contemporary Lost Tribe literature on the *Book of Mormon* is clearcut. Western New York State, in which Smith lived, was a hotbed of Jewish Indian theory, an area dotted with ancient burial sites like the Pittsfield one that were attributed to a vanished people known as the Mound Builders. As a young man Smith was fascinated by these sites. The same year that his golden plates were "found" he had been reading a book called *View of the Hebrews; or the Ten Tribes of Israel in America.* Written by a Vermont minister, Ethan Smith, *View of the Hebrews* maintained that the Mound Builders had been ancient tribes of Israel — some of which, falling into a "savage state," went to war with their more civilized brethren, exterminated them, and put an end to the biblical heritage of the American Indians.

This is precisely the "plot" of the *Book of Mormon*, which tells the saga of the family of the Hebrew prophet Lehi, who, with his sons Nephi, Laman, Lemuel, Sam, Jacob, and Joseph, leaves Jerusalem shortly before the destruction of the First Temple and makes a long ocean voyage to America. There Laman and Lemuel are cursed by God and beget evil, red-skinned descendants, whereas Nephi and his brothers find favor in the eyes of the Lord and have white offspring granted a revelatory visitation by Jesus Christ. These two families, one piously monotheistic and the other barbarically idolatrous, war for a thousand years, the "Lamanites" gradually getting the better of the "Nephites," who bury their dead after each battle in great mounds. Finally, the Nephites are wiped out completely, so that by the time European colonists arrive on the scene they encounter only the Red Indians and the archeological remains of the Mound Builders. It is left to Joseph Smith to discover the Nephites' scriptures, recorded for posterity by the Nephite prophet Moroni and buried near Palmyra.

One might ask why so gross a fiction, narrated in pseudo-biblical fustian, should have inspired thousands of Americans to face violence and contumely while following Smith through the Midwest in search of territory to settle, and then, after his lynching by an Illinois mob, to brave even greater hazards trekking to Utah with Brigham Young. Smith's personal charisma had much to do with it, as did his American nativism that blotted out with one startling stroke the entire European history of Christianity — a religion, according to the *Book of Mormon*, whose true message Jesus entrusted to the Nephites. Hawked on the frontier, the Mormon gospel was a snake oil for bad consciences, making America's white pioneers the country's owners by hereditary right, engaged not in taking it from its native inhabitants, but in taking it back. Mormonism also soothed another sore point that had nagged Christians, often subliminally, over the centuries, namely, how their Savior could have emerged from a people as known for its bad qualities as the Jews. If the

Nephites — brave, honest, hardworking, and morally exemplary — represented the *real* Jews, a pristine biblical version of a race that later degenerated, Jesus was born into a good family after all.

Indeed, perhaps this was the motivation for much of Christian Lost Tribism. It had never been easy for Christianity to accept Jesus' Jewishness, a matter traditionally played down in different ways. For some Christians, the discovery of ancient Israelites surviving as noble savages far removed from the anti-Semitic caricature of the sneaking Pharisee or the craven Shylock was a welcome solution to an old dilemma. In the Christian no less than the Jewish imagination, the Lost Tribes stood for a different kind of Jew, one whom no one had to be ashamed of.

Or else — as the myth of the Lost Tribes played itself out to its final demise in a parody of the parody — they stood for no Jew at all. Such was the trajectory of that strange movement known as the British Israelites, which commenced as a sedate British counterpart of Mormonism and concluded as an American hate group.

The Joseph Smith of the British Israel movement was the Englishman Richard Brothers. Brothers, an ex–naval officer who called himself "the nephew of the Almighty," because he thought himself a descendant of James, the brother of Jesus, published a book in 1800 entitled *A Correct Account of the Invasion of England by the Saxons, Showing the English Nation to be Descendants of the Lost Ten Tribes.* Although he spent the following years in a lunatic asylum, he attracted disciples. The most influential of them, Edward Hine, wrote his own book in 1871, *The English and American Nation Identified With the Lost House of Israel,* which put forth forty-seven "identifications" based on resemblances between Jews and Englishmen. Other British Israelite pamphleteers argued that the Saxons were the ancient Scythians, descended from Israelite tribes who had migrated across the English Channel after being exiled to the steppes of Russia; that "British" came from Hebrew *brit,* "covenant," and *ish,* "man"; that Queen Victoria was of Davidic lineage; and that the Stone of Scone in Westminster Abbey, brought by the prophet Jeremiah to Ireland before its transfer to London for the coronation of Edward I, was the pillow slept on by Jacob in his flight from Esau. Hines's book was said to have sold a quarter of a million copies, and a British Israel World Federation, claiming hundreds of thousands of members, was established in London.

Such numbers were undoubtedly inflated. Unlike the Mormons, the British Israelites never became a religion and amounted to little more than a seedy Victorian amalgam of eccentrics, obsessives, misinformed autodidacts, lonely widows, and bored pensioners of the kind who also attended lectures on Mesmerism in rented halls and the afternoon teas of Theosophist societies. Before petering out, shortly after World War II, they managed to enlist in their ranks one bishop, one brigadier general, and one admiral, and to produce a large library of publications — one of which, the Reverend Canon Jonathan Holt Titcomb's *A Résumé of the Scriptural Argument Proving the Identity of the British Race With the Lost Ten Tribes of Israel*, went through, by the author's count, 2,005 editions. By the early twentieth century the movement had spread to the United States and fallen into the hands of America First white supremacists, spawning such offshoots as the Great Pyramid Club, the Kingdom of Yahweh, and the Anglo-Saxon Federation of America. In 1928 the last of these issued a statement of principles, among them:

- "The Bible does not state or infer that the Jews are God's Chosen People. Judah and Israel are entirely distinct."
- "The Celtic-Anglo-Saxons are Israel, the Chosen People of God."
- "In 1776 the Lord divided Israel into two nations, England and America, so that God's promises to both Ephraim and Manasseh might be realized."

Born in Nazareth in northern Palestine, in other words, Jesus was not a Jew but a forerunner of Englishmen killed by Jews, a descendant of that portion of the lily-white "house of Joseph," which remained on its soil when the Aryan kingdom of Israel was dispatched to Scythia by Shalmaneser. The Lost Tribes had been found at last — by the anti-Semitic lunatic fringe. It was the tawdry end of a once grand notion.

⚶

Yet not quite the end. Imitations of British Israelism popped up everywhere. The Lost Tribes were the Welsh, the Dutch, the Danes, the Armenians, the Japanese, the Eskimos, the Zulus, the Madagascans, the Maori of New Zealand. A few enthusiasts were enough to start a local chapter.

Meanwhile, the actual facts of the matter had grown clearer. Alongside the fantasts and the frauds (among the most notable of them, the notorious antiquities forger Abraham Firkowitsch, who produced in 1840 a Hebrew document, purportedly written by a descendant in the Crimea of the tribe of Naphtali, that fooled even the great Jewish historian Heinrich Graetz), inquisitive observers with an interest in the Lost Tribes — missionaries, travelers, and ethnographers — had contributed by the end of the nineteenth century to a considerable body of information. Two findings were paramount. One was that no people, Jewish or Gentile, could be proven to descend from the Assyrian exiles. Even the most far-flung and historically isolated of Jewish communities, such as the Falashas of Ethiopia, the Cochin and Bene Israel Jews of India, and the tiny remnant of the Chinese Jews of Kaifeng, could be more plausibly traced to other, post-biblical origins. There was not a single document, artifact, or tradition that could establish a Lost Tribe link for anyone.

On the other hand, not every claim could be automatically dismissed. Some local traditions of Lost Tribe descent were not necessarily absurd. These were mainly concentrated in two areas. One, already cited by the Talmud, was the mountains of the Caucasus stretching south into Kurdistan, where Westerners like the American Protestant minister Asahel Grant and the Jewish traveler Joseph Israel Benjamin (better known to his readers as Benjamin the Second) were impressed by the strong belief among Jews and Christians alike that (as Benjamin put it) "their settlement in these countries took place before the destruction of the first Temple." The other was farther east, among the Pashtuns of Afghanistan. The most comprehensive treatment of Lost Tribe traditions there was by H. W. Bellew, a British surgeon-general in India who presented his *Inquiry Into the Ethnography of Afghanistan* to the Ninth International Congress of Orientalists in London in 1891. Remarking that many Pashtun tribes believed they were descended from the Bani Isra'il, or Children of Israel, Bellew pointed out that this did not mean the disdained "Yahud," or Jew, any connection with whom was indignantly rejected. These tribes held that they had been *Taurat-khwan*, observers of the Torah, until they embraced Islam in Mohammed's time.

The few serious scholars to inquire into a field by now infamous for its quackery differed as to whether the Lost Tribes had left any footprints. In a study entitled *Where Are the Ten Tribes?* (1889), the Jewish Orientalist Adolf Neubauer concluded that the seekers had been chasing a chimera. Only the "influential part" of the northern kingdom of Israel, Neubauer thought, had been exiled by the Assyrians, the "humbler classes" having been left on their land, where they eventually merged with the newcomers brought from "Cutha, Ava, Hamath, and Sepharvaim" to form the Samaritans — a people who accepted Mosaic law but later quarreled with the Judeans and went their own way. As for the exiles, some were soon assimilated by the indigenous peoples they settled among and others by the Judeans deported in a later age by the Babylonians. In either case, they soon disappeared as a discrete group. Neubauer's conclusion to the question "Where are the Ten Tribes?" was "We can only answer, Nowhere."

Some of Neubauer's ideas were endorsed by two Hebrew writers who followed him. In *The Ten Tribes and Their Solution* (1908), Simon Menachem Lazar hypothesized that the northern exiles had retained their identity long enough to return to Palestine and merge there with their southern brethren of Judah under the Persian restoration of 538 B.C.E. Tsvi Kasdai's *The Tribes of Jacob and the Vanished of Israel* (1928), on the other hand, argued for an Israelite-Judean recombination in the Diaspora — specifically, in the Kurdo-Caucasus, the cloud-covered peaks of which were the ancient rabbis' Mountains of Darkness. The many Lost Tribe traditions found in this area, Kasdai believed, had a genuine historical basis.

These three men were Jews. In 1930 appeared the first major study of the subject by a Gentile, the 800-page tome *The Lost Tribes: A Myth*, by Allen Godbey, a professor of biblical studies at Duke. The history of the tribes was Godbey's life's work, and the book was a veritable encyclopedia of every historical reference to them or anything connected to them that could be tracked down. Massively footnoted, it ranged from Timbuctoo to Tamerlane and from ancient Iranian trade routes to Berber sororities, its heavy erudition leavened by a crusty polemical tone; for its author had a Christian bone to pick not only with deluded Lost Tribe hunters but with Judaism itself — a religion that, in his opinion, was obsessed with race and heredity, to the detriment of its implicitly universalistic message. The title of his book notwithstanding, however, Godbey never argued that the Lost Tribes had not existed. Rather, he proposed that both in their exile and their many pre-exilic trading outposts, the more open Israelites of the north, unlike the isolationist Judeans of the south, had sought to bring the universal God to the Gentiles, converting to biblical monotheism large numbers of them, from North Africa to Central Asia and India. Of these converts, some had remained Jewish and others had subsequently become Christian or Moslem, in both cases retaining fragmentary memories of an ancient association with the northern tribes. Far from being religiously assimilated, Godbey contended, the Lost Tribes had assimilated others until they themselves lost their tribal nature and became nonbiological communities of faith.

Godbey's work was such a scholarly blockbuster that, despite its idiosyncrasies, it proved a hard act to follow; seventy-two years had to pass before the publication of another book-length investigation of the subject, this one by the London academic Tudor Parfitt. Thanks to the related disciplines of biblical archeology and Assyriology, however, much more is now known about the northern kingdom of Israel's downfall in the context of Assyrian history and imperial procedures. Summarized in books by the Israeli scholar Bustenay Oded and his Dutch colleague Bob Becking, this knowledge began in the mid-nineteenth century with the discovery of two Assyrian cuneiform inscriptions by French archeologists. Both were in the name of Sargon II and confirmed the essentials of the account in Kings. In one of them Sargon declares, "In the beginning of my reign and in the first years of my reign . . . I besieged Samaria . . . [its] inhabitants I carried away. Fifty chariots I collected there as a royal force. . . . I set [Samaria] up again and made [it] more populous than before. People from lands which I had taken I settled there. My men I set over them as governors. Tribute and taxes [like those paid by ordinary Assyrians] I set over them." The second text has the Assyrian king say, "I besieged and captured Samaria. I carried away 27,290 of its inhabitants. I collected there fifty chariots. The remainder of them I permitted to retain their goods. I put my governors over them, and I laid the tribute of former kings upon them."

Both inscriptions refer to the fall of Samaria in 720 B.C.E. In addition, more recently discovered Assyrian texts indicate that another 13,500 Israelites were deported in Tiglath-Pileser's campaign of 734–32.* Unlike

---

* Yet another Assyrian document dealing with deportations from Palestine dates from 701, four years after the end of Sargon's reign, when his successor, Sennacherib, moved an army south from conquered Samaria into independent Judea. Although Sennacherib, according to this text, besieged but did not capture Jerusalem, which was then under the rule of King Hezekiah, he subdued elsewhere in Judea "46 strong cities with walls" and "brought forth from them and counted as booty 200,150 men, young, old, male, female." Yet while the Book of Kings contains a lengthy passage about Sennacherib's siege of Jerusalem, and tells of his taking the "walled cities" of Hezekiah's kingdom, it makes no mention of the inhabitants being exiled, much less in

the biblical versions of these two events, which imply a total deportation, the Assyrian records depict a partial one; for although it is unknown what the exact population of the northern kingdom was, it must have been considerably greater than 40,000. As Oded and Becking described them, such deportations were standard Assyrian practice, especially from the start of Tiglath-Pileser's reign. Only in extreme cases were populations exiled *in toto*. What was more common, as Neubauer had surmised, was that the Assyrians culled crucial elements — the royal family, the aristocracy, the priesthood, the army, and skilled craftsmen, particularly those who could produce weapons — and left the peasantry in place. Their purpose was to deprive the conquered inhabitants of leadership and the capacity for armed rebellion. Groups brought in from elsewhere to replace the deportees were assembled from different places so as to minimize the chances of their forming a common front, as in the biblical account of the repopulation of Samaria.

Becking and Oded also discussed the probable fate of the 40,000 Israelite exiles. Populations deported by the Assyrians were broken into small groups, granted the legal status of Assyrian subjects, and allowed to retain their communal structures and religious and cultural identities. While their situation after resettlement was far from uniform, there being among them rich and poor, freemen and slaves, soldiers and civilians, townsmen and villagers, they were on the whole treated well. The Assyrian government had no reason to fear them. Far from home and settled among natives who resented their intrusive presence, they depended on the government for protection. Their warrior class, its military units kept intact, was impressed into the Assyrian army and sent to guard distant frontiers. The "fifty chariots" that Sargon "collected" from Samaria would in all likelihood have included charioteers and archers, the ancient version of a mechanized brigade. Assyrian cavalry rosters referring to a Samaritan cohort have been found from this period.

Where were the Israelites deported to? Although the Assyrian rec-

---

such great numbers. On the contrary, attributing Jerusalem's deliverance to a miraculous plague in Sennacherib's army, it tells of 185,000 Assyrian soldiers struck dead. It is impossible to harmonize these two accounts. Perhaps the author of the pro-Judean Book of Kings, who regarded the exile of the northern Israelites as a punishment for their sins, did not wish to mention a worse catastrophe taking place in Judea under Hezekiah, who did "that which was right in the sight of the Lord." Perhaps, too, the Assyrian figures, which seem disproportionately large, were exaggerated.

ords fail to say, there is no reason to doubt the Bible's mention of "Halah," "Habor by the river of Gozan," and "the cities of the Medes," since each of these refers to an identifiable frontier region that the Assyrians would have been eager to settle with trustworthy populations. Halah is the Assyrian Halahhu on the upper Tigris, on the border of what is now Iraqi Kurdistan; Gozan was an ancient city on the Habor River (the redactor of Kings confused the two), a tributary of the Euphrates just south of today's Syrian-Turkish frontier; and the Assyrian Madaya, or land of the Medes, was in the Zagros Mountains of Iranian Kurdistan. Remarkably, ancient Assyrian commercial, administrative, and military documents found in all three sites contain numerous Israelite names. Becking identified some fifty of them, an analysis of which led him to the conclusion that "although some or even many Israelite deportees were forced into lower social positions, some of the exiles attained important positions in the Assyrian army and others were in a position to appear as witnesses in contracts and judicial procedures."

Could some of these Israelites have maintained their identity over time? We know of ancient peoples exiled under similar circumstances who did so for generations. A settlement of Tyrians deported to Nippur in the early sixth century B.C.E. by the Babylonian emperor Nebuchadnezzar, for example, was still in existence 150 years later. But 150 years is not the several thousand that the Lost Tribe legends suppose, and we have no way of looking for Israelite communities very far past the time of their deportation. The Assyrians' records break off with the Babylonian conquest of their empire in 606, and the annals of the Babylonians, or of the Persians, who sacked Babylon in 550, are useless; for inasmuch as the peoples of Judah and Israel spoke the same tongue, any Hebrew names found in cuneiform inscriptions after 586 could date from that year's Babylonian exile of the Judeans, making further tracking of the northern tribes impossible. Perhaps, as Lazar thought, they returned with the southerners to Palestine. Perhaps, as Kasdai thought, they reunited with them in the Diaspora. Perhaps, as most contemporary scholars think, they were swallowed up by other peoples. Perhaps, as Godbey thought, they were the swallowers. We do not know.

⚜

There was an innocence about Avichail's obsession and a futility. Thousands before him had looked for the Lost Tribes, and he was going to find

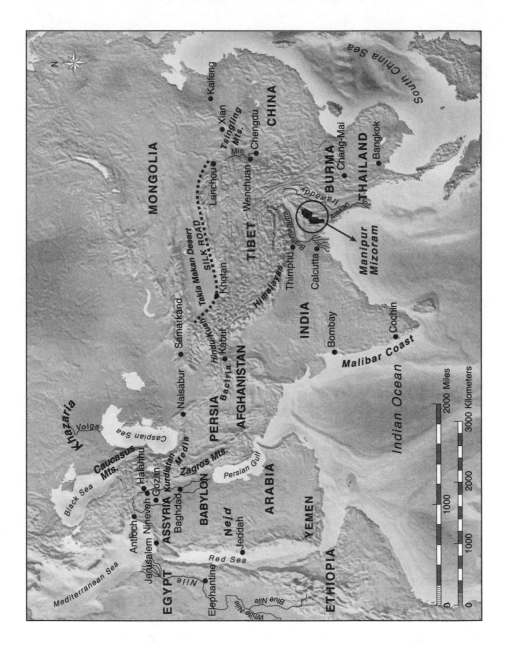

NORTHEAST AFRICA,
THE MIDDLE EAST, AND ASIA

them. He may as well have donned Spanish armor and gone looking for the Fountain of Youth. At bottom, he was doing what the conquistadors and the Puritans had done. They too had discovered native parallels with Israelite religion. They too had heard native stories like the Bible's. They too thought they had found Hebrew words and names in native languages. They too had been wrong.

He was not the only Lost Tribe hunter left. A handful of others were still beating the bushes beside him. There was Tudor Parfitt, who had written about a tribe in southern Africa, called the Lemba, that claimed Israelite descent. Hoping to make use of new techniques of DNA analysis, he had now returned to Africa for genetic testing that might determine the Lembas' origins. (Avichail, for his part, was adamantly opposed to genetic studies of the B'nei Menashe. No DNA test, he held, could determine whether a soul had stood at Sinai.) There was Simha Jacobovici, a Canadian-Israeli filmmaker and producer of a documentary on the Lost Tribes. Naïvely purporting to find them all, he was like a child in a last game of hide-and-seek, who, not knowing that it is over and all the players have gone to bed, goes on searching through the night.

Yet what was I to make of my week in Aizawl? I had seen and heard strange things there, none stranger than Yosi Hualngo's document. Nor were all my suspicions of it necessarily justified. Back in Israel, and browsing in Herodotus one day, I came across a passage in which the Greek historian — writing in the fifth century B.C.E., a mere three hundred years after the Assyrian exile — mentioned a "very long narrow gulf" between Egypt and Arabia "running up from the Red Sea (as it is called)." A verse in Kings suggested an explanation for this geographical term, which the Greeks must have taken from a Hebraic or Semitic source. One reads there, in the King James Version, "And King Solomon made a navy of ships in Ezion-Geber . . . on the shore of the Red Sea, in the land of Edom." Although the Hebrew rendered as "Red Sea" is indeed *yam suf*, or Reed Sea, the word "Edom" — the biblical name for the arid, mountainous land along the northeastern shore of the Gulf of Aqaba — comes from *adom*, Hebrew for "red." (Whoever has seen a sunset on the mountains of Edom can vouch for the fiery crimson they then turn.) If the gulf had also been known in biblical times as *yam edom*, "the Sea of Edom," or *ha-yam he-adom*, "the Red Sea," an ancient "red sea song" would not have been out of the question.

And how was I to explain a 1955 news report in a Hebrew daily, to which I was led by a reference in a book, appearing under the headline REMNANTS OF THE TRIBE OF MENASHE DISCOVERED IN BURMA? In it was a description of a people in the Arakan Hills who worshiped in "a strange combination of an Indochinese pagoda and the Temple in Jerusalem," had virgin priestesses who danced in the moonlight, and required married men to go wandering while their wives ran the household. It had no byline and — as far as I could determine — no follow-up.

Of course it was easy to laugh at such a tale, just as it was easy to dismiss the Mizos' belief that they were a Lost Tribe as a twentieth-century myth fabricated under the influence of, and in partial rebellion against, the Christianization of traditional Mizo culture. This was the argument put forth by Myer Samra, an anthropologist at the University of Sidney, in a short paper published in 1992, the only academic treatment of the subject on record. When I discussed the Mizos with Shalva Weiss, a Hebrew University ethnologist and curator of a Lost Tribes exhibit at Tel Aviv's Diaspora Museum, she cited Samra's paper as definitive. The one or two other scholars with any interest in the matter agreed.

There were only two ways to think about it. Either a Tibeto-Burmese people in a remote corner of southeast Asia had a mysterious connection with ancient Israel, or they were the victims of a mass delusion. Either way, there was a story to be written.

That meant going back — without Avichail. I wrote a book proposal and obtained a contract from a publisher, then got in touch with Zaithanchhungi and was assured that an inner-line permit would be available. I asked Avichail to find me a pair of translators from the B'nei Menashe community in Israel, one for Mizoram and one for Manipur, where a Kuki language called Thado was widely spoken. He recommended two young men, Samuel Joram from Aizawl and Isaac Thangjom from Imphal. I met Shmuel and Yitzhak — the Hebrew names by which they preferred to be known — at the plastic table of a kiosk outside the Jerusalem yeshiva where they studied, and I liked them both. They spoke English well — in fact, they spoke it to each other, since each had difficulty understanding the other's dialect — and were interested in joining me.

Before we had set a date for our departure, a printed invitation arrived in the mail. It was from Lalchhanhima Sailo.

> We are please to invite you on the occasion of our true iden-
> tity referendum to a historic meeting of the CHHINLUNG ISRAEL
> PEOPLE CONVENTION. For many years our movement have in-
> vestigated, repromoted, and rekindled the old truth and belief
> widespread among our People that we the CHHINLUNG CHHUAK
> called by different names — Mizo and Kuki in India, Chin in
> Myanmar, and Lushai in Bangladesh — are the descendants of
> the biblical tribes of the Northern Kingdom of Israel, convinced
> that the time has come to declare our true Identity to the World.
>
> So, we are convening the Leaders of our movement in Aizawl,
> the Capital of Mizoram State, on the 27th of October, 1999, in
> Vanapa Hall, to hold a referendum of our true Identity. The pro-
> ceeding will be at 11:00 A.M. Indian Standard Time (IST) and
> your presence as an observer will be appreciated.

I booked a flight for October 17. By then, Yitzhak and Shmuel assured
me, the monsoon rains would be over.

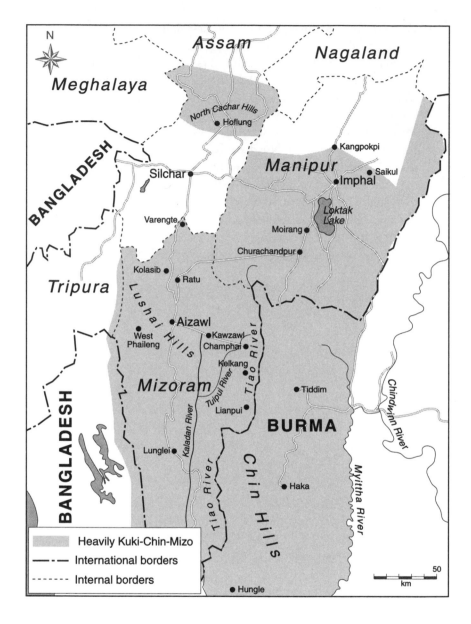

THE PRESENT TERRITORY OF
THE KUKI-CHIN-MIZO

⚝ 5 ⚝

Chhinlung Israel Mipuite

THE CID BLOTTER in Aizawl had me down as the forty-fifth foreign tourist of 1999. Our plan was to be four weeks in Mizoram and one in Manipur. Even though the fighting around Imphal had subsided, it seemed pointless to spend much time there. Whereas Mizoram was ethnically homogeneous, Manipur was a hodgepodge, a once independent Hindu raj with a majority of Hinduized Tibeto-Burmans called Meiteis and mutually hostile Christian Kukis and Christian Nagas. As a minority group in a multicultural society, I reasoned, the Kukis would have been more subject to outside influences and less likely to have preserved pre-Christian memories than the more insular Mizos, to whom they were closely related. Although this proved to be a miscalculation, it seemed logical at the time.

Before our departure I received a letter from Yosi Hualngo. Even had I given it more thought than I did, there was not much I could have done about it. It read:

> Shalom! Shalom! I hope that you are keeping as well by the grace of Hashem as we do overhere.
>
> Some time ago, I went to Myanmar (Burma) to try to know more historical facts. But, unluckily, the military people arrested me and seized my things like my TV camera and so on. I got myself released by paying the fine of 15 thousand of Indian money. I had been suffering from malaria, liver trouble, boil for the last

one month. Now I am on my way to recovery and will try to go again.

As you know, you are our only hope to recognize us as the Israelites. When you came here last time, I did not want to tell you, my interpreter was not good as he interpreted things on his own whimsical way. Now I'm very happy to tell you that I have a good and truthful interpretor. When you come, we shall help you in full swing.

In order to enter into the Holy Land, we need evidence as a whole. But the B'nei Menashe overthere and overhere cannot understand this very point. They are divided into two parties, favouring their relatives and friends to enter into the Holy Land; so, they are deeply fighting amongst themselves for unreasonable reasons. That's why I humbly advise you not to bring B'nei Menashe from there. I am here for you to collect the historical facts for you which will surely be the best thing for all the B'nei Menashe of the world. So, when you come again, please let us avoid all these childish and stupid things so that you can have a progress in historical facts.

Please do bring some water of the Dead Sea and a little dust of Jerusalem (near the Wailing Wall).

May the good Hashem bless us all everywhere we are.

What worried me most about the letter was its warning not to trust any information received from Sailo, who "whimsically" put words in people's mouths when he translated. If this was true, most of my notes on the old Mizo religion were worthless. I could only hope — Yosi's letter being meant to persuade me to hire a translator of his choice — that the accusation was baseless. I wrote back that, while I understood his distress over the dissension in the B'nei Menashe community, I had confidence in Shmuel and Yitzhak and intended to bring them. I didn't stop to wonder how Yosi, who knew no English, could have written such a letter at all.

This set the scene for an unfortunate incident. On our third or fourth day in Mizoram we were approached by two men as we stood on a street in Kawzawl, a village on the Champhai-Aizawl road, beside a sign that said:

Young Mizo Association Motto
1. Spend Your Free Time Productively.

2. Always Put The Mizo People First.
3. Always Behave Like A True Christian.

The men, like us, were headed for Aizawl and were looking for a ride. One was bound for Sailo's Identity Referendum. The other reminded me of Yosi Hualngo, but was more gaunt, with the weary, stubbled face of a man who had not seen clean sheets or hot water for days. "He's on his way back from Burma," Shmuel reported after a brief conversation with him. "Probably a smuggler." Although we could have squeezed one of the men into the back seat of our car, we did not make the offer.

Back in Aizawl, I went to find Yosi. I had his Dead Sea water and Jerusalem soil and needed to talk to him. As it was a Friday night, and Shmuel was spending the Sabbath with a sister, I was guided to Yosi's residence, in a shabby building called the Hotel Zodin, by a niece of Zaithanchhungi's, who spoke a bit of English. Steps led down to the dim front room of a basement apartment lit by the stubs of Sabbath candles on a bare table. Two men were sitting there. One, paunchy, straddled a bench near the door. The other, gaunt, sat facing him. It was Yosi Hualngo. Clean-shaven and rested, he was the man we had met on the street in Kawzawl.

I was too bewildered to ask why he hadn't said hello to me then. Afterward, when I put the question to Yitzhak, he said, "From his point of view, you outranked him. If you didn't make the first move, he had to assume you had your reasons. Anything else would have been a breach of Mizo etiquette."

"What reasons could I have had?"

"Look, he's a Mizo." Although he got along well with them, Yitzhak considered Mizos more primitive than Kukis. "He may have thought Shmuel was saying to you, in English, 'Here's that stupid man who didn't want me as your translator. Let's pretend we don't know him.'"

"But Shmuel didn't know him."

"Of course he did. All the Aizawl B'nei Menashe know each other."

"Then why did he tell me he was just some smuggler?"

"He's a Mizo, too."

It was a bad beginning.

We had gone to Champhai to attend the Young Mizo Association's annual jamboree. That was Zai's idea, and she had been firm about it, writing to remind me to schedule my trip accordingly. I didn't understand why she thought it so important. Only when I was sitting beside her in a row of dignitaries, looking down from a platform at a large tent filled with thousands of bright-faced Young Mizos, did I grasp her purpose. I was not there to see the YMA. I was there to be seen by it. It was her way of demonstrating that I was in Mizoram as her guest and not (for he had spread word that I had come especially for his Referendum) as Sailo's. And perhaps, I thought, as I listened to chirpy Mizo speeches and patriotic songs that sounded like English church hymns, she was not thinking only of herself. Sailo was widely distrusted, especially in church circles, which were the circles that mattered in Mizoram. It might not be in my best interest to be identified with him too closely. She was a smart woman, Zai.

She was not the primly starched figure I had taken her for. She had left Aizawl for Champhai ahead of us in her jeep, and we'd followed an hour later in a rented van with a driver named Tana. The route ran south and east toward the Burmese border, clinging to the midriffs of mountains that plunged to invisible depths. Close up, the jungle was so thick that it seemed bottomless, a green ziggurat without a foundation. Streams of water ran across the road. Despite assurances I'd been given, the monsoon rains were still falling, and mudslides were everywhere. Pushed against the mountainside by gangs of dark-skinned Bihari workers, they left messy scrapings to be churned through. There were no Mizos in those gangs, which went on working in the rain in pairs, one Bihari holding an umbrella for a second, who shoveled mud. A Mizo, Shmuel said, would *volunteer* to clear a road. He would never do it for money. That was *vai* work.

Vai was Mizo for a non-Mizo. It sounded like "goy."

A little past Kawzawl a fresh slide blocked the road. A Champhai-bound bus of YMA-ers, too big to turn around, awaited help. Dusk had fallen. It was raining again. We made a fractured U-turn and headed back toward Kawzawl, with no idea of where to spend the night. When we were a few hundred yards into the village, a flashlight beam intercepted us. Words were exchanged, and we followed a vehicle to a house. Inside a table was set. A hearth glowed in the corner. A woman crouched by it on long haunches, stirring a pot. It was Zai.

I never learned how we were found in the dark, or how Zai was so certain we would be that she had gone ahead and set the dinner table for us. It was the kind of thing that happened in Mizoram for which no one offered explanations. The Mizos had no need for them. They were at a stage of development at which they spread human pheromones no longer secreted by others. So quickly had they made the leap to modern life that one foot still trailed on the jungle floor. There was Zai, ladeling out supper by the hearth, heels beneath her in that immemorial squat of the race that no one brought up on chairs can be at home with. The Aizawl representative of a large Delhi insurance firm, she rose and brought bowls of steaming lentil stew to the table.

The Young Mizo Association was anchored in the pre-Christian past, too. The largest nonchurch organization in Mizoram, it was a sort of senior Scout movement in which young men and women socialized in a framework of community service. Such public-spiritedness was known to the Mizos as *tlawmngaihna* and had traditionally been a feature of the *zawlbuk*, a bachelor home for the unmarried young men of a village. The *zawlbuk* was a social and athletic club, a college dormitory, a volunteer fire brigade, and a military barracks all in one. Responsible for a variety of village chores and activities, its residents doubled as an emergency force in case of an enemy attack or other danger. Although the YMA, the *zawlbuk*'s latter-day metamorphosis, was co-ed and stripped of martial functions, you could still see the mixture of *tlawmngaihna* and village warfare in the buses we'd passed on the road with their banners saying Seling, Phullen, Lunglei, Varengte, Phaileng, and Sihphir, now stopping to push each other out of the mud and now razzing and hooting one another.

But the pre-Christian past was no more recoverable from such things than limestone is from marble. Asked by Zai to say a few words of greeting to those assembled, I explained my purpose in Mizoram and ended with a request. While I did not, I said, expect any of the Young Mizos to know much about the old religion, I would appreciate being told about grandparents or other kin who might know more. No one approached me at the evening's end.

Zai tried making it up to me. The oldest living Mizo on record, she said, resided in Kelkang, an hour's drive from Champhai. His name was Pu Chere and he was ninety-eight and had all his wits about him. She would take us to see him the next day.

Champhai meant "great plain" in Mizo and sat on a hill overlooking the country's largest valley. The valley was stippled with hillocks like green warts and dense with the only paddies I was ever to see in Mizoram, where rice grew dry on the hillsides. It took five minutes to cross it.

Then we were back in the mountains. The clouds had lifted, and we could see far into Burma. For a while we followed the looping line of the Tiao River, which formed the border officially sealed by the Burmese. Clumps of bushes stood along its banks, good places to hide in while waiting to cross in the dark. I gathered that this was not especially dangerous. The Mizos and Burma Chin were practically one people. It was easy to blend in on either side, and a bribe in the guise of a fine, growing steeper as you scaled the ladder of justice, could extricate you if you were caught. Those unable to afford it went to jail. I was told by one man of being sentenced by a Burmese judge to as many days as it took a hot chili nailed to his cell door to shrivel up and fall off.

The country was of a vast and monotonous beauty. It first stunned you with its bounty and then rendered you indifferent as you saw that all its gifts were the same. It was a green desert whose only signs of human presence were the tin roofs of the villages in the distant outfield of the mountains, catching the sunbeams and flinging them back at you, and the rice fields branded into the hills. Shmuel translated their colors for me. The wheaten yellows were ready for harvest. The apple greens were still a few weeks short. The furry browns were cut jungle, waiting to be fired in the spring for a new crop to be planted in their ashes. The mangy buffs had just been reaped. Soon the jungle would invade them and start a new cycle until they were ready to be slashed and burned once more — *jhumed* was the word used in India.

Zai talked as she drove about the difficulties of investigating the Mizo past. The missionaries had not only fought the old religion; they had done everything in their power to eradicate all knowledge of it. Children were warned that asking their parents about it was sinful; parents were threatened with damnation for telling their children. Sacred relics were destroyed. Zai knew of an old man in Lunglei who had inherited a *pathian bom*, an old "god box," from his father. Although not sure what this was, she believed it to be some kind of "holy ark." When the local pastor insisted that the man get rid of it, he hid it in the roofbeams of his home. One day the pastor came when the man was out, took the god box from the roofbeams, and demolished it.

Kelkang ran along a level hilltop. Pu Chere's house was like any other, a two-room dwelling of plaited bamboo with a low tower, serving as a chimney above and a pantry below, over the hearth. Pu Chere sat scrunched beside it, a blanket thrown over him. Though he let Zai kneel in homage before him and take his face in her hands, he refused help to get to the bench where our interview took place. Using a low stool as a walker, he pushed it in front of him while extending one leg at a time, his back bent parallel to the floor, creeping across it like a bony old turkey. His family picked him up when he reached the bench and set him down on it, unstraightened, as if he were a piece of rusted machinery.

He was clear-minded enough, however, even if his pupils had leaked into the whites of his eyes like broken yolks and Shmuel had to shout at him to be heard. Pu Chere remembered many things. He remembered when the British first came to Kelkang; since he was a boy of nine at the time, that must have been in 1910. He remembered the village's first Christians, Pu Kura and his wife; this was six or seven years later. Pu Kura counted the nameless days of the week — a novel concept — by drawing a line for each in the ashes of his hearth until he came to Sunday, when he refused to work. Yet this was considered less strange than his abstention from *zu*, the rice beer drunk by everyone.

The village chief in those days was Lianola. Being one of the few grown-ups who had learned to write, Pu Chere worked as Lianola's *kohchhiar,* or secretary, keeping village records for the British. Lianola didn't like the British missionaries. None of the chiefs or priests did, because the missionaries deprived them of their power. They even took away the chief's slaves by getting the government to ban slavery. Lianola stole the village churchbells to keep them from ringing, and the missionaries made him give them back. Pu Chere sided with the missionaries. He thought Christianity was a good thing.

As a Christian, Pu Chere kept his distance from the old religion, which lingered on in Kelkang until about 1950. Its main rituals were sacrifices performed on a hill beyond the village. These were offered to Pathian on a four-cornered bamboo altar on which lay a banana leaf sprinkled with flour; the blood of the sacrifice, usually a goat or mythun, a wild ox, was poured over the leaf. Sometimes a pig was sacrificed to

Ram Huai, the devil spirit. Ram Huai lived in the swamps and made you sick. If you had a stomachache, you were said to have Ram Huai in your belly.

Pu Chere remembered two kinds of priests. One, who was "more personal," cured sicknesses and prevented accidents; the other was "more for the community." The first was called a *bawlpu*; the second, a *sadawt*. For example, suppose the chief and elders wished to know whether the next day would be a good one for hunting. That night the *sadawt* would spread ashes on the ground and examine them in the morning for an augury of animal tracks. Or suppose it was a day for clearing roads in the jungle, a task in which all the men joined. The *sadawt* led them back to the village when they were done, knocked on the chief's door, and announced, "Let us in. We are the children of Manasa!"

"I asked who Manasa was."

Pu Chere said he was the son of Joseph.

"How does he know?"

"It's in the Bible."

"But the Bible was brought by Christianity. Who was Manasa before that?"

Pu Chere didn't know. There were many things he didn't know. He didn't know about Ya or Za. He had no knowledge of circumcision, though he knew the meaning of the word. He had never heard a song about a sea. He was growing tired of so many questions. He wanted to know if there were more.

"How does it feel to be ninety-eight?" I asked.

"Not so good," Pu Chere said.

The interview was over. Pu Chere made a remark. His family laughed.

Shmuel translated:

"He said, 'Whew! The things that fellow asked!'"

ﯼ

Two young plainclothesmen from the CID were waiting for us in the Holiday Home Hotel in Champhai when we returned from Kelkang. They examined my inner-line permit and asked whether, if they joined the B'nei Menashe, they could fight in the Israeli army. I answered that, given the number of tourists needing surveillance in Mizoram, they could probably fight in the Israeli army and keep their present jobs. They found that funny.

It wasn't the only time I was asked such a question. At first it struck me as strange. There was a large military recruitment billboard next to the Assam Rifles base in Aizawl, and Mizo youngsters anxious to test their mettle in battle did not lack opportunities in India. In fact, on the plane with us from Calcutta had been the coffin, received with military pomp at the new airport, of a Mizo boy killed in action in Kashmir. But fighting for India did not appeal to many Mizos. Had it been practical, they would have preferred to fight against it. They envied the B'nei Menashe their military service in Israel.

They came from warrior stock. Yet there was nothing bellicose about them. With one another they were soft-spoken and trusting. On our way to Champhai we were sideswiped by a minibus that crowded us to the edge of a precipice as it tried passing. In Israel, both drivers would have jumped from their vehicles, screaming. Tana got out of the car, inspected the damage, spoke quietly to the other driver, climbed back behind the wheel, and drove off. I expressed surprise that he wasn't angry. Shmuel said, "There's nothing to be angry about. The other driver took the blame. He'll pay for the repairs."

"Does Tana know him?"

"No. They arranged to meet in a garage in Aizawl."

"But Tana didn't even ask to see his license. Suppose he doesn't show up?"

"Why shouldn't he show up?" Tana said. "He's no *vai*."

This was one side of the Mizos' character. Back in 1870, Captain T. H. Lewin, one of the first British officers to make their acquaintance, described seeing a drunken Lushai shove an unprotesting chief off a village path. Asked why he put up with such insolence, the chief replied, "On the warpath I am chief and my words are obeyed; behavior like that would be punished by death. Here, in the village, that drunkard is my fellow and equal." But on the warpath the Lushais could be ruthless. In another incident related by Lewin, a young warrior was ordered to spear a captive Bengali woman his own age who could not keep up with the march. "It was pitiful!" he told the British captain. "When the girl saw me take the spear and come toward her, she fell weeping, and caught my garments and my hands, and all my heart thumped, and I could not hurt her. So the chief began to laugh at me and said, 'O white-livered son of a female dog, when we return to the village I will tell the young maidens of your courage,' so I shut my eyes and speared her. The chief made me lick the spear. The blood of Bengallees is very salt. Since then I have not been afraid to spear any one."

⚜

Between YMA sessions, Zai turned up with someone she knew. His name was Zana, and staying with him in Champhai were two friends from Burma, one of them a priest in the old religion. If I wished, Zana would bring them to the Holiday Home Hotel for breakfast the next morning.

Of course I wished! I had been told many times that Burma held the keys to the old religion. At one point I had thought of flying to Rangoon and trying to reach Chin State on the Indian border. In the end, I gave up the idea. The Burmese barred tourists west of Mandalay, and I wasn't eager to test the strength of a Burmese chili.

The little red Mizo chilis were strong enough. The size of a baby's pinky, they torpedoed your nose and flooded its inner chambers. At the Holiday Home Hotel they were served for breakfast as part of the standard Mizo fare: a bland stew of potatoes and bony meat known as "curry," a dish of dahl, one or two local vegetables like jungle spinach or the small, bitter-tasting Mizo eggplant, and solid slabs of hard mountain rice over which the rest was poured. It was dull going without the peppers, especially since the Mizos, who ate but two meals a day — a late breakfast and an early dinner — never varied the menu. They sat down to curry, rice, spinach, eggplant, and dahl morning and evening, seven days a week, and washed everything down with cold water. They liked it that way. Once, when Yitzhak, Shmuel, and I chose to breakfast on sticky rice cakes at a teahouse, Tana walked off grumpily to look for a proper eatery, complaining that he could not start the day without his "grub." Now he was digging into it, scooping it up with dripping fingers like Zana and his Burmese friends, Ying Kaw and Suangolian. Both came from Tiddim in the Chin Hills and appeared not to have eaten in days. They finished a first big helping in silence, put away a second, worked their way more slowly through a third, wiped their hands on the tablecloth, and leaned back, burping bashfully.

Suangolian — his friends called him Liana — was the priest, a diminutive fellow, wearing a child's windbreaker, with delicate features and the bright liquid eyes of a small animal that might dart up a tree at any moment. On his chin was the wee number of untweezed hairs that passed in southeast Asia for a beard. Although he spoke a good Mizo, he and Ying Kaw were Paites, like the petitioners from Manipur who had come to see Avichail in Aizawl the summer before. He had been a practicing priest for fifteen years, having learned the trade from his grandfather after his father died when Liana was young.

Yet Liana proved a disappointment. The priesthood was not his full-time job. Although he officiated at the odd occasion, his main line was gem smuggling, and he knew or was prepared to divulge less than I had hoped. He had never heard of circumcision. He had never heard of Manasa. He had never heard of Ya or Za. He *had* heard a song about the sea.

"He has?"

Yes. About the sea, and the land, and the trees and the sky, and how Pasian (as he pronounced it) made them all. He just didn't remember the words.

Liana belonged to the Chinglut clan and sacrificed only to Pasian. Mostly he did house purifications and child namings, for which he offered a chicken on the fifth, seventh, or ninth day after birth. Sometimes he performed a road-clearing ceremony, slaughtering a dog and hanging its head on a post. This was done in a small hut outside the village on two stones called "the husband" and "the wife," on which the victim's blood was smeared. If a goat was slaughtered, Liana's share was the liver and the heart. He didn't do sicknesses or good luck sacrifices. Those were for a Ram Huai priest. Ram Huai priests sacrificed pigs. They didn't eat any part of them, though. The entire pig went to the family.

"Tell Liana," I said to Shmuel, "that we'd like to hear a sacrificial chant."

Liana glanced around as though looking for a tree to climb.

"Just one."

Liana moved his lips and murmured something that sounded like *ka pasian*. Shmuel translated this as "O my God . . ." and waited for more. Liana broke off and stared at the ballpoint pen in Yitzhak's hand.

"He's afraid," Shmuel said.

"Maybe that's all he knows," said Yitzhak. "He could keep mumbling a few words like that at a sacrifice, and nobody would know the difference."

"Well," I said, "there must be priests in Burma who know more than that. Let's bring them to Champhai."

There was a consultation in Paite. Yes, there were such priests. It would be possible to bring some. It would just cost money.

"How much?"

Calculations were made on a page from Yitzhak's notebook. Bus fare to and from the Tiao was 200 rupees. Food along the way was 100 more. That came to 600 rupees per round trip. Liana and two priests made three round trips.

"They're too polite to ask, but you'll have to pay them for their time, too," Yitzhak said.

All in all it came to 3300 rupees — about eighty dollars. I asked, "How long will it take them to get there and back?"

More calculations. "A week."

We arranged to meet in Champhai in eight days' time, and I handed over half the sum in advance. There were differences of opinion as to whether we'd see Liana again. Yitzhak thought we would. Shmuel was doubtful.

The two of them were opposites. Shmuel was tall, brown, thin-faced, and taciturn. Yitzhak was short, yellow, round-faced, and outgoing. He came from the Gangte tribe, which, like the Raltes, had a reputation for loquacity. (According to the old Lushai myth of Chhinlung, the great rock pushed aside when mankind clambered up to the earth's surface from the underworld, the first two Raltes to emerge made so much noise that Pathian rolled the rock back into place again.) He also had the more Western mind and the freer attitude toward religion. I had noticed that, while Shmuel's Orthodox skullcap remained on his head after we boarded the plane in Israel for our flight to Bombay, Yitzhak's came off and stayed off. It was easier to share my thoughts with him. On our return trip from Champhai, while waiting in a teahouse in Kawzawl for Shmuel, who had gone to look for some local B'nei Menashe, I remarked, "It's odd that those Burmese were our only informants so far who haven't heard of Manasa. It doesn't fit our picture of Burma as the last stronghold of the old religion. Unless Manasa wasn't part of it."

"Time hasn't stood still in Burma either," Yitzhak said. "The old religion may have degenerated there."

"Maybe. Did you notice, by the way, that Liana confirmed what we've been told about a double priesthood, one half of which doesn't sacrifice pig? I heard something similar last year from Lalthuari, a Burmese woman. If I were to let my imagination go, I could propose a theory about that."

"I'm listening."

"Suppose, for the sake of argument, that Manasa is the biblical Manasseh and the Kuki-Chin-Mizo really are a Lost Tribe. You people are obviously not pure descendants of that tribe, because your appearance is Tibeto-Burmese. That means that at least two different racial strands met and intertwined at some point in your past, one from the Middle East and one from southeast Asia. The two kinds of priests — *sadawt* and *bawlpu*, we've heard them called — could reflect that. Pathian and Ram Huai could too. We may be looking at a fusion of two religions, a pork-avoiding Middle Eastern one and a pork-eating local one, in which the god of the first won out and the god of the second was demoted to head devil. That's been known to happen to losing gods."

"Do you believe that?"

"I might if there were any real evidence for it. But there isn't. If Yosi Hualngo is right about Sailo, we can't even count on Lalthuari, because it was Sailo who translated what she told me. We can't even count on Yosi himself. That doesn't leave much to go on."

We rose to join Shmuel, who was coming up the street. That's when we ran into Yosi Hualngo.

Perhaps it was because of the vaguely Slavic-sounding name, but the scene at the Hotel Zodin had a Dostoyevskyan ambience. The bare, candle-lit room was largely in shadow, and its two occupants made an incongruous pair. The gaunt one was wearing a T-shirt, his thin arms hard with muscle below the sleeves. He did not rise to greet me but gave me a tight-lipped smile as if acknowledging our botched encounter. On the smile's other, invisible side, the deep hollows of his cheeks seemed to meet. I failed to understand how a few days' beard on such a face could have fooled me. Odder yet, how could I, the forty-fifth foreigner of the year — and one expected by him! — have fooled him? The only explanation I came up with was that he had deliberately snubbed me for bringing Shmuel from Israel.

The paunchy man wore a rumpled gray suit and had the bright red lips of a betel chewer. As if mistaking me for Rabbi Avichail, he reached into his pocket and placed a large skullcap on his head. "Daniel Israelo," he introduced himself with a curtain-call bow. The skullcap slipped from his head and fell to the floor. "A.k.a. George Lawma. Georgie-porgie-pudding-and-pie at your service!"

I assumed he was drunk. There were beads of sweat on his puffy face. He spoke English with an American accent or, rather, with the accent of someone who had lived for a while in the States. In Seattle, Washington, to be exact. "The Chinook state. La-a-a-nd that I lo-o-ove." He sang the off-tune bar of "God Bless America" with a hand solemnly placed over his heart. A spasm of laughter swept over him. His stomach wobbled, and he jigged like a dancing bear. "Oh, sorry, sorry," he gasped. "Georgie-boy will be good."

I looked for assistance to Yosi. Although he regarded the red-lipped man with distaste, he made no move to intervene. The two of them did not go together. And it was then that the obvious occurred to me. Yosi's letter had not been written by Yosi. It could not have been. It had been written by ("Yessiree! At your service! I speak English, Mizo, Kuki, Chin, Indian! I am co-author of the authorized Grand Mizo-English Dictionary, soon to be published in Aizawl!") "the good and truthful interpretor," George Lawma himself.

It was a bizarre situation. Zaithanchhungi's niece had departed and would have been no help if she hadn't. I needed to explain to Yosi that even had I not brought Shmuel to Mizoram, I would by no means have employed the buffoon now waving in my face a thin packet of paper representing the first letter of the Grand Mizo-English Dictionary — and the only way to explain it was via the buffoon.

I placed the Dead Sea water and the Jerusalem soil on the table, wished both men a good Sabbath, and told George Lawma that I was pleased to meet him. "Please tell Yosi," I said, "that I would like to discuss with him the document he gave me and Rabbi Avichail in the Hotel Ritz last year. I can see this isn't a good time. Let's set a date when I can come with Samuel Joram."

Shmuel's name dropped like a tray of dirty dishes. My turning up without him, it appeared, had been taken for my agreeing to hire George in his place, so my proposal now came as a shock. George sobered up at once and spoke in Mizo to Yosi, who made a sharp reply. George asked, "Did you not receive Yosi's letter?"

"I received a letter. I answered it."

"Then you do not understand. Mr. Samuel Joram is not acceptable. He will not interpret truly."

"He will interpret truly. I would not have chosen him otherwise."

"But you do not understand!" This time it was an accusation. I was naïve. I knew nothing about the B'nei Menashe community. I knew nothing about Mr. Samuel Joram. Mr. Samuel Joram was one of its leaders. He would deceive me. He would manipulate what was said to me without my knowing it. "Sir, I am the author of a dictionary. I know the English and American lingo. What for do you need Mr. Samuel Joram?"

The last thing I wanted was a confrontation. They would have to accept Shmuel when the time came. "Let's not argue about it," I said. "I want to hear from Yosi how Ezra is. And to ask about his trip to Burma."

The change of subject passed without challenge. Ezra was fine and sent his regards. He was working in a welding shop in Bombay and was sorry that he wouldn't get to see me. As for Burma, Yosi had gone back illegally a second time after his release by the Burmese authorities; he had been on his way home when we ran into him in Kawzawl. He took a sheet of paper and drew a line on it to show me his Burmese route. Writing N at the top and S at the bottom, he made a number of circles to represent his stops on the way. The southernmost stop was Muchhip Mountain, where he had attended a sacrifice. But he had not found what he was looking for. "They have forgotten the holy name of Hasem," George said. "They only pray, 'Pasien, Pasien.' Yosi knows where the holy name is spoken. It is further south, in Arakan."

"You mean Ya?"

Yosi nodded at the sacred syllable. He seemed loath to pronounce it.

It was the Lost Tribe legend in a nutshell: the dreamed-of prize was always farther on, beyond the last village, over the last mountain. I said, "Look, George. I need to talk to Yosi about his document. Let's set a time for it."

But Yosi was not ready to discuss the document. First, he had other plans for me. George would tell me about them. George said, "Here's the scoop."

The scoop was not to think I had understood Yosi's document just because it was written in the King's English. The fragments of chants in it came from old sacrifices. I would have to see the sacrifices in order to understand the chants. That was why Yosi was arranging a demonstration of them. "A real happening," George said. "We'll bring gents from Burma, experts. You'll come with your VCR and ask questions. We'll get their answers down in depositions. Thumbprints for folks that can't write. We'll deposit 'em all."

"I don't have a VCR," I said. "Where does all this take place?"

"Lianpui village. Champhai side."

"Why so far?"

George gave me a conspiratorial look. "Some Christian folks ain't gonna like this. We need a safe, quiet joint."

The co-author of the Grand Mizo-English Dictionary needed to update his slang. But if Yosi's happening could be combined with Liana and his priests, it was not an inconvenient venue. The rendezvous with Liana in Champhai was set for the last day of October. Today was the twenty-second. Could we schedule the sacrifices for November 1?

Yosi and George went into a huddle. George said, "We can swing it. Just don't bring Joram. And we'll need some bucks."

He and Yosi made a Mizo list, which George recopied into English. The English list looked longer than the Mizo one. It read:

Nite bus to Champhai, round trip (2)	R800.
Taxi Champhai-Lianpui " "	R1600
Transport Burma Side	R4000
Grub	R1600
1 gote	R1000
Chickies	R600
2 bags rice (25k's) for the missus	R800
Personal expenses	R5000
Total	R15400

I went through it item by item.

"Why two taxis to Lianpui?"

"I go tomorrow night to set things up. Yosi comes later."

"What's this for transport and grub?"

"Burma folks. Gotta feed 'em."

"Who's the missus?"

"Mine."

"*Fifty* kilos of rice?"

"The kids are big eaters."

The largest item was "personal expenses."

"My honorarium," George explained.

I bargained him down to 12,000 rupees while Yosi studied the Hebrew label on the bottle of Dead Sea medicinal water. He had followed George's briefing intently, anxious to ascertain whether his instructions were being carried out. Now, disdainful of our haggling, he was impatient to be done. George took the bills I gave him, divided them into wads, slipped each into a different pocket, and patted them all. "Yes, sir, yes, sir, three bags full," he sang. I was never to find out what he had done in Seattle apart from acquiring a functional command of Mother Goose rhymes.

Clearly the two men needed each other. Something was driving Yosi — something I wasn't sure I understood. If it was his desire to convince me that the Mizos were a Lost Tribe, why should this matter to him more than it did to others in the B'nei Menashe community? Perhaps he wanted to get his family to Israel. The lists of emigrants were drawn up by the community's leaders in Aizawl and forwarded to Jerusalem for review by Avichail. If Yosi was on bad terms with these leaders, he and his family stood no chance. His only hope was a direct link to Avichail through someone like me.

Was that was why he had kept his knowledge to himself until Avichail and I came to Aizawl? But why, then, had he run the risk of taking two trips to Burma? Or did he simply belong to that race of men, more curious and adventurous than most, who are the natural truth-seekers in any society?

Whatever the answer, he had found in George Lawma a small-time operator with a commodity, dirt-cheap in many places, that was worth a great deal to him: a knowledge of English, a language few Mizos spoke. Without it, he had no access to the outside world. He might as well have been in a locked room.

Of course, he could have gone to Sailo. He *had* gone to Sailo the night they came to the Ritz. Perhaps he had believed this would guarantee him a hearing, whereas George could have easily ruined things with his clowning. But Sailo was ambitious, and Yosi did not trust him. George was nickel-and-dime. Although his list of expenses remained padded even after I'd driven it down, the profit, able to feed a Mizo family for a month, was negligible in Western terms. Presumably, he and Yosi would share it.

I hoped this accounted for their opposition to Shmuel. I hated to think there might be another reason. It could have occurred to them that a gullible Lost Tribe hunter with dollars was a better game than a Mizo-English dictionary. Maybe they already had this in mind when they dangled the bait of the Hotel Ritz document, which probably had been translated by George. That could have been why they didn't want Shmuel around to contradict their version of what the "Burma gents" or anyone else told me.

Or else George was conning us both. I had no idea how he had translated what Yosi and I said to each other. I didn't even know if Yosi knew about the letter George had sent me in Yosi's name. I could find out only by asking Yosi without George's being present, and for that I needed Shmuel, to whom Yosi refused to talk. Or so George said. It was like one of those phony mathematical equations in which you need to know X to solve for Y and Y to solve for X, so that you go on spinning around inside it forever.

☙

Vanapa Hall was packed. A thousand delegates to Sailo's Identity Referendum filled the floor and balcony and waved little paper Chhinlung Israel People flags. Young hostesses in the colors of the *langlap* ushered guests of honor to their places. A banner at the back of the stage proclaimed:

Chhinlung Israel Mipuite Hi Thendarh Leh
Tihtluk Kan Ni Tawh Ngai Lovang.

The Chhinlung Israel People Shall Not
Be Scattered Nor Fall Again.

There was excitement in the air.
I had to admit that I was surprised. I hadn't believed Sailo could pull it

off. The number of supporters claimed by him had struck me as wildly exaggerated. Probably it was. You didn't need 100,000 people to fill Vanapa Hall. But the sight, when I turned around in my front-row seat, was impressive. The crowd was lively and boisterous. I recognized faces. Peter Tlau was there, and Elisabeth Zodingliani, and Brigadier Sapliana the ex–Salvation Army general, and Saidinga of the Ephraim National Conference, and Lalthuari, the woman from Burma.

Sailo had scheduled his speech as the day's main event, led up to by preliminaries. These began with an opening hymn and a prayer for "Lord and country" by a Presbyterian minister, who told the story of the prodigal son. "We were like this son," he said, "but no longer. We were like a coin that is lost and does not know it is lost. Now we know who we are!" His high pulpitry was balanced by a Pentecostal prayer group with drums and hallelujahs; possessed by the Spirit, a tumbler did a handstand and somersaulted across the stage. "We will build a new Israel in Mizoram!" someone in the audience called. There was a prayer for Israel read by a B'nei Menashe in halting Hebrew, followed by the Israeli anthem in a key and tempo never heard in Jerusalem. There were dances and songs to which everyone clapped along. The Mizos loved to sing. They had different styles — the church hymn style with its bright soaring lilt, a plunky Asian pop style with electric guitar, and a slow, dirgelike style accompanied by a solemn drum. Sailo had mixed them equally.

An old woman dressed in *langlap* colors, "our oldest daughter of Ephraim and Menashe," was brought onstage to greet the audience. *Chibai, chibai,* she waved to hearty cheers. All stood in silence for "the martyrs of our people who could not live to see this day" — there was no need to rouse the nodding CID men in the audience by referring to the dead of the Mizo insurgency more explicitly — and then former Mizo chief minister Lalthanhawla introduced the red sea song. "If we were not Israelites," he declared, "our forefathers would not have sung this song. It is fitting for us to perform it here today."

The performers were dressed in old Lushai costume and led by a long-haired man with a drum. They circled with a monkeylike shuffle, arms hanging loose and backs bent low; while the long-haired man drummed, someone else struck a gong, and a singer called out each line and then sang it along with the dancers. Her blend of old-time dirge and Asian pop did not seem quite authentic. When the words were later transcribed by Shmuel from my cassette deck, however, I had my first full version of the song. It was in the dialect of the Hmar, a northern tribal group, and differed from the fragments in the Hotel Ritz document. Shmuel's translation of it was:

> We Hmar are the offspring of Manmasi.
> We dance the *sikpui* at the peak of the feast.
> This is the way of the Manmasi Hmar.
> When Khuavang has set forth,
> The sea stands still.
> Even though the land is very high,
> We do not tire.
> Ephraim the good name,
> Paving the way.
> Boys, is any one missing
> Of those who went to fight the enemy?
> Your friendly maidens, Miriam,
> Tukbander, and Zermanziak,
> Come home.
> We have taken the head of the enemy
> Rejoice by singing.

Manmasi, Shmuel said, was the Hmar form of Manasa or Manasia. The *sikpui* was a Hmar celebration. Khuavang, he thought, was a name for God. More he didn't know.

But I did. It was something I remembered from Zai's little book. In it she had mentioned a Mizo folksong about three maidens, Riami, Zermanziaki, and Tukbanderi. The first of these, she had observed, had a name like that of Moses's sister Miriam — who, according to the Bible, after Pharaoh's hosts drowned in the Red Sea, "took a timbrel in her hand, and all the women went out after her with timbrels and with dances." Sailo had turned "a name like" into "the same name as" and stuck all three maidens into the red sea song.

The performance was followed by an English "keynote address," given by David Ashkenazi, an Israeli businessman with dealings in Mizoram. Then at last came Sailo's turn. He, too, began in English "for our friends from the foreign media" — meaning, as far as I could see, a sole Indian TV crew and me. But he worked the crowd well in his clear, ringing voice. When he had aroused it sufficiently by accusing the gov-

ernment in Delhi, in violation of the Indian constitution, of the "geno-
cide of neocolonialism" perpetrated by the "administrative fragmenta-
tion" of the Chin-Mizo-Kuki people, he put his Identity Referendum to
a vote. First came a long peroration. "We the Chhinlung Chhuak . . . the
Lost Tribes of Israel . . . with all our heart and sincerity . . . firmly uphold
universal human rights . . . adopt the principle of nonviolence . . . and sincerely appeal to the conscience of all heads of States and Government . . .
to recognize and acknowledge . . . our just struggle for the recognition of
our historical, political, and identity rights . . . and seal this document . . .
upon the altar of universal human rights. All in favor raise your hands!"

A thousand paper flags shot into the air.

"Long live the Chhinlung Israel People!"

"Long live the Chhinlung Israel People!" the delegates shouted back.

*"Chhinlung Israel mipuite hi thendarh leh tihtluk kan ti tawh ngai
lovang!"* Sailo cried into the microphone.

*"Chhinlung Israel mipuite hi thendarh leh tihtluk kan ti tawh ngai
lovang!"*

"Chhinlung Israel mipuite!"

"Chhinlung Israel mipuite!"

He put his hand to his ear.

"CHHINLUNG ISRAEL MIPUITE!"

"CHHINLUNG ISRAEL MIPUITE!"

It still wasn't loud enough.

"CHHINLUNG ISRAEL MIPUITE!"

"CHHINLUNG ISRAEL MIPUITE!"

It was the most shopworn of oratorical tricks, one every camp coun-
selor knew how to use in a color war, but it had Vanapa Hall on its feet.
The delegates had voted themselves a Lost Tribe. The Referendum had
passed unanimously.

What Sailo intended to do with it, besides send it out to his international mailing list, was anybody's guess. As if to put off the decision, he
went on talking for two more hours. After a while I left Shmuel in the
hall and went out for lunch with Yitzhak. Joining us was the keynote
speaker, David Ashkenazi, who was half hill-tribe himself, the son of an
Israeli father and a Khasi mother from the state of Meghalaya. Ashkenazi
had spoken poignantly of his attachment to Mizoram while avoiding all
reference to the Referendum, concluding with the plea: "You have a

lovely land — please don't lose it." Over hamburgers and French fries in Aizawl's one American-style diner, I asked him what he had meant by that.

"The Mizos are a wonderful people," he said. "I love them. I'm afraid all this Israel business is going to get them into trouble."

"With the Indian government?"

He nodded. "They paid a terrible price in the Insurgency. Thousands killed, dozens of villages burned. I'd hate to see some hothead lead them into a new fight they can't win."

"I doubt if that's what Sailo has in mind," I said. "He may have the lungs of a Fidel Castro, but he seems to know how far he can go."

"I hope so. These things can get out of hand."

It was hard to believe that anyone in Mizoram seriously wanted to go another round with the Indian army. The Insurgency had been fought during the Cold War, when foreign governments seeking to destabilize had provided the Mizos with military aid; in any uprising now, they would have to fight alone against impossible odds. In small ways, the Indian army took care to remind them of these. Each day, the Assam Rifles went on a predawn run through the streets of Aizawl, carrying their packs and weapons past the windows of my room in the Hotel Chief. First, like a messenger sent by the silent night, came the fleet solo steps of the leader, boots clattering on the sidewalk; then, those of the man behind him. Clinging to sleep, I half-dreamed of a chase through the dark streets of a city, someone running from a mugger or a policeman. But then came more boots, and still more, until the whole pack galloped by like a frightened herd. You could hear the heavy breathing and the curses and grunts of the men. At last the stampede receded, and only the stragglers were left. Again lone footsteps sounded in the night, this time weary and plodding. The steps of those who would never catch up, they fell slowly out of my sleep.

And sometimes it was sleep that fell away. Unable to regain it, I would rise and sit by the window, writing, while awaiting the dawn. It began with milky bands that striped the darkness. As it grew lighter, these turned to rivers of fog in the north-south gorges outside the city. Yitzhak had told me a Gangte story about these fogs, which were typical of the Mizo landscape. Reaching the banks of one, a party of hunters challenged one another to swim to the other side. The bravest of them offered to go first, it being agreed that, if he crossed safely, he would sound a call like a bird's to let the others know. He dived headlong into the fog and disappeared — and a few minutes later, just as his comrades were despairing of him, the *tu-tu-tu* of a real bird sounded from across the gorge. Thinking it was the cloud swimmer, a second hunter dived in, and soon the call came again. And so, hunter after hunter, they plunged to their death. To this day, Yitzhak said, a Gangte proposing something brave but foolish was told by his friends, "Don't be a cloud swimmer!"

Then I went down for breakfast. The Chief was ritzier than the Ritz, in which hot water had to be ordered in a bucket from room service. It had a good kitchen. The food was Indian. So was the staff. It stood at attention while you studied the menu, and later solicitously transferred your prawn biryani or vindaloo chicken from a silver tureen to your plate, tucking it into a bed of fluffy *vai* rice. It was *vai* work that no Mizo would stoop to. No Mizo girl would go out with the young *vai* waiters, who sometimes spent the between-meal hours dancing with one another in the dining room to music from a radio.

Awaiting the dawn I wrote, "The ultimate proof the Mizos are Jews: a small and never civilized people, they think they are better than everyone."

☙

Bualhranga, who owned one of the little bookstalls on the street below the CIPC office, had served in the Insurgency, going high up into Burma to run guns from China. The Mizo revolt had been in the making since Indian independence in 1947. As this was about to take place, three schools of thought contended in the Lushai Hills. One called for integration with India, one for an independent Mizo state, one for a continued British protectorate. The Mizo Union, the main political party, split the same three ways, with a main faction taking a pro-Indian line. The new Indian government used this to justify annexing the region, which was renamed the Mizo Hills District and incorporated into the state of Assam. In the late 1950s, the mishandling by Assam of a severe famine in the Mizo Hills led to the creation of the Mizo National Famine Front, soon to become the militantly anti-Indian Mizo National Front. Under its popular leader, Laldenga, the MNF wrested power from the Mizo Union and declared unilateral independence in 1966 while launching an armed attack against Indian forces. The worst of the bitter fighting that followed, in which the Mizos were aided by China and Pakistan, was over by 1971. Five years later Laldenga returned to India from exile and commenced drawn-out peace negotiations. MNF hardliners branded him a traitor.

Unlike Sailo, Bualhranga did not judge Laldenga harshly. Further armed resistance against the Indians had been hopeless, and the peace terms were reasonable. If he had a poor opinion of anyone it was of Sailo — who, he said, had been involved in shady dealings after returning to Aizawl from Delhi and was using the CIPC for his own ends. Of Sailo's Identity Referendum, Bualhranga declared, "The prophet Amos has put it well. 'I despise your solemn assemblies.'" Nor did he think much of the B'nei Menashe. "Lower-class types" who were "not of the mainstream," they had drifted from one Pentecostal group to another until winding up in Judaism. It made them feel important.

Zai and her husband disapproved of Sailo, too. Although not eager to discuss it, they dropped hints of a scam involving government loans. The CIPC was Sailo's bid for a political career after failing at conventional politics.

I learned more about this failure from Chawngkunga, a former state minister of art and culture. I had gone to see him regarding the stone inscription in the Aizawl museum, about which he was said to be knowledgeable. But he also knew about Sailo, once his aide in the Mizo People's Congress Party, the local affiliate of the national Congress Party, then headed by Indira Gandhi. In 1993, Sailo had sought its nomination to the state legislature. Turned down, he had founded the CIPC.

Chawngkunga disabused me of the notion that the mysterious inscription in the museum might be Semitic. It was written, he said, in a script invented by a Chin Hills religious leader named Paucinhau, who died as an old man in 1948. Paucinhau had been a reformer who reacted to the influence of Christianity by trying to purify the old religion from within. He had emphasized the belief in Pathian, the one God and Creator, and called for abolishing the sacrifices to the jungle spirits. In one of his many visions, he was commanded by Pathian to learn the art of writing. So ardent was his desire to obey, he told his disciples, that he thought of nothing else, day and night, until a script was miraculously revealed to him. Actually, Chawngkunga said, Paucinhau's script was an adaptation of an old syllabic system of writing called *laisui*, used by priests of the Sukte clan in Burma. Chawngkunga showed me a chart of *laisui* characters that did not look Semitic in the least.

Talking with Chawnkunga was frustrating. Just when I was lulled into thinking I was conversing with a rational mind, along came some remark of his to demonstrate that this was a misunderstanding on my part. I'd experienced this in talking with other Mizos. After a quite lucid discussion of the Sukte script, for example, Chawngkunga might suddenly say that it was the writing of the lost scroll destroyed by Emperor Shi Huang Ti of China in 213 B.C.E. — the proof being that in Lushai legend this scroll had been eaten by a dog; that "dog" was a term of abuse for a Chinese; and that Shi Huang Ti had burned books that year. Or he might point to the genealogical chart on his wall, with its standard twenty-five generations — the number of ancestors a Lushai traditionally was expected to remember — and insist that Zo, the first name on it, was the biblical Joseph; or declare that the red sea song was "at least fourteen hundred years old," because there were traditions that it came from Burma, which was reached by the Mizos in their migrations by 600 C.E. That Burma might have been reached without the red sea song apparently had not occurred to him.

Yet although Chawngkunga was confident that the Mizos were a Lost Tribe, he did not think Sailo's version of the song was correct. The authentic one could be found in an anthology of ancient Mizo poetry edited by a man named Lalbiakliana. It, too, was in Hmar dialect, but made no mention of Miriam or Ephraim. There was no Ephraim in Mizo tradition. That was an invention of Sailo's. He had done it to appeal to Christians reluctant to call themselves by the name Manasseh because they associated it with the Jewish B'nei Menashe.

It took awhile to find Lalbiakliana. Sailo, though, was in the CIPC office when I dropped by that week. He denied Chawngkunga's accusation. Reliable informants, he said, had told him the name Ephraim occurred in chants from Burma. The two brotherly tribes, both descended from Joseph, must have wandered to southeast Asia together. Pleased with his Referendum, he was pondering his next step. "I'd like to go to Arakan," he said. However, that was "very tough these days." He had tried sending two of his people there. One was arrested and the other disappeared. Although you could buy a pass from Burmese army officers at the border for 30,000 rupees, the Burmese Communist Party, whose armed forces controlled much of the Arakan region, was unlikely to honor it.

Still lingering in Aizawl, several out-of-town delegates to the Referendum were in the office. They had many questions for me. Now that they were an official Lost Tribe, would the government of Israel recognize them? Should they seek the protection of the United Nations as in East Timor? What would I write about them in my book? A man from Hrawlhong, south of Lunglei, said, "We will still be Israel even if you say we aren't."

Among those present was Darkapi, the old woman displayed in the *langlap* colors. To a question about her age she replied, "I'm told I'm ninety-three. But all I really know is that I was born three years before the bamboos flowered."

There was laughter. The bamboos were said to flower in Mizoram once every fifty years — a catastrophic event, since the temporary abundance of bamboo fruit led to a sharp rise in the jungle rat population, which wreaked havoc in the rice fields the following year. In 1911, as in 1959, this had led to a great famine.

"You couldn't have kept me away," Darkapi answered when asked why she had attended Sailo's Referendum. "Our old religion was the same as the Bible's. I've always known that. I've known it since Lalchhanhima's grandfather, Saikulara the chief of Kawnpui, announced we were Israel." She thought that had happened before World War II but said, "Lalchhanhima knows these things better than I do. He's the only leader I trust."

Sailo translated the last words for me into English with a mock salute, delivered as if from a reviewing stand. There was laughter again. It grew louder when Darkapi added, "That may be very foolish of me."

Sailo laughed harder than anyone.

She was a tiny, shrunken thing. The skin of her face looked smoked, like a mackerel's. Age had pared the breasts from her body and made it a small girl's again. All she remembered of the old religion was that once — she must have been four or five years old — her parents had performed a sacrifice for her health. The priest had chanted many names. Later, her family was baptized. This took place in "the year of the shaking." That was the year a "shaking preacher" had come to her village. He was followed by Pastor Haochhoma, who had scolded the children for dancing the "Entering Zion" dance.

"But why did he scold you?" I objected. "The missionaries taught you that dance."

Darkapi thought the notion that she had been taught the "Entering Zion" dance by a missionary was the funniest thing she had ever heard. It was so funny that she grabbed the eighty-three-year-old woman next to her and began to dance it with her. They joined hands, raised them high, and revolved through the arch they made, first facing each other, then do-si-do, then face to face again. Next, Darkapi seized the back of her friend's blouse and the two of them snaked through the office. Soon there was a whole line following them. It wound past the chairs and benches, singing *lut theng theng, lut theng theng,* and stopped only when Darkapi collapsed on a bench, laughing helplessly. "This old lady is very stiff," she gasped. "That's a dance for children."

She wiped the tears from her eyes. "Oh, I miss those days. There were so many beautiful things. Maybe Lalchhanhima will bring some of them back."

☩

There was one more old person I had been advised to see. His name was Liankeuva and he lived in West Phaileng, a five-hour drive from Aizawl. The asphalt surface of the road had crumbled in many places, and Tana swore as we jounced over them.

Pu Liankeuva was a vigorous ninety-one. Removing his orange stocking cap with its pompom, he revealed a full head of white hair. But he could not tell us much about the old religion. Most of his knowledge of it came from Pu Savitsa, the name given to Frederick Savidge, one of the first two English missionaries to have entered Mizoram, in 1894. He was stationed in the south, where Liankeuva grew up with an uncle in the village of Pupui. Savitsa told the children many stories. Once he said to them, "There will come a time when you will call yourselves children of Israel."

Liankeuva was not sure what Savitsa had meant by that. While he himself believed the Mizos were a Lost Tribe, he had arrived at this conclusion only in the 1960s. He had never heard of Ya or Za. He had never heard of circumcision, though he knew of an old ritual in which a newborn male child was passed through a coiled vine on the seventh day after birth and named on the eighth. He did remember the two kinds of priests, the *bawlpu* and *sadawt:* one sacrificed to Ram Huai, who had seven names and was an "enemy of human beings," and one to Khuavang and Pu Vana, who were "supporters of human beings." Liankeuva had also heard of Manasia. As a young man he had heard the name chanted during a road-clearing ceremony in the jungle. That was where Ram Huai lived. The men clearing the road had called out, "Evildoers, run away! You are blocking the children of Manasia!" That must have been about 1923.

As we spoke, the house filled up with several generations of Pu Liankeuva's family. The older offspring occupied the chairs and floor, and the younger ones crowded outside the open window and stuck their heads through its bars. Even the children in Mizoram were keen to know their true identity.

Pu Liankeuva remembered a few snatches of the old songs and chants. One had the names of different places in Burma. He had also once known the words of the red sea song. He had some lines of it written down somewhere and would mail them to us if he found them.

Several days later a letter arrived at the Hotel Chief with the lines Liankeuva had found. They were difficult for Shmuel to translate. Some of the words were very old. He came up with:

> When we celebrate the *sikpui*,
> The red sea was cut in two.
> Tera, [unclear word] my enemies,
> Cloud by day, fire by night, rising.

☙

On Saturday morning I went to services at the Shalom Zion Synagogue. The main street near the Hotel Chief was lined with the vendors who came to Aizawl for the weekly market. Wrapped in shawls and blankets, they had arrived before dawn in buses from the villages, spread their mats and cloths on the sidewalks, and set themselves down with their produce: little Mizo bananas, little Mizo oranges, tiny Mizo peppers and squashes and potatoes and eggplants and succulents and tubers from the jungle, gnarled fruitlike roots and rootlike fruits and little Mizo fish from the rivers. The people were little, too. After a while, a European of normal height began to feel like a giant in Mizoram. It gave one a sense of unnatural confidence, heightened by the deference shown a Westerner.

I hadn't been to the synagogue since my visit with Avichail the year before. Along the muddy lane leading down to it, with its pastry and butcher stalls, still hung the storefront sign that said "Office of Israel Luseithar, Chief Founder & Dictator, International Reformed Church Of India." The entrance, too, was unchanged. It was reached by a flight of steps through an opening in the sidewalk as though you were descending through a concrete trapdoor.

The service was under way when I arrived. The synagogue was emptier than I remembered it; some of the old faces were gone. The prayer was quiet, subdued. A bona fide parchment Torah scroll donated from Israel was now in the Holy Ark. Taken out for the Torah reading, it was kept unopened on the lectern while the weekly portion was recited from a Mizo Bible.

The portion was the third one in Genesis. It began with the commandment to Abraham: "Get thee out of thy country, and from thy kindred, and from thy father's house, unto a land that I will show thee." When it was finished, I was asked to speak. I was unprepared and didn't know what to say. In the year that had gone by, hardly a Jew from the outside world had been to Aizawl. One or two groups of B'nei Menashe had left for Israel and joined earlier contingents in religious settlements in the West Bank and Gaza Strip, which alone were ready to shoulder their absorption costs. Those remaining in India fought for places on the next list. The prospects for increasing the annual quota were slim. Together with Avichail, I had testified in Jerusalem at a session of a Knesset committee on immigration; most of the witnesses were unfriendly. They regarded the B'nei Menashe as either Third World imposters or pawns of nationalist extremists. Yet in Aizawl it was believed that a favorable book by an Israeli author would open the gates. What was I to tell them?

I stood by the lectern with Shmuel and let the words come by themselves. I was deeply moved, I said, to be in the Shalom Zion Synagogue again. More than any other experience, my previous visit to Mizoram had taught me the strength of the ties binding Jews. Here I was, far from home, in a country as removed from my own in race and language as it was possible to be — yet the minute I stepped into this synagogue, I *was* home. "It is important for you to understand," I said, "that this has nothing to do with your ancestors or mine. I do not know who my distant forefathers were. My more recent ones lived in Russia. The color of my eyes and complexion tells me that they probably did not all descend from an ancient tribe of Israel. And there are many descendants of Jews in the world today who have nothing Jewish about them. With you I share the same prayers and the same God. Everywhere today we are reading the story of Abraham. This makes us one people."

There was no expression on the faces staring at me. One belonged to Yosi Hualngo, sitting in the second row. I had not expected him to be there. I ended, "You know that I hope to write a book about your possible descent from the tribe of Menashe. It would be exciting to discover that this belief is true. But it would not make you less Jewish if it isn't. Abraham did not have Jewish ancestors. He became a Jew by having the courage to be one. When he told his neighbors he was setting out for an unknown country because of a promise made by God, they must have laughed. You have the same courage. This matters more than anything I could say in a book."

Though I meant it sincerely, it fell flat. The somber eyes did not light up. I had not told them what they wanted to hear. I was palming off on them a currency that could not buy them anything they needed. And perhaps they were thinking, "This writer of books, what does he take us for? Does he not know we understand from his words what his conclusions will be?" At the end of the service they shook my hand and said their *sabbat saloms* dispiritedly, as if I had already betrayed them.

I went over to Yosi, who was folding his prayer shawl. "Come," I said, putting my arm around him. For a moment he let his slight body be pulled without resistance. Then, seeing it was in the direction of Samuel Joram, he locked his legs. I had to drag him the last steps to where Shmuel was standing with a look of consternation. "All right," I said, "now talk to each other!"

Neither said a word.

I said, "Look, this can't go on. Shmuel, make Yosi tell you what he has against you. Yosi, tell him why you're angry. I need you both."

But it could go on. Yosi stubbornly kept his head down. Shmuel turned his face away. "Not today," he said, as if the concession demanded of him, bad enough on any day of the week, would be a desecration on the Sabbath.

I threw up my hands, feeling foolish.

At Minchah time I paid a visit to Aizawl's latest synagogue. Peter Tlau picked me up at the Hotel Chief. The South Aizawl Synagogue had been disbanded, and Peter had joined a new congregation. He took me to a room near Vanapa Hall. Over the door was the sign:

Beth Midrash Hashem, Inc.
Messianic Judaism
Synagogue
Aizawl, Mizoram

About twenty people were in the room. One was Zohmengaiha, who nodded to me when I entered. Another was Elisabeth Zodingliani. It was soon apparent that I had been invited not to Minchah but to a theological dispute. The Beth Midrash Hashem was divided into pro- and anti-Jesus factions. The antis, led by Zohmengaiha and Peter, were eager to enlist me on their side.

I was reluctant to comply. I did not wish to debate the nature of Jesus, a Jew I happened to be fond of. The Mizos loved to assure you that they would become Jews tomorrow if you could prove they were a Lost Tribe, or if Israel would recognize them, or if they did not have to be circumcised, or if they could go on believing in Jesus — and while the last of these was like offering to become a vegetarian provided you could go on eating steak, I tried (unlike Yitzhak and Shmuel, who had an enthusiasm for their new religion) to avoid arguments. Despite my disagreements with Avichail, I had no desire to make a Jew of anyone. Being Jewish, it seemed to me, was a fate, marvelous and perverse, best appreciated with a dash of humor rarely found among converts. But this was not something I could tell the Mizos, who took their religion seriously and believed in comparative shopping. They were as keen to match verses from the Bible as were Americans to discuss their CD/ROMS. Christianity was a product still new enough to keep them hopping from brand to brand.

For many of them, Judaism was one more brand of Christianity. Maneuvered by Peter, I now found myself telling the Beth Midrash Hashem that this was not the case. Not all of its members wished to concede the point. But there were people in Israel who believed in Jesus, too! There were Jews for Jesus in America! Why did the Jews of the world not want them? "I come from the village of Lungphun," one man protested. "We have a CIPC chapter with a hundred members. Sixty would become Jews tomorrow if ——"

Fill in the blank.

In the back, a thin, pretty woman listened intently while rocking back and forth with a nursing baby. It was imbibing a taste for hermeneutics with its mother's milk.

Peter and Zohmengaiha walked me back to the hotel. They were hopeful that I'd tipped the scales in their favor. "Oh, those B'nei Menashe!" Peter exclaimed, justifying his defection from the Aizawl community. "They think only of themselves! How do they expect the word of Hasem to spread if they do not spread it?" He and Zohmengaiha would win the Messianic Jews for true Judaism. They would rid them of their foolish belief in Jesus. "We must tear the New Testament from their heart as I have tear it from my Bible. See, I have done it."

He really had. He showed me the Bible he was carrying. It had been his mother's. The entire New Testament was torn out of it.

By the statue of Gandhi near Vanapa Hall, Peter made a rude sound. "The whole world think that man a hero. No, no, no, no, no! He must go back to Delhi. Let India leave us Mizos alone."

⚶

Perhaps it was my talk in the Shalom Zion Synagogue, perhaps it was the company I kept: the B'nei Menashe of Aizawl regarded me with suspicion. They did not flock to the Hotel Chief as they had flocked to the Ritz and were content to leave me to my own devices.

But I did not lack visitors. They arrived around the clock, from early morning until late at night. One of the early birds, a CID man, was waiting in the dining room one day when I came down for breakfast. I bristled when he pulled out a small black book and said he had seen me at Sailo's Identity Referendum. However, he was a hidden sympathizer. He opened the book to a blank page, drew two irregular but similar shapes, and asked whether I knew what they were. One resembled a map of Israel. I hadn't a clue to the second.

"Mizoram downside up!" The man turned his book around to show me. He wrote some numbers. "Area Israel: 20,170 square kilometers. Area Mizoram: 21,081." This appeared to have kabbalistic significance. "Mr. Sailo have the good idea!"

I had a visit from Lalnaglinga and his wife of the Church of Gethsemane. They wished to discuss the Old Testament. They kept its commandments and lived by its laws. Nevertheless, when Isaiah said, "He was wounded for our transgressions, he was bruised for our iniquities, and with his stripes we are healed," whom but Jesus could he have been speaking of?

I had a visit from Sapchhunga, the retired police officer. Sapchhunga was eighty-eight and troubled. "It is difficult to know what to think," he said. "During the Great War I was a British quartermaster in Assam. There I met a Christian minister from China who had fled the Communists. He said to me, 'You Mizos look and talk like the Yi in Yunnan.' So! If we resemble a minority people in China how can we be . . . ?"

"Israelites?"

"That is my presumption."

He wished he could help me more with my research. But his parents, whose marriage in 1904 was the first Christian wedding in Mizoram, had refused to tell their children about the heathen practices they had abandoned. "My father detested those old things. Truthfully, I never liked them either. Now I am old and have come to take a deep interest in our history. But I fear that many of our people have concocted things. I am walking in the valley of the shadow of death and would like to know the truth ere I leave it."

I was visited by Lalsanga, president of the Ephraim Union. The Ephraim Union was a different organization from Saidinga's National Ephraim Conference. It was a political party that had run in the last state elections, receiving $1\frac{1}{2}$ percent of the vote. Soon it would win a majority and form the government. Lalsanga had come to invite me to dinner in his home.

I had a visit from V. L. Ngawta. He had invented a revolutionary new gear box that would enable motor vehicles to recharge large batteries, thus ushering in the age of mass electric transportation. "I have by assumption and logic," he told me, "applied the law of the lever to the law of the wheel and axle to magnify the power of a spinning shaft." Making a prototype, however, was complicated. He had received no response from the numerous Indian business firms he had written to. Perhaps I could find him backers in Israel.

I had a visit from Zohminga. Zohminga worked for the ministry of tourism, which meant he had a lot of free time. He spent part of it riding around Aizawl on a motorcycle with Israeli flags. He wished to know how he might acquire some Israeli army fatigues.

There was also Ram Peng, who came from Haka in the Chin Hills. He had walked for two weeks to get to Sailo's Referendum. As if still exhausted by the effort, he breathed heavily. He had a bad heart and no money for medicines.

The CIPC was illegal in Burma. Ram Peng thought it had about 10,000 members there. "All Chin people know they are Israel," he said. Raised a Baptist, he belonged to a group that observed the Jewish Sabbath and dietary laws. They met secretly in the jungle to pray. It was hard to be a Jew. There were no teachers, no schools, no books. Ram Peng asked to borrow $100 for medicines.

C. Fung Kung and Nithanthluai came to visit me too. C. Fung Kung was a Burmese living in Aizawl. Nithanthluai had come from Haka for the Referendum. She brought me a photograph of a silver-banded gunpowder horn. It belonged to a family in Burma, and Nithanthluai thought it might be an Israelite shofar.

C. Fung Kung solved a mystery. He was the "reliable informant" who had told Sailo about Ephraim. As a boy in the Chin Hills, he had heard the word in the chants of hunters. Only it wasn't Ephraim, it was *erfihm*, and he wasn't sure if it was a proper name. Sailo had reversed the first two consonants.

I invited the two of them to stay for lunch. Our *vai* waiter stood waiting for them to order. After a while went by without their opening their menus, I realized they did not know what these were. Mizo restaurants did not have them. "We'll eat what you do," Nithanthluai said when I tried explaining the principle of the thing. The idea of three people sitting down to a single meal at which each ate something different was more than she could digest.

She was a mother of ten, with thick glasses and the waistline of a debutante, and she told a curious story. For years, she had sought confirmation of her Israelite roots. A year ago, after the monsoon rains, she had gone south to the region of Hungle, halfway to Arakan. The mountains there were very high. There were no roads, and she had walked from village to village, four months of walking all in all. To her amazement, the inhabitants of ten villages told her they were Israel. Secretive about their faith, they had refused to discuss it until convinced she was Israel too. Then they let her attend their sacrifices. There she heard them pray to the God of Abraham, Isaac, and Jacob.

She had a guileless face. It could have been a schoolteacher's if not for the dreamy look that came over it when the conversation left her, as if she then went somewhere else. Called back, she returned with a smile so radiant that I felt blessed.

"Are you sure that's what you heard?" I asked.

She was sure. Apraham Pasian, Izak Pasian, Zakop Pasian. If only she had had a tape recorder. It was stupid of her not to have brought one.

Did the villagers near Hungle circumcise?

Nithanthluai did not think so.

Did they observe the Sabbath? Refrain from pork?

Not as far as she knew. "But that is because they are ignorant," she said. "I tried telling them this."

I offered to buy her a cassette deck in Aizawl if she would return to the Hungle region with it.

I had a visit from C. Ngura. He wanted my collaboration in a research project. He told me, "To differentiate the Zo descendants and the Hebrews in course of a research, it is necessary to examine the bone and the hair. For this I need a microscope."

I was visited by K. Lian Cung, who came from Falam, between Haka and Tiddim. He brought with him five manuscripts on Chin history and folklore written in the Lai language. He had heard I was a writer too. He would be grateful if I would arrange for the publication of his manuscripts abroad.

"But they're in Lai," I said.

He would be grateful if I would arrange for their translation.

K. Lian Cung had heard of the villagers near Hungle who prayed to the God of Abraham, Isaac, and Jacob. They belonged to the Zaotang tribe, but the custom was not old. The Zaotangs were mostly Christians and had picked it up from the Bible. They did not call themselves "children of Manasa." This expression was purely Mizo and did not exist among the Chin.

I visited Reverend Zairema. Zairema was an influential Presbyterian minister considered to be Aizawl's leading Bible scholar. He had even taught himself some Hebrew. "None of it is true" was his opinion of the Mizos' supposed Israelite origins. The belief had originated in the 1950s in the hamlet of Buolawng among a group of Pentecostalists, or *mi hlim*, a phrase that literally meant "happy people." Buolawng was in Hmar territory near the Manipur border. In 1973 Zairema had sought to visit it, only to discover it had been razed during the Insurgency and its inhabitants regrouped in the nearby town of Ratu. There were about thirty Judaizing families in Ratu at the time. Zairema did not think highly of the B'nei Menashe. Like Bualhranga, he regarded them as lost souls who had drifted from one church to another until they ended up in Judaism.

Zairema had written his doctoral thesis on the concept of God in the old Mizo religion. Besides Pathian, "the Eternal One," the religion had deities like Pu Vana or "Grandfather Heaven," Khuava, Khuapa, Khuanu, and Khuavang. A *khua* was a friendly spirit that helped mankind. It was ministered to by a *sadawt* priest, whose name meant "meat spearer," because he sacrificed large animals by stabbing them in the heart. A *bawlpu* priest sacrificed to Ram Huai. Zairema did not think this duality reflected a merger of two religions. Nor was it the case that pigs were sacrificed only to Ram Huai. The difference was that a pig sacrificed by a *sadawt* was eaten, whereas one sacrificed by a *bawlpu* was not. The meat was taboo not because it was pork but because it was offered to evil spirits.

Zairema had never heard of a Mizo god named Ya or Za. He did not know if Pathian, Pu Vana, and the various *khuas* were best thought of as one god or many. "That's something I would like dearly to comprehend," he said. "However, there is no way of reconstructing these things. Historically, Mizo civilization was wiped out. Even the physical landscape is gone. There's not a bit of jungle left."

"But I've seen jungle everywhere," I said.

He laughed at my ignorance. "What you saw was second growth. Perhaps third or fourth. The entire jungle has been *jhumed*. It no longer exists."

He did not know who Manasia was. "I never looked into that. *Man* means to catch or grab hold of. *Sia*–" He played with several possibilities and gave up. "No, it has no meaning. That's exceptional. Mizo names always mean something."

I was leaving when he asked, "Have you thought of genetic testing?"

"Yes," I said, "but if you're so certain you're not a Lost Tribe, what would be the point?"

"Well, we must make it watertight." He smiled sadly as if caught out at the last moment. "You see, I don't know what my origins are. None of us do."

I visited John Vanlal Hluna, dean of T. Romana College. Hluna was a pleasantly moon-faced man, a leader of the Mizo National Conference Party and the author of *Church and Political Upheaval in Mizoram: A Study of the Impact of Christianity on Political Development*. He had his own theory about the Lost Tribe claim, in which he put even less credence than did Zairema. At the time of the Insurgency, Hluna said, a wave of anti-Mizo feeling had swept India. Mizos were treated badly. It was hard for them to find work. "To be a Mizo was a crime. People were ashamed to be identified as one. They would say, 'I'm not a Mizo, I'm a Paite,' or a Hmar, or some other tribe. Many fled to Burma. Many were sent back and jailed in India. The news that we were a Lost Tribe — that it was possible to exchange a Mizo identity for an Israelite one — was highly welcome." Hluna did not think the British missionaries had had anything to do with it. On the contrary, they were traditionally opposed to such Pentecostal enthusiasms.

I visited Zaliana, head of the religion department at Aizawl's Tribal Research Institute. Zaliana doubted the Mizos had ever been monotheists. In his opinion, Pu Vana and the different *khuas* were distinct from Pathian.

He had no more idea than did Reverend Zairema of who Manasia was. To the best of his knowledge, the Hmar form of "Manmasi" was not a corruption but the original name. He disagreed, however, with the assumption, made by Vumson in *Zo History* and Pudaihte in *The Education of the Hmar People*, that Manmasi was the Hmars' first ancestor. In Hmar tradition this was Luahpuia, who lived five generations after Kinminga and Chinhila, the supposed progenitors of all Mizos. Zaliana questioned the antiquity of the red sea song, too. Most of the oldest Mizo folk songs were in Lai, more correctly known as Pawi, and the red sea song had no Pawi version. Pawi was closest to the original speech from which all Mizo dialects had developed. The oldest of these dialects was spoken by the Hmar. They were the pioneer group to break away from the other tribes by migrating from the Chin Hills into present-day Mizoram, near Champhai, in the sixteenth century, first moving along the Tuipui River valley in a southwesterly direction before turning and heading north through the Lushai Hills. The word *hmar* meant "northerners."

We had crossed the Tuipui near its headwaters, coming in and out of Champhai. There was a wooden bridge there, with a sign saying ONE VE-HICLE AT A TIME, onto which I had seen three busloads of YMA-ers pile together. "Aren't *tuipui sen* the words in the song that mean 'red sea'?" I asked, remembering the lines sent us by Liankeuva.

Yes, Zaliana replied. *Sen* meant "red" and *tuipui* meant "big water" or "sea." But it was also the name of a river.

Could *tuipui sen* then refer to that river?

In theory it could.

"In short," I summed up, "you see no reason to believe the Mizos have anything to do with ancient Israel."

"Ah!"

Zaliana raised a finger, single and salutary. There was a reason. One alone. But irrefutable.

"It's like this." He drew a box to represent a village. Leading away from it, a line stood for a road. At the line's end was a circle filled with dots that indicated ashes. The ashes were sprinkled by a priest on the night before a planned hunt. In the morning the priest looked for tracks in them. If they pointed toward the village, the hunt would go well. If not, it was best postponed.

So? Although I had heard of this custom from Pu Chere, I failed to see its relevance.

So! It was simple. The circle was made by coiling a vine called a *vawm hrui*. The *vawm hrui* was a species of wild grape rare in Mizoram. It was so treasured that a villager seeing one in the jungle marked the spot so that he could find it again.

"So?"

"So! To whom else is the grape vine so important? To Israel! In your Sabbath meal, do you not bless the fruit of the vine? No one else does this thing."

I visited Doliana. Back when Chala started the Buolawng movement, Doliana had been Chala's *kohchhiar*. Now he lived in a little house on the outskirts of Aizawl, reached by a descending stone path. He had moved to Aizawl in 1969 from Ratu, where he was regrouped with the Buolawng refugees.

In 1954, Doliana related, the Holy Spirit came to Buolawng. Two men had visions in that year, Darnghaka and Chala. Visions were common in the United Pentecostal Church, to which most of the villagers belonged. They were called *zel* and often occurred during the singing and dancing in church. Sometimes those having them fell to the floor in a trance. A *zel* might last for a minute or much longer. It was like a waking dream.

But these two visions were special. Darnghaka's came first. In it he was told that the Mizos were Israel and should return to their forefathers' land. Then Chala had a *zel* in which he saw a large fruit cut in half. A voice declared this fruit to be the Mizo people. Half should go to Israel and half should build a new Israel in Mizoram.

The two men related their visions to the church elders. This was the practice in the UPC. An important vision was brought before the elders to determine whether it came from God or from men's hearts. The elders investigated and found that both Darnghaka's and Chala's visions came from God.

"On what grounds?"

On various grounds, Doliana said. Many customs of the old religion proved to be the same as those in the Bible. It was thus established that the Mizos were descended from Joseph's son Manasseh, called "Manmasi" by the Hmar. At their sacrifices the priests had prayed, "God who is above, God who is below, we the children of Manmasi make you this offering." Or suppose a jungle spirit caused a tree to shrivel and die: the spirit was driven out by the priest's chanting, "Go away, get out, Manmasi forbids you to live here." "And there was one more wonderful thing," Doliana added.

"What was that?"

There had been an old Hmar celebration. In it was a dance. The dancers stood in two lines and sang. Doliana sang the words in a creaky voice, in the old dirgelike style. They were similar to those sent us by Liankeuva. "These were chanted by our forefathers," he said. "When we looked into the Bible, we found them there."

After Darnghaka's and Chala's visions were confirmed by the elders, Chala founded an organization called the Israel Association and appointed Doliana its secretary. One of his first acts was to make contact with the Israeli consul in Calcutta, a Jewish dentist who headed an emigration committee aiding Indian Jews to move to Israel. The consul visited them in Buolawng and called them his "lost brothers" but explained that, as there were many Jews in the world who wanted to go to Israel, they would have to wait their turn. Doliana then wrote a long letter to Mr. David Ben-Gurion, Israel's chief minister, detailing the chants and customs confirmed by the elders. He received no answer.

Most of the records Doliana kept for Chala concerned more trivial things, like organizational meetings, correspondences, and dues. These were lost during the Insurgency, when the villagers were forced to abandon Buolawng and take the jungle path to Ratu, pursued by gunfire and smoke. The Indian army ransacked the village and the insurgents later took what was left. They did not approve of Chala. Laldenga was a Marxist and antireligious. He thought Chala and his followers should forget their visions and devote themselves to the Mizos' war of liberation.

Chala died in 1958. Buolawng was never resettled. For a while, the members of the Israel Association stuck together. Then they went their separate ways. Some eventually were circumcised and began to live as Jews; Doliana thought this had happened in the mid-1970s. "They said the Messiah hadn't come yet," he said. Others, like himself, went on believing that "Christ was born in Bethlehem." For a long time he had been disappointed in the government of Israel for failing to recognize them. However, "now that Lalchhanima has shown us a way of being Israel in Mizoram," he was no longer sure this mattered. He had seen Sailo's Identity Referendum on TV. He had even seen Shmuel, Yitzhak, and me.

As for Darnghaka, he was still alive, in Ratu. Never a leader like Chala, he was remembered by few people. Doliana was no longer in touch with him. He thought it would be easy for us to find him, though.

⚚ 6 ⚚

Ratu

WE HAD A NEW DRIVER, Moya. Every few minutes, without slowing down, he opened the car door and stuck his head out as if looking at the ground.

"Something wrong with the tires?" I asked from the back.

"No," Shmuel answered. "It's Moya's window."

Moya was chewing betel. His window was jammed. Each time he had to spit, he leaned out the opened door while steering blindly with one arm.

We were driving north toward Manipur, through villages like Langpui, Twakzawl, and East Phaileng. The sun was out, and mats of freshly winnowed rice were spread out to dry. In places where the road was the only level ground between the uphill and downhill slopes, the mats were laid directly on it. Moya drove over them. It helped husk the rice, he said.

The day was languid. From time to time, as monotonous as the jungle on either side of us, a cicada called the *nirleng* buzzed like a high-tension wire. The sound grew louder on the turns, whirling us around them like a slingshot and releasing us on the straightaways.

Near East Phaileng, Moya pointed out a game sanctuary. He knew some men who had gone poaching in it. They were on a path when they saw a bamboo shake. As soon as they reached it, the shaking stopped. Then it started in a second tree. Curious, they made for that, and so were lured deeper and deeper into the jungle until they were lost. It took them a week to find their way out. This was the work of a *huai*, a jungle spirit.

There were lots of *huais* in the jungle. Moya had heard of them too often to doubt it. A friend of his, a truck driver, had once given a ride to a *huai* in the form of a beautiful lady. As they were chatting, the lady laughed, baring snake fangs instead of teeth. Moya's friend stopped the truck and jumped out, and the *huai* vanished.

Huais were attracted to people. Moya knew of a girl who had befriended a group of them. It had happened about fifteen years ago. A handsome young *huai* appeared to her in the fields and beckoned her to follow him. Her parents, working alongside her, did not see him. She told them she had to "go somewhere," and they, thinking it was to relieve herself, let her wander into the jungle.

Time passed, and she did not return. Her parents sent her brothers off to look for her. They followed her tracks and found her sitting at the edge of a cliff, surrounded, she said, by "friends" she did not want to leave. The brothers dragged her home and stood watch over her when she pleaded to be allowed to go back. "My friends are waiting for me," she told them, describing the *huais'* beautiful dwelling place. Finally, they agreed to escort her there. While she waxed ecstatic over its lavish appearance, they saw only a bare cave.

The *huais* lived on, though the old religion was dead. People like Moya had a healthy respect for them. Already the first Christian missionaries had observed that, while the Lushais honored Pathian as the Supreme Being, they put little stock in his providence. It was the *huais* they were concerned with. Perpetual mischief makers, these had to be watched out for, outwitted, propitiated. Generally taking the shape of human beings, or of one-legged or grotesquely headed monsters, they could also turn themselves into snakes, tigers, even flowers. The missionaries exploited the fear of them by identifying them with the servants of Satan, who was none other than their ruler Ram Huai, and offered in the person of Jesus the protection Pathian failed to provide. This was a powerful selling point.

The jungle was the *huais'* home. For the Lushais it was more of a habitat. Perhaps their sense of living in and off it without being entirely of it went back to the days when their ancestors first entered its dark tangle from the expansive Sino-Tibetan borderlands. It was only abstractly, after all, that Mizoram had vast open spaces. All that was really open were the clearings of the villages and *jhums*. In olden times a Lushai left the safety of his village, stockaded against wild animals and enemy attack, to hunt, forage, fetch water, *jhum*, raid, or ambush, and returned to it with relief — for as long, that is, as it was there. Lushai villages were notoriously impermanent. *Jhuming* quickly exhausted the soil; before the British came, when uninhabited land had no owner, whole settlements often packed up and moved on when their surroundings were *jhumed* out. Given the paucity of a family's possessions and the speed with which a traditional dwelling could be constructed, this was easier than moving in Manhattan. In Kawzawl I had watched a man weave a house from strips of bamboo he had prepared by cutting stalks in the nearby jungle, slitting them lengthwise, softening them by soaking, pressing them flat, and leaving them to dry. He would make the floor of bamboo struts and the roof of thatch or — if he could afford them — tin sheets. Working alone, he said, he could finish the job in two weeks. The only part he needed help with was sinking the timber stilts on which the downhill side of most Mizo houses stood.

Choosing the site for a new village was simple. It required a suitable hilltop, several roosters (favorable if they crowed before dawn), and a hard-boiled egg (inauspicious if foaming from a cracked shell). Nor did a discontented Lushai have to wait for these. He could try his luck elsewhere on his own, since any village he chose to settle in was obliged to stake him to *jhum* land. Sometimes, unhappy with their chief, groups of villagers migrated together. The Lushais, their British governor Colonel J. Shakespear observed, had a "peculiar vagabond strain." Shakespear contrasted them with the stay-at-home Nagas, who had an intense love for their ancestral abodes.

This explained something I had found puzzling — namely, why so many of the villages razed during the Insurgency had never been resettled. Take Buolawng, for example. Although its inhabitants, "regrouped" in Ratu, to which we were now traveling to look for Darnghaka, could have rebuilt it once the fighting was over, they never did. To a Naga this would have been incomprehensible. A Mizo, accustomed to routinely abandoning homes to the jungle, found it normal.

An hour short of Ratu, in the village of Khawruhlian, we stopped for a drink in a place called Mr. Tea Stall. Within minutes we had attracted a gathering. People came to shake hands. The Mizos were great hand shakers. They took your hand and gripped it between their own as if it were a car battery on which they'd clamped two cables.

Others wanted to talk. They belonged to a group called Ephraim Israel and were eager to conduct a religious colloquium. While they were arguing with Yitzhak and Shmuel about Jesus, I watched two men and a woman prepare cooking wood. They worked in an assembly line, one man opening short logs with a hammer and wedge, the second splitting them with an ax, the woman shaving the split halves with a hoe-shaped plane so that they would fit beneath the grate of a Mizo cooking hearth. Then they were stacked upright in a basket, like baguettes, and carried away for sale.

We had left Mr. Tea Stall and were passing through the marketplace when Shmuel spotted someone he knew. It was Chala's nephew Ramhawngmina, the son of Ramsiami, the widow of Chala's younger brother. Ramsiami lived in Khanpui, the next village up the road, and Ramhawngmina offered to take us to see her. *Siyata di-shmaya!*

A mezuzah, the talisman that marks the entrance to a Jewish home, was nailed to the side of Ramsiami's door. Busy at the hearth when we arrived, she did not mind letting Ramhawngmina tend the fire while she talked about the days in Buolawng. They were happy ones. She and her friends in the United Pentecostal Church had been "happy people." The term she used, *mi hlim*, was the same one I had heard from Zairema. I asked about Chala's and Darnghaka's visions.

Ramsiami said she had forgotten much but would tell us what she remembered. Chala, whose widow still lived in Ratu, had had many visions; Darnghaka, Ramsiami thought, had had but one. His spirit had left his body and his eyes were closed. Ramsiami remembered that clearly. She remembered kneeling by his side and praying. Prayer was the *mi hlims'* way of bringing back a spirit. As she prayed, she shut her eyes and had a vision of her own. "I saw Darnghaka become a small child and enter a house," she said. "I couldn't see inside, so I put his head in my lap and went on praying. Then I saw him come out. His head was surrounded by light. I asked what had happened, but he wouldn't tell me. I wanted so badly to know."

Darnghaka related his vision to the UPC elders. "We all assumed it was God's spirit," Ramsiami said. "We didn't know for sure, though, until the elders summoned us and said, 'You are the children of Manasseh.'

When we heard that, we were in much joy and sang and danced all around."

The next vision, Ramsiami recalled, was Chala's. "He fell unconscious to the floor in church. When he awoke, he told us we must return to Israel."

The elders sent three men, Darnghaka, Sankhuma, and Dothanga, to Silchar, the nearest big city, to find out how to get to Israel. They walked all the way. In Silchar they were informed that an Israeli consul resided in Calcutta. Before setting out for there (Darnghaka remained in Buolawng), Sankhuma and Dothanga were told by Chala, "You are going to bring back good news. Be sure to tell no one about it until you return."

And indeed the consul in Calcutta told Sankhuma and Dothanga that all the children of Manasseh could go to Israel. The two were overjoyed. Unable to restrain themselves, they revealed the glad tidings to everyone on the train they took back to Silchar. The consequences were immediate. The story was published in the newspapers, and the CID sent investigators to nip the emigration movement in the bud.

"They told us only slackers wished to go to Israel," Ramsiami said. (Good in the 1990s, Indian-Israeli relations were poor in the 1950s, when Jawaharlal Nehru was courting the Moslem world.) Although she tried to be accurate, tapping her little palm with a forefinger as if to match each detail against a checklist in her memory, her account of the consul's declaration was different from Doliana's and less probable. The story of the "train of the good news," as she called it, with its Pandora-like secret, sounded like folklore. Indeed, the entire episode was already encrusted with legend. In Israel I had been told that all of Chala's followers had set out on foot for Silchar, intending to walk the rest of the way to Jerusalem. "How many were you?" I asked.

Ramsiami thought the Buolawng movement had numbered one or two hundred people. Once they realized they were not going to Israel, they left the UPC and founded a church of their own, called the Church of God. The break occurred when Chala instructed them to observe the Old Testament Sabbath in place of the Christian Sunday. Subsequently, they stopped eating pork and reinstituted biblical sacrifice on a hilltop outside the village.

"What about Jesus?" Yitzhak asked. He was still hot from his argument in Mr. Tea Stall.

Ramsiami thought Jesus was still believed in, because each Church of

God prayer session ended with an invocation of his name. She said, "We knew nothing about Judaism. We didn't know what a Jew was. We never used that word. We said 'Israel.'"

Judaism came later. First the Buolawng movement spread north into Manipur along the Ratu-Churachandpur road; then it returned from there in Jewish guise. The first to come preaching Judaism from Manipur was Gideon Ray.

I had met Ray, a legendary figure, at a B'nei Menashe wedding in Israel. He had come with a busload of guests from a settlement in the Gaza Strip, where he lived. It was a noisy, happy affair, presided over by a beaming Rabbi Avichail. There was a modern Orthodox wedding canopy and a modern Orthodox ceremony and modern Orthodox singing and dancing. The bride was greeted in modern Orthodox fashion by ho-ho-ing ranks of young men, and the groom was carried on the traditional chair. The men and women danced and sat separately, and the young ladies wore long-sleeved modern Orthodox dresses instead of Mizo wraparound skirts. There was nothing Mizo in evidence except Mizos. A few were in Israeli army uniform, one with sergeant's stripes. More than a wedding, it was a celebration of a remarkably swift process of acculturation.

It saddened me, although perhaps it shouldn't have. It was the same perfect mimicry that had so impressed me on my first visit to the Shalom Zion Synagogue — only then it had been bravely dissident, whereas now it was dutifully conformist. There was nothing wrong with Israelification, of course. The B'nei Menashe wanted it. They were eager to try on their new identity, on which they had made a large down payment. They were heady with the ease of slipping into it — and it was this that gave one pause. Once more an old life had been abandoned like a village in the jungle. When all was said and done, Avichail was not much different from the missionaries.

One wondered whether the children and grandchildren of the young couple beneath the wedding canopy would have to search for their true identity again. The older people lacked the excitement of the younger ones. They sat passively at their tables, half-pleased and half-befuddled. You could see in them the realization that they had been left behind by what they had launched. Gideon Ray had proud, mocking lips. A large man, taller than most Mizos, he wore with flair a buckskin shirt and a maroon cowboy hat. "I know I am no one now," those mocking lips said. "Yet remember that I started all this. Remember that thou wentest after me in a land that was not sown. I, Gideon Ray, who came from Manipur — I was the first Jew."

᠅

We found Darnghaka's house easily, but Darnghaka wasn't in. He was on his *jhum* land in the jungle, harvesting the rice. He spent the nights there, his wife told us, and would not be back before the weekend.

We asked how far it was. About an hour-and-a-half's walk, said Darnghaka's wife. The neighbor's son was going that way in the morning, and it would be best to go with him, since we'd never find the path by ourselves.

The neighbor's son lived in a house beside a water tank painted with a large Star of David. We arranged to meet him there early the next morning. Then we found the woman with the key to the Forest Rest House, a state-run bungalow for the hypothetical tourist to Ratu. We paid her to clean away the cobwebs, make the beds, and shake out the mosquito nets, and went to see Chala's widow.

It was getting dark. The house was lit by a kerosene lamp. Chala's widow and Shmuel sat on either side of it, sharing its glow. Chala's son, born the year his father died, listened from a corner beneath a picture of Jesus and Mary. He was bare-chested and had a head of curly hair — "uncommon among the Mizos," according to Shakespear, "and much objected to" — and looked more like a teenager than a man of forty. By now I was used to Mizos looking younger than they were. They rarely suffered from baldness until extreme old age, and their skin kept the smooth sheen of a well-oiled boot or baseball glove.

There were others in the room. A young lady was seated at what resembled a vanity on which she had arranged her cosmetics. She was manufacturing two products, rolling cigarettes from a pile of shredded tobacco in front of her, and then, when tiring of this, switching to betel-and-lime-on-areca-leaf sandwiches. A boy by the window sliced the betel for her while singing softly to himself. On a bench behind me, apparently fast asleep, lay a man. A dog was curled beneath the table by its rice bowl. People came in and out. They went to a back room with Chala's son and returned with packages wrapped in newspaper.

"They're doing a nice business," I remarked to Shmuel when Chala's widow rose to serve dinner. At first we had protested that we wanted none. Then we sent Yitzhak out to buy a chicken as our contribution. But he'd come back empty-handed, and a Mizo curry of tinned fish was now simmering on the hearth.

"I think," Shmuel said softly, "that they're selling *zu* in the back."

"Then we'll have some for supper," I declared. I was curious to taste *zu*. Made of fermented rice mash, it was banned in Mizoram, a dry state. The missionaries had fought *zu* tooth and nail, both for reasons of Christian temperance and because its consumption was basic to the old religion, whose sacrifices and celebrations made copious use of it. Nowadays, however, even tipplers, or at least the ones I had encountered in Aizawl, preferred the bootleg rum or Scotch with fake British labels jocularly known as IMFOL — Indian-Made Foreign Liquor. Yitzhak agreed with them that *zu* was a bad idea.

"I wouldn't," he said. "You never know what rot goes into these home brews. Wait until you get to Manipur."

Zu was sold openly there. And so we ate our fish curry, rice, and bitter eggplant without it and talked about Chala, whose widow recalled little of his visions and did not even have a photograph of him. She did remember the Saturday on which he broke with the UPC. He had told his followers to observe their first biblical Sabbath by neither working nor lighting a fire, and the UPC elders had retaliated by declaring it a public road-clearing day. Out of fifty families in the village, thirty showed up for work. The shirkers were fined, and as none had any money, their pots and pans were confiscated. Chala's widow laughed as she pointed to the neat stack of aluminum utensils on the shelves by her hearth. The loss of her kitchenware was her most vivid memory from her years as a *mi hlim*.

The man on the bench sat up suddenly. The pots and pans had tumbled into his sleeping brain and jarred loose a bothersome question. "*Kapu!*" he addressed Shmuel. "How many lost tribes are we? I know about Manasseh, but what's all this about Ephraim?"

Everyone, the man said, was talking about Ephraim these days. We told him what we knew. Although so many people were into the Ephraim game by now that it couldn't be pinned just on Sailo, he was doing his share to promote it. The last time I had seen him at the CIPC office, he had had two new Ephraimite chants for me.

We drove back to the Forest Rest House, which stood on a low hill overlooking Ratu. The moon was nearly full. Most of the houses in the village were dark. In the distance, out to the east, perhaps over the Manipur border, the glow of moonlight on mist marked a river valley.

A dog barked. The village had gone to sleep early. Yet from somewhere came the beating of a drum. At first I heard it as a snake hears, more with my skin than my ears, mistaking its quick rhythm for the excited beating of my heart.

"Someone's drumming."

"Singing, too," Yitzhak said.

I strained to hear. There was more than one voice. The sound ebbed and came back. It grew stronger, fainter, faded, surged again.

It seemed to be traveling from afar. But Shmuel motioned from the top of the hill for us to join him, and the voices grew clearer when we did. They were coming from a house on the other side of a gully. A window was lit. Figures moved across it. They crossed it three or four at a time, holding hands. Although there appeared to be an endless line of them, this was because they were moving in a circle. They flickered in the bright window as though on a screen.

They were men and women. They stopped and swayed and circled some more, their movement half a walk and half a dance. Their singing was not like any I had heard in Mizoram. It was not old-time dirge or English church or Western at all. It rose and fell in waves of longing, wave after wave. It was a longing so pure and unformed that it did not yet know what it was, only knew it was a fullness and an emptiness. The fullness bore it forward on the crest of each wave, and the emptiness sucked it back down. The drum beat quickly. It had the feverish pulse of someone ill with a jungle spirit.

A voice sang beside me. It was Shmuel's. He knew the words of the song. They were about standing on the banks of the Jordan and waiting to enter the Promised Land. "It's a revival meeting," he said.

"UPC?" The drumming was steady, hypnotic. It was easy to imagine being put into a trance by it.

"No. The drum is too slow. It sounds Presbyterian."

"Slow?" I held my watch to the moon for fifteen seconds. Forty drumbeats. A heart beating like that, unless from strenuous exertion, would have a bad case of tachycardia.

But Shmuel was sure. He had drummed at revivals himself, before becoming Jewish, in a church called the Assembly of God. A Pentecostal
drum was faster.

I took his word for it. In the early years, Presbyterian missionaries like
Savidge had not allowed drumming in their churches. They considered it
un-Christian. Yet although in the end they relented, they had capped it,
so it seemed, with a speed limit.

The revival went on for another hour. Even when the songs changed,
the quality of emotion stayed the same. The next day we were told that a
"crusader" from East Phaileng had come for a week of nightly sessions.
The one we had witnessed was the last.

⚕

The neighbor's son was waiting by the water tank. The dawn light was
still muddy with shadow. Darngakha's *jhum* land was on the Buolawng
ridge, the first line of hills to the west. This meant descending the Ratu
side of a deep ravine and ascending the Buolawng side. Little more than a
mile as the crow flies, the distance was several times that on foot. The
path twisted and turned, running alternately across the slope and down
it. Meticulously cleared of jungle growth, it was wide enough for two
men to pass each other. In the steeper parts, steps cut in the jungle floor
made an earthen staircase. No doubt slippery in the rain, they were dry
now, after several days of clear weather.

The jungle formed a wall on either side of us. Scorned by Reverend
Zairema as second growth, it was still too thick to see through and too
high to see over. The minute we entered it, it blocked out all else. Even
the rising sun was snarled in its foliage. On its floor grew wild ginger, and
taller than the ginger were the ginger lilies, and above the ginger lilies
hung the wild yam vines, and over the wild yam vines waved the bamboos, and looking down on the bamboos were the sissoo trees, and up the
sissoo trees grew the stag moss, and higher than the stag moss were the
teak trees, and dwarfing the teak trees were the great banyans, and from
the great banyans descended snaky air roots to the jungle floor. Shmuel
knew the Mizo names and uses of still other plants. The tendrils of a bush
we had passed made an excellent broom. When roasted, the edible ker-
nels of that stalk blew up like popcorn. These fluffy fibers filled pillows
and mattresses. You could fashion hoops for children's games from the
huge pods of that tree and a swing from the vine growing next to it. Here

Arriving in Mizoram. Avichail, in a skullcap, his back to the camera, is being greeted by Eliezer Sela. Jeremiah Hnamte, carrying bags, is behind him.

Above: Avichail giving a lesson in the Shalom Zion synagogue. Rivka Sela is his translator.

Right: An Aizawl street scene. Note the "Zion Hardware Store" sign behind the policeman.

Below: Aizawl from Zai's balcony.

A discussion in the synagogue.

A B'nei Menashe family in Kawzawl.

A Mizoram landscape. The foreground is jungle. The lighter patches farther off are *jhum* land.

Yitzhak (right), Shmuel (left), and the author on the way to Doliana's house.

Darnghaka (right) and Ngakhuma sitting on a bed of winnowed rice.

A street in a Mizo village. The house in the middle is of traditional bamboo-and-thatch construction. It stands on a downward slope, its rear stilts higher than its front ones.

Dancing "Enter, Enter Zion" at the CIPC office. From left to right: Darkapi, Lalchhanhima Sailo, Yosi Hualngo, and Sailo's wife.

The delegates to the CIPC Referendum voting themselves a lost tribe.

Stuck in the mud on the way to Lianpui. From left to right: Shmuel, Yitzhak, and Moya.

Neihhrima helping Yosi Hualngo to dress for the sacrifice in Lianpui. George Lawma looks on.

Lalbiakliana explaining the red sea song.

Liana in his priestly garments in our hotel room in Champhai.

Left: Lianpuisuaka (right) and his brother Piangrangchhuna.
Courtesy of Yosi Hualngo.

Below: Lianpuisuaka's will. Note the effaced words written in ballpoint pen, and in a different hand, in a number of lines.

The Khuplams' yard in Saikul. Mrs. Khuplam has her back to the camera. Dr. Khuplam is standing in the doorway.

Above: Dr. Milui Khuplam Lenthang. *Courtesy of Shlomo Gangte.*

Right: Mrs. Khuplam and the author in the Thangjoms' apartment in Imphal.

Zankothang Haokip, the buffalo herder (left), and Thintang Lenthang talking to Yitzhak.

Laokhalet Haokip, the village chief, dancing like a great bird.

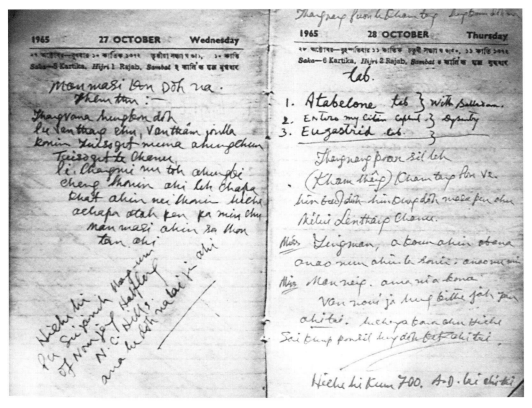

Two pages of Dr. Khuplam's diary from October 27–28, 1965. The Pu Vanthang *themthu* appears on the left-hand page. A note at the bottom records that the informant was Seijaneh Langhun of Namjong village in the North Cachar Hills. At the top of the right-hand page are medical prescriptions. *Courtesy of Shlomo Gangte.*

was the jungle spinach I had eaten, and these leaves were for rubbing on wounds, and those could be blown like a horn, and the roots of that tree were good to eat. From bamboo could be made, besides a house, a sturdy walking stick. Borrowing a machete-like knife called a *dao* from the little haversack on our guide's shoulder, Shmuel cut a rattan cane for me with a few sharp strokes. He had learned these things as a boy in Aizawl. In those days, the jungle grew right into the city.

For the first time I understood the old Mizo practice of "clearing the road." Paths like this were the lifelines of a village. Left untended, they were soon choked by the jungle. Failure to maintain them cut a village off from its rice fields, its hunting grounds, other villages; without new paths there was no fresh land to *jhum*. The priest chanting, "Here we come, you who block our way, above the road, below the road, move aside," was not performing an occult rite. He was protecting a crew of *dao* wielders hacking a route across a slope infested with snakes, thorny creepers, biting ants, clinging leeches, stinging centipedes, and tarantulas — the defensive weapons of the *huais*. "Flee those up there, flee those down there, flee, flee, vipers and all the biters," he had chanted. "Manmasi's sons are coming."

The path dropped toward a streambed at the bottom of the ravine and crossed it on a spur. Then the uphill climb began. We walked in silence. Apart from the shrill of the *nirleng* and the *tu-tu-tu* of a cloud-swimmer bird, the jungle was quiet. I had never thought of jungles that way. I had imagined them as noisy as zoos. But the Mizo jungle was hunted out. The big game — the elephants, the tigers, the rhinos, the bears — was all gone. So were the lemurs and the gibbons, shot out of the trees. The smaller animals were vanishing too. Shmuel pointed out a trap for them concealed in the brush. It was made of a pole resting on the fulcrum of a notched log, its shorter end tied to a noose staked to the ground. The bait, attached to the stake, was reached through the noose, which swung up with a pheasant or squirrel when the stake was dislodged. Once, a Lushai warrior who wished after death to avoid the bleak underworld of Mi-thi-khua and reach the happy hunting ground of Pial-ral had to take in his lifetime, besides a human head, an elephant, a black bear, a sambar, a barking deer, a wild boar, a mythun, a king cobra, and an eagle. Now, only poachers like Moya's friends could hope to see any of these. The keys to heaven had passed to the Christian ministers.

We reached the top of the ridge and followed a path along it. Here the village of Buolawng had stood. Nothing remained. It had rotted back into earth like the leavings in a compost pile. An archeologist would find only the stone altar built by Chala's followers for their biblical sacrifices. That was somewhere off in the jungle to our left. Our guide had heard of it but never seen it.

We headed downhill again. The jungle wall thinned. Then we stepped through it. A valley lay in front of us. Harvested *jhum* fields ran down its steep sides. Wan against the green hills, they looked like Alpine meadows before a first snow.

We skirted one of them. Its ears of rice had been cut close to the top, leaving the headless stalks standing. At its bottom the field leveled off and then dropped to another field. Our guide hallooed down this. He spoke to Shmuel, who shaded his eyes and stared. After a while, Shmuel said, "I see his basket."

I followed his stare. At first I saw nothing. Then a basket appeared among the rice stalks. Next came a blue-and-red stocking cap. Beneath the cap were a face and a khaki shirt. It was Darnghaka, climbing the lower field to greet us. A second man went on working there. He moved among the ripe stalks, seizing the tops with one hand and lopping them off with a small sickle. With every few flicks of the sickle he tossed what he had seized into a basket on his back.

Darnghaka's basket was half full. Strapped to his body, it was the regulation Mizo carrying gear, round on top and tapering gracefully to a small, square bottom. He shook our hands without removing it. "So!" he said. "I saw you fellows on TV." He, too, had watched Sailo's Referendum. He seemed to consider our presence at it sufficient explanation for our turning up in his field, about which he asked no questions.

Of course, it was difficult to tell with Mizos. They were not an outwardly expressive people. What might appear to be a lack of curiosity or emotion was often just a sense of tact. But there was a gravity about Darngakha. Perhaps it came from his vision. Once in his life he had been touched by the Spirit. That singularity was its validation. Had he been deluded or self-seeking or disturbed, it surely would have happened again. But the Spirit came and moved on, choosing and dropping him with the same sublime caprice. "It was all in God's honor," he remarked, with none of the pride, or resentment at being passed by, that I had sensed in Gideon Ray. "We are only his messengers."

Actually, there was more than one vision. Like the tremors before an earthquake, there were little ones first. The big one came in April 1951. Lying down for an afternoon nap, he had lapsed into a dream, from which he did not wake for three whole days. (This must have been the time Ramsiami tried bringing back his spirit.) At one point an angel spoke to him. He never saw it, because it covered him with its wings as a brooding hen covers its chicks. He only heard its voice. The angel told him that Armageddon was near. "I will save only Jerusalem," the angel said. "You must go there to be saved."

The angel did not tell Darnghaka that the Mizos were Israel. That happened later, when he was on the road to Silchar with Sankhuma and Dothanga. Then the angel came again. The new revelation struck him with great force. He was eager to return to Buolawng and tell the elders. He felt pregnant with God's word. "I was like a woman carrying a baby," he said. "The Mizos were my children."

He was seated on a heap of threshed paddy, a small man in faded brown corduroys and what looked like suspenders but were the shoulder straps of the basket he had slipped off. The paddy lay in a shaded storage bin whose low bamboo walls reached halfway to a thatch roof supported by wooden posts. The ground around it was littered with chaff. Darnghaka and his partner, Ngakhuma, threshed the rice by treading on it and winnowed the grain on a canvas sheet that they snapped up and down as if airing a blanket.

The UPC elders were not totally surprised. As far back as 1945, a Hmar named Zakaithanga had been told from heaven that Manmasi was Manasseh. The elders appointed a committee of seven men, two of them, Chala and Suakliana, "Bible scholars." They went to Hrangliana, a Hmar expert on the past. Hrangliana told them the Hmar used to chant:

> When we celebrate the feast,
> The great big water was parted sideways.

Nor was this the only point of resemblance between old Hmar customs and the Bible. For example, the Hmar practiced engagement before marriage, as did the Israelites. The Hmar confined their women after childbirth, and the Israelites did too. Homosexuals were punished by both peoples. Both left a corner of their fields unharvested so that the poor could find food. In both it was the elders who interpreted the laws. Chala and Suakliana had looked these things up in the Bible.

I didn't bother to tell Darnghaka they were Torrancisms. In any event, he was now engaged in a friendly dispute with Nghakuma, who had put down his sickle and joined us. Ngakhuma was Suakliana's son, and he was certain that an angel had told Chala to keep the laws of Moses. Darnghaka was dubious about this. "But how else would we have known we had to keep them?" Ngakhuma asked. "Did your angel tell you that?"

Darnghaka admitted that his angel had not.

It was Chala who persuaded the villagers to perform the Old Testament sacrifices. Nghakuma's father was one of two men chosen to officiate. The other was Thuama. Priestly robes were made for them according to instructions in the Book of Exodus. The sacrifices continued up to the time of the Insurgency. Suakliana's garments were burned with the village. Nghakuma thought Thuama's were in the possession of his son Mansamna.

Darnghaka's vision on the way to Silchar was his last. He had no idea why the visions stopped. "They just did," was all he could say.

He let some rice grains trickle through his fist.

"Sometimes," he said, "I've felt the whole thing was a catastrophe."

What else could being embraced by an angel be?

But he didn't mean that. "No one understood us," he said. "The CID was angry. They said, 'How could you organize an emigration movement to Israel without government consent?'" He was called in for questioning. "Then the MNF came along and said we were lazy and wanted Israel to take care of us. So! We didn't convince many people."

"But you did," I told him. "Here are two of them." I pointed to Yitzhak and Shmuel. "They're in Israel because of you. So are hundreds of others. You made history."

Darnghaka said nothing. Perhaps he was thinking the angel had told him that history was ending, not being made. He fastened his basket to its shoulder straps, eighty-six years old and returning to his harvest. Lazy! You could tell that the insult still rankled.

Nghakuma stayed behind. He, too, had had a vision he wanted to share with us. It occurred in 1965, a year before Buolawng was torched. The archangel Michael appeared to him, "dressed like a soldier," Ngakhuma said. "Look to your right!" Michael commanded, and Ngakhuma looked to his right and saw a land rising at the end of the sky. The land was Mizoram. Indian soldiers were looting and burning it. "Regard the world!" Michael said. The world was dark with smoke. "Because you are Israel," Michael said, "you will be the light of the world." Then Nghakuma saw a light shine forth from Mizoram and pierce the darkness. And Michael said, "Look to the north!" And Nghakuma looked to the north and saw . . .

I wasn't listening. I was looking at a *zouzon*. The *zouzon* was the national flower of Mizoram. Although few Mizos tended flower gardens, I had seen this one planted in front of homes and had heard a song about it at the YMA jamboree. It was said to keep away *huais*. Its tall red stalks fluttered with velvet-ribboned petals like the fins of tropical fish. "I have multiplied visions," God told the prophet Hosea, and He had not yet even been to Mizoram.

⚜

We walked back to Ratu through the jungle and went to Mansamna's house to ask about Thuama's robe. Mansamna, a genial schoolteacher, did not take his father's career as an Old Testament priest very seriously. The garment in question, he said, had long ago been torn up for rags. Like most of Chala's followers, Thuama had stayed in the Church of God. He did not go over to Judaism when it came from Manipur.

I was tired and went to bed early, crawling under the mosquito netting in the Forest Rest House. Several hours into sleep I was awakened by a strange sound. It was not rain, because none was drumming on the tin roof. It was not a motor, because none could be running at this hour.

It was the wind. I had forgotten the sound of pure, empty wind. I dressed and slipped outside quietly to avoid waking Shmuel and Yitzhak.

The moon was out again. The sleeping village lay below. The river valley out toward Manipur had overflowed its banks in a flood of fog. The wind was coming from the northeast. A stiff, dry breeze, it blew steadily without gusting, as if pacing itself in the knowledge that it still had far to go. It remembered the way, which it had not taken for many a month: down from the high Tibetan plateau, across the valley of the Brahmaputra, over the Naga and the Kuki and the Lushai hills, low on the delta of the Ganges, piling up waves on the Bay of Bengal to Ceylon, the Andamans, Sumatra.

For six months it had blown the other way, carrying the monsoon rains to Asia. Now, while I slept, it had turned. Once, in the great ports of the Orient, this was the moment the berthed ships had waited for. In Quilon and Cranganore and Calicut, in Malacca and Pelambang and Canton and Foochao, they had sat low in the water, their holds crammed with spices, sugar, silks, incense, camphor, porcelain, cotton prints, dyed goods, parrots, ivories, bamboo, lacquerware, bound for Muscat, Hormuz, Siraf, Basra, Baghdad, Dhofar, Aden. At last they could set sail for home.

I was still taking on cargo.

There was no Lost Tribe in it. I had found nothing to confirm a connection between the Mizos and ancient Israel. None of the evidence pointing to it had stood up. Even its most tantalizing item, the red sea song, could be dismissed. If this song was Hmar, and Hrangliana knew only the two lines of it quoted by Darnghaka, the whole thing was a soap bubble, especially since these lines most likely referred to the Tuipui River, down which the Hmar had migrated from the Chin Hills. Whatever "parting of the big water" took place had been near Champhai, not in Egypt. All the biblical extras — fire by day, and cloud by night, and enemies drowned, and a sister of Moses — had accrued like barnacles when the belief in Lost Tribehood began making waves after World War II.

It was no accident that this had started with the Hmar. Whether a real ancestor or a mythical eponym, Manmasi came from Hmar tradition. Although the name had spread southward as Manasa or Manasia long before being equated with the biblical Manasseh by Zakaithanga, it had remained better known in the north and was unfamiliar to the Chin in Burma. And yet it was the key to the whole story. It was Zakaithanga who had primed Darnghaka for his vision. He and the establishment of the state of Israel in 1948. News of that event must have penetrated even a remote place like Buolawng. It would have been the villagers' first intimation, though they knew nothing yet about Jews, that the people of the Bible still existed and were living in their land. This was something the missionaries hadn't told them.

The UPC, founded in Mizoram in 1949, was the largest of a number of Christian denominations to have grown out of the revival movements that periodically swept the Lushai Hills during British rule. There had been mass revivals in 1906, in 1913, in 1919, and in 1935, each more frenzied than the one before. Christians gathered in great hymn-singing "love feasts"; bands of preaching evangelists walked from village to village; recipients of the spirit sang, danced, drummed, laid on hands, spoke in tongues, had visions. Visions had always been a part of Lushai religion, its one form of free expression independent of sacrifice and priestly ritual. There had been specifically Christian visions as early as 1901, when a man named Darphawka saw in a trance two great lights that came from across the sea. Soon afterward the Welsh Baptist David Evan Jones and the Scots Presybterian Edwin Rolands came to preach the Gospel, and Darphawka was honored as a prophet.

Both the Baptists in the south and the Presbyterians in the north, the first two established churches in Mizoram, had mixed feelings toward revivalism. They recognized its potency and feared its disruptiveness. On at least one occasion, it had to be quelled by British troops. This happened in Kelkang, where local revivalists prophesied the end of the world, persuaded the population to stop cultivating the *jhums* because God would rain food from the sky, and drove the local minister from his pulpit. A detachment of Ghurkas arriving from Aizawl to restore order found the villagers on the verge of starvation.

The *mi hlim* were equally ambivalent toward the Christian establishment. It had brought them the word of God — but in a milk-tea English version that substituted a new elite of British-trained pastors and government clerks for the old one of priests and chiefs. The traditional Lushai religious festivals had been rowdy affairs, marked by gorging, partying, large amounts of *zu* drinking, and a general loss of social inhibition. The *mi hlim* sought their emotional equivalent in Christianity. Sometimes it was hard to tell which influenced which. In an account of a "sudden resurgence of heathenism" in the Lushai Hills in 1908, the Welsh missionary J. Meirion Lloyd related that this had begun with an old Lushai song, set to new words believed to have been sung by a jungle spirit. This song, Lloyd wrote, "spread like wild fire to all parts of the hills. Amazing manifestations of feeling accompanied the singing — almost as though the Revivals were being parodied. Great feasts were held during which the young men and girls danced in ecstasy. These demonstrations were made in every village. The cause of Christ seemed doomed in Lushai." The "heathen resurgence" collapsed during the 1911 famine, when the Christian churches alone distributed emergency relief.

The *mi hlims'* apocalyptic views were characteristic of Christian revivalism everywhere, just as they were of many societies in radical transition. The world was expected to end when it *had* ended — when an old way of life was dead or dying and a new one was still in the throes of birth. The hysteria that gripped Kelkang, like Darnghaka's "big vision," bore the coded message: Yes, Jesus is the Way . . . and since this Way has been the ruin of everything we knew, it is time for the wonders and the flames in which, according to the Way's holy book, everything will be consumed.

The Australian anthropologist Myer Samra had been right. It was their unconscious uncertainty about Christianity that accounted for the Mizos' Lost Tribe fever. Psychologically, they had a problem. They were indebted to the Christian church. It had brought them great benefits: education, modern health care, an association with a British ruling class that favored them over their non-Christian neighbors. Unlike many so-called primitive peoples demoralized by their encounter with Western culture, the Mizos had kept their pride intact by introjecting the colonial religion so deeply that it seemed to come entirely from within themselves. It had enabled them, a devoutly Christian people surrounded by Moslems, Hindus, and Buddhists, to retain the sense of superiority over their *vai* neighbors that once came from their fighting prowess. Former headhunters and stalkers and slayers of animals in the jungle and upon the altar, they had become one of the best educated people in India. They did well in the civil service, *jhumed* their rice on peaceful hillsides, tended shops with names like Zion Hardware and Jerusalem Minimarket, and listened to Sunday sermons. They even believed that New Testament love was a Lushai virtue. Was it not the same as *tlawmngainha?*

Yet deep in their hearts the Mizos knew Christianity had killed something vital. Had they read the Hebrew Bible, they might have recognized what this was. The missionaries did recognize it, for they avoided teaching the Old Testament and delayed translating it for decades. Knowingly or not, they feared its dangers. Here was a book in which there were no saintly apostles but real men and women who fought, killed, lusted, took slaves and prisoners, and worshiped God with animal blood. And were God's chosen! Only when these stories began appearing in their own language could the Mizos read for the first time about the people Jesus came from — about Abraham, Isaac, Jacob, and Joseph, and the twelve tribes, and how ten were lost, one of which was Manasseh. Suppose — just suppose — that Manasseh was Manmasi and they were his lost descendants. Then this, the world of Genesis, Leviticus, Joshua, Judges, and Kings, had all been theirs, and the Christianity that brought them the Bible had destroyed nothing. On the contrary, it had restored them to their truest selves.

It was not surprising that this belief was so popular. It was the perfect solution. And it was a purely indigenous one. The British missionaries had indeed had nothing to do with it. Nowhere in anything written by or about them was there a single reference to the possibility of the Mizos being a Lost Tribe. The idea had never occurred to them.

Indirectly, of course, anything learned from them could become "proof" of Israelite origins. Edwin Rowlands told an instructive story of how, coming one day to a Lushai village in which no Englishman had ever set foot and in which no Christian was to be found, he overheard two boys singing a hymn about Jesus that he himself had translated into Mizo! Looking back as adults, these boys could honestly have sworn that Jesus was known in their village before Christianity came to it, just as Darkapi could swear that the Entering Zion dance predated the missionaries. Such convictions, alas, meant nothing.

The same was true of all the other "proofs" — circumcision, four-cornered altars, seven days of mourning, a God called Ya, and all the rest. Examined closely, every one of these was trivial, inexact, or based on hearsay. A four-cornered altar was about as unusual as a four-cornered table, and the seven days of Mizo mourning turned out to have also been three or five or almost any odd number. No Mizo had ever seen a circumcision, just as none had ever heard a prayer to Ya. It was always I-was-told-it-by-So-and-So-who-heard-it-from-Such-and-Such-who-got-it-from-I-can't-remember-his-name.

It needn't have been a hoax on anyone's part, not even on Sailo's. When all was said and done, he too was doing history's work. There wasn't a people worthy of the name that didn't have its founding legend. The Kuki-Chin-Mizos were still looking for theirs. In the not distant past they had been an amalgam of culturally and linguistically related tribes that warred with one another and lacked all sense of unity. A Ralte was a Ralte and a Paite was a Paite, just as Lombards were Lombards and Tuscans were Tuscans in medieval Italy, or even just Milanese and Florentines. The creation of Mizoram in the wake of the MNF uprising had forged a Mizo identity while excluding the Kukis and the Chins. Sailo had found a way to count them in. Laughable or dangerous, he aspired to be their Garibaldi.

There was nothing unique about the B'nei Menashe either. Judaizers in remote places were an old story. Some formed major episodes in Jewish history. The mysterious kingdom of Khazaria that held sway along the Volga between the eighth and tenth centuries was one of these. Its Turkic royal house was converted, according to the medieval Hebrew poet Yehuda Halevi's *Book of the Kuzari*, by a single rabbi coming from afar like Avichail, after which it propagated Judaism among its subjects. The Falashas of Ethiopia were considered by many scholars to be a similar case, the descendants of medieval Christians who, despite no or minimal contact with the outside Jewish world, adopted Old Testament beliefs and practices. Small groups living or claiming to live as Jews in the absence of a known Jewish history, like the Sefwe of Ghana, the Abayudaya of Uganda, the B'nei Abraham of Peru, and the Black Hebrews of the United States could be found all over the world. They owed their existence to a complex of factors: charismatic leaders convinced that the Old Testament was truer than the New; the desire to be religiously differentiated from their neighbors; the attractiveness of being linked to an international people deemed wealthy and caring of their own; the hope of immigrating to Israel. The B'nei Menashe belonged to a larger picture.

So did I. Of course, the unexpected could still happen. Yosi Hualngo or Liana's priests from Burma might yet surprise me. As it stood, however, I was one more unsuccessful Lost Tribe hunter.

My face to the wind out of Asia, I was not distressed by this. Although it would have been grand to come home with a unicorn on a leash, merely chasing one was good fun too. There was a satisfaction in solving a puzzle even if the solution was mundane.

Not a light shone in the houses of Ratu. At three in the morning I could have been the only person awake in Mizoram. The great river of fog out toward Manipur was still rising in the moonlight. It was a perfect night for cloud swimming.

⚜ 7 ⚜

To Lianpui and Back

But the wind in Ratu was just a trial run. By the time we set out for Champhai, two days later, the wet weather was back. Halfway there we were hit by a cloudburst. It broke without warning, like a pot boiling over, one moment a lazy drizzle and the next the world's highest waterfall.

It fell over a large area, slicing off chunks of jungle all the way to Champhai. Trees writhed in fresh mudslides, roots gasping in air. Through the bamboo sluices outside the villages, the jungle plumbing used for bathing and laundry, water gushed as though from a broken main. The Tuipui River licked its wooden bridge.

Yitzhak won his bet with Shmuel. Liana was waiting for us in Champhai with his party of two from Burma. They had gone twice to the Holiday Home Hotel to ask for us and had left a message that they were at Zana's.

Shmuel went to get them. Only one of the two was a priest. His name was Ningzenawng, and he spoke only Chin Paite and did not make a brilliant impression. He had a hang-jaw mouth and eyes that jerked from speaker to speaker belatedly, as if he were concentrating so hard on the uncomprehended words of each that he failed to notice they'd stopped. He looked as astounded by his surroundings in the Holiday Home Hotel as he might have been by the lobby of the Waldorf. Yet once we got down to business, he gained confidence. Though not your village-intellectual type of priest, he was every bit the professional Liana had promised us.

The second man was Kawbzedawr. Perhaps Liana had brought him so that we could meet a fellow Jew, or perhaps he had wanted to meet us. He had been preaching Judaism in the Chin Hills and had won, so he said, hundreds of souls for it, and he sat beneath the dome of his blue skullcap with his hands folded agreeably over his stomach like a rabbi waiting to give his weekly sermon. His Judaism, however, was not quite rabbinical. Although he obeyed the biblical commandments and did not believe in Jesus, he did believe in "Joshua." This was because Jesus belonged "to the religion of the Greeks," whereas Joshua was "he who was born in Bethlehem." Jesus was dead; Joshua would return as the Messiah. It was not clear whether Kawbzedawr was talking about two different people or a single multiple personality.

The two had just come from celebrating Mim Kut, the old pre-Christian harvest festival equated by some Mizos with the Feast of Tabernacles. Indeed, said Kawbzedawr, Mim Kut had once been held for seven days like the biblical holiday. Nowadays, it was only three, because no one could afford so much food and drink. Apart from eating, *zu* drinking, singing and dancing, there were no special rituals. No sacrifices were performed, and priests like Ningzenawng had time off like everyone else.

Ningzenawng belonged to the Hualkawng clan and had inherited his position from his father. He was a "private priest" and dealt only with individuals. Public sacrifices, such as an annual one in which a pig was offered "for everyone," were not in his domain. The two positions were distinct and their holders wore different robes — red for the private priest, white for the public one.

Ningzenawng's repertoire included twelve sacrifices. Most were for treating illness. If a complaint was caused by a *huai*, for example, he went to the jungle, picked a spot near running water, and built an altar by erecting four corner posts of forked branches, laying bamboo poles between them, and making a platform of cross-poles covered with green leaves. Then he slaughtered a pig or chicken — the first with a bamboo spear to the heart, the second by wringing its neck — and chanted. This sacrifice was known as *gunram*. He also performed a "doorpost sacrifice" called *kawnglai*; *sumtawng*, a sacrifice for the health of animals and crops; a sacrifice to counter bad dreams; and a *zu*-making sacrifice. Each had its own name and chant.

I asked whether he would let us hear the *gunram* chant. He had no objection. In fact, he looked pleased by the cassette deck placed on the table. The only tapes he had ever heard were of popular singers and musicians. He liked being in their company.

He shut his eyes as if to picture a jungle altar. Then he threw back his head and released a long, high note, pushing off on it as far as it would go: *heyyyy-y-y-y-y-y!* A call for attention from a god or votary, it made the *vai* desk clerk of the hotel leave his post and come to the entrance of the dining room. Ningzenawng let it ring and slowly fade like a gong, took a breath, and shifted on the glide of the last long strains to a rapid incantation. Now the words ran nipping at each other's heels, the syllables *ah-mee* recurring. Bearing down on each *ah*, he rose a tone higher on it: ta-ta AH-*mee*, tum-tum AH-*mee*, tak-tak AH-*mee*, tu-tu AH-*mee*, tam-tam AH-*mee*. . . . His voice, raw and plangent, seemed less to beseech a higher power than to cajole a stubborn or indolent one whose resistance had to be worn down. Tee-tee AH-*mee*, tay-tay AH-*mee*, tie-tie AH-*mee*. . . . He kept it up, a fretful bellows breathing on coals that might catch fire if he didn't stop too soon. Even when the *ah-mees* ceased, the rapid strokes of syllables persisted. Then they ended abruptly on a long ringing note like the first: *heyyyy-y-y-y-y-y!*

And perhaps it was merely the old religion's Mincha murmur, sounds so old and worn that they signified nothing.

No one could tell me what all the words meant. Even Liana had trouble with them. By the time the double translation from Chin Paite and Mizo reached English, I understood only that *ami* referred to "some kind of being." Most of the chant, Liana said, was a list of places.

It was not until reaching Imphal that I was able to have the *gunram* chant translated from my tape. It came out as:

> O Being who lives at the great river
> O Being who lives at the riverbank,
> O Being who lives in the South,
> O Being who lives in the mountain wilderness,
> O Being who lives at Panghawk,
> O Being who lives at Tamchi,
> O Being who lives at Letlui,
> O Being who lives at Lolawn,
> [There were fifteen more lines like this]

Those that follow the elder kin, the younger kin,
Those whose names I have mistakenly not included,
Those whose names I have mistakenly included,
One by one, whom I am to redeem,
Whose arms I am to redeem —
The pains of the arms,
The pains of the loins —
I am here to redeem the running water.
Reached by day,
Reached by night,
I am unshackling this man's illness.
O my ancestors and my ancestresses!

The places mentioned were all in Burma. Although different from those in the Hotel Ritz document, they seemed to form a similar sequence of migration stops. At least this confirmed that the old chants had such formulas.

I asked who the "Being" of the chant was. Ningzenawng gaped. Liana said it was Pasian. All the chants were addressed to Pasian. Yet no one could point to the word in Ningzenawng's *gunram*. Kawbzedawr said, "This is because it is not God's real name. The real name of God cannot be said."

"You mean it's too holy?"

"Aw."

"Like God's name in the Bible?"

"Aw."

But this was no cause for excitement. Kawbzedawr was a Judaizer with an agenda of his own, and Ningzenawng for his part denied knowing any secret names of God. I believed him. Far from having been best preserved in the Chin Hills, the so-called Israelite elements in the old religion, I now was certain, had first been imagined in northern Mizoram and had never existed in Burma. Perhaps the whole Ya or Za belief had its roots in a phonetic confusion. All of Ningzenawng's chants started and ended with the same *heyyy-y-y-y-y-y*. Relaxing the tensed jaw at the end of them could have produced a *heyyy-y-y-y-y-ya*, which might have been heard as "O Ya" or "O Za."

It seemed a plausible explanation. In any event, when Ningzenawng's chants were translated in Imphal, neither Pasian nor Ya was in any of them. Other beings were. One chant went:

Hehluanu, Hehluanpa, Dahluanu, Dahluanpa,
It is you:
You who follow the sun and the moon,
You who grip the back and the belly,
The body's right, the body's left.
In the day and in the night,
Let it burst!
You will not take this man by force!
Like the luster of a precious stone,
Like the new sun rising,
Like the new moon rising,
I have retained this man's soul.

Nu and *pa*, I was told, were feminine and masculine endings, the dual aspects of jungle spirits named Hehlua and Dahlua. Ningzenawng was a typical southeast Asian shaman, charged with freeing his clients from the clutches of the *huais* and keeping their souls safely in their bodies. He officiated, he told us, only at sacrifices. Unlike an Old Testament priest, he did not rule on ritual matters. He had never heard of Manmasi or Manasa. He knew nothing about the tradition of circumcision. He knew no old stories or legends of ancient origins.

But he was enjoying himself immensely. "This is as good as the real thing!" he exclaimed after recording the last sacrifice, a *zu* blessing known as *banglung*. It was better than the real thing. He was a celebrity.

The time had come to settle accounts and give gifts. Before leaving Israel I had bought dozens of little items — key chains with menorahs and Stars of David, ceramic ashtrays with scenes of Jerusalem, miniature Psalm and prayer books, gilded mezuzah casings. I gave mezuzah casings to Liana and Ningzenawng and a miniature Torah scroll to Kawbzedawr. Liana stuck his gift in the pocket of his windbreaker and kept a hand there to make sure it stayed put. Ningzenawng palmed his wonderingly. I had told them it was a powerful charm against *huais*. Although without its parchment verses from the Bible a mezuzah had no such power, perhaps the *huais* would fail to realize this.

Kawbzedawr was visibly moved by his Torah scroll. He had been to a synagogue in Imphal and knew how to hold it by its tiny stanchions. He bowed and said rabbinically, *"Barukh se-natan mi-khuavo le-basar ve-dam."*

Had I heard right? Despite some garbled syllables, he had not only recited a Hebrew blessing, he had recited one so rare that the average Jew never said it in a lifetime, for it was to be uttered only in the presence of a potentate or king.

"Blessed is He who bestows His glory on flesh and blood."

"Thank you," I said, honored. "Where did you learn that?"

He was pleased that I had recognized it. "From a B'nei Menashe in Manipur."

Ningzenawng asked whether he and Kawbezedawr were still needed. If not, they would head back for Burma in the morning.

"Actually," I said to Shmuel, "why don't we ask Ninzenawng to come with us to Lianpui tomorrow? He can give us a professional opinion on Yosi's sacrifices. With all the food George bought, one more mouth to feed won't be a problem."

Ningzenawng, however, begged off. Walking to and from Burma was one thing. Cars were another. They made him sick.

"What about me?" little Liana piped up shyly.

It sounded like, "Hey, I'm a priest, too!"

We had forgotten that. And so Liana came with us the next day to Lianpui.

ᨭ

But we never made it to Lianpui the next day.

We set out in a heavy fog, following the route to Kelkang. Soon after climbing out of the Champhai Valley we passed two men walking on either side of the road. They were the rabbi and the priest, each with his haversack on his shoulder. They waved and were swallowed by the fog. Liana reckoned they had four more hours of walking to reach the Tiao. They would sleep away the rest of the day there and cross at night.

Liana was losing his shyness. No longer were his responses confined to brief murmurs. Now, I questioned him about traditional Chin Paite birth and death customs. There was nothing biblical about them. A baby, he said, was named on the third day after birth, when a bag or box was opened to release its spirit into the world. The coiled vine ceremony was performed only if the child was ill and on no particular day. The dead were mourned for three days, not seven. They were dressed in their best clothes and displayed to the accompaniment of singing, dancing, and gong playing. The day after the burial a feast was held.

Yet though he knew of no special reason to believe that he was descended from ancient Israelites, Liana believed it anyway. So, he said, did many Chin Paites. Perhaps this was why he didn't seem to mind that the old religion was dying even in Burma, since its soul would live on in the Bible after its body had perished. It was being replaced by Christianity. Despite being treated badly by the pro-Buddhist government, the Christians were thriving. People feared their hell more than the government's. "We'll be gone by the year 2000," Liana said of the old believers. He appeared to conceive of this date not as a real one two months distant but as a figure of speech for a relentlessly approaching future.

He had only one regret. There would be no one to bury him properly. That much at least was Jewish. *Who will say the Kaddish when I'm gone?*

We stopped for breakfast at Matloangi's tea stall in Dilkawn. Moya had eaten there before and was enamored of Matloangi. "Bee-yoo-dee-ful lay-dee," he repeated in English so often between Kelkang and Dilkawn that we were all in a state of pleasurable suspense. Both Yitzhak and Shmuel had a lively interest in Mizo girls and sometimes practiced Hebrew by discussing their physical attractions in their presence. Perhaps the prospect of a local beauty who might agree to come to Israel as a bride had been an incentive for joining me. Shmuel already had a candidate in Lunglei, a young lady he had been corresponding with. He hoped to visit her during our trip.

Matloangi was not beautiful and was missing some front teeth, but she and Moya had a fine time flirting, and her breakfast was a welcome change from the usual fare: fried pooris with a tasty chili-and-onion relish and a piping hot yellow chickpea porridge. The place was jumping. Men wrapped in blankets against the morning chill drank milk tea and talked loudly. A woman came over to tell Shmuel that her father was the first person in the area to decide the Mizos were Israel. This was in the 1950s. As no one was much interested in the idea at the time, he had remained a good Presbyterian.

From Dilkawn we drove to Khuangleng, near the Burmese border. Here, we had to make a decision. Our two hours of traveling from Champhai — twice the time George had said it would take to get all the way to Lianpui — had been on paved roads. The remaining sixteen kilometers, we now discovered, were on dirt track. The first five were a "secondary truck route" to the village of Sessih. The final eleven were "jeepable." Although Moya's Indian-made Maruthi had good springs and a sturdy chassis, its 800 cc. engine and rear-wheel drive were no jeep's. Moreover, what was passable before yesterday's downpour might not be so now. Even if we made it to Sessih, we might have to walk from there.

"What could Yosi and George have been thinking of?" I asked irritably.

"A cheaper place than Vanapa Hall," Yitzhak said.

Moya was for giving it a try. We careened down a rutted incline to the secondary truck route and started out with Burma on our left. The road was about three meters wide, with a steep drop on the downhill side. Old water from the uphill side had carved little gullies in it that were bridged with bamboo struts that rattled nervously beneath our wheels. New water ran along it before resuming its downward plunge, turning the surface to mud in some places and pitting it like a streambed in others. At each of these Moya got out of the car to study the lay of the land. Sometimes before traversing it he ordered us out, too.

We made Sessih in half an hour. The secondary truck route passed some houses and ended in a football field. Moya drove through the goal posts and stopped to ask about the rest of the way. It was, he was told, not much worse than what we had driven. He decided to go for it.

For a while all was well. The road, which ran at a steady downhill grade, even improved. Then it hit a level stretch in which water had collected in the troughs. The mud was deep and we had to get out and push while Moya jockeyed the car back and forth. Once, reversing with us in it, he spun his wheels, suddenly gained traction, and lurched into a gully through which water chuted down the mountain. Another foot and we would have been over the side.

We were the only vehicle. Now and then we passed villagers walking to Sessih. A group of men carrying hoes and shovels came by while we were pushing the Maruthi. No one offered to help. No one said hello or did more than shrug when asked about the road up ahead. I had never seen such unfriendly Mizos.

"That's because they know why we're coming," Shmuel said. He sounded morose. He wasn't looking forward to Lianpui or to the scene his arrival might touch off. He considered George and Yosi dangerous, "Burmese."

"I thought they were Mizos," I said.

"They're Hualngos."

The Hualngos, Shmuel explained, were the one Lushai tribe never to have joined the migration from the Chin Hills. While some lived on the Mizo side of the Tiao, most were still in Burma. They were, like everyone there, untrustworthy and hot-headed. George Lawma had once stabbed a B'nei Menashe in a quarrel. He had been unwelcome in the community ever since.

I swore at Shmuel's Mizo tact for not revealing this to me earlier. Then I swore at Yosi and George and at their "safe joint" — a Hualngo village whose inhabitants refused to talk to us because we had come to watch a pre-Christian sacrifice. The two of them could have slaughtered their goat in Aizawl and spared us all this mud.

We were stuck in it again. This time it was serious. The Maruthi's rear wheels were dug in to the hubcaps. Each time Moya gave the car gas, they just pawed deeper. We were thirty or forty yards into a quagmire that ran for another hundred; even if we managed to cross it, there were sure to be more like it before the road rose back up toward Lianpui. The only sensible course was to back out and turn around where we could. Continuing on foot while Moya drove back to Sessih was out of the question. He would never make it without us to push.

We broke off branches from the jungle, placed them beneath the wheels, and hurled ourselves at the car. The wheels spun wildly, spattering us with mud. Yitzhak shouted "One! Two! Three!" and we pushed again. A rear wheel caught a branch, moved the car, and lost traction. We put fresh branches beneath the wheels and pushed some more. Slowly we headed for Sessih's goal posts, running the same ground play over and over, picking up a few yards, held at the line of scrimmage, making another a small gain. Before each new charge Liana scrambled into the jungle, broke off branches, and passed them down to us. Looking like a festive welcome mat beneath the wheels, they were soon a tossed salad of mud, bark, and leaf. Moya steered and laughed at each shout of "Three!" He was having a whale of a time.

Filthy and exhausted, we made it back to Sessih by midafternoon. There, we paid a boy to take a note to Lianpui. "Dear Yosi and George," said my English postscript to Shmuel's Mizo. "You chose one hell of a place for your sacrifice. Couldn't you have told us we needed a 4×4? We'll look for one tomorrow. This better be worth it!"

From there we drove back to Khuangleng. Now Burma was on our right. Although the Tiao was hidden between two ridges, Rih Lake, the watery gateway to Mi-thi-khua, the village of the dead, was visible beyond the second ridge, dark beneath a gray sky. It formed a nearly perfect circle, as perfect and dark as death itself.

According to old Lushai legend, Rih Lake was the first obstacle reached by the departed soul on its way to Mi-thi-kua, a place poor, shadowy, and lacking in substance. Once it crossed the lake, the soul came to a junction of seven roads. Here stood the home of Pupawla, the first man on earth to have died. Pupawla guarded the junction and shot pellets at the souls that tried to pass. It was their task to elude him and reach the Lunglo or Never-Feel-Again River, on whose banks grew the flower called the *hawilo*, or look-back-no-more. Drinking the Lunglo's waters and tucking a *hawilo* behind one ear, the dead lost all desire to return to the land of the living. Those hit by Pupawla's pellets had to remain in Mi-thi-khua. Only the soul unscarred by them could continue to Pial-ral, the abode of bliss.

Though small, Rih Lake was treacherous. Once a year, as though receiving a foul greeting from the underworld, its clear waters grew cloudy with mud mysteriously erupting from its bottom. There were stories of people drowning in it. Once, in the old days, Shmuel said, a party of hunters mortally wounded an elephant and pursued it to the lake's shores. As elephants were hunted in teams, it was customary for the first man mounting the carcass to be credited with the kill — a highly sought honor, since slaying an elephant was a requirement for entering Pial-ral. The hunters ran toward the shore, and the swiftest, reaching the dying elephant first, leaped onto its back as it plunged into the lake. Refusing to abandon it lest he forfeit his claim, he chanted his victory song as he sank into the water.

In Khuangleng we found the owner of a Nissan Patrol truck who agreed to take us to Lianpui in the morning. Then, stopping for tea at Matloangi's, we drove back to Champhai. There was no closer place with a hotel.

⚜

The Nissan Patrol was Indian army surplus. It had no springs. Sandwiched in the front seat between the owner and his assistant, I could see the road through the floor. There was no switch, and the engine had to be jump-started. It was killed by a homemade choke, a wire sticking out from beneath the broken fuel gauge. This was yanked by the assistant each time the Nissan coughed and emitted billows of smoke. He then opened the hood, stood on the front fender, and manually primed the fuel pump. When the pump was primed, the truck was jump-started again. If it came to rest on level ground and could not be rolled by the release of the brake, its owner bounced up and down in his seat while working the gas pedal. Vigorously performed, this maneuver bucked us forward enough to turn over the engine.

In Sessih we found the boy who had taken our note to Lianpui. He had given it to Yosi and George and reported that they were waiting for us.

We headed on. The Nissan forged ahead, slithering ominously when the mud thinned to a fine film like an oil slick. The worst part was the jolting. After a while my stomach felt stomped on. But the Maruthi would never have made it. The muddy stretch we had turned back at was far from the worst. It took us an hour and a quarter to reach a sign in the middle of the jungle that said, WEL-COME TO LIANPUI.

George Lawma was waiting there. He must have heard us grinding up the road long beforehand, because the Nissan was as noisy as a bulldozer. Now, facing its roar, he made hand signals like a ground controller's. *Hello! Go slow! This way! Follow me!* Plumply, he turned and trotted ahead of us through the streets of the village in his gray suit, his paisley tie flopping over one shoulder. A few barefoot children ran beside him. The adults paid no attention.

We stopped by a house with a tin roof. Yosi Hualngo was standing outside it. This was the moment Shmuel had feared.

He needn't have. No knives were drawn when he stepped out of the car. In fact, he could just as well not have been there. Yosi and George ignored him completely. Yosi spoke some words of welcome, and the co-author of the Grand Mizo-English Dictionary rendered them freely into three languages:

"Salom! *Chibai!* How-de-do! Sorry for your getting all stuck up. We thought you understood the need for a four-wheeler of your choice. So! Being late for an important date, you will excuse Mr. Yosi for departing to prepare the sacrification. Our program begins after your grub. First number: Q and A with yours truly."

Yosi went off to prepare the sacrifice, and George led us to our grub.

The house had a Mizo main room with a table by one wall and a hearth and shelves along another. Long gourds were drying above the hearth. A man squatted next to them, smoking a cigarette. Another sat on a crate, looking at nothing. Two more men were dishing out food. When they finished, one carried the dishes to the table, and the other sat down with a cup of tea.

"Where is everybody?" I asked.

"Everybody who?" George said.

"Your gents from Burma."

"They're here."

"Where?"

"You're looking at 'em."

"*These* men?"

"What's wrong with them?"

"There are only four."

"The best informers we could find."

"George! I gave you four thousand rupees for transportation from Burma. I gave you sixteen hundred for food. You said you were bringing lots of people."

"We did our best," George said plaintively. "It's harvest time. Folks are out in their *jhums*. They just finished Mim Kut. They're too busy for happenings."

"But you knew that before coming down here."

"The date was set by you."

"You had enough money to bring these four men in a limousine to Aizawl and put them up at the Hotel Chief."

"With a goat?"

It was useless to argue. The money was now part of George's honorarium. We finished our grub and went to a back room, where the four informers were waiting on a bench.

There *was* something wrong with them. I could tell at a glance.

It was clear from the way none of them looked at me. By now I had interviewed dozens of Mizos. Even the bashful ones kept their eyes on you when you spoke. They tried to read in your face what your foreign words and intonations did not disclose. Their eyes fingered you like blind men.

Not these eyes. They avoided contact.

George introduced the four, and I asked each for his age and residence. Only two were from Burma. They were Neihhrima, seventy, and Hrangchina, seventy-six. Hrangchina was the man who'd been sitting on the crate; he was thin, with a broad forehead and a narrow, pointy chin, a triangle balanced on a stick. Neihhrima had the quizzical mug of an old monkey that wonders what life in the trees has been all about. After a while he shut his eyes and fell asleep.

The other two were from Lianpui: Huallotahuangza, fifty-one, a lanky fellow, and Riliana, sixty-two. Riliana was smoking another cigarette. He had a hard, sullen face. Huallotahuangza looked like someone just found with another man's wallet in his pocket. All four looked guilty of something. They sat on the bench like old hoods picked up in a police sweep.

It was Q and A time. George took some folded pages from the pocket of his gray suit and read from the first page like a catechist: "What is the exact name of your God according to your fathers?"

No one answered. George looked at Riliana. Riliana said as though reciting the alphabet, "Apram, Tera, Akupta, Sinai, Iaksak, Jordan, Babylon, Himaloi, Tibet, Khuanu, Khuahpu, Khuavang. . . ."

He had answered a different question on George's list. George pretended not to notice and asked, "How do you know this?"

"This I know," Riliana said, "from my fathers and my fathers' fathers."

Yitzhak leaned toward me. "It's a put-up job," he said behind his hand.

Of course it was. George had even improved on the Hotel Ritz document. "Jordan" and "Babylon" were his own additions — unless they were afterthoughts of Yosi's.

I said, "Perhaps Riliana can tell us in what sacrifice he heard these names."

George put my request to Riliana. Riliana said something in a low voice. "Our informer here," George said, "says he heard them at the *khuangchawi.*"

I looked at Shmuel, who nodded to confirm this.

But the *khuangchawi* was not a sacrifice. It was a series of prestigious public feasts traditionally given by those who could afford to pay for the honor. Various sacrifices were performed in the course of it. Which of them was Riliana referring to?

Riliana could not say. He stared glumly at George's shiny shoes.

Then, remembering the correct answer to George's first question, he said, "In my father's time, no one was allowed to pronounce the name of God."

George pounced on the cue. "Would you like to hear it?" he asked me. "Go to Riliana, and he will whisper it in your ear."

He made it sound salacious.

I went to Riliana, who had risen from the bench. Cupping both hands to a mouth hot with cigarette smoke and chilis, he whispered, "Zya!"

It was too corny for words. There was no time for them anyway, because George was already asking the next question. "How did you treat the newborn baby?"

"We bathed it and passed it through a vine," Riliana said.

"What else?"

Riliana could not think of anything else. He didn't see Hrangchina prompting him with cutting movements of his hand. Huallotahuangza, who did, volunteered in Riliana's place. George summarized. "The baby boy is passed through the vine on the third day. On the eighth or ninth day a pretended cut is made in the foreskin. The baby's head is then combed with a porcupine quill. In Burma there still are places where this is done. It is called *bawrh keu*."

Yosi Hualngo had reappeared and stood listening, his lips tight, in the doorway.

George turned to the men on the bench. "Sometimes," he said, "a child is born circumcised. Who knows what that was called?"

No one did.

"An ancient. . . ."

"Penis!"

The word came in a chorus.

George shuffled his notes. "When two people met on the road to ask forgiveness from the trees and stones for clearing them," he asked, "what did they say?"

Neihhrima awoke and murmured dreamily, "Tera . . . Apram . . . Iasak. . . ."

George cut him short.

Yosi Hualngo walked away.

George called on Huallotahuangza, who answered, "When two people met to clear the road they said, 'We are coming, O trees, we are coming, O stones, we the children of Manmasi are coming. We do not do this because we are a cruel people, but because we must."

I asked whether he'd actually heard those words.

Neihrima answered for him. "Old people said them," he said.

"Did *you* hear them?"

Neihrima mumbled something.

"He says he did," George said.

"He said he didn't," said Shmuel.

George glared at Shmuel.

Riliana had something to say. He had suddenly remembered where the names starting with "Tera" came from. They weren't from the *khuangchawi.* They were from an old priest named Lianpuisuaka. Riliana had once asked him about the words in the old sacrifices. Riliana said, "We children had to watch from a distance. Even if we had been closer, we couldn't have understood what the priests were saying. I wanted to know what that was."

"And Lianpuisuaka told you?"

"Not at first. He said, 'Oh, what's the use! What good are the old chants? Everyone is worshiping the bearded man.'"

"The bearded man?"

"Jesus."

"If a person had an ulcer or a cancer," George asked, "what did the priest say?"

And so it went, Q and A with George Lawma and the Four Informers. It took an effort not to laugh. No wonder George had come back from Seattle. The bush leagues were more his speed.

Mine too. He had ripped me off for nearly $300.

And yet it was worth every penny. How often did you see a theory confirmed before your eyes? It was one thing to conclude that something was a crock. It was another to observe a feeding crocodile.

And I was curious about Yosi Hualngo. I wanted to know why he'd looked at George the way he did.

⚶

The goat to be sacrificed was small and white with black bags around its eyes, no doubt from sleeping badly. A shirtless young man in a motorcycle jacket led it by a rope to a field in back of the village. George strode after it in his gray suit, all three jacket buttons buttoned as usual. Liana, Shmuel, Yitzhak, the Four Informers, and a procession of children trailed after him. The rest of Lianpui was absent, represented by its opprobrium.

Yosi Hualngo was already in the field, hanging a *langlap* over an altar like the one described by Ningzenawng. A faggot of bamboo sticks lay beneath it, and green branches were stuck in the ground on either side. When the *langlap* was hung, he unfolded two sheets of white cotton, wound the smaller one around his head to make a turban, and wrapped himself in the other, adjusting its folds with Neihhrima's help. It looked like a costume for a school play.

Riliana and Huallotahuangza laid the goat on the ground and trussed its legs. Sprawled on its side, it nibbled greedily at the grass. The idiocy of its appetite was appalling. Or was this frantic eating, the last meal before the execution, the wise brain's lie to the terrified body that it was just an ordinary moment in an ordinary day?

The two men placed the goat on the altar, and Yosi sprinkled it with water from a bowl. Holding a *dao*, he circled the altar seven times. Then, kneeling, he placed his hands on the goat and uttered a long prayer. The opening part, said softly, had in it the names "Za," "Tera," "Apram," "Iasak," and others that I recognized from the Hotel Ritz document. Toward the end, Yosi raised his voice. When he was finished, Riliana handed him the *dao*. The young man in the motorcycle jacket yanked the goat back by the ears and Yosi slit its throat expertly, cutting through the muscle and the spinal tissue. He left the head hanging by a flap of skin, bled the throat into the water bowl, and tossed the carcass on the ground, where it started to twitch as if it meant to resume eating. Dipping a hand in the bowl, he sprinkled blood on the altar and painted the corner posts red. He placed the goat back on the altar, lit the faggot, and, after a few seconds, blew it out.

This was the *tlangrai thawi*, the first of several sacrifices he meant to show us. I should realize, he said, that I had not seen a true replica. The priestly garments were not real. The altar should have been sprinkled with *zu* instead of water. The traditional victim was a mythun, for the *tlangrai thawi* was a public sacrifice that had to be performed on an animal large enough to feed a village. It was killed with a spear by a *sadawt*, and the sacred pieces of the ears and legs were burned together with the altar; the fire he'd lit was only symbolic. Nor had he chanted the priest's words as Ningzenawng had done but rather recited them in a flat voice. He had last witnessed the *tlangrai thawi* as a child and did not remember the chant notes.

Yosi said all this matter-of-factly, making me wonder again what he and George were doing together. Either he was an even worse actor than George or a far better one. Judged as a school play, the *tlangrai thawi* was a flop, its stagecraft crude, its lines spoken without conviction, its audience of children kept from drifting away only by the promise of a bloody last act. And even then Ningzenawng's chanting in the Holiday Home Hotel had been more evocative than the gore on Yosi's altar . . . which was what puzzled me. Yosi had been to Burma many times. He had attended sacrifices and heard chants like Ningzenawng's. If he had invented the biblical names in the *tlangrai thawi*, he could just as easily have made up a chant for them. Why hadn't he?

The next demonstration was of the road-clearing ceremony. Still in his cloak and turban, Yosi took a green branch from the ground by the altar and walked back to the village, sweeping the path with it as he went. He said, "We are coming, we are coming! The children of Manmasi, the elder son of Zo-a, we are coming! You who are above and below the road, who may harm us, go away! The children of Manmasi are making the road! Go away, those who block our way!"

We entered the village, our entourage having shrunk to George and our carload from Champhai. The children had disappeared, as had the Four Informers. Yosi walked to the house with the tin roof, bent to pick up some pebbles, and threw one at the house. "Open the door!" he called.

A voice like Riliana's answered from inside, "Who are you? Are you good or bad visitors?"

"We are good visitors," Yosi called back. "We are the children of our forefather Manmasi, who is the eldest son of Zo-a, and we have come from clearing the road. We have brought blessings of fruitfulness and prosperity for you and your animals."

Riliana replied, "If you are the children of Manmasi our forefather, please do come in."

The door was opened, and we entered. Yosi went to the table and placed the remaining pebbles on it. "These are blessings of fruitfulness, prosperity, and health for your animals," he said.

The Four Informers were sitting at the table. They answered, "The children of Manmasi our forefather have brought us so many blessings!"

Then we all drank milk tea in place of *zu*.

Now Yosi became a *bawlpu*. Someone was ill. It was Neihhrima, who sat on the floor clutching his side. Yosi crouched behind him, a live red chicken in one hand and a long stick in the other. He brushed Neihhrima's back with the chicken, brandished the stick, and said, "I call in the name of this man! Whoever is making him sick, get out! Get out at once! Sentenu, Sentepa, are you leaving? If you do not leave, I will pierce you with my spear. I will cut you into pieces!"

He made menacing motions with the stick. Riliana, Huallotahuangza, and Hranchina all said, "Oh, don't harm him! He is leaving! He is leaving!"

Yosi put down the stick and waved the chicken. "I have made you leave by this chicken," he announced. "You have no more power over this man."

With a knife, he cut the chicken's throat, held it over the bowl of blood from the *tlangrai thawi*, and smeared some of the blood on Neihhrima's forehead. When Neihhrima lifted his shirt, Yosi smeared blood on Neihhrima's side. He smeared more blood on the branch that had swept the path and painted the doorposts with it. He said, "Let this chicken carry away all disease and death and iniquity that come into the village of the children of our forefather Manmasi," and flung it into the street.

The chicken squawked and flapped away, its throat uncut after all. It was the day's best stage effect.

Actually, Yosi explained, this ceremony called for two birds, one slaughtered and one set free. He had decided, however, to economize. When he professed not to know of a similar custom described in the Book of Leviticus, I took the little Bible I always carried with me and read it to him.

There were two more sacrifices. One, performed with the retrieved chicken, was for a house dedication. Yosi circled the room seven times, swinging the bird and saying, "O Za, O Za," before feigning its slaughter as before. The second was a family thanksgiving offering called *kelkhal*. Now it was the turn of the dead goat, its head still clinging to its body, to be recycled. Yosi recited a prayer, passed the *dao* over the goat's yawning throat, smeared blood on the doorposts with the green branch, and tied it to the outside of the door. This was a sign, he said, that the house was *hrilh*, off-limits to strangers. After slitting the goat's belly, he removed the heart and liver, wrapped them in a leaf, and laid them on a shelf above the door. These were for Pathian. The *kelkhal* sacrifice was performed after sunset, and its meat was consumed in one sitting before dawn, the eaters making sure to break none of its bones. Any remnants were buried by the priest. Although in the past the meat had been roasted, nowadays it was boiled, in Mizo fashion.

I opened my Bible to Exodus and read aloud:

> And the Lord spake unto Moses and Aaron in the land of Egypt, saying . . . Speak ye unto all the congregation of Israel, saying, In the tenth day of the month they shall take to them every man a lamb, according to the house of their fathers. . . . And the whole assembly of the congregation of Israel shall kill it in the evening. And they shall take of the blood and strike it on the two doorposts of the houses, wherein they shall eat it. And they shall eat the flesh in that night, roast with fire and unleavened bread . . . And ye shall let nothing of it remain until the morning; and that which remaineth of it until the morning ye shall burn with fire . . . neither shall ye break a bone thereof.

Had Yosi deliberately made the old sacrifices seem more like biblical ones? We were discussing the parallels between the Passover sacrifice and the *kelkhal* when a horn honked. It was the Nissan Patrol, whose owner was anxious to start back for Khuangleng. He wanted to make it before dark.

We started to say our goodbyes. Yosi looked upset. George said, "Why all the rush-rush? We thought you were going to sleep here in Lianpui."

"I'm sorry, George," I said. No one had told us we were to be overnight guests. "This has been very enlightening. Tell Yosi I'll look him up in Aizawl."

The Nissan honked again.

"Wait," George said. "You owe me for the goat."

"I paid you in Aizawl."

"There's an extra charge."

"For what?"

"A special goat for the sacrifice. Its fleece was white as snow."

"You can return it to Mary," I said.

It was a relief to get out of Lianpui. It was a relief to reach

Khuangleng, too, because it was growing dark, and the Nissan Patrol, which had no battery, drove without headlights.

We paid its owner and set out for Champhai. After a while I asked Liana about Yosi's sacrifices. I was curious to know what he thought of them.

Liana answered carefully. It was hard to say, he said. Some of the things Yosi did were familiar; others were not. The first sacrifice, for instance. At first he thought it was *gunram*, but then it wasn't. Or the *kelkhal*, which started out like *kawnglai* and ended up more like *sumtawng*. He couldn't say they weren't genuine. Hualngo sacrifices might be different from Chin Paite ones. Hualngo chants, too. Chants were old and in difficult language.

Halfway to Dilkawn we had a flat tire. Moya jacked up the car and Shmuel loosened with a wrench the bolts that held the spare in place. A soft rain was falling. We had stopped by a lone house. The light coming from its windows and from Yitzhak's flashlight was the only light in the world. The only sounds were Shmuel and Moya working. A man stepped out of the house to see what the matter was. Between the jungle in front of him and the jungle in back of him were nothing but his house and the road. That was the thing about Mizoram. There was so much space and so little of it.

We drove on in silence. I must have dozed off, because the next thing I knew, Yitzhak was shaking me. "Wake up," he was saying. "This is something you should hear."

I opened my eyes.

"It's Liana," Yitzhak said. "He's been telling us something strange. It's about a ceremony he performs. He goes to this place and asks for forgiveness and says the secret name of God and —"

"Hold on," I said. "Tell him to start again from the beginning."

Liana started from the beginning. Once a year there was a holiday on which he performed a public sacrifice. He was one of four priests in his clan with the authority to do this. That was because he was a *tulpi pa*, or highest priest, being the eldest son of a *tulpi pa* before him. Only he was allowed to be present at the sacrifice. While his household and relatives waited outside, he donned his priestly clothes and entered a room in which lay a trussed pig. "He calls the room the most holy place," Shmuel said.

"Go on."

Liana entered the most holy place and said a prayer. In it he addressed God by a name never used at any other time. He said, "*Ka pasian, ka pa Za*, O my God, my father Za! Today in this house we are going to ask forgiveness from you and our forefathers. I swear to perform my task today as surely as there is smoke from fire." He then killed the pig with a thrust of a spear and emerged from the room to tell those waiting outside that they were forgiven.

"What happens then?"

This, the first day of the holiday, was called the Day of Forgiveness. On the second day, called the Day of Impaling, the carcass of the pig was removed from the room and its head was stuck on a post. The rest of the animal was cooked and eaten, with a portion set aside for Pasian. Liana's only other duty was to bring a bamboo branch from the jungle, which was hung on the doorpost of the sacrificial house.

"Ask Liana," I said, "whether he can eat on the Day of Forgiveness."

Liana said he could eat all he wanted, both before the sacrifice and after.

Fasting — "afflicting your soul," in the Hebrew phrase — was part of the biblical Day of Atonement. But even without it the resemblance was eerie. I didn't have to look that up in the Bible. I knew how, once a year, a High Priest from the lineage of Aaron asked for forgiveness for the people of Israel; how he put on his vestments and entered the sanctuary by himself; how he sacrificed a young bull there "to make an atonement in the holy place for himself and for his household and for all the people." I knew the ancient rabbis' account of the Yom Kippur service in the Temple, read in synagogue on that day. Having performed the sacrifice in the Holy of Holies, the High Priest called out the sacred name of God, uttered at no other time, and said, "I beseech Thee, O Yahweh! We have sinned, trespassed, and transgressed before Thee, I and my house. Forgive, I beseech Thee, all our sins, trespasses, and transgressions." And when the priests and people waiting outside heard "the most sublime, awesome, and ineffable name of God uttered in holiness and sanctity from the mouth of the High Priest, they knelt and bowed and fell on their faces and said, 'Blessed be the Name of the Glory of His Kingdom forever and ever!'"

"But a *pig*? It's like a joke," Yitzhak said.

"Maybe the joke's on us," I said. An hour ago I had left Lianpui with the Mizo-Israel theory buried for good — and here I was, in a car with a little man from Burma who was telling me that he performed each year something very much like the most sacred of ancient Israelite rituals! The pig hardly made it any stranger. "I suppose the sacrifice could have survived while the taboo on pork didn't," I mused. "What I don't get is why, when Kawbzedawr told us two days ago that God had a secret name, Liana didn't say a word."

"He's been feeling us out," Yitzhak said. "Do you remember our first meeting in Champhai, when he began reciting a prayer and stopped? It was the same one. You don't reveal God's secret name to someone you've just met over breakfast."

A column of fire was floating in the night ahead of us. Then it was a woman with a torch. Then it was a column of fire behind us.

A biblical priest was subject to various restrictions. He was not allowed to shave his beard. He was not allowed to marry a divorced woman or a widow. He was not allowed to touch a dead body or attend a funeral. He could not be blind, deaf, lame, or physically impaired. "Ask Liana," I said, "if there are things a *tulpi pa* mustn't do."

At first Liana said no. Then he said yes. A *tulpi pa* mustn't touch a dead body. He mustn't dig a grave or stand near one.

"Wow!"

That was Yitzhak.

"Anything else?"

A *tulpi pa* mustn't marry inside his clan. He mustn't enter a Christian church. He mustn't wash his clothes after sunset. He could wash them whenever he wanted as long as the sun hadn't set.

"Wow!"

That was me. Mosaic law decreed that a person rendered unclean must bathe and wash his clothes "before evening." To wait any longer was a sin.

"Can he marry a widow? A divorcée?"

Liana thought he could.

"Suppose he's deaf or lame?"

Liana wasn't sure about that. All those rules could be found in a book written by his great-grandfather before Liana was born.

"Who has this book?"

Yitzhak said, "Liana does."

"We need to see it."

Moya pulled into Matloangi's. Although the place looked deserted, he hoped she was still there. But Matloangi was gone, leaving two boys sitting in darkness beside the embers in the hearth. They had to be coaxed into making us tea. One took a candle stub from his pocket, held a match to it, dripped some tallow on the table, and set the candle in the tallow. Its light twirled upward to form a halo around little Liana's head. He was not eager to go back to Burma for his great-grandfather's book. He had just been there to fetch Ningzenawng and had been counting on catching a ride with us to Aizawl, where he wanted to peddle some gems.

"We'll pay him," I said. "We'll photocopy the book and return it."

Liana looked doubtful.

"Ten thousand rupees."

Shmuel was shocked by the sum.

"Tell him."

Shmuel spoke to Liana. Yitzhak laughed.

"What's so funny?"

"Shmuel offered him five."

Liana was wavering.

"Ten, Shmuel. Paid on delivery."

Liana agreed.

Back in Champhai, we examined a calendar. It was November 2. Liana thought he could be in Aizawl with the book by the ninth. By then Yitzhak would be in Imphal, where he'd be going ahead of me. "I wonder," he said after Liana left our room. "Do you think he made all that up?"

"No," I answered. "Ningzenawng mentioned something about an annual pig sacrifice 'for everyone,' so it can't be entirely imaginary. Liana seems pretty honest."

"Ten thousand rupees is a lot for him."

"He didn't know I was going to offer him that. He only mentioned his great-grandfather's book at the last minute."

"He could have been planning to mention it. He saw the game Yosi and George were playing. Maybe he thought, if they can do it, so can I."

"That would make him awfully cunning. How would he know about the Day of Atonement? Even if he knew some Bible stories, they wouldn't include the priestly laws in Leviticus."

"He could have heard about them from Kawbzedawr."

Little Liana returned with his haversack. He wanted, he said, to use our toilet before going to Zana's for the night.

It was a ruse. When he emerged from the bathroom, he was wearing priestly garments over his windbreaker and he was not so little anymore.

He looked a foot taller. He had on a white headband with brown and purple scrolling and an eagle's feather sticking up from it. A white robe, banded red and green across the back, fell to the floor behind him. In front it was shorter and open, fastened at the breast; the hem above the knees was striped and fringed like a prayer shawl. Draped over his hidden arms, the colored bands swept the line of them downward, adding to his stature. The light of the electric bulb on the wall was effulgent in the teak varnish of his face. He stood transfigured, beaming at our astonishment.

The robe had been in his haversack all along. He had not been certain he would show it to us when he set out from Burma. It was an option he had left open. First, as Yitzhak said, he had wanted to see what he thought of us — and after two days in the car and in the mud and in Lianpui, he thought pretty well of us. He was telling us that.

He was telling us more. He had had the words to describe what he did when he entered the most holy place but not what it was like. He wanted us to know that it was not a school play or the twitching of a brain-dead faith; that in donning the sacred robe over his tatty windbreaker he, little Liana, became Suangolian, a *tulpi pa* of his people coming before his father Za. There was a glory in that.

"Like the morning star in the bounds of the east," the prayer book said of the High Priest emerging from the Holy of Holies. "Happy is the eye that has seen all this. For the hearing of the ear alone our souls have ached." Liana took off his priestly clothes and returned them to his haversack. "I wish you could see me wear them in Burma," he said wistfully. "As soon as your government lets me, I will," I promised. "It will too late then," he said.

⚜

One of the first things we did on getting back to Aizawl was to track down H.K.R. Lalbiakliana, the anthologist of Mizo poetry recommended by Chhunkunga as an expert on the red sea song. Like most people in Aizawl, he did not have an address or telephone. He had a neighborhood, and one could find him by going there and asking for him.

Aizawl had no street names; it consisted of districts called *vengs*, parishes centered on a Presbyterian church. In the old days, the larger Lushai villages had also been divided into *vengs*, each with its own *zawlbuk*. There were no posh *vengs* or slum *vengs*. Better-off and poorer Mizos lived side by side. Zaithanchhungi and Yosi Hualngo, for instance, were neighbors in Electric Veng.

Lalbiakliana, we were told, lived in a *veng* called Ramhlun South. No one there could direct us to him, however. In front of the parish church we encountered a man named Chhuanvawra who knew "Aitch-Kay-Ar" well, since they both taught Mizo literature at North Aizawl College. But although Chhuanvawra knew that "Aitch" stood for "Hmar," he did not know where Lalbiakliana lived. Told why we were looking for him, he said he himself had written two books on Mizo poetry and that "You can't take those biblical parallels seriously. Most are universal motifs. If you compared Mizo and Russian folklore, you could prove we came from Russia." Pretty soon several bystanders joined the discussion. They suggested that we ask for Lalbiakliana at a Hmar house down the street. Yet the lady of the house, who was conversing in her front yard with a friend holding a piglet in a bamboo poke, was not a Hmar. The Hmar was her husband, and he had gone out.

Shmuel remembered that Jeremiah Hnamte's parents lived in Ramhlun South and decided to ask them. Although they, too, were not home, Jeremiah's sister-in-law was in the family candy store around the corner, preparing five-rupee plastic bags of betel. She made a face that said "Do I look like one?" when asked if she belonged to the B'nei Menashe and told us she didn't know where Lalbiakliana lived.

In the end we found him in Ramhlun North. We met with him twice, once at the home of a neighbor and once in his own home, to which we were invited for a Mizo breakfast, together with a friend named Rozika. A quiet, broad-shouldered man with a rare Mizo mustache, Lalbiakliana warmed to the subject when he saw that I was genuinely interested. "As much as you want," he said of the time he had to give me, and both meetings lasted several hours. They strengthened my theory about the red sea song — and weakened it.

Lalbiakliana thought the most authentic text of this song was the one in his 1995 collection *Mizo Zaite*, or "Mizo Poems." It appeared in a chapter on the Sikpui dance verses. He believed that these were the oldest surviving Mizo poetry. Their language was a practically extinct sub-dialect of Hmar, called Triac, spoken by a clan near the Manipur border. The text he published had been recorded in Sakawrdai, a village north of Ratu, from an eighty-eight-year-old man. A nearly identical version had also turned up in Phulpui, across the border in Manipur.

The Sikpui — literally, Big Winter — Festival was not held annually. It was a Hmar holiday of thanksgiving that took place, Lalbakliana said, once every ten years in late winter, provided that a suitable village could be found. That meant a village in which no death had occurred during the previous year. If there was no such village, the feast was deferred. The last Sikpui held in Mizoram before Christianity put an end to the practice was at Saiphum, in the Champhai area, around 1915.

The Sikpui had no set duration. It lasted for as many days as people had food and drink, three being the usual number. In addition to the feasting, singing, and dancing, a formal ceremony was held in a field outside the village. It could be performed on any day of the holiday. A large, flat stone called a *lungdaw* was placed in the center of the field, and the celebrants arranged themselves around it by age, the older ones in the inner circles and the younger in the outer circles. Several men stood on the *lungdaw*. One played a gong and another called out two lines at a time of the *hlapui* or "great hymn," which were then sung by the circles. The singers swayed in place as they sang, holding hands and swinging their arms.

The "great hymn" was the Hmar term for the red sea song. Lalbiakliana took a copy of *Mizo Zaite* and went over the Triac words line by line with me. First, he read each line aloud; next, he explained the literal meaning of every word; and last, he offered a free translation of the whole in standard Mizo, which Shmuel helped me to put into English. Given that the "great hymn" was in old, poetic language and that Kuki-Chin-Mizo dialects are quite different from English grammatically, this took a long time. There were six and a half distichs, or thirteen lines in all.*

"While we prepare for the famous big winter feast,
I tell O! of the parting of the lurking big red water.
My enemies from the time of Tera, O!

---

* For those who are interested, Lalbiakliana's line-by-line analysis can be found in the end notes.

Like clouds in the daytime, like a fire that goes by night.
O how great and determined was their cruelty in coming to fight!
You have come with your mythun shields and weapons.
? [unclear word] like my enemy, O!
From the time of Tera, fire that came and went like a cloud.
? like my enemy, O!
All the mortals were swallowed by the lurking big water as
    though devoured by beasts.
All of you, take the birds,
Take the water that gushes out on the big rock.
O how frightening to see their determination!"

Yet while these lines, or fragments or variations of them, were the ones frequently cited in support of the assertion that the song referred to the biblical crossing of the Red Sea, they were not, Lalbiakliana said, the entire "great hymn." Eleven more lines were traditionally sung around the *lungdaw* on the same occasion, making twenty-four in all. We reviewed them in similar fashion. In English they were:

Our village Zielong,* from which we came out secretly, is now
    in the south.
Verily, a grown-up *thlutli*† is singing.
You still remain the same beloved in my heart.
Have we been too long on the banks of the Tiao River?
The beautiful woman is blossoming like a flower.
You are all the beautiful women in the world for me.
You are the most beautiful of views for me.
When I visited Durlai Valley** down below,
How very clean and happy were its babies!
I wish you the very best things,
The *vawkchal*‡ meat, the mythun meat, the *zang*§ meat.

At first glance these eleven lines seemed completely unrelated to the thirteen preceding ones. And yet though the "great hymn" appeared to

---

* The Triac equivalent of the Mizo "Chhinlung," the mythical rock through which mankind emerged upon the earth from the underworld.
† A legendary bird having the power of speech.
** Lalbiakliana did not know where the Durlai Valley was. It seemed reasonable to assume from the context that it was on or near the banks of the Tiao.
‡ A male pig.
§ The meat from an animal's back, considered the choicest cut.

be composed of two different poems that had been spliced together, Lalbiakliana firmly believed that it was a single composition, even though he had trouble explaining why. "I *feel* it" was all that he — a poet himself — could say.

Perhaps he was right. The fact was that the "great hymn" could be read as one unit by the simple procedure of reversing its parts. If its first thirteen lines, that is, were a description of a battle fought by the migrating Hmar against an enemy blocking their progress down the Tuipui River, perhaps turned red from the blood of the warring armies, the next eleven could be construed as a poignant goodbye said *before this battle* to a woman loved by the poet. Standing on a hilltop overlooking the Tiao River valley in which she lived, at the point where the Chin Hills and the Lushai Hills met, her lover thought of it as a blessed place filled with happy infants, and wished for her the greatest symbol of Mizo esteem: the choice meat from a sacrifice. He was about to join the Hmar push into Mizoram, leaving behind in Burma an ancestral land so old that the first men to have emerged on earth from the underworld were thought to have lived in it.

Such a reading supported the assumption that the "big red water" of the "great hymn" was the Tuipui River, not the Red Sea. The only problem was that Lalbiakliana insisted that all the "biblical" details in lines 1 to 13 — the cloud by day, the fire by night, the water split in two, the enemy drowned, the thirst quenched from a rock, the birds gathered by hand like the miraculous quail of the Book of Exodus — were also authentically old. Had some or all of them been added after the spread of the Buolawng movement in the 1950s, it was inconceivable that they would be found most fully in a vanishing archaic dialect spoken only by a few old people. Moreover, Lalbiakliana's Triac-speaking informants had told him that they learned the *hlapui* from people even older than they were. There was no reason to suspect them of lying.

Could these details be coincidental? *Six* of them? (Eight, if you counted Tera and the red water.) That did not seem statistically possible. And so two long mornings with Lalbiakliana left me with the conclusion that (a) the red sea song had nothing to do with the Bible and (b) it had everything to do with the Bible.

I asked Lalbiakliana whether he could sing the "great hymn." Unfortunately, he said, he could not. He had not taped the old man's singing and did not recall the melody. Few people in Mizoram still knew it. Once it had been sung not only at the Sikpui but at bouts of *zu* drinking. Like all the old songs, it was accompanied by a drum.

I mentioned having heard such drumming in Ratu. Lalbiakliana's friend Rozika, who had been following all this intently, now demurred. What I had heard in Ratu was not the old drumming at all, he said. Mizo revival singing had a modern tempo. The old drumming was very, very slow. So was the singing that accompanied it. "I'll give you an example," Rozika said. "First, old." He sang a few dirgelike lines in vocal slow motion, slowly tapping the arm of his chair with his hand. His voice dragged like my cassette deck when its batteries were low. "Now, today." His hand fluttered hurriedly. It was like the drumming in Ratu. Rozika made a disapproving face as though listening through a stethoscope to a sick heart.

᭙

On Saturday morning I was handed a note left for me at the desk of the Hotel Chief.

> Dear Hilel,
>   Please come to my house this evening at about 6 or 6-½. If you come, please come alone without anybody. I'll send my son to take you from your hotel at 6 P.M.
>   Remember please come alone.
>
> Yours,
Yosi Hualngo

The handwriting was George's. My first thought was to reply with a note of my own saying I would not come without Shmuel. My second thought was to be downstairs at 5:55.

I followed a teenager, Ezra's younger brother, down a long flight of steps to the Hotel Zodin. Having walked there previously from Zai's house, I hadn't realized how close to it I was. Yosi lived on the street right below the terrace of my hotel room.

George was there. So was his brother Anthony. Anthony was the co-author of the Grand Mizo-English Dictionary. Heavyset, like George, he was more suave and less antic. "How do you do," he said when introduced by George as "my bro and co."

But we were not there to talk about the dictionary. We had gathered to discuss Yosi's research. Now that I had seen the sacrifices, I was in a position to understand it better. It was the key to the Mizo mystery. "Anyone who looks for the answer by going to this old person or that old person will not find his happiness," George said with a pointed glance at me. "He will go hither and thither, spending his precious time and money, and all will be null and void. Everyone looks in books and each man reads the other's books and knows nothing. Only Yosi has gone to the source." However, there was a need to be frank. The visit to Lianpui had not gone well. "Yosi here is disjected. He thought you came for a serious colloquium. We intended to solve all your questions. But Mr. Samuel Joram and the Manipuri, they only kept looking at their watch. You were advised not to bring Mr. Samuel. Already in Kawzawl he showed his bad nature. And what for did you bring the little Paite? Paites have no religious manners. This is known."

I tried being conciliatory. I apologized for Kawzawl once again while standing by Shmuel's merits as an interpreter. Still, I was willing to do without his presence if Yosi felt that strongly about it. It was not our fault, in any case, that we had run out of time in Lianpui. We had been told the village was an hour from Champhai and had not been warned about the road, which made us lose a day in getting there. But none of this really mattered. "If Yosi has the key to the mystery," I said, "we can open the lock here in Aizawl."

I did not believe this would reveal a secret trove of knowledge. Yet three weeks of searching in Mizoram had turned up no one else claiming to have one. I had nothing to lose but more rupees by playing the game to the end.

And Yosi was ready to state his price. He had not brought me to the Hotel Zodin just to scold me. As if to upgrade the negotiations, he now turned to Anthony and spoke through him. He accepted my apology, he said, and would not dwell on what had happened. He wished to discuss future plans. He had much material, which he had spent years collecting. The first time he saw me with Rabbi Avichail he realized I could be the person to bring his findings to the world. However, I knew no Mizo. In my hands, he feared, his research might end up mistranslated and misinterpreted.

"Tell Yosi," I said to Anthony, "that I understand his concerns. I've worked as a translator. I know the pitfalls of being one. But now I'm writing a book. Without Yosi's help, I may come to the wrong conclusions. I'm ready to sit down with him and George here in Aizawl and translate the relevant texts together. It will be a collaboration."

Anthony conveyed this to Yosi. There was an exchange, joined by George. After a while it grew heated. George was arguing. Yosi rebuked him. Anthony said to me, "Your proposal is accepted in principle. We must work out the modalities."

Modalities! A word for the Grand Mizo-English Dictionary. *1. Methods of procedure. 2. Money.* "The modalities are of course crucial," I said. "I'm afraid I can't afford very much. But I'll do my best."

I was prepared to go as high as forty thousand rupees.

Anthony said, "Yosi has two requests. First, he wishes you to print his texts in Mizo as well as in English so that Western scholars can have access to them in the original language. Second, he wants to read your book before publication in order to correct any errors."

He had started with Definition 1. Although yielding on it would have made it easier to hold the line on 2, this wasn't possible. I could not, I explained, commit my publisher to numerous pages in Mizo, nor was there any practical way for Yosi to review the manuscript in a language he couldn't read. "What else does he want?" I asked. I'd go to fifty thousand if I had to.

Anthony conferred again with Yosi. "Nothing," he said.

"Nothing?"

"Nothing. Yosi wishes to start work tomorrow morning."

George spread his arms and watched a fortune sail away like a child's balloon. "I have no say," he lamented in a stage whisper. "I say and I say and I have no say."

I owed Yosi an apology for more than just Kawzawl.

᳕

George was in a better mood the next morning. Dripping wet from a washtub on the floor behind him, his lower half wrapped in a towel, he opened the door at the Hotel Zodin to let me in. It was my first view of him out of his gray suit. "I'm sweating like a pig," he said gaily. You couldn't trust a word he said.

Yosi was in the kitchen area, fussing over some pots. Less gloomy by day, the basement apartment was still threadbare. It had three rooms — a vestibule with a bench and television set, the equivalent of a village veranda; a large living space with a stove in the back like a Mizo hearth and shelves for pots and dishes; and a curtained-off bedroom. There was a table, some chairs, a fridge, clotheslines in lieu of closets along the walls, a sink, a water tank, and a canister of cooking gas connected to a burner be-neath the washtub. A suitcase lay on the floor in a corner. Yosi chided me when I declined the morning meal that he and George had already fin-ished. "It's time you learned to eat Mizo food," he said, putting a plate of it in front of me. I couldn't convince him that I had already eaten enough jungle spinach and bitter eggplant to last me forever.

I ate while he explained why it had been foolish of me to bring little Liana to Lianpui. The Paites, Yosi said, had stopped observing the au-thentic practices of the old religion long ago. Even their priests no longer knew anything about them. This was the result of an incident in the Bur-mese village of Pangrawn. In ancient times, all the tribes had gathered in Pangrawn every year for a great *tlangrai thawi* sacrifice. On one such oc-casion, when the sacrificial meat was served, the Paite chief was so hun-gry that he started eating before the priest had taken the first bite. He was reproved by the Hualngos for his poor manners, and the ensuing quarrel led to the Paites' ejection from the feast. Subsequently, they lost religious contact with the other tribes and went their own way. They were so igno-rant that they did not even sacrifice with a *langlap*. If I wanted knowledge of the old religion, I would not find it among the Paites. I would find it in the suitcase on the floor.

Yosi opened it. "Have a look," George said.

I peered into the suitcase: in a disorderly heap of notebooks, typed and handwritten manuscripts, writing pads, loose sheets of paper, photo-graphs, and correspondences in envelopes lay Yosi's research. It was as if the entire contents of a large desk had been emptied into one medium-sized piece of luggage. "A life's work," George said grandly.

It looked like that. There were thousands of pages, every one of them in Mizo. I would be flying to Imphal in a week. There was no way, even working day and night, that I could make a dent in all that.

I tried explaining this to Yosi. The only way to proceed, I said, was by means of a rigorous selection. He would have to go through the suitcase and choose only the most important items bearing directly on the Hotel Ritz document or a possible link between the Mizos and ancient Israel.

Yosi agreed. In fact, he had a better idea. He would take these items and copy them into a notebook for me. That way I would have the origi-nal Mizo texts as well as the translations. It would take him two or three days.

I hoped this would leave us enough time to go over everything. "The thing to remember," I told George before leaving, "is that it all has to be documented. Every chant, text, and memory — I need to be told when and where it's from. If I write in a book that the Mizos sacrificed to X and had chants with Y and Z, my readers will ask how I know. Saying 'Yosi Hualngo says so' won't cut any ice. If it's not tagged with a name, place, and date, it's unclaimable baggage."

George stared at me. He froze for a moment with one hand on his bath towel and the other on his soft belly, which was the shape and color of a large scoop of chocolate ice cream. You could see the penny drop. For the first time in his life the co-author of the Grand Mizo-English Dictionary had glimpsed the idea known as scholarship. He may not have comprehended its full grandeur, but something had gotten through. You could hear it in the sudden tone of authority with which he now spoke to Yosi. He was explaining scholarship to him.

Yosi nodded. George said, "Confirmed! We will provide you with pictures, names, dates, persons, places, designations, and all what-nots. We start today!"

He spoke like a man turning over a new leaf.

⚜

Yitzhak left for Imphal on Monday, November 8. I was to join him on the fifteenth. I did my best to keep busy while waiting for Yosi to finish his notebook and Liana to return from Burma.

I went with Shmuel to the Tribal Research Institute to speak to Genkhanda, its chief archeologist. Mainly, I wanted to determine if there was archeological evidence of a Hmar migration down the Tuipui River. Although Genkhanda knew of none, he agreed with Zaliana that the Tuipui was a logical route into the Lushai Hills. The one Hmar relic from the area was a large *lungdaw*, weighing over three tons and found in a field outside the village of Zote near Champhai. On it was an inscription by the Sailo chief Zahula, who had conquered the village in British times. It said: "This is the Sikpui stone of Hmars of the past and we occupied this place from 28.2.1918."

I had dinner at the house of Lalsanga, the president of the Ephraim Union. I was taken there in a taxi by Anthony, whose wife, Sangnuni, was vice president. On the way, he talked about himself and "Georgie." They had been raised as Catholics, an uncommon faith in Mizoram, and were sent to study at Catholic schools in the United States. Georgie had even considered the priesthood when he was young. Now they were working on their dictionary. It was to have fifty thousand entries, ten times as many as its largest rival. Once they received the ministry of culture grant they were applying for, they would proceed to the letter *B*. But the ministry of culture was taking its time.

The evening at Lalsanga's was less a dinner than a photo-opportunity. I was photographed alone with Lalsanga, with the other guests, with the neighbors, with Lalsanga, with his children, with their cousins, with Lalsanga. The flash bulbs popped while we ate and I asked Lalsanga about his political aims. These were, he said, to change the name of Mizoram to Ephraimram. "I suppose that's easier than changing Mizoram," I remarked. But Lalsanga did not want to change Mizoram. He wanted to retire to the living room for more photographs. The young man who took me back to my hotel on his motor scooter after we couldn't order a return taxi because Lalsanga's phone line was dead thought Ephraimram was only Stage One. "Bang-bang," he said, firing a finger at the night sky for Stage Two.

I attended a luncheon of the Mizo Writers' Association. The afternoon progressed in triadic cycles — a speech by a dignitary about the uniqueness of Mizoram, some jokes by an MC about the foibles of Mizoram, a church-hymn-style song about the beauties of Mizoram, and a repetition of the sequence. Then the repetition was repeated. Everyone joined in the singing.

C. Fung Kung and Nithanthluai came to see me. I gave Nithanthluai the cassette deck I had bought her and showed her how she could use it when she went back to Hungle. Then I gave each of them a little book of Psalms in English and Hebrew. Nithanthluai's smile when I put hers in her hand was pure light.

Peter Tlau and Elisabeth Zodingliani dropped by. They were disgruntled with the Messianic Jews. "They will never give up their Jesus!" Peter exclaimed. "I tell them Judaism has one God, and they want two." Peter and Elisabeth were planning to start a new synagogue to be called The Sephardic Jews of Mizoram. It would challenge the Ashkenazi hegemony of the Shalom Zion Synagogue.

They had brought along a surprise companion. It was Gideon Ray, on a visit from Israel. Now that he was in Aizawl, he was considering staying for a while. Perhaps he would open a Hebrew school. Although his Hebrew was rudimentary, he had discovered, like many a Zionist leader before him, that the Diaspora had its allures.

Elisabeth returned the next day to escort me to the CIPC office. Not to be outdone by Yosi Hualngo, Sailo had also decided to stage a sacrifice in my honor. A sizable audience had turned out for it. If Lianpui was a school play, this was *opéra bouffe*. It began, on a stage set with an altar made from a bamboo tray propped on four cans of soda pop, with two turbaned warriors in striped lungis. Peering into the jungle, they fiercely waved wooden swords to protect a fat priest who appeared, swinging a chicken. The priest circled the altar while chanting in a rich baritone and pretended to slaughter the chicken over a bowl. When he smeared the altar with the bowl's thin contents, these dribbled down to the soda cans.

Afterward Sailo was apologetic. As Indian law forbade the public killing of animals, he had had to forgo a live sacrifice. That would have been more exciting.

"Well," I said, "it was only a reconstruction. A dead chicken still wouldn't have made it a UPC meeting."

He and I had attended such a meeting together. Although I had wanted to see a Pentecostal service, I'd felt awkward about asking Shmuel to accompany me. Having crossed the lines to Judaism, I thought, he wouldn't be comfortable crossing them back as my guide. And so I asked Sailo to come with me.

We went to a church in Armed Veng, called that because of an old armory. All the way there you could hear the Sunday drums of Aizawl. They came from churches and homes. Like the whir of the *nirleng*, they peaked and waned. The sound went on all day. Close up you heard the singing, but mostly it was just the drumming, a steady throb. The city sounded like one big trance party.

The congregation was singing as we entered. The men sat to the left of the aisle; the women, wearing white kerchiefs, to the right. A drum was beating, and several people circled in a space up front, their arms swinging slowly at their sides. The singing came in waves, as it had at Ratu. The drum raced wildly, faster than Ratu.

Sailo and I sat in the last row. After a while there was a break in the service for anyone wishing to speak. A few men rose and addressed the meeting. One welcomed me. "We are very happy," he said. "Until now we have only read about Israelites in the Bible. Now we see an Israelite face."

A leader recited a prayer. Then everyone prayed on his own. Within seconds the church was a babble of voices. Some clamored to be heard with a long "Ho-o-o-o!" or "O-o-o-o!" that sounded like Ningzenawng's *Heyyyy-y-y-y-y-y*, followed by a rapid outburst like the *gunram* chant. The drum urged them on, driving them ahead of it. Whoever reached his prayer's end sang out a loud "Amen!" or "Hallelujah!" The word was then repeated until it became a song of its own, a one-word Pentecostal scat.

The discord was total. No two people seemed aware of each other. And yet slowly, out of the chaos of voices, an order was emerging. As the "amens" and "hallelujahs" multiplied, they sought each other out. Mergers and alliances were formed, runged ladders and linked chains of sound. The last of the shouted prayers ceased. Timbreled harmonies were born, silver-toned, diapasoned. They grew more intricate, turned into architectural structures. Sonorous, they filled the air like the strains of organ pipes. Now all the men and all the women were singing one "amen" and one "hallelujah" like two competing choirs of angels. Then the competition ceased, and they came together in a single wordless chord, a long, last heavenly diminuendo.

A woman rose to her feet. "I have something to say," she declared. She began calmly, dispassionately. She was talking — Sailo told me — about love. Without love nought availed. Love overcame her, inflamed her. All at once she fell to her knees. She pressed her face to the floor and prayed for love. She sat up and prayed on her knees. The words streamed forth in long cadences, each exhausting itself before another rose within her. The drumming resumed. Some women rose from their pews and went to the front of the church, where they danced before the kneeling woman. Half-crouching, they spun slowly, their arms extended. They spun and spun as if groping for something to hold on to. One toppled to the floor. Others staggered. The drumming stopped. All but one of the spinning women stopped, too. The one who didn't spun back to her seat in the rear of the church. Still spinning, she tumbled onto it, crashing into the woman beside her. The woman beside her was nearly thrown off the bench. She put her arms around the spinner and held her until the spinning went out of her and she lay on the bench, her shoulders heaving. Then she sat up and adjusted her kerchief. No one paid her any attention. People were gathered around the woman on the floor.

"They're returning her spirit," Sailo said. After a while the woman on the floor rose, looking perfectly normal.

A preacher gave the sermon. He had tailored it to Sailo's visit. The UPC, he said, was distinguished by one feature. This was "not being ashamed of our feelings." Because of this, many Presbyterians had joined it. If Presbyterianism was a strict home in which you had to be on your best behavior, Pentacostalism was a loving home in which you were free to be yourself. Yet the UPC had grown up with Presbyterian parents and would remain forever grateful to them. Nowadays many people were asking why, if the Mizos had always been Israel, the missionaries were needed in the first place. Many were suggesting that the Mizos would have been better off without them. But this was not so. Though not Gentiles, the Mizos had lacked Christ. The New Testament spoke of two missions — Paul's to the Gentiles and Peter's to the Jews. The mission to the Mizos was the mission of Peter. So! Peter said, "Ye are the children of the prophets, and of the covenant which God made with our fathers, saying unto Abraham, And in thy seed shall all the kindreds of the earth be blessed. Unto you first God, having raised up his Son Jesus, sent him to bless you, in turning away every one of you from his iniquities."

Afterward, I told Sailo that I had found the service quite beautiful. "Do you really want to take all this away from them?" I asked.

"I don't want to take away anything," he answered peevishly. "Let them know who they are and be what they want — Christians, Jews, fire worshipers. I'm the grandson of a chief. I know what Christianity took from me." He blamed it for the moral dissolution of his father — who, the institution of chiefdom having been abolished, joined the British army and retired, Sailo said, "with the rank of drunkard." Although he became a Christian late in life, "he never took a bit of it seriously."

And so Sailo, it seemed, had been circumcised by his father as a drunken protest. Perhaps his own great dream was only to be a Sailo chief again.

Another note in George's handwriting was at the hotel desk.

> Dear Hilel,
> Today I went out to find out one elderly man. Unluckily, that man died three months ago. So I went to send George to bring some more people who know the chantings in the form of singing. George would visit two villages and bring some important words and people from Vaphai and Sazep side.
> In the meantime, I am briefing out the important words from my suitcase. I am doing the work now itself.
> So, please, come down itself in the morning, so that George can go at once and come back soon.
> Yours,
> Yosi Hualngo.

I came down itself in the morning. Yosi, wearing his reading glasses, was seated at the table, copying into a notebook from a pile of papers in front of him. Hard at work, he barely looked up. George got down to business at once. Vaphai and Sazep were near Lianpui. He needed 3700 rupees for transportation.

At least he wasn't charging me for the old man's funeral. "Why didn't you bring these people to Lianpui while we were down there?" I asked.

"This was our intention. You did not stay."

I was beginning to feel sorry for him. The Grand Mizo-English Dictionary was stuck at A, and Yosi's decision to share his research with me gratis had sent George's shares in their joint venture plummeting. I gave him two thousand rupees, and we agreed to meet again on the afternoon of Thursday, November 11. George would be there with his "people," and Yosi's notebook would be ready.

It wasn't quite. There were several pages still to go when I arrived. Yosi was writing in the same position as when I'd left him. George had brought three men. One, in a Chicago Bulls jacket, was writing too. Meanwhile, George played nursery school with the other two. They sang "Entering Zion" for me; a ditty about Tera, Moses, a brass mythun, some tablets, and a furnace; and the chant of a children's game in which each player tried to place an object noticed only by God — that is, Khuavang — on someone's head. For a while they chased each other around the table and Yosi put down his pen and scampered with them. But George needn't have gone to Sazep for such stuff or even (as I suspected he had) around the corner in Aizawl. I had enough versions of "Entering Zion"; Khuavang had nothing to do with anything; and I did not believe that even the children of a Lost Tribe had played for thousands of years at being Moses burning the golden calf after breaking the tablets of the Law.

The Chicago Bull, a Hualngo named Zakemlova, finished his writing and handed it to Yosi, who read it silently, and then said, "These are the true words of the song of the crossing of the Red Sea."

He gave Zakemlova a signal to sing it. Zakemlova sang in deep, slow tones. He sang the way Rozika had sung when demonstrating the Mizos' old music. At one point Yosi joined him with a clear tenor. Then his voice quivered and broke off. When they were done, George wrote the words for me in English.

> Long ago, our master Musian by the still big water.
> Khuavang came and the big water was still.
>
> Khuavang came and the big water was still.
> Maidens of friendship, Riami, Thansangi.
>
> Friendly maidens, Riami, Thansangi,
> Come home, you, Tukbander, Zermanziaki, and Bahawngi.
>
> The heads of our enemies, we rejoiced by singing.
> Displaying the heads on stakes, Zermanziaki, Bahawngi.

This was curious! It was the first time I had encountered Moses — "Pu Musian" — in any version of the red sea song. The "friendly maidens" were known to me from Sailo's Referendum, but now there were five of them, not three. If it wasn't Sailo who had inserted them, who was it? The same person who had added the lines about impaled heads in an apparent reference to Pharaoh's slain host? And why were the biblical allusions in Lalbiakliana's text — the fire by day and the cloud by night and all the rest — left out?

"Where is this from?" I asked.

Zakemlova said he had learned the song from his grandfather Darneihpinga, who died in his nineties in the Chin Hills in 1994. Never a Christian, Darneihpinga was a practicing priest in the old religion until his death. Zakemlova once saw him drive a *huai* from a woman by commanding it, "Come out of Phaichungi and go back to the jungle! I am an ancient priest and we are the children of Manmasi, a holy people!" He had liked to drink *zu;* this was one of the songs he sang with his drinking friends. The more they drank, the sadder the songs became. They called the really sad ones "Zion songs," *saion zaite.* But the red sea song was not a Zion song. It was an ordinary drinking song. Many people in the Chin Hills still sang songs like it. "Some are old and some are new," Zakemlova said, rolling himself a cigarette.

I asked if the new ones had a quicker tempo.

No, Zakemlova said. The music stayed the same. People just put new words to it.

So the dirgelike style he had sung in did not mean the song was old. Yet who in Christian times would make up such a thing, mixing Moses and the "big still water" and the friendly maidens and the heads of enemies in one crazy jumble?

As soon as Zakemlova and his two friends departed, I was eager to start work on Yosi's notebook. Yosi, however, wanted to finish it first. He needed a few more hours, he said. George would bring it to be photocopied in the morning, and each of us would have his own text. Then we could begin.

⚶

Back in the Hotel Chief, I found little Liana asleep on the floor by the reception desk. He could have been mistaken for a small mail sack. Picking himself up, he pointed to his haversack to let me know it contained his great-grandfather's book. I slapped his back so hard with excitement that I nearly knocked him down again. There was even less of him than usual, because he hadn't eaten all day. I ordered a chicken biryani and a Coke for him and took him to my room. Then I went to get Shmuel.

My heart sank as the two of us watched Liana take the book from his haversack. It wasn't the old handwritten manuscript I had expected. It was mimeographed and stapled and bore the date 1993.

"This book was supposed to have been written before you were born," I said.

Liana reaffirmed that it was. He had brought the second edition. He didn't own a copy of the first.

"What's in it?"

Shmuel thumbed through it. He couldn't understand most of the Chin Paite. There were many names and dates. "And family trees," he said. "It looks like a history of a Paite clan."

"What about the laws of the *tulpi pa?* Ask Liana where they are. Ask where it says a priest mustn't touch a dead body."

Liana took the book and stared at it helplessly, as if he had no idea of what was in it. He had probably never read it. Convinced of its value by my eagerness to see it, he had assumed it would speak for itself. Now he tried reading it, his lips forming each word. He wet a finger, turned a page, and read some more. It had only now dawned on him that ten thousand rupees was riding on his ability to find what he had promised us. "Here," he said, pointing to a passage.

"Tell him to translate it," I told Shmuel.

The passage Liana read to us dealt with lines of succession in a priestly clan. When a priest died, his office passed to his eldest son. If his eldest son was ineligible, it went to the next eldest.

I said, "That's not what we're looking for. We want what we heard in the car. The sacrifice of atonement. Ask where that is."

Liana licked his finger again. He placed it on some words and read haltingly, as if the print were unclear. Shmuel interrupted him angrily.

"What's wrong?" I asked.

"He's making it up. I told him to stick to what's written."

Liana turned some more pages. He had his frightened-animal look. After a while he stopped and sat with his hands in his lap, as if awaiting the inevitable blow.

There was no point in tormenting him further. "Tell him to leave the book with us," I said. "We'll find someone who can read it. If it's what Liana said, he'll get his money. This is for his travel expenses." Liana took what I gave him and stuck it in the pocket of his windbreaker. He did not protest. He had not gotten through life by protesting. He ate his chicken biryani, drank his Coke, and said he would return the next day.

Shmuel knew a Chin Paite in Aizawl. He went looking for him and came back a few hours later. It was as he had thought. The book was a clan history with nothing about priestly laws. "Liana knew it all along," he said. He was as disdainful of my innocence as he was of Liana's treachery.

"I'm not so sure," I told him. I wouldn't be seeing him for a few days. He was taking a bus to Lunglei in the morning so that he could spend the Sabbath there with his brother, a B'nei Menashe. And he wanted to see the girl he had been corresponding with. Afterward, he would fly to join me in Imphal, and we would return together to Israel.

⚡ 8 ⚡

Lianpuisuaka's Will

Yosi's notebook was finished. Its red cover said "Good Boy Exercise Book." He had filled three-quarters of it, numbering the pages from 1 to 65.

We spent two days working our way through it. The procedure was simple. First George translated a few lines from his photocopy while I scribbled a digest of them in the margins of mine; then I questioned Yosi about them and scribbled some more. Later, when we were back in Israel, I had Shmuel retranslate the entire notebook.*

It began with an introduction:

> This is the story of my research into who we are, where we came from, what our religion was, and who our God was. It is looking at the way our forefathers worshiped and practiced their religion.
>
> I did not copy anything from books but gathered everything from my father and the elders.
>
> I was often present when my uncle Hualkhaia offered sacrifices. At the age of 13, when I learned to read and write, I also started traveling to my mother's family in Seipui, Burma, and collecting as much information as I could there.
>
> Unfortunately, at the time of the Insurgency, the army burned down my house and all my valuable written materials.

* I have used his translation in this chapter, with some minor editing on my part.

Therefore, these words that I have written are reconstructed from memory as well as collected from others.

When Rabbi Eliahu Avichail first came from Israel, I told him about the sacrificial chants that I learned from my father. Beginning in 1998, when Rabbi Eliahu, Hillel Halkin, and a third person came from Israel, I began doing more research.

In October 1999, Hillel Halkin came again. I helped him as best I could, using George Lawma as my interpreter.

Since all these customs go back to the times when our forefathers were illiterate, no single person's knowledge is enough. I have therefore spent much time collecting information from others.

In many towns and villages that I visited, people were wary and not forthcoming, since, being Christians, they were afraid of what might be done to them. For this reason, they would not tell me what they knew.

As I am not a journalist or a writer, I may not have ordered my paragraphs or sentences in the best manner.

Yosi Hualngo (Biakenga)
Electric Veng
Aizawl, Mizoram

The first third of the notebook was devoted to descriptions of the sacrifices we had seen in Lianpui. Yosi had written out the words of the chants. It was evident at a glance that much of the Hotel Ritz document derived from these. The words for the *tlangrai thawi* chant, for example, were:

You who are above, whom I worship, Pathian, Khuanu, Khuapa, Thlaropa, Chungkhuanuleng, Hualmintu, Za, Tera, Apram, Iasak, Muria, Iakop, Akoptan, Big Red Water, Sin-ai Mountain, the Place of the Covenant, Marah, the Place You Gave Us Water,* Entering Saion, Suraluido, Apnitan, Himalawi, at Lungding, at Kunming, at Mongoloi, at Moirang, at Mangding,

---

* Chapter 15 of Exodus relates how, after leaving Egypt, the children of Israel came to a place of bitter (*marah* in Hebrew) water that was miraculously sweetened for them. The reader comparing the *tlangrai thawi* chant with the Hotel Ritz document will notice that the phrase "Marah, the place you gave us water" does not appear in the latter, which has instead "the place where we used to go up and down." There are also a number of discrepancies in the two lists of Burmese place names.

at Thinkuazing, at Tingtun, at Vawngran, at Sangring, at Airawdung, at Hommalen, at Chundung, at Awksatlang, at Khampah, at Thanghem, at Ngatan, at Run, at Suklui, at Pangrawn, at the Tiao River, the Protector of wherever we go, Za, Khuavang, the Place Where the Sun Rises, Where the Moon Rises, Where the Buffalo Dwell, Where the Cattle Dwell, Under the Eight Folds of the Earth, Under the Eight Folds of the Sea, Omnipresent, Protector.

All this, Yosi wrote, was chanted by the priest in a low voice. He then chanted more loudly:

O One Who Is Above, whom I worship, answer me, protect us! Protect the village where dwell the holy children of our fore-father Manmasi, the elder son of Zo-a! Arise and protect us from Muriah, Akuptan, the Big Red Water, the Si-nai Mountain, Marah, Saion! You above whom I worship, Khuanu, Khuapa, an-swer my sacrifice with unblemished *zu!* Answer us, answer us! We are the children of our forefather Manmasi who is the elder son of Zo-a. Protect our dwelling place! Protect us from conta-gious disease, from fire and storm, and from our enemies! Pro-tect us with the blessings of hundreds of children, crops, and animals!

The chants for the other sacrifices were similar. As a boy, Yosi said, he had heard them from different people — especially from his uncle, his father's elder brother Hualkhaia, who was a village priest. Before becom-ing a Christian, Yosi had liked to help his uncle prepare the sacrifices. One of his jobs was making the *langlap,* which afterward he got to keep. He wrote down and memorized his uncle's chants because he dreamed of being a priest himself. He even told Hualkhaia, "Uncle, I want to per-form the sacrifices in your place." Hualkhaia answered that he wasn't ready yet.

When he was little, he sometimes played at being a priest. Once, after watching his uncle paint the doorposts of a neighbor's home with the blood of a chicken, he obtained some buffalo dung, the only suitable ma-terial he could find, smeared it over the doorposts of his own home, and received a good scolding. Another time, the village children marched through the village in a road-clearing ceremony, with Yosi as the priest. He rose from the table to show me, taking a broom as his green branch and laughing as he swept dust with it onto George's pants. George brushed the dust off with forbearance and explained, "This Yosi did to the children behind him."

When Yosi was baptized, his uncle was angry. They had an argument in which he told Hualkhaia to stop worshiping Ram Huai and believe in Jesus. Hualkhaia answered, "Biakenga, I'll never believe in your make-believe God. The God of our forefather Manmasi has no beginning and no end. I don't worship Ram Huai. But he is almost as powerful as God and can harm us, and we do things to please him so that he does no harm."

Yosi's father, Piangriangchhunga, was also opposed to Yosi's baptism. But by the early 1950s all the children in school were Christian, and Yosi wanted to be like them. The boys in his class made fun of him. He begged his father to let him convert, as his elder brothers Chalchuama and Thlangtansiama had done. But Piangriangchhunga told him, "My son, our God is not a God invented by human beings who can be killed and sacrificed. I spit on the bearded man who can be crucified! My God is the master of the sun and moon. He is beneath the eight layers of the water. His true name must not even be spoken. I am a priest. When I speak God's name, I mustn't move. I mustn't blink."

He lowered his voice and said, "This name is Za."

And added, "Do you see that stick over there? If you ever utter that name out loud, or tell any of your friends, I'll beat you with it."

Yet in the end Piangriangchhunga not only agreed to Yosi's baptism, he himself became a Christian for his children's sake. This caused his eldest brother Lianpuisuaka, who was none other than the old priest I had heard about in Lianpui, to break off relations with him. For years the two didn't speak. Then, Lianpuisuaka approached Piangriang-chhunga to ask a favor: he wanted to perform the *khuangchawi* ceremony in honor of his wife, and he needed help to buy a mythun for a sacrifice. Piangriangchhunga refused. It was not because he was now a Christian, he said. He still spat on the bearded man. On the contrary, it was because Lianpuisuaka was corrupting the old religion.

He said to him, "You know very well how the *khuangchawi* originated. It was a celebration in honor of the spiritual scroll of the covenant. All this changed when the Chinese dogs attacked us in Sangring village in Burma. They killed four hundred of our priests and took away our scroll. Then, when we were in Pangrawn village, some rich man said, 'As we no longer have a scroll, I will celebrate the *khuangchawi* of the scroll in honor of my family.' Soon everyone was doing the same."

And Piangriangchhunga continued, "Brother, you know this is so. Don't ask me to help you celebrate the *khuangchawi* for your wife. We Hualngos are the clan who composed the song 'The scroll from the mount of Si-nai has been eaten by the dog, aie, ie, ue, aw, e!'"

Lianpuisuaka was indignant. Who was a Christian like Piangriangchhunga to accuse him of corrupting the old religion? "Don't be cross with me," Piangriangchhunga replied. "I was baptized only to please my children. A crazy *huai* got into them." The two brothers burst into laughter. They were reconciled, and Piangriangchhunga helped Lianpuisuaka buy his mythun. Yosi was a witness to this. His father never forgave himself for becoming a Christian. He once said to Yosi, "Biakenga, after I'm dead, your children won't know anything about us. I am not worthy of being my father's son."

Piangriangchhunga died in 1981 and Lianpuisuaka in 1990, the same year as Hualkhaia. In addition to the sacrificial chants that Yosi had learned from them, he recorded the chants of two Chin Hills relatives on his mother's side, Chalkuma and Pakthanga.

I said to Yosi, "There's something I don't understand. If all these biblical names — Abraham and Isaac and Jacob and Mount Sinai — were really in the old chants, how come no one noticed them? How could the missionaries not have known about them, either from hearing them or being told, 'Hey, all these names from your Bible are also in our prayers!' Why didn't they run to tell the world that they'd found a Lost Tribe? And if these *were* the words of the old chants, how is it possible that today, in all Mizoram, you alone know them?"

It was a question with several parts, and it took George a while to convey them all. In his Mizo translation I heard "CNN," "BBC," and "ABC" — apparently his idea, or his idea of my idea, of how the missionaries should have told the world of their discovery. Yosi's answer, too, broke down into parts:

1. "I can't speak the mind of the missionaries." He did not know what they were or were not aware of. But he did know that no one ever discussed the old religion with them. This only led to being scolded for taking an interest in it.

2. Very few people knew what was in the chants. As I had seen in

Lianpui, portions of them were recited so quietly that they were audible only to those standing beside the priest. These were the portions containing the name Za. In the louder parts, God was addressed by other names. But those were chanted rapidly. No one tried to make them out. They were considered the exclusive business of the priests.

3. Even Mizos who knew the chants did not know the stories in the Old Testament. The missionaries preached only about Jesus, and by the time the Old Testament was translated into Mizo, the old religion had all but disappeared. For this reason, Old Testament names in the chants did not ring a bell.

4. Every Mizo tribe had its own chants. Each tribe listed the different places its ancestors had passed through. Yosi knew the Hualngo chants, which were highly conservative. The Hualngos "did not change things like the others" and may have retained old prayers that others had forgotten or altered. In general, the Hualngos looked down on the other tribes, who, in turn, considered them snobbish. For example, it was customary among the Mizos to lend one's hair comb only to social equals, since contact with an inferior rendered it unclean. A Hualngo, however, lent his comb only to another Hualngo. If he had to lend it to someone else, he threw it away when it was returned.

I asked why the names "Babylon" and "Jordan," recited by Riliana in Lianpui, were not in the notebook. Although I was fairly sure they had been planted by George, I was curious to see the reaction. George's was to try changing the subject. Yosi made an irritable remark. "Yosi here is not responsible for Riliana's names" was George's translation.

He added, in an injured tone, "I am telling you very frankly, I have not been telling you any lies. But as I am under your and Mr. Yosi's employment, I cannot say my own findings."

We returned to the *tlangrai thawi* chant. Why, I asked, were personal names like "Tera" and "Apram" mixed with place names like "Muriah" and "Sin-ai"? And what were the words of a children's dance like "Entering Zion" doing among them?

Yosi had no explanation. He could say only that these were the words he had recorded.

"But all your records were destroyed in the Insurgency!"

That was correct. Lianpui was burned in 1966, and its inhabitants were regrouped. At the time, Yosi was commanding an MNF force near

Champhai. Soon afterward, the Indian army launched an offensive, and his men retreated across the border into Burma. When the MNF laid down its arms, they fought on for a while with a faction called the Chhinlung Democratic Party. Yet even after the fighting stopped, he did not return to Lianpui, which was resettled in 1971. He crossed back into Mizoram and wandered from place to place, working as an itinerant dentist, a skill he had learned from treating his troops. In 1975 he was arrested by the CID and sentenced to three years in prison for his part in the Insurgency, and on his release he settled in Aizawl.

When, then, did he recopy the chants that were destroyed in 1966?

"Only in 1996," Yosi said. "But I had often thought of them over the years. In my heart I had wanted to write about them as history." History mattered to him. He didn't like myths. "All that Ephraim talk of Sailo's . . ." He made a face.

George put in, helpfully, "Yosi here doesn't believe in all that Chhinlung rock stuff. The real lowdown is the Garden of Eden."

It was also in 1996 that Yosi, having decided the Mizos were a Lost Tribe, grew interested in Judaism and was circumcised. As it happened, his son Ezra had himself circumcised at that time, too. When the two found out about each other, they took it as a providential sign.

"But how could you have remembered in 1996 words that had been destroyed thirty years earlier?" I asked.

"I went back and asked Hualkhaia."

"But Hualkhaia was dead! You told me he died in 1990."

Had we been in a courtroom, this would have been the time for a telling glance at the jury. Yosi was indeed confused. He talked with George and then went to speak to his wife, who had come back from the market and was watching television in the outer room. He returned and spoke again to George.

George said, "So! It's like this. The correct year is 1988." That was the year Yosi had taken Ezra, then a boy of fifteen, on a visit to Lianpui. Although Hualkhaia was very old, Yosi talked to him and he "remembered everything." From Lianpui, Yosi crossed into Burma and went to see Chalkuma and Pakthanga. Pakthanga was deaf and unapproachable, but Chalkuma was clear of mind. He, too, remembered the old chants.

"So the chants in this notebook date from 1988?"

"That is correct," George said.

"In that case," I said, "I'd like to see Yosi's notes from that year."

There was another time-out. George said, "So! There were no notes. Yosi did not write this matter down then. He spoke to Hualkhaia and Chalkunga. They refreshed his memory."

Yosi assured me it still was fresh. "Remembering is not difficult for us," he said. It was an ability the Mizos had. "We never depended on books like you. Our forefathers could not read or write. They had to remember everything. I can remember every word of my conversations with you last summer."

I didn't put him to the test, although perhaps I should have. The nub of it was that there wasn't a scrap of paper in his suitcase to prove that he hadn't made up the chants himself. "What you're asking of me," I said, "is to rely on your memory from ten years ago of what priests relying on their memories from . . . George, ask Yosi. When was the last time Hualkhaia sacrificed in Lianpui?"

That was in 1966 too, Yosi said. He was sure of it because he was MNF commander in the Lianpui sector before his unit moved to Champhai. It was he who had ordered the sacrifices stopped. They were having a bad effect on his troops. The men used them as an excuse to drink *zu* and get drunk.

"A Mizo," George remarked, "just has to touch a drop of *zu* and he's whammo-out-of-control."

"Let me get this straight, George," I said. "It was Yosi who ordered his own uncle to stop sacrificing?"

That was correct. This was the MNF line. All religions were considered reactionary. Yosi went along with it. He didn't know the MNF was just the tool of Laldenga, who would betray the cause of independence. The fighting was going badly, and he had to put the safety of his men first. Many were killed. Each time he sent them into battle, he knew some would never again see their wives or girlfriends.

His voice quivered familiarly.

When else had I heard it do that? When he was singing with Zakem-lova

> Maidens of friendship, Riami, Thansangi,
> Friendly maidens, Riami, Thansangi,
> Come home, you, Tukbander, Zermanziaki, Bahawngi.

"George," I said, "ask Yosi if the other day — when Zakemlova was here — you remember, he was singing — and Yosi joined him and stopped. . . . Ask if he was thinking about those men."

George asked and said, "Yes, it was a song the soldiers sang."

So it was an MNF song. That explained the lines I had heard at Sailo's Referendum, the ones that went, *Boys, is any one missing of those who went to fight the enemy?* The soldiers of the Insurgency had taken the red sea song and put new words to it. There was nothing unusual about that; it was done all over. As a teenager I had often sat on the floor at parties, drinking cheap wine and singing Spanish Civil War songs that were retoolings of older Spanish ballads.

Yosi said, "You asked what I was thinking. I was thinking also about my parents and my uncles. I was thinking about my people."

"George," I said, "ask Yosi if that's why he's doing this."

George asked. He said, "Yosi is doing this because he is now clear about his people."

It was the nearest thing to a statement of purpose I was able to get from him.

"Let's go on," I said.

The next section of the notebook dealt with old Hualngo customs of birth and death. It described the mock-circumcision ceremony called *bawrh keu* and related:

> When a baby is born, the father is not allowed to do any work. He ties a bamboo rope to the wooden post that supports the main beam of the house. In case he is compelled to leave the house for unavoidable reasons, this rope will represent him.
>
> The person (generally a woman) who helps the mother deliver the baby gives the newborn child a temporary name. On the eighth day after birth a torch is placed below a vine shaped as a circle. If the child is male, the priest or father makes it hold a hand tool like a knife, spear, or bow. Then the priest passes the baby through the round vine and blesses the baby, who is given a permanent name. The priest or father chants, "Protect So-and-So, the son of our forefather Manmasi, the elder son of Zo-a. Protect and bless him with a hundred blessings, a hundred children, a hundred portions of food, a hundred years of age, and big-horned animals. Grant him wealth and success in hunting."

He then picks up the quill of a porcupine, brushes the baby's fontanel, and throws the quill away, saying, "You, the disease, go away!" Pulling the baby's foreskin in one hand and holding a knife in the other, he pretends to cut while he says, "In the olden days we, the children of Manmasi our forefather, elder son of Zo-a, used to circumcise with sharp stones." He turns the knife upside down, with the blunt side toward the penis, and rubs it against the penis.

If the baby is a girl, she is passed through the round vine and blessed. If she has health problems or is sick, the father unties the bamboo rope from the post, and the baby is cured.

I asked Yosi whether he had ever seen a *bawrh keu*. Yes, he said. His nephew Tanchiama, Chalchuama's son, had had one. That was in the early 1950s in Lianpui. Perhaps he could find other people who had witnessed one.

The pages that came next were the strangest. They told of a letter from Yosi's cousin Laltaithuama, his mother's sister's son. Laltaithuama was a Christian pastor who traveled a lot and knew many languages, among them Nepali. In 1976, hearing of a place in Tibet called Lungding, a name mentioned in the *tlangrai thawi* chant, he decided to look for it. On his return he wrote to Yosi:

After many difficulties I reached a town near the old town of Lungding, where I was guided to the house of an old man, Tenzing, 145 years of age. He could no longer stand up but was happy to see me and asked me to hug him by bending down. After this warm welcome, knowing what I had come for, he said to me, "My son, be happy that you have met me, as I am also happy. You said you are the descendant of Manmasi, but you are very small and have a stranger's face. When our forefathers were living here together with your forefathers, your forefathers were strong, stubborn, and powerful people. You were those who worshiped the Creator of the heaven and earth, sun, moon, and stars, by making an altar with four corners and offering animal blood. Though you used to look down upon those who didn't worship Him as you did and called them dogs, you never harmed us at all. You used to have a scroll and would never mix with us. After the second downfall of the town of Lungding, one group of your people went toward the south, beyond the lake, where there are hills and slopes like the place where you are living — the Chin Hills. There were also those who went eastward. I once traveled to Manipur and Burma to sell medicines. (I too am interested in tracing the past of our ancestors.) I wish you all the best success, and I hope you are as happy about having met me as I am in meeting you."

Then [wrote Laltaithuama] I was guided by four young men to the site of Lungding, but I was disappointed to see an empty, abandoned place with few trees and much grass. I saw only rocks, plains, and a few hills. But I am glad that I saw Lungding with my own eyes, since it is mentioned in the sacrificial chants of the priests.

I found this account beyond belief. Quite apart from the unlikelihood of a 145-year-old man, the idea of a Mizo searching for ancient sites in Tibet in the 1970s was absurd. "Tenzing may be a genuine Tibetan name," I said, "but Tibet was totally closed to foreigners back then. Even if your cousin had managed to enter it from India or Nepal, he would have been arrested in no time."

Yosi stuck to his guns. He was well acquainted with Laltaithuama, who died in 1986. His aunt's son was a respected figure, not a teller of tall tales.

We moved on. The notebook now sought to trace the route of the children of Manmasi from Tibet into Burma. Basing himself on Laltaithuama's story, the place name "Moirang" from the *tlangrai thawi* chant, and a traditional song, Yosi had written:

We went south from Lungding and allowed those in the front to form a group, each one holding on to a chain made of vines, and singing, "We are the people who carry the vine chain toward the south" . . . Still others went farther ahead and reached the land beyond the lake. The name of a place, Moirang, which is in Manipur and also in the chants, indicates that once we were living there. Moirang is on the shore of Tuipaugpui, now known as Loktak Lake.

Yosi took a towel, rolled it into a vine, and danced as he sang the traditional song, a cigarette dangling from his mouth. He held out the vine to George, and both men capered with it, George heavy as a bear, Yosi light as a boy. And perhaps, I thought, the coiled will that drove him was a boy's too. *He feels as close to the truth of his childhood as I do to mine*, I wrote in the margin of my photocopy. Perhaps that was why I wanted so badly to believe him.

From Manipur the Hualngos migrated south to the Chin Hills. Yosi took a piece of paper from the table and drew two lines, a straight one for the migration route and a wiggly one for the Tiao River. He circled their junction at Pangrawn, on the river's Burmese side. This was where the Paite chief had been ejected from the feast and the *khuangchawi* corrupted.

Next in the notebook were a number of sayings and songs. I had seen some of these in the Hotel Ritz document. Here, though, Yosi gave his sources. To Lawmchungnunga of Khopuichep village in Burma he attributed the line "Parova's armies who were on the horses were swallowed up by the red sea," as well as "There was a big thunder with the fire and cloud of Tera on the mountain of Sin-ai. Musia received the tablet of stone but could not keep it for long and broke it and burned the golden calf in fire."

Lawmchungnunga had also given Yosi his own version of the red sea song. Yosi recalled with amusement how he had had to go out and buy Lawmchungnunga and his friends jugs of *zu* before they would agree to sing it. It went:

> While preparations for the great Siktui [sic] feast are on,
> The fire of Tera flares skyward by day and by night.
> My enemies of day and night are swallowed by the sea.
> Collect those birds for food,
> Drink that water from the rock.

There followed descriptions of several children's games. There was the "Entering Zion" dance and an elimination game, in which players raced for a line while others called out, "Tera's fire is burning! The last one will be caught!" The last child was seized and sent to the sidelines, and the race was repeated until a single winner remained. Since George was too tired to get to his feet, Yosi staged a solo demonstration by running in place with his arms and legs pumping madly, staggering backward as if seized by an invisible hand, and then joining the chorus on the side.

We were all tired. A model of comportment until now, George was showing signs of strain. He had been working overtime without recompense, and as we began the notebook's final section, an anti-Christian last will and testament attributed to Yosi's uncle Lianpuisuaka, the retaining walls of his self-pity began to crack. He now revealed the "findings" that he had withheld before. The scandal of Christianity was worse than Yosi's uncle had thought. "Though I am exceedingly sorrowful that I never became a Catholic priest," George declared, "I will now tell you why Christianity is bull. It is all based on a lie. The pope says Jesus was the son of Joseph. But Jesus was truthfully the bastard of Zachariah. This I can prove. How then could Mary have been a virgin?"

His unshaven cheeks were covered with gray grizzle; betel had turned his lips a garish, hermaphroditic red. "George," I asked, "why then are you sorrowful?"

"I am sorrowful," said the might-have-been swinger of censers, "not in the name of George Lawma. It is the climax of George Lawma to throw away the New Testament and the bearded man. I am sorrowful in the name of my parents, who did not see their Georgie attain his entitled position."

Cassocked-and-chasubled! Knelt-and-confessed-to! The George the world had lost.

Lianpuisuaka's will, under the caption "A Hidden Treasure Is Found," read as follows:

> A hidden treasure written by Lianpuisuaka, son of Tlangthanga, from the village of Sazep, to his children.
>
> I, Lianpuisuaka, son of Tlangthanga, am not going to give up the religion of my ancestors. I am not going to worship or believe in your Christian God, who can die. I don't want it. This religion of the white people is not the religion of the children of Manmasi our forefather. Therefore, please remember to keep this treasure that has been passed on from our forefathers — that our forefathers used to remember the names of places they had gone through or come from and which we still do remember today by the children of Manmasi our forefather and whisper them only out at the time of worship, which are:
>
> "You, who are above and whom I worship, Patian, Khuanu, Khuapa, Thlaropa, Thlanrawkpa, Thlanropa, Chunkhuanuleng,

Hualhimtu, Khuanu, Khuavang, Tera, Apram, Iaksak, Muriah, Iakkawp, Akuptan, Big Red Water, Sin-ai Mountain, the Place of the Covenant, Marah, the Place You Gave Us Water, the Place Where We Went Up and Down, Enter Enter Si-awn, Surraleido, Apnitan, Himmalawi, at Lungding, at Kunming, at Mawngkawlawi, at Moirang, at Tuippangpui, at Mangding, at Thimkawzing, at Tingtun, at Vangrawn, at Sangring, at Airawhdung, at Homalen, at Chindung, at Mount Awksaw, at Khampa, at Thanghem, at Nghatan, at Run, at Suk River, at Pangrawn, at Seipui, at Tiao River — who guided us wherever we went — Za, Khuanu — who is in the place where the sun rises, where the moon rises, where the buffalo dwell, where the cattle dwell, under the eight folds of the earth, under the eight folds of the sea, Omnipresent, Za, Khuavang."

As Za is the name of God, do not ever pronounce it in vain. Since his name has been guarded and pronounced secretly by our forefathers, in order to hide the greatness of the name, they instead used to say:

> Patian, Khuanu, Khuapa, Thlaropa,
> Thlanrawpa, Thlanrawkpa, Chungkhuanuleng,
> Hualhimtu, Khuavang, Khua.

Although there are many kinds of sacrifice, we, our own family, do not want to copy from any invented sacrifice that others perform. You should obey me and keep my religion, go only according to what I have told you, and do not copy from others. And do not bury me as the Christians do when I die.

Written in the month of Min Kut, Sazep.

To this Yosi had added:

Fortunately, this written treasure was given to me by my cousin, to whom I had sent my nephew to ask if he could help me in the writing of our past history, as I was confused about where to begin because of all the material I had collected. And this treasure was not written by my cousins, as they were Christians and looked down upon the older practices and did not want to write it. Therefore, I do not know who wrote it down from my uncle, and the writer is unknown to this day. The document was found only after my uncle died.

It didn't seem such a great treasure to me. Lianpuisuaka had died in 1990. Even had these really been his last words, they came too late in the day to carry much historical weight.

But the will, I now was told, was not written in 1990. It was written in 1948. "In that year," George said, "Yosi's uncle, having reached the half-century time of his life, chose to leave his children this writing."

That was another story. The year 1948 was before Buolawng movement. The Lost Tribe belief didn't exist among the Mizos then. There would have been no motive for anyone, least of all for an anti-Christian diehard of the old religion, to insert biblical names in old chants. "I don't suppose," I said, trying to fight back my excitement, "that Yosi knows where the original copy of his uncle's will is."

Of course he didn't. He would have been waving it in my face if he did.

"As a matter of fact," George answered, "the original was recently here in Aizawl. Now it's back in Sessih."

"*What?*"

"It's like this. When Yosi was in Lianpui for the sacrifications, he asked for info regarding our research. Two days ago Lianpuisuaka's son, Yosi's cousin Hrangtawnga, sent a messenger from Sessih with said document. So! Yosi copied it into his notebook and returned it to Sessih."

"Just a minute!" I said. "Are you telling me that Yosi sat here two days ago with the original of Lianpuisuaka's will and sent it back to Sessih without letting me see it? Without photographing it? After everything I've said to you? I must be dreaming."

Yosi uttered a Mizo expletive. George clapped a hand to his mouth, the whole thing too dreadful for words.

"What did Yosi just say?"

"He says there would be no room for anything if he had to keep every damn piece of paper." George's hands went to his ears. "Oh, sorry! Sorry!" he said. "Mr. Yosi does not understand. He is not a writer like you. I have tried to explain this to him many times but he does not understand."

Yosi swore again. He pushed across the table toward me the piece of paper on which he had drawn the Hualngo migration route and spoke to George. George held the paper in the air. "Here, see, see," he said. "Mr. Yosi is telling the truth. This comes from Hrangtawnga."

I took the paper. On one side, written in English, was:

B.H.P. Urgent Please
To
Biakenga
Electric Veng
Aizawl

On the other side, upside down to the wiggly Tiao, the same hand had written, in Mizo:

"To My Younger Cousin Biakenga,

"I hope you are well. I am also well. This is the testament of our father Lianpuisuaka, the son of Thlantanga. It tells the story of our forefathers and how they worshiped, although not in detail. Keep it safely with you always."*

Hrangtawnga hadn't even wanted it back. But he had sent it. His note was proof of that. "May I have this?" I asked.

Yosi began tearing off Hrangtawnga's note.

"No, no! The whole thing!"

He handed me the paper intact.

"We'll get you the original document," George said. "We'll send a boy to Sessih posthaste. He'll leave tomorrow morning."

"He won't be back in time," I said. "Today's Saturday. I'm flying to Imphal on Monday."

"Then we will give the document to Mr. Samuel Joram. He will bring it to you in Imphal."

Suddenly, Shmuel was kosher.

"Fine," I said. "I want it accompanied by a signed statement from Hrangtawnga. I want him to declare that his father's will is genuine. Is that clear?"

My plan was for Shmuel to cancel his flight to Imphal, go to Sessih with Hrangtawnga's statement, and verify that he had actually written it. If Lianpuisuaka's will was my first smoking gun, I wanted it with all the fingerprints.

☙

---

* George's translation of these words was later confirmed by Shmuel.

I returned to the Hotel Zodin the next morning to say goodbye. George was sleeping on the bench in the outer room. A button had come off the jacket of his gray suit, on which a loose thread lay like a fallen hair. He looked derelict. Yosi was at the table, addressing an envelope to Hrangtawnga.

I woke George and told him I had something to say. I wanted to thank him and Yosi for all their help. "Please tell Yosi," I said, "that although I know he did not do this for the money, I would like to make a contribution to his research."

I held out some hundred-dollar bills. George reached for them. I evaded his hand and gave them to Yosi. George said, hopefully, "Half and half, isn't it?"

Yosi put the money in his shirt pocket. He, too, had something to say. He hoped that through me the true history of his people would be made known. He had indeed not pursued it for personal gain. Now that we were done, however, he had a request. He wrote on a piece of paper a list of names:

> Yosi Hualngo
> Ruth Hualngo
> Ezra Hualngo
> Semida Hualngo
> Azriel Hualngo

He wanted my help in getting his family to Israel.

George took the pen and added to the list: Daniel Israelo.

Yosi laughed.

I saw George one more time, the next morning. I was waiting for Zai to take me to the airport when he knocked on the door of my room. His eyes were bloodshot and he still was unshaven. He had, he said, a "secret" to tell me. I let him in and remained standing by the door.

"Because you have not seen me in synagogue," George said, "you may think I am not a good Jew."

I said nothing.

"In Aizawl town they talk behind my back. They do not know I was with Gideon Ray in Manipur when they still worshiped the bearded man. They say I am a drunkard — a thief — that I cut throats." He put a hand to his throat with a horrified expression, as if the throat being slit were his own. "So! I cannot associate with such people. I cannot pray with them. There, that is my secret! In Israel I can pray with everyone."

I remained silent. He glanced at the chair by the window, but I made no move to invite him in. After a while he said, "Well, I guess I'll be going home."

The thought came as a revelation that he had no home. The "missus," the hungry mouths — figments, like all else.

He stuck his hand in the pocket of his gray suit and pulled out a few tattered rupee notes. "These are all the bucks I have left."

I gave him a thousand rupees from my wallet.

"Salom," he said, hugging me.

His grizzled cheek scraped mine. He must have picked that up in Seattle. Mizos never hugged or kissed. They thought it unmanly.

From Imphal I telephoned Shmuel at the Hotel Chief to ask whether he'd received Lianpuisuaka's will.

"No," he said. "I spoke to Yosi, and he said the messenger came back from Sessih without it. It couldn't be found."

"That's impossible! It was just sent there from Aizawl. It couldn't have gotten lost in a few days."

Shmuel had no comment. He knew I knew what he thought of Yosi Hualngo.

"All right," I said. "Here's what you'll do. You'll go to Sessih anyway. You'll find Hrangtawnga, and you'll clear this matter up."

"I can't."

"Why not?"

"I'm getting married this week in Lunglei. The girl and I hit it off."

It took a moment for me to absorb that. "Mazal tov," I said. "That's wonderful news."

It was terrible news. After the wedding he would barely have time to catch the Imphal-Aizawl-Calcutta flight that I'd be on. I would never know whether or not there was a will.

"That's wonderful news," I said again.

⚜ 9 ⚜

Introducing Dr. Khuplam

Imphal was a sinister town. Although the ethnic warfare was in abeyance, the streets emptied quickly at night. Frequent power failures left them dark, and Indian army patrols stopped cars to search for weapons and explosives. The local English press ran daily reports of clashes with Kuki, Naga, and Meitei "militants," "ultras," "insurgents," and "underground cadres" belonging to an alphabet soup of organizations with names like the KLA, the MLF, the UNLF, the PLA, the NSCN. Most of these, Yitzhak said, were criminal gangs masquerading as ethnic militias. Representatives of one, the Kuki Liberation Army, dropped by his family's home one day while I was conducting interviews. They parleyed and left with — as he put it wryly — a "patriotic donation."

Yitzhak's parents, the Thangjoms, were wealthy by local standards. They lived on a dusty thoroughfare, called Gaol Road, that teemed by day with cars and tricycle rickshaws whose drivers, faces masked against the fumes of the traffic, all looked headed for the same bank robbery. There had been no rickshaws in Aizawl, in which — even without the hills — no Mizo would have pedaled anyone around for a fee. But Meiteis and Nagas had no such scruples, and Imphal lay in a valley, a 2000-square-kilometer ellipse, in the center of the state of Manipur, whose southern half was occupied by Loktak Lake. The mountains farther south, running toward Mizoram and Burma, were heavily Kuki; to the east and west they were mostly Meitei in the foothills, Kuki in

the lower ranges, and Naga higher up; while the north, through which
ran the road to Kohima, the capital of the state of Nagaland, was Naga-
dominated. Yitzhak and I drove part of this road one day to Kangpokpi,
a mixed Kuki-Meitei village with a B'nei Menashe community. He
thought it unsafe to venture beyond that.

The Kuki-Naga enmity was old. It went back hundreds of years, to
when the first Lushai tribes, having pushed into Mizoram from Burma,
advanced north into the Manipur hills. There, they encroached on
the indigenous Nagas, some of whom retreated before superior Kuki
strength while others became vassals of Kuki chiefs.* Outside the Imphal
Valley, long controlled by a Hindu dynasty of Meitei kings, the more
warlike Kukis lorded it over the Nagas right through British times; the
greater aggressiveness of their culture was often remarked on by the British, who tended to favor them. With Indian independence, however, the
tables were turned. Less divided by tribal rivalries than the Kukis, the
equally nationalistic Nagas took up arms in a battle to secede from Assam
as early as 1956 and were granted statehood by New Delhi in 1962. During the major Naga-Kuki violence that broke out in those years, and continued sporadically into the 1990s, they generally had the upper hand.
The Kukis, an estimated quarter of Manipur's population of 1.8 million,
were unable to form a common front. Some were Kuki separatists. Some
clung to their tribal identities — Thado, Paite, Vaihte, Ralte, Gangte,
Mate, and Kom. Some were for union with a Greater Mizoram. The
latter, too, however, resented being called "Mizo" and did not regard that
as their name. The main obstacle to Kuki-Chin-Mizo unity, they gave
the impression, was the problem of nomenclature.

The ethnic complexity of Manipur, which I had assumed would have
plunged the old Kuki-Chin-Mizo religion into an oblivion even deeper
than that in Mizoram, turned out — so I discovered in Imphal — to have
had the opposite effect. Although the Kukis were Christians like the
Mizos, the old religion had lived on longer among them and was remembered more vividly. This was mainly because the British missionaries had

* The word "Kuki," originally a Bengali term for any wild mountain tribe, eventually came to
denote these Lushai migrants into Manipur, who in turn were divided by the date of their arrival
into "Old Kukis," like the Hmar, and "New Kukis," like the Thado. The latter, though present
in Manipur only from the late eighteenth century, grew into the largest and most dominant
Kuki tribe, and their language became the lingua franca spoken by most Kukis.

had less power in Manipur. Whereas in Mizoram they had been adjuncts of a British administration that placed the educational system in their hands, Manipur's Hindu character had precluded this. Meitei resistance to Christianity was more effective than that of Mizo priests and chiefs. It was backed by a political structure and a sophisticated religious tradition, and it threatened to arouse the passions of Hindus elsewhere, a reaction the British were anxious to avoid. Under Hindu pressure, the early Baptist missions were banished from the more heavily populated Imphal Valley and restricted to the hill country around it, and the Hindu Meiteis never became Christians.

Hinduism, though it neither attracted nor reached out to the Kukis, slowed the pace of Christianization in yet another way; for as the religion of a great civilization capable of holding its own against the colonial faith, it moderated the impression, so powerful among the Mizos, of Christianity as an irresistible force. A lesser awe of the British contributed to the 1917–1919 "Kuki Rebellion," an insurrection against the conscription of native labor brigades for the war in Europe that, led by the Thado tribe, never spread to Mizoram. Nor could Christianity serve the Kukis as a unifying force against their neighbors, since the Nagas, among whom missionaries from Assam had been active as far back as the 1840s, were adopting it even faster. The Kukis did become Christians — it was their only practical option for material and cultural advancement — but more gradually and with less ardor than did the Mizos.

My first hours in Imphal brought this home to me. From the airport I was taken to Amishav House, a three-story building named for Eliahu Avichail's "My People Returneth" organization. It housed the B'nei Menashe synagogue and community center, and was only a few hundred yards from the Thangjoms' home. Yitzhak's father, Yehoshua, a retired senior government official, was the community's leader, and many of its activities took place along this strip of Gaol Road. Now, he had prepared a small reception for me to which he had invited some of his B'nei Menashe colleagues. One was Elitsur Haokip, who was to translate Ningzenawng's Chin Paite chants into Thado so that Yitzhak could put them into English. Another, Peniel Haokip, was the kapellmeister. Peniel led a small choir that sang songs of welcome to the old dirgelike music, including an ode composed in my honor. I was given an English version of it.

My brethren from the womb, Menashe,
Awake and rise, our beloved guest is now cometh!
He is our guest, he is our brother from the womb,
He has arrived in India, the land of our playground.

Grieve not thy soul of thy fate,
For Zion weeps for thy presence, day after day.
If our mother weeps for her children,
Take me home to our mother to console her.

Peniel accompanied the singers on the gong and drum and performed a solo on an instrument called a *gusem*, a round, high-necked gourd with bamboo pipes. Fingering their stops while blowing into the neck of the gourd, he played a mournful melody that resembled a bagpipe's. Not many people, he said, could still play the *gusem*.

I had a question. To my ears, the old music was haunting but uniformly sad. Was this just my Western reaction?

The question intrigued them. They had never heard a Western reaction to their music. Someone said, "No, it is sad for us, too. It is full of. . . ." Yitzhak groped for the right English word. He finally hit on "nostalgia."

"For what?"

No one was sure. One man answered, "We don't know. We Kukis seem to be in a perpetual state of mourning."

This was cheerfully agreed to by everyone. A woman said there were even slower and sadder songs than those I had heard. To sing them, there had to be *zu*. You couldn't sing the really sad songs without it.

"Zion songs?"

Yes, they were familiar with the expression. "They're our blues," the woman said.

Peniel was a small, dapper man of fifty-seven. He had been raised as a child in the old religion and baptized at the age of nine by his parents, though his mother refused to become a Christian herself. During refreshment time after the music, he reminisced about standing in the ashes of a fired *jhum* field with his father and hearing him ask for forgiveness. "Grandfather Manmasi," his father had prayed, "I have only done like my ancestors, though my burning has killed many animals." Peniel remembered a special corner in the back part of his family's home used for sacrifice. There had once been such a corner, called "the most holy place," in every Thado house. (In every Chin Paite house, too, it stood to reason. That explained Liana's "holy of holies.") While Peniel's mother hushed the children in the outer room, his father would sacrifice a pig or chicken there and say, "God of my forefathers! Today I sacrifice this animal for my whole family, that we may have health and food." Emerging from the holy place, he would announce, "Our God and the God of our forefathers is very happy!"

Peniel's mother would respond, "We are very happy!"

And Peniel and his four brothers would say after her: "We are happy, happy!"

When the family sat down to eat the sacrificial meat, Peniel's father asked God to "bless us as you blessed our forefathers" and gave a portion of food to his wife and to each of his children in descending order of age. Peniel, the youngest, received a double portion.

Sometimes Gam Huoi, the Kukis' Ram Huai, stole a soul and made its owner sick. Then a house sacrifice was not enough, and Peniel's father would turn to a priest, who cast lots to determine whether to offer the king of the jungle spirits, or *thilhas*, as they were called in Thado, a hen, cock, or pig. In Thado this priest was called a *doipu*. There was also a *thempu*, a priest who performed public sacrifices, and a *themzong*, who took care of burying the dead.

Peniel's friend Navi Songtiniam remembered the *themzong* well. He was the only priest allowed to visit a home made unclean by death. He did this, Navi said, on the third day and on the seventh, the last day of mourning, sprinkling the house with purifying water carried in a large leaf from a stream. As he did so, he chanted, "All evil spirits, all misfortune, go away! This is the house of the children of Manmasi." After the second purification, the mourners washed themselves and their clothes in the stream and were clean.

The Book of Numbers prescribed similar third- and seventh-day rituals for mourners. Yet by now I had learned to take such parallels with a grain of salt. Navi had already cited several others that struck me as implausibly exact. I did not suspect him of deliberate deception — he had a kindly, absent-minded air far from subterfuge — but of unconsciously adjusting childhood memories of the old religion to adult knowledge of the Bible. Most of us rewrite our childhoods in such ways.

Like Kawbzedawr, the "rabbi" from Burma, Navi believed in both Judaism and "Joshua." In Aizawl this would have cost him his place in the B'nei Menashe community. The B'nei Menashe of Imphal, however, had a greater tolerance for heterodoxy. They were more relaxed about their Judaism and less fearful of Avichail's disapproval — a confidence deriving, Yitzhak thought, from their better education and higher status. "Manipur isn't a Christian society like Mizoram," he explained. "People here don't look down on us. My father was a government commissioner. No Mizo B'nei Menashe could be that. Well-placed Mizos would never become Jewish because it would cost them their social position." Many of the Imphal B'nei Menashe had been born into the old religion, had become conventional Christians, and had then experimented with a Judaizing Christianity before adopting a more normative Jewish faith. They didn't mind that others, like Navi, were still traveling the same path.

Peniel was a case in point. Educated as a Baptist, he was so devout that in 1973, at the age of thirty-two, he quit his job to become an evangelical circuit rider, going from village to village to win souls for Christ. But he had already then begun to resent the Baptist clergy, which was wary of enthusiastic lay preachers and sought to keep them on a tight rein. One day he went to preach in the Hmar village of Mapo. Living there was a Judaizer named Rama, who had a reputation as a crack debater. Rama was an expert at citing chapter and verse and was said to be invincible.

Peniel knew his Bible, too, and was persuaded to take Rama on. For a while it was touch-and-go. Peniel had a parry for every thrust of Rama's and Rama had a riposte for each attack of Peniel's. But then Rama delivered the coup de grâce. "Tell me this," he said to Peniel. "The Bible speaks of God's feasts: the Feast of Tabernacles, the Feast of Unleavened Bread, the Feast of Weeks. But where does it say anything about your Baptist holidays, such as Christmas and Easter? By what authority do you observe them?" Peniel had no answer. He could not think of a single verse in the New Testament that mentioned Christmas or Easter. He lost the debate and his certainty.

The question gnawed at him. Although he continued his life as a Baptist preacher, his heart was no longer in it. It became harder and harder for him to understand how, if the God of the New Testament was also the God of the Old, He could abrogate His own laws. In 1979 Peniel had himself rebaptized in a Judaizing church called the Kenesiyah. He was circumcised and began observing the Sabbath and the biblical dietary laws while continuing to believe in Jesus — not as God, but as the Messiah. Several years later he was sent by the Kenesiyah to preach in Imphal.

Yet he was still not at peace. In Imphal he studied the Bible "more and more deeply" and came to acknowledge that he was living a contradiction. The Kenesiyah, too, didn't observe the holidays of Moses. Its members simply conducted Christian prayers on Old Testament dates. Instead of building booths and living in them during the Feast of Tabernacles, for example, they gathered on those days to pray to Jesus. And Jesus, Peniel had gradually become convinced, could not have been the Messiah. The Book of Psalms said, "Now I know that the Lord saveth his Anointed One." How was dying on the cross being saved? By now Peniel also believed that he was descended from the tribe of Manasseh. On July 23, 1994 — he remembered the exact date — he joined the B'nei Menashe. It made him happy to be praying again to the God of his ancestors, as his father had done. He had come full circle.

The stories told me over the next few days by people like Peniel added incrementally to my knowledge. Although most of the information corroborated things I had already learned in Mizoram, more of it was based on personal experience. The categories were familiar:

1. Manmasi. There was abundant evidence that the phrase "children of Manmasi" had been widely used by the Kukis in a ritual context, especially in times of danger. Navi Songtiniam remembered people from his village exclaiming, during a bad storm, "We are alive, the children of Manmasi are still alive, save us!" In Samson Dochang's village the women had burned leaves, calling, as the smoke blew away, "O wind, O wind, slow down, slow down, we the children of Manmasi are still alive!" Samson recalled people shouting at the time of a tremor, "Heyyyy-yyyyy, we Children of Manmasi are still alive!" When there was a lunar eclipse, Zosi Thouthang had heard the cry, "We are the Children of Manmasi. Let go of the moon! Let go of my big moon!" He had also heard a *thempu* implore Gam Huoi in the jungle, "Let go of this sick man. He is a son of Manmasi. You'll be in trouble if you don't!" Peniel Haokip remembered how, at the funeral of a child, sesame seeds were inserted between the child's fingers so that "the seed of the children of Manmasi" would multiply. Navi Songtiniam had heard a priest chant at a sacrifice:

Manmasi who crossed the small and great water,
The small mountains and great mountains, you crossed them —
You who desire the heart and the liver,
Partake of the heart and the liver!

There were alleged Kuki genealogies going back to Manmasi and beyond. One was given to me by Jimmy Jamkhomang Haokip, chairman of the Thado Tribal Council. A secular nationalist, like Sailo, keen to unite the Kukis under the Manasseh banner, he presented me with a "Genealogical Tree of the Thados Through Pu Abraham the Great Progenitor." It started with:

Abraham
|
Isaac
|
Jacob
|
Joseph
|
Manmasi
|
Machir
|
Gilead
|
Sechem

When I pointed out that this sequence was taken from the genealogies of the tribe of Manasseh in Chapter 26 of the Book of Numbers, I was answered that it had been prepared "in consultation with leading clan leaders" and reflected genuine Thado traditions. What form these traditions took, no one could say.

2. Priests and Sacrifice. The public priest–private priest dichotomy known to the Mizos and Chin Paites had also existed among the Kukis. Private priests mostly sacrificed to the *thilhas*, and public priests to Pathen. Both offered pigs, dogs, chickens, and goats. Pigs were killed in-

side the home with a spear thrust, goats outside by a slitting of the throat. Only Navi Songtiniam claimed to have heard the public priest address Pathen as *Pu Za* or "Father Za"; this was, he said, "barely audible" and part of the "soft chant" preceding the "loud chant." There was agreement that the "soft chants" sounded like a "strange language" and that only the priests knew what was in them. In the "loud chants," people remembered hearing God variously addressed as Pathen, Noimangpa, Vanleng, Lungzei, Nungzai, and Ningzai. The last three were clearly variants of the same name. Some took them to be synonymous with Pathen; others, to belong to a divine companion or consort — a being that served God but was distinct from him.

3. The red sea song. Everyone had heard of it. I found one person, Samson Dochang, who could sing it. He did so in the old dirgelike style. The words were:

> When the great feast was celebrated by us,
> The vast red water was divided.
> Led by cloud by day, by pillar of fire by night,
> They were swallowed by the sea.
> Rush to catch those birds for food.
> Drink the pure water from the mountain rock.

4. Circumcision. No one had witnessed or even heard of an old-religion circumcision. There was general knowledge of a naming ceremony, performed on the eighth day after birth, at which the newborn child's ears were pierced with a porcupine quill. There was also knowledge of the term "an old-time penis," which I had heard in Lianpui. It was used for a male member lacking a foreskin at birth.

In addition, there were, like Navi's priestly house calls on mourners, the usual miscellaneous parallels between old customs and biblical law. One day I was chatting with a young B'nei Menashe in his early thirties, a photographer named Shlomo Gangte. Shlomo was excited because he had come across a prohibition in the Bible against taking eggs from a nesting bird. He now understood, he told me, something that had happened to him as a boy. Spying a nest in a tree while walking with his father, he had started to climb the tree for the eggs, only to be warned to leave them alone. "Why can't I take them?" he had asked. "Because we mustn't," his father replied. His father didn't know why this was so. He knew only that it was the rule and always had been. "Now *I* know," Shlomo said.

⚜

Yehoshua Thangjom, Yitzhak's father, had one brown eye and one blue one. Although the blue eye was partially sightless, a memento from an unsuccessful cornea transplant, Mr. Thangjom bore his peculiar color scheme with good humor. He was a short, round, opinionated man, and the blue eye had a piercing quality.

He liked to argue. "It is up to you to prove me wrong!" he told me in good English after declaring, on my first evening in Imphal, that he was "of the tribe of Manasseh."

"On the contrary," I said. "It is up to you to prove yourself right. When a claim goes against all educated opinion, the burden of proof is on the claimant."

He sputtered at that but understood. What he really was saying was that his belief in being a member of a Lost Tribe was so much a part of him that I had better have good reasons for undermining it. His own reasons were emotional and psychological. "We Kukis do not belong to this place," he said of Manipur. "We have been here for hundreds of years, yet it is not ours. Have you ever heard of an entire people feeling out of place where their ancestors were born?"

Apart from the Jews, I confessed, I never had. "There you are!" he said, vindicated. "You see, we are not a happy people. We are always yearning."

"Nostalgic."

"Yes."

"For somewhere else."

"Exactly!" He was so happy that I understood.

"I've noticed that," I said. I had noticed it that night in Ratu, listening to the singers yearn for the Jordan. So had William Shaw, the British superintendent of Manipur's Northwest Subdistrict. In *The Thadou Kukis*, Shaw attributed the Kukis' nostalgia to their migratory, slash-and-burn life. Although generally "truculent," and with "a tremendous idea of his own importance," a Kuki, Shaw observed, particularly a Kuki woman, "will often be heard weeping in a village one is visiting because someone has turned up who looks like or has the same name as a long departed child, relation, or friend, or some conversation has recalled some sad day in her life. When deserting a village, the men will walk gaily off with anticipatory feelings of new ventures while the women will stay behind a while to shed a tear over the graves of their children and relatives, before catching up with the men, because they may never see them again."

"You're wanderers." I said to Yehoshua Thangjom. "You always have been. You have a permanent sense of impermanence. You look at others who feel at home and you envy them. It's that feeling you yearn for. It doesn't make you a Lost Tribe."

"We yearn for Zion," Mr. Thangjom said. "Have some more *zu*."

I filled another water glass from the unlabeled bottle that Yitzhak had bought for me. A cloudy yellow liquid with a cloying sweet-and-sour taste that fizzed on the tongue, it wasn't much to my liking. Yet I was curious to gauge its effects. Its alcoholic content, not great, was masked, as in a punch. It was definitely there, though. The second glass made me feel tingly. Several more might be seriously destabilizing.

Mr. Thangjom was eager to go over my schedule with me. It was he who had drawn it up, far in excess of my intentions when I told Yitzhak, before he left Aizawl, that we should plan my week in Imphal efficiently by arranging meetings in advance. The retired commissioner had taken to the task with administrative zeal. The two printed pages he handed me looked like the course load of an overambitious undergraduate. The first page was an "interview chart":

November 16, 1999 (Tuesday)

MORNING — 9:00 A.M. to 1:00 P.M.
9:00   Dr. H. Kamkenthang, Director Tribal Research, Govt. of Manipur
9:30   Pu Holkholun Lhungdim, Sociologist, Churachandpur
10:00   Pu T. Dongjakai Gangte, Chairman, Manmasi People's Congress
        Etc.

AFTERNOON — 2:00 P.M. to 6:30 P.M.
2:00   Dr. Lalnghorlien, Sr. Lecturer, Churachandpur College
2:30   Dr. Rev. T. Lunkim

3:00   Pu Haokholal Thangjom, Adviser to the Chief Minister, Govt. of Manipur
Etc.

November 18, 1999 (Thursday)

MORNING — 9:00 A.M. to 1:00 P.M.

9:00   Dr. Lal Dena, Professor in History, Manipur University
Etc.

AFTERNOON — 2:00 P.M. to 6:00 P.M.

2:00   Pu Jimmy Jamkhomang Haokip, Chairman, Thadou Tribal Council
Etc.

The second page said:

RECEPTION PROGRAMME
in honour of
Mr. Hillel Halkin and his friends
Kuki Inn
Wednesday, the 17th November 1999
11 A.M. onwards

Grander than my reception at Amishav House, this was to be in two parts. Part I would include a "welcome speech" by Mr. Thangjom; a "traditional welcome song"; more songs; some "cultural dances"; more speeches; more dances; a "short speech, if any"; and "words of thanks." Part II would be a demonstration of a sacrifice. If anything was capable of reviving the institution of sacrifice among the Kuki-Chin-Mizo, it was apparently a visit by an author from Israel.

☙

Fortunately, perhaps, half those on the interview chart never showed up. Mr. Thangjom did not seem to be put out by this. He had overbooked with it in mind.

The half that came to see me in the top-floor apartment of the Gaol Road building were not of much help. Most of them believed they were descendants of the biblical tribe of Manasseh, and none of them had anything new to say — or rather, anything remotely logical, since of outright lunacy there was no end. This started with Dr. H. Kamkenthang, Pu Holkholun Lhungdim, and Pu T. Dongjakai Gangte, who arrived together like the Three Wise Men of the East and had a riddle apiece for me. Dr. H. Kamkenthang's was: "There is, sir, an old Thado poem in which occur the words *ana* and *thoth*, the meanings of which are unknown. Do you not agree that they must be the village of Anatoth, from which hailed the prophet Jeremiah?"

Pu Holkholun Lungdhim propounded: "Sir! The Thado word for 'ocean,' *tuisogiet*, meant 'eight flowing waters.' Must not these have been the arms of the Nile? Surely they were not the arms of the Ganges flowing into the Bay of Bengal, for of these there are more than eight."

Pu T. Dongjakai Gangte proposed: "There is in Kuki folklore a great bird of prey called the *mulaopi*, so large that it carries men in its claws. A similar bird, called the roc, is described in the well-known book *Arabia's Nights*. But you see, sir, the roc is not native to Manipur. We cannot have encountered it here. Would you not say this proves that we come from the Middle East?"

The three were chagrined by my evasive replies. They whispered to one another, and T. Dongjakai Gangte said, reprovingly, "We feel, sir, that you deny us."

Before they left, they presented me with the constitution of the Manmasi People's Congress. Its preamble stated, "From time immemorial, our forefathers called upon Manmasi of old for safety from natural forces like hurricane, earthquake, etc and evil spirits throughout their migratory routes to the present habitats, whence originated the dialectical division." Article XV proposed overcoming this division by making Hebrew "the official language of the Congress." Prudently, it added, "However, English shall be in use so long as the Hebrew language is not mastered by the masses." Alas, the masses knew no English either.

The affair at the Kuki Inn was a large one. Hundreds of people turned out for it, B'nei Menashe from all over Manipur. They arrived in chartered buses from Muolkoi, from Moreh, from Kangpokpi, from Tuibong, from Tuipiphai, and from Churachandpur. They came less to honor me than for the entertainment and for the sacrifices and for one another. The sacrifices were a big draw. Their backsliding was not the problem that it was for the villagers of Lianpui. Judaism *was* backsliding, all the way back to the fathers. The younger people had never seen a sacrifice. Curious, they crowded on the grass outside the Kuki Inn.

Two sacrifices were performed, a private and a public one, each by a different priest. Both men had already appeared in Part I of the program, the private priest as the director of the "cultural dance" troupe, one of whose numbers was "Enter, Enter Zion." Choreographed to music, this started out with the dancers in a single long line. Two of them formed a gate through which the line wound, the last member peeling off on each pass to become a new gatepost; then, once the entire line had joined the gate, it reversed itself by unwinding. Although the dance resembled an English reel, I was assured by several of the onlookers that they had learned it as children long before seeing their first missionary. It was called "the Snake," they said, and was old.

The public priest had begun the reception by blowing a fanfare on a *gushomkol*, a traditional bamboo trumpet. His name was Zephaniah Haokip, and he was a short, wizened man with slit eyes like a lizard's in the heavy folds of his cheeks. The bamboo altar constructed for him was as tall as he was and rested on four posts supported by crossties. Seven bamboo tubes filled with *zu* were arranged along one side of it; seven empty tubes along another; and a seven-rung bamboo ladder leaned against it. At the foot of the ladder was a goat. Zephaniah Haokip stood by the goat, spraying it and the altar seven times from the seven tubes of *zu*. He used his mouth as a shower nozzle, as La Aa had done in A Gai Nei, and chanted:

> Pure, whatever animal it may be,
> Let what I offer you be pure
> To build my ladder.
> Build it like the *gopiphan*,
> Build it like the twinings of the *khaopi*,
> Build it like the curve of the tooth of the boar,
> Build it like the good blade.
> Pathen, upon this village I offer feasts.
> Choicest of the feasts I offer.
> Here, the bones unbroken and whole I put.
> I am continuing the ways of Pu Manmasi.
> I am continuing the ways of Pu Chongthu.
> I am continuing the ways of the Doikungpa.
> I am continuing the ways of Galgnam.

He laid the dull edge of his knife on the neck of the goat and tried cutting with it. Stymied, he apologized to the goat for having to use the sharp edge. It was necessary for the success of the year's crops. He cut the goat's throat, filled the seven empty tubes with blood, and placed them back on the altar. Opening the animal's chest, he removed the heart and liver, sliced each into seven pieces, and placed these by the blood-filled tubes. Then he severed the goat's head and four feet and put them on the altar, too. He said:

> Seven vessels of bamboo,
> Seven parts of the liver,
> Seven parts of the heart,
> Seven vessels of blood do I offer.
> For the biggest to the smallest,
> The old and the young,
> For their health during this year.
> May there be no dearth!
> For our well-being do I offer this.
> May you be fulfilled!
> Pathen-nu, may you be fulfilled!
> Pathen-pa, may you be fulfilled!
> My ancestor Manmasi, may you be fulfilled!
> Pu Doikungpa, may you be fulfilled!
> Pu Galgnam, may you be fulfilled!
> If I have said anything wrong, O my ancestors,
> May you forgive me.
> I am but continuing your ways.
> I am but continuing your deeds.
> I am but continuing your words.
> I may have left something unsaid.
> I may have left something undone.
> Forgive me for all left unsaid.
> Forgive me for all left undone.

That was the end of the sacrifice. Soon after, the guests climbed into their buses and went home.

I returned to my room in Amishav House. Toward evening I went to the Thangjoms' and drove back with Yitzhak and his father to the Kuki Inn.

A goat stew was bubbling in a tureen. Some B'nei Menashe were standing near it, passing around a bottle of IMFOL. By now I knew most of them: Peniel Haokip, and Elitsur Haokip, and Navi Songtiniam, and

Samson Dochang, and Zosi Thouthang, and Shlomo Gangte, and Zephaniah Haokip. Zephaniah was the oldest. He had performed his last real sacrifice, he told me, in 1970. The words he had recited today were from memory. He hadn't needed to rehearse them. It had felt good to pray to God again in the old way. But he had something to say.

"It's like this," Yitzhak said to me. "Zephaniah has two children in Israel. He knows he may never see them again. He understands why Rabbi Avichail chooses to send the young people. He's just sad that he can't convert to Judaism here in Manipur. He would like to die as a Jew."

While I was telling Zephaniah that Avichail was considering the dispatch of a rabbinical conversion court to India, Navi Songtiniam approached me. He had a question. The Hebrew word for "judge" was *shofet*, yet the Book of Judges was called *Shofetim*. Why?

Shofetim, I told Navi, was the plural; *–im* was the masculine plural ending.

He nodded, looking worried. That's what he had thought, but he had wanted to make sure. His real question was this: Why, then, was the Hebrew word for God, *elohim*, in the plural form too? Was the Bible saying God was many?

"Did someone tell you that?" I asked.

Yes, Navi said. A Christian friend had said it during an argument. The friend had said that the plural God was the Father, Son, and Holy Ghost. Navi hadn't known what to answer.

"You can tell your friend," I said, "that a small number of Hebrew nouns like *mayim*, meaning 'water,' have a plural ending because they indicate a single substance that is everywhere. It's the same with *elohim*. But tell him, too, that Hebrew has singular and plural verbs and that *elohim* always takes the singular verb. The Bible says, *bereshit bara elohim*. 'In the beginning God created — *singly* — heaven and earth.'"

Navi looked relieved. He knit his bushy brows, committing my words to memory.

It was remarkable. His question, posed by a Christian heretic to a rabbi, could be found in Bereshit Rabba, a fourth-century midrash on the Book of Genesis. My answer could be found there, too. Nothing was new in the old quarrel between Judaism and Christianity. And yet something was. Now it was Christianity that was the smug parent and Judaism the rebellious child. The two had changed places but not positions.

The bottle of IMFOL kept going around. Peniel put down his glass, slipped a drum strap over his shoulder, and tapped out a slow beat on a drum. Elitsur Haokip and Samson Dochang began to sing.

A circle formed. More people joined in the singing. They sang in the old dirgelike style, men and women together. They swayed in place as they sang, holding onto each long, mournful note as if about to part from it forever.

And in a sense they were doing just that. Theirs was the last generation that would sing these songs in Manipur.

Peniel drummed more slowly. The singers slowed down, too. Refusing to let the departing notes go, they clasped each in a long embrace.

They were singing the Kuki blues. The slower they sang, the happier they became. A plural grin ran like water through the folds of old Zephaniah Haokip's face. Elitsur conducted with one hand, a glass of IMFOL in the other. He pumped his arm slowly, juicing the fruit of sorrow to the pulp. He slowed the singers still more, until the stilled heart of time was barely beating.

> O my clansmen, that we have been torn
> Upon the big Samakai range.
> My sadness spreads from north to south.
> Like the water that is flowing, I move on.

Samson Dochang took the drum from Peniel. The circle began to dance. At first each dancer remained in place, exaggerating the swaying, one knee bending as the hip extended outward and straightening as the hip came back. Then the movement grew more pronounced and the foot took the lead: step to the left, bend the knee, straighten the knee, step back again; step to the right, bend the knee, straighten the knee, step back. Finally the steps were unshackled. As the dancers moved in a clockwise direction, Elitsur and Peniel entered the circle and danced against the clock. They crouched with knees low and arms extended, raising and lowering them from the shoulders. "We Kukis say," Yitzhak murmured in my ear, "that you must dance like an eagle, covering the earth with your wings."

The dancers indeed looked like great, flapping birds of prey. Speed them up, and you had the spinning women in Armed Veng. Slow down the singing in Ratu, and you had the Kuki blues. Perhaps loss, longing, and *mi-hlim*-ity were all the same emotion at different RPMs of the soul.

Elitsur left the circle and came over to me. The silk foulard he always wore around his neck made him the dandy of Manipur. "I am so-o happy," he said. He was happy because his dream had come true. Many years ago he had dreamed that two doves came from afar and fluttered around a tree. The tree was Imphal. How sad he was in his dream that the doves did not alight! Then Rabbi Avichail came to Imphal. He was the first dove. Now I had come, the second. Elitsur improvised a song about two doves, and Samson Dochang drummed. Elitsur called out each line, and everyone sang it back. It was turning into a Kuki jam session.

Yehoshua Thangjom was excited. "We're all drunk; we're all drunk!" he exclaimed, as if this were an exceptional feat. But though no one was misbehaving, Yitzhak thought it best to go home. The streets of Imphal were not safe at night, especially for a foreigner like me. They were roamed by armed gangs of hijackers and extortionists.

We bundled into the Thangjoms' car — Yitzhak, his father, several bodyguards, a pot of boiled goat, and I. Twice on our way we were stopped by army patrols, who shone flashlights into the car. The word "ex-commissioner" quickly released us. More bodyguards were waiting outside the house on Gaol Road. Upstairs, a new bottle of *zu* was on the table. I liked it better than the first one. Tangy, it tasted like a whiskey sour. *Zu* was beginning to grow on me.

⚜

From the synagogue upstairs came the sound of the morning prayer. Too lazy to rise for it, I followed it from my bed: the *p'sukei de-zimra*, the *ashrei*, the *barkhu*, the *shema*, the *shemoneh esrei*, the *aleinu*. There was no need to make out the words. The buzz and timbre, Avichail's, sufficed to identify them.

It was Friday. The night before, Shmuel had called from Aizawl. With Lianpuisuaka's will now reduced to a magic trick, a now-you-see-it-now-you-don't proposition, my inquiries had reached their end. There was nothing left for me to do in Imphal. A city without sights, its unsightliness, too, had been placed off-limits to me for "security reasons." Gaol Road, with its skulking pariah dogs and rickshaw desperados, was as good as its name.

I went to the Thangjoms' for my breakfast. Yitzhak was already gone, having driven to the village of Saikul to fetch a man who claimed to have "important evidence" for me — perhaps the slingshot with which David slew Goliath or another tale from *The Arabian Nights*. I was still sipping my milk tea when the day's first visitor arrived. He was K. L. Samuel and he sat on "the board of directors of the B'nei Yisrael of Northeast India." As we talked, he painfully kneaded his fingers, which he'd caught in the accordion bars of the Thangjoms' security gate.

Mr. Samuel was a Rongmei, or Kacha Naga, a member of a tribe of Nagafied Old Kukis that other Kukis denied all kinship with. Yet, though spurned, the Rongmeis, he had come to tell me, were a Lost Tribe, too. They too were "children of Manmasi." They too had once prayed to Za. They too had practiced eighth-day ear piercing. They had had a holiday called *ngat nuh ngai*, "the feast of the unseen foreskin." Although this holiday was no longer observed, what but circumcision could render a foreskin unseen?

Mr. Samuel was aggrieved by the B'nei Menashe's rejection of Rongmeis like him returning to their biblical roots. But the real culprit, he admonished me, was "your Chief Rabbi Eliahu Avichail." It was Avichail who had incited the B'nei Menashe to turn their backs on their Rongmei brethren. "We know," Mr. Samuel said, "that he is the one deputed by your government to make a feverish search for the lost Israelites. But since he has introduced the Judaism conversion system, his people have isolated themselves in this way." Avichail had "sown the seed of disharmony." As direct descendants of Manasseh, the Rongmeis could not accept the conversion system. And yet they had been attacked in the recent fighting by the Nagas, with the loss of over a thousand lives. "The Nagas say," Mr. Samuel told me, "that if we are Israelites, we do not belong in India. So! Please inform your government to take us home to Zion."

By now another visitor had arrived and taken a seat on the bench in the vestibule. Upon K. L. Samuel's departure he presented himself as Hemkhochon Chongloi. He taught theology at Kuki Christian College, whose dean, the Reverend T. Lumkin, had sent him to convey his apologies for missing his interview with me and to answer any questions I might have about the old Kuki religion. Hemkhochon Chongloi had written his M.A. thesis on that very subject.

I did not spend much time with him for two reasons. The first was that, asked whether he had ever come across the name "Za" or "Pu Za" in priestly chants, he replied, "I believe a *puja* is a Hindu ritual offering," and added, "To tell you the truth, I never took much interest in those old chants." Presumably he had researched for his thesis by reading medieval works of Kuki theology. He was not the first such academic I had met in northeast India. Men like him thought fieldwork was demeaning. They looked shocked when you suggested it, as if you had proposed banishing them from their desks to the rice paddies. They had not fought their way up from the paddies in order to return to them.

The second reason for cutting short Hemkhochon Chongloi's visit was that three more people were waiting in the vestibule. They had arrived with Yitzhak and were an odd-looking group. One was a pudgy man with thin gray hair combed straight back and knotted in a chignon behind his head, a sparse mustache, and two beards, the first growing wispily from his chin and the second from beneath his lower lip. He wore a white turtleneck shirt; white, baggy cotton slacks; a V-neck pullover embroidered with bright geometric patterns and two large Stars of David; and a plug of amber in each ear. Over his shoulder was a haversack. He looked like a middle-aged Manipuri hippie.

Beside him sat a slightly built woman with many necklaces and gold bangles. Her hairdo, which circled her head in a crown of stiff ringlets, appeared to be pomaded with glue.

The third person was dressed in a blanket. When the man and the woman rose from the bench, he walked behind them, carrying a tall paper scroll.

I glanced at my watch. Breakfast was ending with fruitcake. I would give them half an hour and get rid of them.

Yitzhak introduced them: Dr. Khuplam Milui Lenthang, his wife, and their son, Thangsei.

Dr. Khuplam *chibai*-ed me. He was "deeply touched," he told Yitzhak in Thado, that someone from "the outside world" had taken an interest in "our old culture." He had wished to see me because this culture was an interest of his, too. But before we talked about it, perhaps he should tell me about himself. I must be curious about the Stars of David.

The clock was running. Let it be the Stars of David.

The Stars of David, Dr. Khuplam said, had to do with his belonging to the Beth Midrash Hashem, the same Messianic movement to whose synagogue Peter Tlau had taken me in Aizawl. Like Kawbzedawr and Navi, he believed in "the teachings of Joshua." The Messiah was still to come. Meanwhile, he strove to live by the verse "And thou shalt love the Lord thy God with all thy heart, and with all thy soul, and with all thy might." That was his religion.

Mrs. Khuplam whispered to her husband. Dr. Khuplam spoke to Yitzhak. Yitzhak said, "Dr. Khuplam asks if you would like to hear about his visions."

Let it be his visions.

"It's like this," Yitzhak said. Dr. Khuplam had been a Baptist. In 1972 he had a dream. He was living then in the Mikir Hills, a region south of the Brahmaputra Valley and north and west of Kuki territory. In his dream he saw seven bodiless heads beckoning him to follow them. This he did and was led to an old, deserted road on which the sun never shone. Although he tried his best to walk it, the darkness was too great. He asked the heads, "What is this road?"

"This," the heads said, "is the road taken by the children of Manmasi."

The heads took him to a mountaintop. From there, he looked down and saw the Kuki-Chin-Mizo people spread out below in the darkness. The heads said, "It is your task to bring the sun to these people and retrieve the lost flock. You must command the sun to rise seven times."

He commanded the sun to rise. Large and dim on the horizon, it rose out of the sea in the east. He commanded it a second time, and it rose again. Each time it rose higher, brighter, and smaller until it shone down overhead, a tiny, brilliantly glowing point. Its heat dried the sea and uncovered fertile land. The children of Manmasi set out for this land on the sunlit road. "Go east to your people," the heads instructed him before he awoke from his dream. And so he moved from the Mikir Hills to Manipur, first to a village named Gelnal and then to Saikul.

In Manipur, Dr. Khuplam continued, he developed an "acute interest" in religion. This culminated in 1983 in another dream, in which he was ordered to "purify and circumcise" himself. He did so without knowing the reason for it. Circumcised, he prayed daily for divine guidance. In particular, he wished to know the true story of the children of Manmasi. He had heard of a lost scroll in which this story was told, and he prayed for it to be revealed to him. This went on for several years. Then, on October 5, 1986, he had a waking vision — his first. "God seized my hand," he said, "and made me write." He wrote strange letters he had never seen before. Several weeks later this happened again, and then again. Usually it took place after midnight, after he had been praying on his knees for a long time. In this way, the entire alphabet of the lost scroll was made known to him. He learned it well enough to write in it.

The half-hour was almost up. I would have a look at his scroll and bid the visionary doctor farewell. I said, "I take it that's what your son is holding. The ancient wisdom eaten by the Chinese dogs."

Dr. Khuplam laughed politely. He wished it were so. But this was not what his visions had revealed to him. They had only revealed the lost scroll's alphabet, the *bulpizam*, as it was called. The scroll Thangsei was now unrolling on the Thangjoms' coffee table was not the lost scroll itself.

I bent to look at it. "Oh, Christ!" I said. The whole thing was written in visionary characters. They reminded me of Paucinhau's. "How is anyone supposed to read this?"

Yitzhak said, "Dr. Khuplam has an English translation for you. He has some other things to show you, too." The haversack was emptied onto the table. Out came a mimeographed manuscript, some white cotton fabric, two antique flints, an old gunpowder horn, a box for bullet caps, a shiny black stone with "living powers," a broken cylinder once used by priests, and one or two other artifacts. They lay meagerly on the table as though in the poorest section of a flea market.

Mrs. Khuplam and Thangsei unfolded the fabric and held it up for display. The size of a large tablecloth, it was covered in different colors of Magic Marker with a large map and several Thado texts. I recognized one of these as the red sea song. The map showed the migration route of the children of Manmasi to southeast Asia. It started in Egypt, crossed the Red Sea to Canaan, passed through the Middle East to Afghanistan and Tibet, and swung far north into Mongolia before looping back to the Indian-Burmese frontier. "Why Mongolia?" I asked, piqued by the illogic of such a great detour to an inhospitable region.

Dr. Khuplam did not know why the children of Manmasi had journeyed to Mongolia. But he knew from their old priestly chants that they had done so.

"Not from your visions?"

He once again laughed politely. No, not from his visions. He knew the difference between a vision and a chant. He had told me about his visions only because he thought they might interest me, not because they were evidence of anything. The evidence he had for me was ethnographic.

He seemed a rather sane man.

An hour after he left, I phoned Yitzhak from Amishav House. I had been reading the English translation of the scroll. It was called *The Wonderful Genealogical Tales of the Kuki-Chin-Mizo*.

"Where's Khuplam?" I asked.

"I don't know," Yitzhak said. "Somewhere in Imphal."

"You're sure he hasn't gone back to Saikul?"

"Positive. I'm driving him this afternoon."

"Don't."

"Why not?"

"I have to talk to him. Listen. You may belong to a Lost Tribe after all."

"Because of Khuplam?" He was incredulous.

I said, "Just keep him in Imphal."

⚜ 10 ⚜

The People Driven from Their Land
by a Long-tailed Wildcat

A T THIS POINT, since I am about to make some large claims based heavily on the findings of one man, I should say a few words to the reader. In the best of circumstances, it is inadvisable to build a case on one man's work — especially when that case, as I put it to Yehoshua Thangjom, goes against educated opinion. Moreover, the circumstances are not the best. My description so far of Dr. Khuplam Milui Lenthang will have done nothing to inspire confidence in him. You have reason to be, like Yitzhak, in a skeptical frame of mind. Stay there. I need you to remain level-headed in the pages ahead.

At the same time, do not prejudge the matter. Appearances are most deceiving across cultural lines. Take Dr. Khuplam's visions, for example. If a native-born Oklahoman were to tell you that he had moved to Ohio at the urging of bodiless heads, you might very well question his sanity. This is because in America, as a general rule, people do not say or do such things. But this is not true, as we have seen, of the Kuki-Chin-Mizo. Many of them who are quite normal view their sleeping and waking dreams as messages from above. In such a society, visions like Dr. Khuplam's are not aberrant.

Nor should you be misled by his and his family's physical appearance. Though unconventional, it was not unconsidered. The Khuplams went about as they did — Dr. Khuplam all the time, his wife and son on special occasions — as a cultural statement. The oddities of their grooming and garb represented traditional Kuki ways that had lapsed. They had adopted them out of an identification with a vanished past.

This past had preoccupied Khuplam Lenthang ever since he could remember. As a boy in the 1920s and '30s in the village of Hoflung in the North Cachar Hills, his favorite pastime had been listening to the old stories passed down from generation to generation. He first heard these as bedtime tales from his maternal grandmother, who was, in effect, his second parent, since his father, Thangzalang Lenthang, a sepoy in the 3rd Assam Rifles, rarely came home from his military postings. The Lenthangs and the Chengsons, closely related clans descended, according to legend, from two brothers, were Hoflung's sole inhabitants in those days. Although they were Thado speakers, they were not Thados or even Kukis in the strict sense. Their traditions held that they had been in northeast India before the Kukis arrived there, an opinion the latter concurred in, since they called them *mi lui*, "the old people."

The Cachar Hills were a northwestern salient of Kuki settlement projecting into the plains of Assam, and Hoflung was a hamlet of thirty houses. All were similar two-room dwellings set on a slope with timber stilts on the downhill side, a front and a rear veranda, and a hearth on the uphill side of the main room. Christianity had not yet come to the village, and there were no schools or books. The population was illiterate. The children spent most of their time playing. Khuplam preferred listening to his grandmother's stories. Next best was gathering other children around him and telling her stories to them. He told them exactly as he had heard them. It never occurred to him to make a story up. As he grew older and wanted to hear new ones, he frequented other houses where good storytellers lived. None was better than his mother's aunt Lhingneng Chengson. Since she was a very old woman who hated housework, the two of them reached an understanding: Khuplam did the chores that Lhingneng most disliked, such as fetching water, gathering firewood, and husking rice, and she paid him with stories. He amassed a large repertoire from her.

All of Hoflung practiced the old religion in those days. Khuplam's maternal grandfather, Lalsazei, was the local *thempu*, or public priest, and often asked the boy to help him. "Here, chop wood for a sacrifice," he would say, or, "Bring me some bamboo for an altar." It was his way of initiating his grandson into these practices, because he wanted him to carry on the priestly line. But although Khuplam liked learning about the old customs, being a priest did not appeal to him. This was partly due to his mother's influence. It was not that she didn't believe in the old religion, but, rather, that she did. A priest's work, she told him, was difficult and dangerous. One slip in a sacrifice or ceremony, a single wrong word or act, and you could bring down a curse on yourself and die young.

She wanted him to study, to learn to read and write. It was what he wanted, too. At the age of seventeen he enrolled in the Bengalee Lower Primary School in Silchar. Bengali was the lingua franca of Assam, and most people in Hoflung knew some. He was put in first grade with a group of seven- and eight-year-olds and several pupils even older than himself. Unused to formal study, he did not do well and was left back at the end of his first year. By his second year, however, he was excelling, and at the end of the third he was sent for advanced schooling to the American Baptist mission school in Golaghat. Before he left for it his mother told him, "Learn what the Christians have to teach you but stay true to your own religion. Remember that you come from a line of priests."

The mission school was his first encounter with Christianity. Mostly this took the form of daily hymn singing, supplemented by exhortations to convert. His teachers' attitude toward native religion was dismissive; they saw nothing of value in it and urged their students to abandon it without looking back. But while the Christians' beliefs did not speak to his soul, he coveted their knowledge. Upon graduating from the mission school he was accepted at a Baptist medical college in Dibrugarh.

The course of studies in Dibrugarh was three years. The medicine taught was rudimentary by Western standards. The Welsh missionaries in charge sought to turn out evangelists as well as doctors, men who would spread the gospel to the villagers they treated. After receiving his degree, he had himself baptized. He didn't do this out of conviction. It was part of obtaining a medical assignment, and he did not feel guilty about it. But his family in Hoflung took it hard. His explanation that it was a mere formality fell on deaf ears, and his mother and grandmother (his grandfather was no longer alive) broke off all ties with him.

This grieved him, yet he was, in any case, far away. His assignment was in the Sibsagar District in the upper Brahmaputra River valley, well to the north of Kuki and even Naga territory. As a traveling mission doc-

tor he tended to his patients and engaged in his old pastime of telling stories — this time from the New Testament. He earned twenty-seven rupees a month, a good salary in those days, and went on foot from village
to village. There were several dozen along his route, which took many
days to traverse. The villagers had no telephones; as ill as they might be,
they simply waited for him to appear. He treated malaria and other fe-
vers, set broken bones, and delivered babies. The remedies in his bag
were three: quinine; M & B, or May & Baker, a compound of sulfa
diamadine advertised as "the medicine for 80 diseases"; and something
called APC, Approved Prevalent Control, for everything else.

In 1949 he made up his mind to return to Hoflung. With the gradual
penetration of Christianity into the Cachar Hills after Word War II, the
stigma of his baptism had faded, and he was now reconciled with his family. And he had had a realization. Passing back and forth through the
Hindu villages of the Sibsagar District and listening to the old people's stories, he had seen how these were dying with their tellers. The
agents of modernization — literacy, newspapers, film — were breaking
the chain of transmission. Hindu folk culture was not his concern; yet it
struck him with a shock that the same thing must be happening among
the Kukis, and that the world of his childhood, with its endless tales and
legends, was about to disappear. Medicine touched no deep place in him.
Stories did. He decided to abandon his medical practice and devote his
life to the collection of Kuki folklore.

He did not wait to reach Hoflung to begin. On his way there he
passed through the Naga Hills and stopped at a Kuki village called
Maove. There was a *thempu* there named Paominthang Lenthang, an elder brother of his grandfather, who knew many chants and old stories.
Dr. Khuplam asked to hear them and wrote them all down. Paominthang
Lenthang was his first proper informant. From then on he kept a diary in
which he recorded everything of interest that he heard. He dated each
entry and noted the name and place of each source. Although his methods were primitive and made no use of tape recorders or cameras, he had
become — without training or guidance, and without even knowing the
word — an ethnographer. The British having left India, he was in fact
the only ethnographer at work in those years in the Kuki-Chin-Mizo
area.

For the next five or six years he lived in Hoflung, treating the occasional patient and traveling widely in the Cachar Hills to collect material. His informants were mainly Kukis, though some also came from neighboring tribal groups like the Khasi and the Garo. Most were old men and women who remembered things no longer known to others. Whenever they told him of a custom, story, chant, or rite, he would press them for confirmation. "Is that true?" he would ask. "Are you sure this is really so?" Back in Hoflung, he went over his latest notes and compared them with others. Sometimes they contained complete oral texts gathered from a single person; often he had to piece these together from different sources. Between field trips he married a cousin, a Lenthang like himself. (Cousin marriages were traditional among the Kukis, it being customary to wed the daughter of one's mother's brother, a system that created complex patterns of kinship on which the social structure depended.) In 1955 he moved farther north to his wife's village, Karbianlang in the Mikir Hills, where he established a small office for his manuscripts and records. He extended his travels, journeying to Manipur, the Chin Hills, and Mizoram; his ultimate goal was to discover the *bulpizam*, the ancient writing of the lost scroll that he believed still existed. In 1967 he "published," in a single handwritten copy, his first book. This was *The Wonderful Genealogical Tales of the Kuki-Chin-Mizo*, which I had just finished reading.

I'd read it in a translation from Thado by a man named Sehkholun Singson, whom I had met at the Thangjoms'. Although Singson's English was frequently comical, I would have been an ingrate to laugh at it, for he had done his heroic best, and I was indebted to him.* The book was divided into two parts, the first a purported digest of old legends and myths pertaining to human and Kuki-Chin-Mizo origins. The opening chapter, "War in Heaven," described a primeval conflict among the gods. In this conflict Pathen and his forces triumphed, and the losing gods were banished from heaven, "never to be of its citizens forever."

Chapter 2, "The Creation of Earth and Man," began: "Soon after the war in heaven was over, the gods met together and resolved that they should make men for their worshipers and obedient in their command-

---

* Although I have generally retained Singson's language in this summary of my first reading of *The Wonderful Genealogical Tales*, I have changed some passages for the sake of greater comprehensibility.

ments and orders. Then the heavenly god created the earth, all kinds of living animals on the earth and at the center most he made a redden earth, which was higher than other earth. . . . He took out a piece of this redden earth and poured it into golden water. He inspired his breath on the golden watered earth. Then this golden watered earth statue could breathe and live. God called this golden statue man three times. But the man would not respond. Then God was angry with him and said, 'This man I have made with my hand has pride and could not reply even after I called three times. He will not obey and worship me.' So the god abolished this golden man."

God then created a second man, this one of silver, who also failed to respond. On his third try, he used "redden earth" alone. "He molded it and inspired his gas into the mouth of the statue. The statue became living man. And God called, 'Oh, my handmade redden earth man!' The statue responded, 'Yes, I am here, my lord and god,' and searched here and there." And so God blessed this man, saying, "You have been made out of redden earth. When I called you only one time, you replied me and searched me. You are also made in the image of myself, and as such, I love you dearly."

Chapter 3, "How Woman Was Formed," told of God's creation of "a female from an ordinary earth." The children of the male and female multiplied until, generations later, there was a great flood. "The waters and rivers were stagnated, and the flooding water covered all the descendants of the redden earth man except a small family."

Chapter 4 began with an account of Kholkip-Kholzang, a place where, after the flood, "human beings and animals were dwelling and communing together in one language. However, after they have been dwelling together for many thousands of years, they quarreled and disputed each other. Then they separated willingly and went away to east, west, north, and south, which caused gradual differentiating of many kinds of skins, languages, and customs." One group reached a "fruitful oiled land," where they lived and grew bountiful harvests of rice, until a great famine struck. Hearing that there was abundant food in "the land of Tuisogiet," they went there. The ruler of Tuisogiet was Pu Vanthang, and his wife was Pi Lhangmi. Together they fought the famine. A text, curiously labeled by Sehkholun Singson "Legendary episode (Secret poetic words)," said of them:

> Coming down from the heaven above,
> Pu Vanthang reached the Tuisogiet
> With Tuisogiet's daughter Pi Lhangmi,
> Married together nuptially,
> And gave birth to a male child.
> This great son's name — Manmasi —
> Was composed lovingly.

Singson explained. "*Van* means 'heaven' . . . *thang* means 'fame.' Taking these two words together, the man's name was told as Vanthang, which means 'a very popular and fame man from heaven.'"

I put down the manuscript to think.

Like practically everything else so far in *The Wonderful Genealogical Tales of the Kuki-Chin-Mizo*, this story — the first I had come across that had specific information about the nebulous figure of Manmasi — could be linked to a biblical narrative in Genesis. If Manmasi was to be identified with Manasseh, then "Tuisogiet" — the land of "the eight flowing waters," as I had learned from Holkhulon Lungdhim — was indeed Egypt, and Pu Vanthang and Pi Lhangmi were Manasseh's parents, Joseph and his wife, Asenath, the daughter of the Egyptian priest Potiphera. Yet, like everything else, the resemblance was only partial. The Joseph of Genesis did not descend from heaven, just as Yahweh did not create three Adams, and men and beasts in the Garden of Eden did not "commune together in one language."* Like the Karen legend of Mu Kaw Lee's tower, these appeared to be biblical narratives reworked by native storytellers.

Next came Chapter 5, "The Migration Of Pu Vanthang's People," beginning "After some time, the people left Tuisogiet for the fruitful oiled land. On the way they had to cross a sea . . ." There followed the red sea song in a version like those I knew. Then, after the people of Pu Vanthang had gone "far and far from the Red Sea and settled here and there in the wildernesses of landlocks," there was another "legendary episode":

> We adore Thee whose art in heaven,
> Seven folds heaven, seven folds earth,

---

* Mankind itself, of course, according to the Bible, did originally speak a single language. As for the "war in heaven," the story of Satan's rebellion and fall, although not in the Old Testament, it can be found in both the New Testament and the Hebrew Apocrypha.

> For the producing of the tales,
> At the fruitful oiled land.
> Forefathers' Ghost and for health
> And for nutrition,
> From the sacred *bulpizam*,
> We the children of Manmasi,
> Shine bloom upon us.

I found this barely comprehensible. Apparently "the sacred *bulpi-zam*," the ancient script "rediscovered" by Dr. Khuplam, was supposed to be the Torah, given on Mount Sinai after the exodus from Egypt. And in Chapter 7, after the people of Pu Vanthang had reached the "fruitful oiled land" and lived there "peacefully and pleasantly," came an even stranger passage. "One day," it related, "the children of the fruitful oiled land wore their colorful dress and danced in the stretched floor gayous and peacefully. They continued dancing and dancing. At last, all the dressing cloths were loosen and get down the floor. At that moment, Sangah Meichol, the long-tailed wildcat, barked and took away the cloths from them secretly. Then all the children of the oiled land were unclothed and naked. At that moment the heaven sounded thunder loudly, and the children of the oiled land were afraid very much and ran away from their city. Then Sangah Meichol occupied the city. The children of Manmasi spread to the east, west, north, and south of the earth, where they could not claim their identities as the children of the fruitful oiled land. This period is believed to be around 722 B.C. and they composed a sacred ballad about it."

A wildcat occupying a city by stealing clothes? Although Dr. Khuplam obviously considered this story to be a description of the fall of Samaria and of the Assyrian exile of the northern tribes of Israel, it sounded like nothing more than a garbled folktale about an animal trickster. Nor did the rest of the chapter clarify anything when it said:

"Anywhere they go, they sung this sacred ballad in remembrance of their past events, which were tearful and tiresome. The other people could not recognise what identities or nation are they. If they announced they were the children of the fruitful oiled land, they would be killed by their foe. . . . Because of this, they dwelled in caves, holes of rocks, holes of earths, and shadows of trees and woods, and in the jungles, so that no one can trace out and kill them. . . . Then they reached the upper city located at the eastern north of the globe, where they made mansion for a long period. For the remembrance of their gallantry and velocities in the southern areas they left, they sung a sacred ballad as follows:

> Through nights while great darkness,
> I aflamed killed beasts' heads,
> I danced up to the cocks crow,
> Then I met the dawn.

"The children of the globe now have this sacred ballad in remembrance of the great darkness. . . . For this reason, they left this city and spread in different all corners of the earth . . . Then they came from southern place for northern place. When they reached the city of northern place, they made the southern city in sacred ballad as follows:

> The southern how bright,
> My migration, Si-on.
> The northern bright, forward it,
> The southern shall perish now.
> The downian's cock shall crow.
> Forward, the children of Manmasi!

"They brought customs, sacred ballads and sacrificial usages for their identities on the ways and settlements. . . . Then, around 300 B.C., they settled in the land of Tibet. . . . Then they migrated to the valley of a big river within Burma. . . . At that time the British government came with power."

It was gibberish.

And then something occurred to me.

The Thado words *sangah meichol* were pronounced "sangametsal." Kuki speakers, like Mizo speakers, could not articulate the palatal *sh*, for which they substituted a sibilant *s*. Furthermore, in the history of languages, the consonants *l*, *m*, and *n* often changed places with each other, as did *l* and *r*. And the Assyrian king who besieged the city of Samaria in 722 B.C.E. was called, in Hebrew, "Shalmaneser." If this name had survived for thousands of years in the memory of an Israelite tribe, or a part of one, that had wandered to southeast Asia — and if, now pronounced, say, "Salnamesel," it was connected with an ancient defeat, disaster, or exile — and if no one knew any longer who or what "Salnamesel" was —

would it not be natural to seek an explanation in a similar-sounding word in one's own southeast Asian language? Suppose what came to mind was *sangah meichol*, the long-tailed wildcat. Might not then a folktale evolve, senseless though it might be, about such an animal driving one's ancestors from their land?

That was when I phoned Yitzhak and told him to keep Dr. Khuplam in Imphal.

⚜

We met again the next morning, after prayer in Amishav House. More spirited than the Sabbath service in Aizawl, it was led by the same men who had sung and danced around the goat stew in the Kuki Inn. They switched styles easily.

Dr. Khuplam was combed and dressed as at our first meeting. Mrs. Khuplam had let down her hair. The stiff ringlets were gone, their place taken by a simple braid that circled her head. Thangsei was not there.

I began with a few remarks. I told the Khuplams about my weeks in Mizoram; touched briefly on my adventures with Yosi and George; and spoke of being astonished by *The Wonderful Genealogical Tales*. Their similarity to the Bible, I said, could not be coincidental. The key question was whether this similarity could be explained by contact with Christianity. If it could not be — if it could be proved that at least some of these tales predated Christianity's first appearance among the Kuki-Chin-Mizo — then a possible link with ancient Israel, as mysterious as it might seem, had to be taken seriously. It was therefore crucial to determine whether such proof existed.

Dr. Khuplam believed that it did. I had to understand, he said, where the material in *The Wonderful Genealogical Tales* came from. Basically, there were three kinds of sources. One was old priestly chants. Known as *themthu* in Thado, these were called by Sehkholun Singson "legendary episodes (secret poetic words)" because they were generally known only by priests, who recited them in low voices. A second category was *lapi*, traditional folk songs like the red sea song, referred to by Singson as "sacred ballads," even though there was nothing particularly sacred about them. (In fact, Yitzhak observed, the songs I had heard at the Kuki Inn were good examples of *lapi*.) Finally, there were folk tales, or *thusim*, such as those Dr. Khuplam had heard as a boy in Hoflung.

Everything in *The Wonderful Genealogical Tales* came from a *themthu*, a *lapi*, or a *thusim*. The most reliably ancient of these were the *themthu*, which, though varying from tribe to tribe, were never knowingly tampered with; transmitted only within priestly families, they were considered to lose their power, even to become harmful, if altered. *Lapi* and *thusim* were more adaptable. It was not unknown for old melodies to be sung with new words or for stories to change. Yet here, too, Dr. Khuplam said, he was confident that the songs and stories he had relied on were genuinely old. New material was usually detectable by its more modern language and content. Furthermore, in the Cachar Hills, where he had done his most intensive collecting, Christianity had arrived very late. The first baptisms did not take place there until the 1940s. People like his grandmother and his aunt Lhingneng had never been exposed to Christianity and knew nothing about it.

"But they could have been influenced by it indirectly," I said. "Bible stories originating elsewhere could have reached Hoflung in a Kuki form without anyone realizing where they'd come from."

He did not think this had happened. For one thing, such stories had never circulated in those parts of northeast India to which Christianity had come earlier, such as Assam and Nagaland. And in Manipur the British missionaries had taught the New Testament exclusively. They did not translate the Old Testament into native languages, and they warned the faithful not to read it even in English, because it was "outdated." He himself, despite his Baptist education, had never read a word of it before 1979. He couldn't have read it much before then even had he wanted to, because its first volumes in Thado started appearing in the late 1960s. Their translator was the Reverend T. Lumkin.

I said, "But you compiled *The Wonderful Genealogical Tales* in 1967. You clearly arranged the tales on the basis of the Old Testament. How could you have done that without knowing the Old Testament?"

The answer, Dr. Khuplam said, was simple. The English translation I'd read was prepared from a second, revised Thado edition, which he had issued in 1986, after the first of his *bulpizam* visions. The express purpose of this edition was to order the material according to the biblical sequence of events. The 1967 edition had been arranged differently.

"Tell Dr. Khuplam," I told Yitzhak, "that you'll need to compare the two."

Dr. Khuplam replied to this at length. "It's like this," Yitzhak said. "I can't compare them. The first edition no longer exists." This was because, when Dr. Khuplam moved from Gelnal to Saikul, he'd left many of his belongings in Gelnal. During a Naga attack on the Gelnal area in September 1993, eighty Kukis were killed and much of the village was burned, including the single 1967 copy of *The Wonderful Genealogical Tales* and Dr. Khuplam's diaries and field notes.

"Not again!" I groaned. First Yosi Hualngo, now this. Or else, in a part of the world where bamboo houses burned like straw, destruction by fire was a convenient alibi for anything nonexistent. I had been counting on seeing those diaries. "All of them?"

No, Dr. Khuplam said, not all. He had taken two of them to Saikul. They were from 1965 and 1972 and contained references to other years. Copies of his other books, as well as earlier drafts of them, had been in Saikul too. Although some of the pages were later used to wrap vegetables, little of value had been lost.

"*Vegetables?*" Now I had heard everything.

"Fruit, too," Yitzhak said. "Dr. Khuplam says even chocolate. There was never enough paper in Saikul, so people walked into his house and helped themselves. He asked them not to, but they didn't always listen."

A legendary episode:

PRICELESS DOCUMENTS
PRESERVED FROM FIRE
PERISH AS PAPER BAGS.

But I didn't dwell on it. I had one more day left in Manipur. "Ask Dr. Khuplam if I can come to Saikul tomorrow," I said. "I'd like to see what he has there."

Dr. Khuplam responded by clasping my hand warmly. As soon as he released it, Mrs. Khuplam seized it and pressed it to her lips, my first Kuki-Chin-Mizo kiss. The gesture struck me as excessive. Yet it needed to be seen in the light of an earlier incident.

Dr. Khuplam had been telling me about his field trips when three soldiers armed with rifles appeared at the Thangjoms' door. With them was a man in civilian clothes. Yehoshua Thangjom hurried to greet the man, whom he introduced as Mr. Matei, the income tax commissioner of Manipur. He had come especially, Mr. Thangjom said, to see me. I felt a current of alarm.

But Mr. Matei, whose armed escort was routine, was not out to arrest me on a tax charge. He was studying for a degree in anthropology and had come to discuss my research. He sat down beside me with an obliging smile and asked me to tell him about it.

I didn't want to interrupt Dr. Khuplam. "You've come at a good time," I told the tax commissioner, explaining that he could best get an idea of what I was doing by sitting in on the interview presently under way.

Mr. Matei settled into his chair with a grunt and listened for a minute to Dr. Khuplam talk about his work. Then, losing interest, he cast around for something to occupy himself with, took a copy of *The Manipur Gazetteer* from a bookshelf, and turned its pages. After a while he rose and went to chat with Mr. Thangjom.

It was typical. Here, ten feet away from him, was the greatest ethnographic resource in the state of Manipur, and the distinguished student of anthropology could not have cared less. No one could. Not one person on my interview chart had so much as mentioned Khuplam. He was, to those who knew of him at all, an eccentric worth nobody's time. Little wonder that he and his wife were grateful to me for wanting to make the trip to Saikul, especially when the roads were not entirely safe.

They sat close to each other on the couch. Several times during the conversation Mrs. Khuplam spoke to her husband. Once he made an annoyed response. After they left I asked Yitzhak about this. He said, "Mrs. Khuplam kept pestering him to tell you more about his visions. In the end he lost his temper."

"What did he say?"

"He said, 'Be quiet, woman! This man hasn't come from Israel to hear about my visions. He wants to know about my field work.'"

He really did know the difference.

ᨆ

I slept badly. Kept up for a long time by my thoughts, I was awakened in the middle of the night by Hindu religious music being chanted over a loudspeaker. The voice was tender, crooning; the loudspeaker, turned up to full volume, blasted the empty streets of Imphal with a lunatic rage. The voice sang of the soul's love for the All; the loudspeaker *was* the All, terrible and tyrannical. When it was finally switched off, the pariah dogs broke into frightful moans. Before sunrise a bugle sounded reveille in the Assam Rifles camp at the end of Gaol Road, past the slimy moat surrounding the remains of the royal compound of the Vaishnavite Manipuri kings.

Since Yehoshua Thangjom needed his car, Yitzhak and I went by taxi to Saikul, taking Shlomo Gangte with us. I wanted him to photograph any important documents.

The road crossed the Imphal Valley and headed northeast into the hills. It followed, upstream, the course of the Gun River, which cut a series of little valleys that descended like steppingstones to the big one we had left. The landscape was two-toned, the dun stubble of the harvested rice fields contrasting with the lime color of freshly planted paddies, grown with water from the river as a second, dry-season crop. The harvest was gathered in horseshoe-shaped stacks. Threshers were at work between the cusps. Their heads turbaned against the flying chaff, they flailed the earth with long stalks, as if beating a tired horse.

In the last of the upland valleys, beyond which the Gun cut a narrower course, we turned off the main road and drove to a scraggly village. This was Saikul. We passed some houses and a billboard with the message LEPROSY? NO PROBLEM! GET CURED! and came to a fence of beanpoles and dried vines. In it was a gate, and beyond the gate a yard, and at the back of the yard a brick house with a tin roof. A sign said:

Office of the
National Research Laboratory
For Conservation of Chin-Kuki-Mizo
Cultural Properties

The office had a desk, some chairs, and two benches, which quickly filled with curious onlookers. The walls were as crowded as the benches. Hanging on them were native baskets and artifacts; animal horns; an art nouveau fresco of a loin-clothed Kuki youth and a Kuki maiden in a wraparound dress; cotton cloths with texts and drawings like the one shown me in Imphal; signs and placards; Dr. Khuplam's medical license; his wife's certificates in "Tailoring & Cutting Training," "Woolknitting Training," and "Horticulture Training"; a map of Asia; and assorted calendars. Dangling from the ceiling was a red-white-and-black *phelep*, the Kuki *langlap*. Off to one side, in a semi-detached alcove, stood a plain table with a seven-branched candelabrum. This was Dr. Khuplam's prayer nook. Now, though, he prayed aloud at his desk while Mrs. Khuplam joined her hands and shut her eyes. Then we got down to work. My first request was for an overview of all that had survived the Gelnal fire. What did this include?

The answer was placed on the desk in three piles. The first was of sixteen bound books, all written on lined paper in a neat, flowing hand, which represented Dr. Khuplam's life's work. Some of these (*The Revelation of Ancient Times, The Mythical Heaven, Theological Reflections*) dealt with his visions and religious speculations. The *Alphabetical Handbook* described the *bulpizam*. There was a volume called *Home Medicine* and another dealing with Kuki history under the British. *Wonderful Things* described memorable people and occasions that had come the author's way. Four books pertained to the more distant past. Beside *The Wonderful Genealogical Tales of the Kuki-Chin-Mizo*, the only volume translated into English, there was a slim collection of *themthu, lapi,* and *thusim,* entitled *Who Was Manmasi?*; a book called *The Origins of the Kukis;* and one of *Folk Songs and Priestly Chants.* Essentially, Dr. Khuplam said, all the important material in the last three books was summarized in *The Wonderful Genealogical Tales.* We could concentrate on that.

The second pile was of unbound and undated manuscript drafts of the books in the first pile. It was from these, Dr. Khuplam said, that the villagers of Saikul had taken their wrapping paper.

The third and smallest pile consisted of two commercially printed diaries, a small notepad, a bundle of ballpoint pens tied with string, and a bigger bundle of ink cartridges. Back in the old days, Dr. Khuplam said, he never threw away a pen or cartridge. He had written many of his burned diaries with these. Perhaps, he joked, a technology would some day be found to extract lost writing from the pen that had written it.

The diaries were pocket-size. About four by six inches, they were dog-eared and frayed at the edges, particularly the 1965 one, which was missing its front cover and the first half of January. Its pages were scrawled on in different directions, and the writing had faded in places. The 1972 diary was in better condition. So was the notepad, which was from the same year. On its front page was printed in English:

DOCTOR PRESCRIPTION
RESEARCH CHEEK BOOK
1972 — up to date.

"Cheek book" was a misspelling of "check book." In 1972, Dr. Khuplam explained, he had decided to check all his diaries and cross-reference them in this pad, in which he had also jotted down medical prescriptions. Unfortunately, it was a task he'd never finished.

"All right," I said. The general picture was now clear. "This is how I suggest we proceed. We'll go over the first seven chapters of *The Wonderful Genealogical Tales*, chapter by chapter. First, I'll make sure I understand the Thado text behind Sehkholun Singson's translation. Then you'll tell me what your sources for it were. After that you'll show me any references to these sources that can be found in the two diaries and the notepad. Shlomo will photograph them."

Dr. Khuplam thought this a reasonable procedure. We turned to Chapter 1 of *The Wonderful Genealogical Tales of the Kuki-Chin-Mizo*.

"War in Heaven"

This story came, Dr. Khuplam said, from a *thusim*. He knew of no *themthu* or *lapi* alluding to it. He had first heard it as an adolescent in Hoflung. There was a reference to it in the 1972 notepad, dated May 10: "In 1938 my aunt Lhingneng Chengsong told me a story about a war in heaven and fighting among the gods." He summarized it as follows:

"Once, long ago, there was a war in heaven. The gods fought with each other. Pathen, who was most powerful and ruled the world, had three assistants. The highest-ranking, whose name was Nungzai or Noimangpa, was Pathen's lieutenant over the 'heavenly earth.' (The 'earthly earth' had not yet been created.). The second-ranking assistant was Pathen's messenger to the other gods, and the third was the commander of his army.

"Time passed, and Nungzai grew envious of Pathen's power and made secret alliances in heaven to depose him. Then he gathered an army and went to war. The second and third assistants remained loyal to Pathen, and the two armies took the field. At first Nungzai challenged Pathen to personal combat in wit, skill, and magic. When he lost all three of the matches, he drew his sword, and the fighting commenced. It lasted seven days and seven nights. Pathen and his army triumphed and flung the losers into a bottomless pit deep in space, beneath the depths of the sevenfold earth. To this day, they drift from place to place there."

Of course, Dr. Khuplam said, this was not how his aunt told the story.

She did it theatrically and with much repetition, acting out the dialogue between the gods and adding dramatic detail. But if he were to relate the old *thusim* in the way they'd been told to him, one day would not be enough.

I mentioned having heard from informants that "Nungzai" and "Noimangpa" were names in priestly chants. Dr. Khuplam confirmed this. However, he said, these chants were *doithu*, not *themthu*, meaning that they were addressed to the *thilhas* rather than to Pathen. They did not reflect the Manmasi tradition.

Although I would have liked to ask why they did not, I also wanted to move ahead. We proceeded to Chapter 2.

"The Creation of Earth and Man"

This legend, Dr. Khuplam said, could be found in two different *themthu*. They were traditionally recited together in late September, when the dry-season rice crop was planted. The priest took fine red clay from an anthill and molded it into a foot-high statue. As a boy in Hoflung, he'd seen many of these. They were of a little man outfitted with a cloth turban, a loincloth, and a seed bag slung over one shoulder. The little man was taken to the jungle, where an altar was built, and the priest chanted over him:

> Coming to life from the water,
> Coming to life from the water,
> The man of gold is strong, he comes to life.
> The man of gold is strong, he comes to life, ei, ei, Za!
> Destroyed is he.

> Coming to life from the water,
> Coming to life from the water,
> The man of silver is strong, he comes to life.
> The man of silver is strong, he comes to life, ei, ei, Za!
> Destroyed is he.

> Coming to life from the water,
> Coming to life from the water,
> The anthill red-earth man is strong, he comes to life.
> The anthill red-earth man is strong, he comes to life, ei, ei, Za!
> In the garden he dwells in peace.

The priest then took two chickens, laid the blunt edge of his knife on the neck of one, pretended to try cutting, declared, "If I must use the sharp edge, this is not because I want to but because I must," reversed the knife, and cut off the chicken's head with one stroke. Setting the other chicken free, he said:

> He who came from above,
> Who created the red-earth man
> Out of an anthill,
> Who has sent forth the red-earth man to make him multiply –
> O shine forth on earth and in heaven!*

At the ceremony's end, the statue was left behind in the jungle. This was a sacrifice made for the success of the rice crop and the fertility of the earth. The text of the first *themthu* appeared in a diary entry for October 10, 1965. It was, Dr. Khuplam said, in very old language. The second *themthu* had been recorded on September 4 of the same year. The informant for both was a seventy-year-old man from a priestly family, Seijaneh Langhun, of Nomzong village in the Cachar Hills.

I asked for the Thado word for "red-earth man." It was, Dr. Khuplam replied, *leisanpa*, which broke down into *lei*, "earth," *san*, "red," and the masculine ending *pa*.

I said, "I'm not sure whether this means anything, but the Hebrew word for both 'man' and 'Adam' in the Bible, *adam*, is also connected to *adom*, 'red,' and *adama*, 'earth.' It's as if an ancient biblical pun preserved in no translation of the Bible has survived in those two *themthu*."

Dr. Khuplam was not sure whether it meant anything either. There was red earth, he observed, all over northeast India. He did, however, agree that the phrase "in the garden he dwells" — *ho na sib sai*, in Thado — was reminiscent of the Garden of Eden story. There was also, he said, a *thusim* about the creation of man. He pointed to a scrawled note beneath the diary entry for the first *themthu*. It said, "I heard this from my aunt Lhingneng." In Lhingneng's version, Pathen created the third Adam by blowing into him — "*f-f-fiiiiii!*" was the sound she'd made — so that he came alive and said, "*Ka pakai, ka Pathen*," "Yes, my Lord." A similar *thusim* was attributed, in the 1972 notepad, to Paominthang

---

* Like all the *themthu* and *lapi* I reviewed with Dr. Khuplam in Saikul, I rendered these two into English on the spot, with his help and Yitzhak's, and revised them at a later date. The versions cited here are the revised ones.

Lengthang. Dr. Khuplam had visited him again in Nagaland in 1954 and heard the red-earth man story from him on April 10 of that year.

We turned to Chapter 3.

"How Woman Was Formed"

After the creation of the red-earth man (Lhingneng's *thusim* continued), Pathen decided to make a companion for him. He made her of plain earth and blessed the two of them, saying, "Everything is yours. You own all the animals and the whole earth. You will have many offspring." Then, the red-earth man and the earth woman multiplied many times.

I said, "Tell me something. Before you began collecting these stories, there were British officials, men like Shakespear, Parry, and Shaw, who had studied the local culture and written some very solid books about it. Why didn't they know about all this? Why didn't they say, 'Good lord, these Kuki-Chin-Mizo have the same stories that the Bible does!'"

Dr. Khuplam assumed that they did know. The British poked their noses into everything. British researchers had even come to Hoflung. "But the British would have heard only *thusim* and *lapi*," he said. "No priest would have revealed his *themthu* to them." And without knowledge of the *themthu*, the British would have come to the same conclusion that I too entertained — namely, that these stories and songs were Christian in origin. For this reason, they probably didn't think them worth mentioning.

The story of the flood was a good example. There was a *thusim* that related how a man named Pumptuhpa was told by Pathen, in a dream, "I am going to plug the bottom of the earth and destroy all the animals and all the birds and all the men, and only you will survive. Build a boat and waterproof it with *bego*."

Bego was a gummy substance. Pumptuhpa went to his family and asked for help. But since everyone thought he was deranged, he had to build the boat by himself. Then Pathen plugged the earth for seven days and seven nights and the rivers backed up and rose higher than the mountains and all mankind drowned. Only Pumptuhpa, his wife, and their three sons were saved. When Pathen saw that all life was destroyed, he pulled the plug, and the flood receded. He told Pumptuhpa to build a four-cornered altar and station himself and his sons at its corners and offer a sacrifice. Then he commanded them to repopulate the world.

Any Englishman hearing this story, Dr. Khuplam said, would natu-

rally have assumed that it was borrowed from the account of Noah's ark
in the Bible. He wouldn't have known that the *tuitobin*, the ancient plug-
ging of the water, was also mentioned in a *themthu* traditionally recited at
the end of the harvest. Here it was, in a diary entry from December 29,
1972, with the notation that it had been recorded on April 13, 1960, from
Seijaneh Langhum of Namzong:

> Hei rhei Za, hei rhei Za, hei rhei Za!
> Flesh of my forefather, flesh of my father!
> There was the beginning, then the red-earth man,
> Then the water plugged —
> I cross the dark water well!
> As the water that flows in torrents,
> So does my victory. I show my sword.
> In the greatness of my triumph
> My enemies fall like mudslides.
> I spear the mythun.
> Henceforth I am strong as a horse to call *elo*.
> I call *elo* ever after.
> I will be free as a bird.
> As the bird that flies over the mountains,
> So will I overcome all obstacles.
> Honor is mine,
> For I am a son of Manmasi!
>   Selah.

I said, "Look. I agree that sounds old. And it makes sense that a great
flood would be explained in local tradition not by incessant rain, as in the
Bible, but by a blocking of drainage. It's what you'd expect from a people
living on hilltops, from which any amount of rain runs off into deep river
valleys. But words like 'selah' or *elo* can't possibly be old. 'Selah' is all over
the Book of Psalms. You can't tell me it wasn't taken from the Bible. And
elo comes from the Hebrew *elohim*. As a matter of fact, it's right there on
your wall."

I pointed to a placard bearing Dr. Khuplam's biblical credo, curiously
rendered: "And thou shalt love the Yahweh of your Elohim with all thy
heart and with all thy soul and with all thy might."

Dr. Khuplam demurred. The words "Yahweh" and "Elohim," he said,
were not in his Christian Bible; he had learned them in the Beth Midrash

Hashem long after recording this *themthu* from Seijaneh Langhum. And as for "selah" — he had spelled it 'shelah' in his diary, with an aspirated Kuki *s** — it was in many *themthu*. They couldn't all have taken it from Christianity.

"What does it mean in them?" I asked. The biblical word *selah* was an enigma. It was confined to the Book of Psalms and three places in Habakkuk, where it generally marked the end of a passage or section. Since the Psalms were originally sung, it was presumed by Bible commentators to be a musical notation — exactly of what, however, nobody knew.

Yitzhak answered, "Dr. Khuplam says it means 'over and over.'"

"What does *that* mean?"

It meant, Dr. Khuplam explained, that each time the priest said "selah," he had to repeat the passage that preceded it. He might have to do this any number of times, although seven was usually the limit. Only when the "selahs" stopped could he proceed to the next passage or part of the ceremony. The "plugged water" *themthu*, for example, had one "selah" at the end, so it was repeated once in its entirety. It was one of the rare priestly chants having the sacred name of Za in it that could also be sung as a *lapi* over a pot of *zu*. (While the name Za was never uttered in conversation, it was permitted in these *themlapi*, as they were called, which women and children were banned from joining.) Its language was ancient and difficult.

I let that sink in, silent, like Keats's Cortez glimpsing the Pacific, with a wild surmise. So a frequent word in the Book of Psalms, a word that no one had understood for thousands of years, meant *repeat the above* — if, that is, I wasn't deceiving myself with sound-alike words, the way so many Lost Tribe hunters before me had done. But the identical positioning of "selah" in the Thado *themthu* and in the biblical Psalm ruled out the possibility that the two were unrelated. This did not prove, of course, that, even if the Kuki-Chin-Mizo had picked up the word from pre-Christian sources, they were a Lost Tribe. Yet unless these sources themselves were very old, how would a long-forgotten biblical meaning have come to be known by southeast Asian priests?

"Let's go on to Chapter 4," I said.

---

* See pronunciation guide on p. 362.

"Kholkip-Kholzang"

"Once upon a time, all birds, beasts, and men lived in Kholkip-Kholzang, the place of getting together." Thus began the version of the story that Dr. Khuplam had heard from Paominthang Lenthang. Among the inhabitants of Kholkip-Kholzang were half-beasts and half-men known as *saheim*, human beings by day who turned into tigers on nights of the full moon by drinking from a special fountain. Like everyone, they lived in peace until one of them killed a fellow animal. In retaliation for this, the first murder in Kholkip-Kholzang, the true humans, known as *maheim*, put the guilty *saheim* to death. One thing led to another, and fighting broke out. The *maheim* lit fires against the *saheim*, who could not stand to look at the flames. After a while both groups realized that they could not get along, and they met to make a pact and part ways. The leader of the *maheim* swore, "If ever I harm a *saheim*, may death come to me through my neck." The leader of the *saheim* swore, "If ever I harm a *maheim*, may death come to me through my forehead." Then all the *maheim* went in one direction and all the *saheim* in another. That is why to this day a tiger kills a man by biting his neck and a man kills a tiger with a blow to its forehead.

Dr. Khuplam regarded Kholkip-Kholzang as analogous to the Garden of Eden. By the same token, he interpreted the "fruitful oiled land" — Sehkholun Singson's translation of the Thado *leiduppi-leithaopi*, literally "land of oil, land of rich soil" — as the biblical Canaan. He based this on a number of oral texts, such as the following *thusim* told him on April 19, 1945, by Palet Lengthang of Kabahpi village in the Cachar Hills:

> Once upon a time there was a place called Tuisogiet. Its chief was Pu Vanthang. Pu Vanthang had a humble beginning. Before becoming a chief he was an ordinary vagabond who herded buffalo and worked as a servant. He was a good man but very strong, and he liked to fight. One day he came to a village and got into a fight with two men. He thrashed them so soundly that they went to the chief and complained. The chief put Pu Vanthang on trial. "Who are you?" he asked. "Where are you from?" Pu Vanthang refused to answer, so the chief found him guilty and tied him up in his yard.
>
> Time passed, and the chief had a dream. In it he saw a big python come out of the water. When he went closer to have a good look at it, however, it turned into a very little snake. The chief

was bewildered and woke up. Then he fell asleep again and had a second dream. This time he saw a lush rice paddy in the distance. Yet when he approached it, he saw that no rice was growing there.

In the morning the chief gathered a council. He related his dreams and asked the elders to interpret them. No one could. For a whole week he went about the village, looking vainly for an interpreter. He thought he had spoken to everyone, but there was one person he had overlooked. "That's Pu Vanthang," an elder pointed out. And so Pu Vanthang was brought before the chief. "Can you interpret my dreams?" asked the chief. "Why don't you tell them to me?" Pu Vanthang said. The chief told Pu Vanthang his dreams of the python and of the paddy. Pu Vanthang interpreted the first dream, saying, "Something good is going to happen in your village, but it will not last long." Then he interpreted the second dream, saying, "There will be prosperity and then will come hunger."

That troubled the chief greatly. "What should I do?" he asked. Pu Vanthang said, "You should appoint someone to store rice for you." The chief was happy to receive this advice and once more gathered the elders, who counseled putting Pu Vanthang himself in charge of storing the rice. The chief untied him, gave him a bath and new clothes, and made him the most important man in the village. He was very pleased with Pu Vanthang and found him a wife. She was Pi Lhangmi, the daughter of the village *themthu*.

And so Pu Vanthang and Pi Lhangmi worked together for the chief. They collected all the rice paid in tribute from the large harvests and stored it in one place. After a while, the good times ended and hunger began. Everyone was starving, even the people of Leiduppi-Leithaopi. They came to Tuisogiet to look for food. "Where are you from?" Pu Vanthang asked. "From Leiduppi-Leithaopi," they said. "Is everything all right there?" asked Pu Vanthang. He went to a corner and cried and gave them rice and sent them back. The next time the Leiduppi-Leithaopi people returned, Pu Vanthang said to them, "If things are so bad in Leiduppi-Leithaopi, I must see them for myself." "Then come with us," they said. And so he did. When they arrived he said, "I'm so happy! I've never seen Leiduppi-Leithaopi before. Things are truly bad here. Come back to Tuisogiet, and I'll feed you." And so they all went to Tuisogiet and lived there happily.

Then Pu Vanthang and Pi Lhangmi had their first child and named him Manmasi.

Dr. Khuplam had recorded similar versions of this *thusim* from his aunt Lhingneng, from Seijaneh Langhum, and from his grandfather Lalsazei. "I don't know where it is," his grandfather had said of Tuisogiet, "but there was always plenty of food there." Despite differences in the details — a village chief instead of Pharoah, or a snake in a paddy in place of cows on the Nile — the story of Pu Vanthang was clearly the same as the biblical tale of Joseph. It had many more parallels with the Bible than did the Pu Vanthang *themthu*. Translated again, this now was:

> Hei, hei, hei, ezei, ezei, ezei, Za!
> Pu Vanthang who came from the famous heaven —
> From between heaven and earth he came to Tuisogiet.
> The daughter of Tuisogiet he married, Pi Lhangmi.
> Then they had a son.
> Since he was the first, they named him Manmasi.
> Because of this, God of the above, God of the below,
> We are the children of Manmasi.
> We are alive, we are well!
> Sustain us well,
> For the sake of Manmasi's children,
> We pray to you.
>   Selah.

The literal meaning of "Pi Lhangmi," Dr. Khuplam said, was Mrs. Mountain of the People. The *themthu* itself was traditionally recited on two occasions. One was when someone suffered a severe illness or was in danger of death. The priest would chant it before performing a sacrifice for deliverance. The other was when a search party was dispatched to look for someone lost in the jungle. In both cases the idea was to remind Pathen that "we are the children of Manmasi. Our ancestor came from heaven! You must not let us perish like this."

We were up to Chapter 5.

"The Migration of Pu Vanthang's People"

Dr. Khuplam knew of no *thusim* or *themthu* that mentioned the children of Manmasi leaving Tuisogiet. At this point, the only oral text link-

ing Kuki-Chin-Mizo traditions to biblical ones was the red sea *lapi*. He
sang me his version of it, and Yitzhak translated.

> During the celebration of the great festival,
> The great red water dried up.
> We were led by clouds by day,
> Columns of fire by night.
> My enemies pursued me day and night,
> Swallowed up by the great sea like a plague.
> The birds, onward!
> Out of the rock, upon the holy mountain,
> That which came flowing, we fetched.

This was the first time I had heard the phrase "holy mountain" in the
song. Dr. Khuplam believed it to be a reference to Mount Sinai. He
showed me a *themthu* about the ancient writing, the *bulpizam*, a word
composed of *bul*, "source" or "beginning," the feminine marker *pi*, and
zam, "script." Sehkholun Singson's all but incomprehensible translation
of this *themthu* in Chapter 6 was now emended to read:

> Pathen who dwells in heaven, I worship you,
> God of the seven folds of the heavens, the seven folds of the earth,
> Revealing the secrets in Leiduppi-Leithaopi,
> Made of my forefather, made of my father.
> For the good of the eyes and the good of the teeth,
> For the health of the mind and the body,
> This *bulpizam* has come to be.
> Let the children of Manmasi
> Shine forth on earth and in heaven.

To the best of Dr. Khuplam's knowledge, there was no oral tradition
about the wanderings of the children of Manmasi from the red sea or
the "holy mountain" to Leiduppi-Leithaopi. Several *themthu*, however,
placed Leiduppi-Leithaopi after Tuisogiet in the order of events. One of
these was traditionally chanted at the founding of a new settlement in the
jungle. The augury of the cracked egg having proved auspicious, the
scouts would spend the night on the hilltop to see if their dreams were
good. If they were, the priest would sacrifice a hen or goat and say:

> Hei, hei, hei, azei, azei, Za!
> Pathen who dwells forever in heaven, I worship you.

God of the seven folds of the heavens, of the seven folds of the earth,
I worship you.
God of the above, God of the below, look upon us.
Look upon us with the sun and the moon:
Who came out of Leisanpa,
Who came out of Tuitobin,
Who came out of Kholkip-Kholzang,
Who came out of Tuisogiet,
Who came out of Leiduppi-Leithaopi,
Endow not your creatures with fault!
Let abundance be ours.
Let good health be ours.
We, the children of Manmasi, ask of you.
　　Aborizah.

I asked, "What was that last word?"

"Aborizah," Yitzhak said.

"What does it mean?"

"I don't know. It doesn't sound like a Thado word. Thado has no *r* sound."

Dr. Khuplam didn't know the meaning of "aborizah" either. "He thinks it may be the opposite of 'selah,'" Yitzhak said. "Something like 'The End.' That's because it always occurs as the last word of a *themthu* that isn't to be repeated. But it's also a magic word in an old folktale, like 'shazam' or 'abracadabra.'"

"Ask Dr. Khuplam," I said, "if he'd like me to tell him what it means."

Yitzhak stared at me.

"Just ask."

Yitzhak asked and said. "Of course he would."

"Then I will. But first I want to hear the folktale."

"The short or the long version?" Dr. Khuplam wanted to know.

I chose the short version. The day was passing quickly.

And so Dr. Khuplam told the short version of the story of Chang-khatpu.

Once upon a time there was a poor but strong and handsome or-phan with nothing in the world whose name was Changkhatpu. In dire straits, he took to wandering from place to place, until he met the owner of a magic dove. "Where are you going, young man?" asked the owner of the dove. "I'm going to seek my fortune," said Changkhatpu. "Then why not marry my daughter?" asked the man. "That's very kind of you," Changkhatpu said, "but I'm afraid I can't. I'll gladly accept a favor from you another time."

And so Changkhatpu wandered on until he met the owner of a magic cow. "Where are you going, young man?" asked the owner of the cow. "To seek my fortune," said Changkhatpu. "Would you like to marry my daughter?" the man asked. "I'm afraid not," Changkhatpu said, "but I'll gladly accept a favor from you another time."

Changkhatpu wandered some more and met the owner of a magic mole. "Young man," said the owner of the mole, "where are you going?" Changkhatpu told him he was going to seek his fortune. "Then marry my daughter," said the man. "I'll accept a favor from you another time," Changkhatpu replied, "but I'm not yet ready to get married."

Changkhatpu kept wandering until he came to the house of a childless old couple who were *doikungpu* — people versed in the practice of *doi*, or magic. "Where are you going, young man?" they asked. "To seek my fortune," said Changkhatpu. "Then why not stay with us for a while?" they said. Changkhatpu agreed and moved into the old couple's home.

And so Changkhatpu lived with the old couple. One day they said to him, "You know, it's not good for a young fellow like you to be alone. You should take yourself a wife. We have a suggestion. Every week the seven daughters of Pathen come to bathe in the river near our home. The youngest one is the most beautiful and would make a good match for you. You only need to snatch her dress while she's bathing and run back with it to this house. Leave the rest to us."

That's just what Changkhatpu did. He waited seven days by the river for Pathen's seven daughters and hid behind a bush while they took off their clothes and went to bathe. As soon as they were splashing in the water, he ran to the riverbank, snatched the dress of the youngest, and ran with it toward the old couple's home. The seven daughters saw him and shouted at him, "Stop! What do you want with that piece of cloth? It's filthy. We'll wash it for you." Changkhatpu looked back at them, and as soon as he did he turned into an anthill. You see, the old couple had forgotten to tell him not to look back.

After a while, the old couple began to wonder what had become of Changkhatpu. "Oh, my goodness!" the *doi* man said. "We forgot to tell him not to look back. Something must have happened to him." They went to search for him and found the anthill and restored his human form by breathing on it — *f-f-f-fiiiiii*, just like that. "We're terribly sorry," they told him. "But you mustn't despair. Next time, just don't turn around when Pathen's daughters call to you. Run straight to our house with the youngest daughter's dress, and she'll be yours."

And so Changkhatpu waited seven more days for the daughters of Pathen to bathe in the river. Then he jumped out of hiding and stole the youngest one's dress and ran without looking back. "Stop!" shouted the seven daughters. "What do you want with that filthy cloth? We'll wash it for you." But Changkhatpu kept running. When the youngest daughter saw that he wasn't turning back, she jumped from the river and ran after him. As soon as she reached the old couple's house, Changkhatpu grabbed her. As he was strong and handsome, she agreed to marry him.

For a while they lived happily together. Then word got around that Changkhatpu had a beautiful new wife. The news reached the chief, who desired her for himself, so he invited Changkhatpu to his home and challenged him to a duel. "Here's what we'll do," said the chief, who was wary of Changkhatpu's strength. "My animals will fight your animals. If your animals win, my kingdom is yours. If my animals win, your wife is mine."

Now, Changkhatpu owned one little dog and one little rooster and one little cat, but the chief owned the biggest mastiffs and the fiercest fighting cocks and the cruelest cats in the village. Changkhatpu knew they would tear his animals apart. Yet he could not refuse the chief's challenge. So he went home in tears, for he did not wish to lose his wife. "Why are you so weepy-eyed?" his wife asked. "I am weeping for you," Changkhatpu said, "because I am going to lose you." And he told her what had happened. "Don't you worry, my dear," his wife said. "Dry your tears and accept the chief's challenge. Go to his house with your dog, your rooster, and your cat. I'll teach you a magic word that will make them win every fight. It is 'aborizah.' Just whisper it and victory is yours."

Changkhatpu did as he was told. He took his little dog and his little rooster and his little cat to the chief's home. The chief gloated when he saw them. He called for his biggest mastiff, which fell at once on Changkhatpu's little dog and was just about to tear it limb from limb when, in the nick of time, Changkhatpu whispered, "Aborizah!" The mastiff froze, and the little dog seized it by the throat and killed it with one bite.

The same thing happened with the rooster and the cat. As soon as Changkhatpu whispered "Aborizah!" his rooster pecked out the eyes of the chief's fiercest cock and his cat clawed the chief's cat to death.

Astonished, the chief refused to accept defeat. Instead, he issued a new challenge. "We'll have another contest," he told Changkhatpu. "Tonight I will scatter a full basket of sesame seeds on the path by my house. If you can pick up every seed by the morning, my kingdom is yours. If one seed is missing, your wife is mine."

Changkhatpu was deeply dejected. He knew he could never find all the little seeds in one night. But then he remembered the owner of the magic dove. He went to him and said, "Do you remember me? I'm the young man to whom you offered your daughter. Now I'd like to ask for the favor you promised me." "By all means," said the owner of the dove. "What can I do for you?" Changkhatpu told him of the chief's challenge, and the man lent him his dove. All night it pecked up and down the path, putting the seeds in the basket. And yet when dawn began to break, the basket was still not full. "Aborizah!" Changkhatpu whispered — and the basket filled to the top.

The treacherous chief would not give up. "I have another challenge for you," he said. "Tonight I will drain the pond by my house. If you can fill it with milk by the morning, my kingdom is yours. If not, your wife is mine."

Now Changkhatpu remembered the owner of the magic cow. He went to him and asked for a favor. "Of course," the man said and lent Changkhatpu his cow. But although Changkhatpu milked the cow into the empty pond all night, the pond was not full when morning came. "Aborizah!" he whispered — and at once the pond was brimming with milk.

The chief was wild with anger. "All right," he said, "this is my very last challenge. I will dig a hole in my garden and fill it with seven bags of dried chilis. Tonight you will climb into the hole.

Then I will set it on fire. If you are alive in the morning, my kingdom is yours. If not, your wife is mine."

This time Changkhatpu went to the owner of the magic mole. "I need that favor you once promised me," he said. "Gladly," said the man and lent him his mole. Changkhatpu had the mole dig a man-sized tunnel as far as the hole filled with chilis. Before he set out that evening for the chief's home, his wife said to him, "This time, when the chief sets the chilis on fire, don't whisper 'aborizah.' Shout it as loud as you can seven times before you escape through the tunnel." And so the chief and all his servants assembled in the chief's garden and Changkhatpu jumped into the hole and the chief set the chilis on fire. "Aborizah! Aborizah! Aborizah! Aborizah! Aborizah! Aborizah! Aborizah!" Changkhatpu shouted. Then he escaped through the tunnel and went home.

In the morning the chief rose happily. He went to look at the hole and saw only ashes. Confident that Changkhatpu was dead, he went to his house to claim Pathen's daughter. Imagine his surprise when he saw Changkhatpu sitting on his veranda as fit as a fiddle! "But how can that be?" the chief fumed, beside himself with rage. "Changkhatpu must be using *doi*." Remembering how Changkhatpu had shouted "aborizah," he realized that it was a magic word. At once he hurried home to test it, certain the world's riches would soon be his. He filled the hole with seven more bags of chilis, set them on fire, and jumped in, shouting "aborizah" with all his might. But because he shouted it only once, he perished. And so Changkhatpu became chief in his place and lived happily ever after with his wife.

The story of Changkhatpu was over. "Are you sure that's the short version?" I asked.

Dr. Khuplam assured me that if his aunt Lhingneng had been telling it, Pathen's daughter would still be bathing in the river. And now he wished to know what "aborizah" meant.

"A bargain is a bargain," I said. "'Aborizah' means 'O God the creator.' It's the Hebrew words *ha-borey Yah.* Long ago, when those saying them understood their meaning, it would have been natural to end a prayer with them. And once they were no longer understood, they came to be thought of as a magical expression."

It sent a shiver down my spine. Good biblical Hebrew, though not an actual phrase that occurred in the Bible, the words had left Palestine 2,700 years ago. They weren't like "selah" or *elo*, which — if I wanted to believe he was an inspired charlatan — Khuplam Milui Lenthang could have planted in his notes. Back in the days when he did his field work, there was no way he could have known about them.

Pleased by the discovery, he reached across the desk to shake my hand.

☙

We now arrived at Chapter 7, with its strange tale of the *sangah meichol*, the long-tailed wildcat. This story was based, Dr. Khuplam said, on two *lapi* and a bit of *thusim*. The main *lapi*, confusingly translated by Sehkholun Singson, was known as "The Song of Grief."

Dr. Khuplam sang it to me. Its name was well-deserved. I had never heard such awful sorrow put to song. Each note was a long wail that dropped as though into an open grave. It was the Kuki blues at their deepest, most dirgelike, down-lowest sea-bottom blue.

> Pathen who lives in the heavens,
> We settled and prospered in Leiduppi-Laithaopi.
> With the cloth we were wrapped and renowned we became,
> Your creatures, the children of Manmasi. Alas!
> In heaven and earth it is known.
> On the veranda, weep!
> The long-tailed wildcat howls.
> The enemy comes with a sword,
> Bringing defeat long to be lamented.

The second *lapi*, Dr. Khuplam said, was more of a lullaby. His mother and grandmother had sung it to him in Hoflung. Joined by Mrs. Khuplam, he now sang it for me. It had a wistful refrain they kept coming back to almost cheerfully, the way it is possible to be cheerful while singing "Down will come baby, cradle and all."

> *Tangkem chunga ka oi oi leh,*
> *Kanau ponsil ka lhahsah.*
> *Galah vatang kati lei o*
> *Sangah meichol a ham meh.*

> On the veranda I do weep
> For the carrying cloth of my baby.
> Each time I seek to pick it up
> I hear the long-tailed wildcat.
>
> Sleep, my baby, go to sleep,
> The sky is full of thunder.
>   On the veranda I do weep. . . .
>
> Sleep, my baby, go to sleep,
> Your father will bring honey.
>   On the veranda I do weep. . . .
>
> Sleep, my baby, go to sleep,
> Your aunt will bring a melon,
>   On the veranda I do weep. . . .
>
> Sleep, my baby, go to sleep,
> Your mother's breast awaits you.
>   On the veranda I do weep.
>   For the carrying cloth of my baby.
>   Each time I seek to pick it up,
>   I hear the long-tailed wildcat.

The *thusim* was a mere fragment. All there was to it was: "We were dancing and haughty and let our cloths fall off. The long-tailed wildcat stole them in his envy and drove us from our land."

I asked, "How can a wildcat drive anyone from a land?"

Dr. Khuplam did not think the wildcat was to be taken literally. It was a metaphor for the enemy. The "cloth" was metaphoric, too. A cloth, or *pon*, like one of those worn by the youth and maiden in the fresco on the wall behind me, was a person's clothing, the covering of nakedness. In the old days, one *pon* was all most people owned. Even Pathen's daughter was at Changkhatpu's mercy without her *pon*. Losing it was symbolic of losing everything.

"But why a wildcat?" I persisted. "A tiger might make sense. Or even a wolf. Not a wildcat."

Shlomo Gangte agreed. "A *sangah* is a chicken thief," he said. "It doesn't attack people. Here, I'll draw you one."

He took an envelope from Dr. Khuplam's desk and drew what looked more like a large-headed coyote than a cat. It had a long tail sticking out behind.

Shlomo Gangte's
Drawing of Sangah Meichol
The Long-Tailed Wildcat

Dr. Khuplam conceded that a *sangah* was unlikely to harm a man. And yet in Kuki folklore it was a feared animal. Mothers threatened naughty children with it. "I hear the *sangah meichol* howling. He'll get you if you're bad!" they'd say. When he was a small boy, one of his favorite Aunt Lhingneng stories was about an egg, a rope, Mr. Mortar, Mrs. Pestle, Mr. and Mrs. Snake, and a chicken turd all deciding one day to get back at Sangah Meichol for his wickedness. They went to his house when he was away and took up positions. The rope hung itself on Sangah Meichol's wall. Mr. and Mrs. Snake hid by the water barrel. The egg lay down in the hot coals of the hearth. The chicken turd curled up in a plate on the table, and Mr. Mortar and Mrs. Pestle waited on the veranda. When hungry Sangah Meichol came home from his rice fields, he sat down to eat and swallowed the chicken turd. Disgusted, he went to the hearth to look for better food, and the egg exploded in his face. He ran to the water barrel to wash his face, and the snakes bit him. He reached for the towel on the rope to dry himself, and the rope cut him. He ran out to the veranda with his bleeding hand, and the mortar and pestle beat him to death.

But Khuplam Lenthang's grandfather had not joked about Sangah Meichol. He had said, "We were too proud, so God sent Sanga Meichol to punish us."

I repeated that a wildcat, wicked or not, could not send a people into exile. True, "The Song of Grief" and the bit of *thusim* had helped me to understand where the story of an exile from *leiduppi-leithaopi*, "the land of oil and rich soil," came from. I could even explain the term "land of oil," for ancient Palestine was an olive-growing region, a major oil exporter referred to in Deuteronomy as "a good land . . . a land of olives, oil, and honey." But beyond that, Chapter 7 of *The Wonderful Genealogical Tales* lost me. Where, after leaving their land, had the children of Manmasi dwelt in "caves, holes of rocks, and holes of earth"? What was Sehkholun

Singson's "upper city at the eastern north of the globe," where they "made mansion for a long period"? On what grounds were they said to have been in Afghanistan and Tibet before reaching southeast Asia? None of this made sense to me.

Dr. Khuplam confessed that it did not entirely make sense to him either. He had tried, in reconstructing the children of Manmasi's post-exilic history, to place certain oral texts in their most likely context. Because a large number of *themthu, lapi,* and *thusim* mentioned people who lived underground and were surrounded by a "great darkness," it had seemed logical to associate this with the catastrophe of leaving Leiduppi-Leithaopi. The underground place was referred to as *noikhopi,* the "lower village" or "lower city," as opposed to *chungkhopi,* the "upper village" or "upper city," in which the Kuki-Chin-Mizo — sometimes called in their *themthu* "the people of Chungkhopi" — eventually came to reside. He was inclined to identify the "upper city" with northeast India. There was mention of it in a *themthu* appearing in a diary entry for December 3, 1965. The informant was once again Seijaneh Langhun. Seijaneh had last heard the chant when he was a young man. By the time he dictated it to Dr. Khuplam, it was no longer in use, since it had been traditionally recited on the occasion of a village's migration, a practice abandoned in British times.

> Hei, hei, hei, ezei, ezei, Zah!
> God of the above, God of the below, we worship you.
> Coming from the Leisanpa,
> Then coming to Tuitobin,
> And upon Kholkip-Kholzang,
> And upon Tuisogiet,
> And under the great red sea which stood still,
> And under the great red sea which stood still
> For seven days and seven nights,
> And upon the darkness,
> And upon Chungkhopi,
> And upon Kabul,
> And upon Taibe,
> And upon Khotan,
> And upon Mongbung,
> And upon Mongalawi,

And upon Kongjam,
And upon Samakai Range,
And upon Khojipui,
And upon Thimphut,
And upon Zongbung,
And upon Thingkangphai,
And if you come out of Tuiting-jiol,
You will come upon Chindung-ingpi.
Onward to the south, onward to the north!
May the faith of our forefathers follow us!
May the good of our eyes and the good of our teeth follow us!
May faithfulness follow us!
For the children of Manmasi,
    Aborizah.

Dr. Khuplam thought he could identify some of these places. "Kabul" was in Afghanistan. "Thimphut" might be Thimpu, the capital of Bhutan. "Taibe" sounded like Tibet, and "Khotan" was the Chinese Ho-Tien; he had found it by looking in an atlas. "Mongalawi" he took to be Mongolia — hence the northern loop on his migration map. Samakai Range was probably in the Himalayas. I had heard a *lapi* sung at the Kuki Inn about being "torn" or parted there.

Parting, Dr. Khuplam said, was the theme of many old *lapi*. The most popular was "The Song of Hope," a great favorite at *zu* gatherings. He remembered such drinking bouts at his grandfather's; the *zu* was passed around in gourds and sipped through a bamboo straw, or was poured into horn beakers. Because "The Song of Hope" contained the word "Sion," it and similar songs were known as "Zion songs." There was a diary entry for it on September 8, 1965:

I am leaving the south.
Sion was my land of sojourning.
I go toward the north. Onward!
Land of the South, I wear a turban
That will soon be lost to me.
The majestic one will come when the rooster crows.
When the dawn comes, I will be joyous in celebration.
I will beat my drum and be glorified.
Onward, children of Manmasi!

A turban, Dr. Khuplam said, was a sign of status. A man like his grandfather always wore one on formal occasions. His grandfather had told him that he too would wear one when he grew up.

He never saw his grandfather again after leaving home for the Bengalee Lower Primary School in Silchar. Lalsazei died in 1940, and when Khuplam Lenthang returned to Hoflung for the funeral, he found his uncles hacking at the doorposts with a sword as a sign of grief. This was a custom that was accompanied by chanting the names of the deceased's most illustrious ancestors in order to impress the *thilhas* and prevent them from hindering the soul's progress in the afterlife. His uncles chanted:

> O God of the above, God of the below,
> We are the children of our forefather Manmasi!
> We are alive, we are well —
> Sustain us well!
> We pray to you,
> O God of the above, God of the below,
> Look upon us, your creatures.
> These are my ancestors.
> Hei, hei, hei, ezei, ezei, ezei, Zah!
> Manmasi, *hitu!*
> Gelet, *hitu!*
> Ulam, *hitu!*
> Lamza, *hitu!*
> Zakip, *hitu!*
> Hangmang, *hitu!*
> Mongoulen, *hitu!*
> Lapa, *hitu!*
> Palen, *hitu!*
> Lengoukhup, *hitu!*
> Lenthang, *hitu!*

There was no diary entry for this chant and Dr. Khuplam recited it by heart. He pushed off on the *Ho-o-o-o-o-hhhhh* of "O God of the above" as Ningzenawng did on his *Heyyyy-y-y-y-y-y* and fell into the same jerky rhythm before calling the ancestral names loudly, as if taking roll call in a noisy classroom.

"What does *hitu* mean?" I asked.

Dr. Khuplam didn't know. It was an archaic word or perhaps one from another language. He guessed it might mean "son of."

It wasn't *hitu* I was thinking about, though. It was the names in the list of Grandfather Lalsazei's ancestors. I did not believe that the similarity of Gelet to "Gilead" — Hebrew Gil'ad, the son of Machir and grandson of Manasseh, according to the Book of Numbers, and the seventh name on Jimmy Jamkhomang Haokip's genealogical chart — could be a coincidence. I especially did not believe it because, though not on Jimmy Jamkhomang's chart or in Numbers, the next name, "Ulam," of which "Lamza" seemed a garbled version, appeared in Chronicles as Machir's grandson. And as if that were not enough, "Zakip" was just what Thado phonetics might have done to the name of Manasseh's grandfather Jacob, the Hebrew Ya'akov.

I asked, "Are you absolutely certain that, when your grandfather died, you heard your uncles say, 'Manmasi *hitu*, Gelet *hitu*, Ulam *hitu*, Lamza *hitu*, Zakip *hitu*'?"

Dr. Khuplam wanted to be precise. He was certain his uncles had *said* it. He was not certain he remembered hearing it. He remembered them striking the doorpost and calling out names, and he knew from his field-work that these were the names the Lenthang clan called. The last name on the list was that of Lenthang himself, the clan's founder. This funeral chant was part of a longer *themthu*, one that was rarely recited in full, since it belonged to a special ceremony performed only when a family without sons was faced with extinction.

I played my trump card.

"Now I'll tell you," I said, "how a long-tailed wildcat drove a people from their land."

Sorting It Out

THE ETHIOPIAN AIRLINES FLIGHT from Bombay and Addis Ababa, routed to Tel Aviv via Cyprus, passed over Egypt. From 30,000 feet I tried counting the arms of the Nile fanning out through the Egyptian delta, the biblical land of Goshen. They vanished, uncountable, in afternoon haze.

It didn't matter. The Nile had shifted channels frequently in the course of its history. Maps of Pharaonic Egypt showed from five to eleven of them emptying into the Mediterranean, and the Manmasi-Manasseh identification did not depend on the "eight flowing waters" of Tuisogiet being numerically precise. It depended on Dr. Khuplam's oral texts being genuine. If they were, a link between the Kuki-Chin-Mizo and ancient Israel would be difficult to deny.

There was no other satisfactory explanation for these texts. Contact with Christianity could account for only some of them. Take the Pu Vanthang *thusim*, for example: it was certainly conceivable that, introduced by Christian missionaries, the biblical story of Joseph in Egypt could have become a Kuki folktale, its Hebrew slave boy recast as a vagabond, its Pharaoh as a village chief, the cows and wheat of his dreams as snakes and rice. But the Pu Vanthang *themthu* was something else. A priestly chant for someone sick or lost in the jungle would not have developed in British times from a Bible story. And if the Pu Vanthang *themthu* was pre-Christian, there was no particular reason to doubt that the Pu Vanthang *thusim* was, too. Moreover, of all the oral texts collected by Dr. Khuplam in his fieldwork, this was the only one that resembled a biblical narrative about the Patriarchs. Why, if missionaries had been the source of it, were there not also stories about figures like Abraham, Isaac, and Jacob? Why, for that matter, was there nothing taken from the New Testament? Why only this one item about Joseph and the birth of Manasseh, a minor character in the Bible whom no missionary would have chosen to dwell on?

Contact with post-biblical Judaism could not be the explanation either. Other than a small nineteenth-century Jewish presence in Calcutta, a product of British rule in India, no Jewish community was known to have lived within a thousand miles or more of Kuki-Chin-Mizo territory or probable Kuki-Chin-Mizo migration routes from the Tibetan highlands — and even had there been a significant encounter with a stray Jewish traveler, the results would have been very different. Nothing in the old Kuki-Chin-Mizo religion or in Dr. Khuplam's oral texts had a single post-biblical Jewish feature. In fact, not very much was biblical either. Apart from the Sangah Meichol story, the small number of narrative parallels with the Bible stopped with the Exodus from Egypt. There was nothing analogous to anything in Joshua, Judges, Samuel, Kings; no names or stories reminiscent of Samson, Samuel, Saul, David, Solomon, Elijah; no allusion to a single biblical king or prophet. This was consistent with such material having been transmitted by exiled Israelites separated from their people in an early period, at a time when most biblical traditions had not yet been consolidated and many biblical events were still to occur. It made no sense if thought of as coming from a later time.

Nor was the agent of transmission Islam. True, this was the only one of the three major monotheistic religions to have old roots in southeast Asia, having spread through Bengal and Assam under the Moghuls in the sixteenth and seventeenth centuries and leapfrogged by sea to southwestern Burma slightly earlier. But, though Islam was heavily influenced by the Bible and had adopted many biblical stories, key elements of what Dr. Khuplam called "the Manmasi tradition" were missing from it, the most salient being Manasseh himself. Although the Koran devoted an entire chapter to Joseph, his marriage and children were not mentioned there. Other strands of biblical narrative known to the Kuki-Chin-Mizo, such as the details of the red sea song, were also nowhere in the Koran. These must have come by a different route.

Unless, that is, Dr. Khuplam had made up the Pu Vanthang *themthu* and other texts out of whole cloth. Was that possible? The more I considered it, the less I thought it was. This was not only because, self-assured yet far from boastful, he had made a favorable impression on me after my first, negative reaction. It was because his story rang true. The only holes I could find in it after hours of conversation with him were minor inconsistencies, easily attributable to slips of memory quite normal for a person his age.

Of course, I could have fallen victim to a master swindler, a man capable of selling George Lawma the Taj Mahal. But thinking of Dr. Khuplam in this way required strenuous mental gymnastics. It meant assuming, first of all, that he had disinterestedly forged, back in the years when the Lost Tribe belief was in its infancy and of no importance to Kuki-Chin-Mizo society, numerous texts in support of it. Next, it meant that, having skillfully fabricated these documents, he had collected them in a small number of handwritten copies that — unlike his *bulpizam* visions — he made no attempt to promulgate when the Lost Tribe belief began to spread. Like a spider who spins its web in a corner without flies and waits to catch a juicy morsel, he had simply trusted in his luck. Not even the arrival in Imphal of Eliahu Avichail, buzzing with Lost Tribe enthusiasm, could coax him from his hiding place in Saikul. Only when an author with an American book contract came along did he pounce. And even then he was so devious, so crafty in his pretense of guilelessness, that said author having handed him, on their parting in Saikul, several hundred unsolicited American dollars as a donation to his National Research Laboratory, he had looked at them wonderingly and said, "I wouldn't know what to do with these. Couldn't you change them in Imphal and bring me rupees?" (Which Yitzhak did.)

If you could believe such a man was a swindler, you could believe anything.

Not that believing he wasn't didn't have its problems too. It raised the question of why, if his material was authentic, no one else in Manipur seemed to have any knowledge of it. Even making allowances for the rapid loss of old Kuki traditions, and for his having been their sole recorder in the years when they were vanishing most rapidly, one might have expected to encounter at least some corroboration of his findings elsewhere. In the hope of doing so, I composed a brief questionnaire before leaving Imphal and gave it to Yitzhak to distribute through his B'nei

Menashe contacts. It contained a list of terms like "Leisanpa," "Tuisogiet," "Pu Vanthang," "Sanga Meichol," "Aborizah," and "Gelet," with the request that the respondent let me know if any of these were familiar and from where.

Yet as I went over my notes from Saikul, it struck me that there was another possible reason for the singular nature of Dr. Khuplam's material. Although his fieldwork had cut a broad swath through Kuki-Chin-Mizo territory, the oral texts on which he had based *The Wonderful Genealogical Tales of the Kuki-Chin-Mizo* came from a small number of informants, nearly all of them Lenthangs and Chensongs. Known (as I have mentioned) as the *mi lui*, or "old people," these two clans, together with a third called the Lumkins, were believed to have inhabited the hills of southern Manipur before the Kukis arrived. According to a Thado legend related by William Shaw, Chongthu, the mythical first ancestor, found Lenthang and Lumkin already living on the earth when he pushed aside the great rock, the *chhin lung*, that sealed the exit from the underworld. Skilled hunters and rice growers, they had survived the *thimzin*, the seven days and seven nights of the primeval "great darkness," by making a bonfire of the skulls and bones of the game they had killed, and they were enlisted by Chongthu as guides to his new habitat. It was Lenthang, too, according to a myth noted by the British anthropologist J. H. Hutton, who finally dispelled the darkness. His life spared by the warlike Thados after they had fled to the hills from the primeval flood because "he, and his, knew the gods of the country," he "caused a white cock to dance on a stone and thus lured the detainer of the sun to come and look, whereby the sun escaped and came out again, restoring light." This story, Hutton believed, was "obviously suggestive of a separate racial origin for the Thado proper and the Chengson and allied [Lenthang and Lumkin] clans, who presumably were in occupation when the Thado arrived in the hills."

Both legends implied that the *mi lui* were valued by the Kukis for their practical and religious knowledge. But where had *they* originally come from? Neither Hutton nor Shaw asked that question. Now I did. Suppose, I speculated, that it was the *mi lui* who were the original "children of Manmasi" — who, well before the first Kuki incursions into Manipur in the fifteenth century, had settled there after a long migration, lasting many hundreds and perhaps thousands of years, that began with the Assyrian exile of the tribe of Manasseh from the northern kingdom of Israel. Suppose this migration was not of the entire tribe but of a single Manassite family or clan that had struck out eastward on its own. Suppose this group passed through many lands, residing in some for long periods and mixing with different peoples. Suppose its old Israelite religion became increasingly diluted along the way and during the sojourn in southeast Asia, so that by the time the Kukis arrived on the scene much or most of it had been lost. And yet suppose remnants of it had survived: a supreme deity named Yah; certain legends of Creation; dim recollections of tribal ancestors; memories of a land, through which branched a great river, in which there always was enough to eat; of crossing a sea in which enemies drowned; of another land of fertile earth and abundant oil that once was home; of being, against all logic, forced to leave this home by a wildcat. Perhaps some scattered customs had survived, too, such as sparing the eggs in a mother bird's nest.

I pushed this line of thought further. Suppose the Hmar, the first Kuki-Chin-Mizo tribe to advance from the Chin Hills into Mizoram and thence northward to Manipur, was also the first to encounter the *mi lui*. Suppose it was followed by the other Old Kukis and then by the New Kukis. Suppose that while the *mi lui* were gradually integrating into Kuki society and adopting its religion and way of life, the Kukis were, in turn, absorbing lore from the *mi lui*. Suppose this lore included a belief in a common ancestor named Manmasi and a knowledge of certain old stories and songs — one of which, the red sea song, was assimilated into a Hmar poem about migrating down the Tuipui River and then became part of the Hmar's Sikpui celebration. Suppose some of it later diffused southward to the Lushai Hills, where it became the property of many Mizos as well.

Shaw, the only British observer to have paid attention to the "children of Manmasi" epithet — "Manmasi *nao*" or "Manmasi *chate*," in Thado — was not quite sure whether "Manmasi" was a proper name or a word. He tended to think it was the latter and that it meant "a human as distinct from a spirit" and was "generally used with reference to the legendary epoch when the distinction was less marked than it is now." He was familiar with a Thado story about this, which he related as follows:

> At that time [when Chongthu first appeared on earth] the mythical ancestors were known as Manmasinao and all spirits as Thilha. They used to live together in peace until the following

happened, after which the Thilha and Manmasinao have always been at enmity.

There was a Manmasinao called Changkhatpu [!], to play with whom a Thilha came one night. Changkhatpu lost his temper and wounded the Thilha with a *dao* on the hand. On this, the Thilha said that the Manmasinao should suffer for it and went off to his cave in the jungle.

In revenge, the Thilhas, during Changkhatpu's absence, killed his younger sister. In consequence of this the Manmasinao gathered and pursued the Thilha, killing all except a pregnant female Thilha, who escaped. This Thilha went to Pathen in the skies. Pathen told her not to worry, as the child in her womb would be a male child, and that she must marry it and so revive the Thilhas. At the same time Pathen gave her a charm called Chollaivom,* instructing her to place it in the water supply of the Manmasinaos and thereby they would not be able to see the Thilhas in future. So to this day the Thilhas cannot be seen by human beings, who are the descendants of the Manmasinao. A male child was born to the pregnant Thilha and by [her] marrying him the Thilhas multiplied to such large numbers that there were more Thilhas than Manmasinao.

But Shaw also knew a Thado folktale, quite similar in parts to Dr. Khuplam's story of Changkhatpu, the hero of which was *named* Manmasi. This was confusing not only to Shaw; it was confusing even to Pathen — who, after Manmasi married his youngest daughter in this tale, and was given a magic, wish-granting fiddle by her, remarked, "In a house where there are many girls, do not some get married to ordinary men and others to Manmasinao?" Thus, Pathen's son-in-law is Manmasi and one of the "children of Manmasi" at one and the same time! Had Shaw realized that Manmasi was the eponymous ancestor of the Manmasinao, he would have understood his error. He failed to do so because, knowing that no one by the name of Manmasi appeared in traditional Kuki genealogies, which started with Chongthu, he had no ancestral line in which to place him. He overlooked the possibility that Manmasi could have been the ancestor of a non-Kuki people, such as the *mi lui*.

There were several important things to be learned from these stories.

---

* *Chollaivom*, Shaw explains, were "yeast cakes with black centres," and when the Manmasinao ate them "the centre of their eyes became black," thus rendering the *thilhas* invisible to them.

They suggested that the Manmasites had once been regarded by the Kukis as spiritually superior beings closer to Pathen. They described them as warring with the *thilha*s, the jungle spirits that all southeast Asian hill tribe religions worshiped and sought to propitiate. The story of Pathen's daughter, in which a Manmasite hero named Changkhatpu was confused with Manmasi himself, strengthened my theory that "aborizah" (replaced in the Kuki version by a magic fiddle) was a Manmasite word. And both stories suggested that the Manmasites and Chongthu's Kuki-Chin-Mizo descendants had different origins, and that the former, like the *mi lui*, were in northeast India first. Indeed, both pointed strongly, once again, to the conclusion that the Manmasites *were* the *mi lui*.

This hypothesis had much to recommend it. It was simple, it was coherent, and it solved certain problems. It explained, for instance, why Dr. Khuplam's Manmasite oral texts were not more widely known, since they must have belonged to that part of *mi lui* tradition that had never spread to the Hmar and the Kukis. All together, the Lenthangs, Chensongs, and Lumkins numbered no more than twenty thousand, and there had been fewer of them in the years of Dr. Khuplam's field trips, before northeast India's twentieth-century demographic expansion had peaked. Even in those years, only a handful of elderly people may still have had a thorough command of *mi lui* traditions.

The *mi lui* hypothesis also explained how a relatively large group like the Kuki-Chin-Mizo could be related to wandering Israelites so few in number that they left no mark in the pages of history. It accounted for the fact that, while traces of biblical religion could be found among the Kuki-Chin-Mizo, they were minuscule. And it indicated why men like Lalchhanimha Sailo and Yosi Hualngo, who assumed that more of these traces could be found farther south in Burma, were wrong. Sailo and Yosi held that since the old Kuki-Chin-Mizo religion had been biblical, its last Burmese strongholds should reflect this most clearly. But the old religion was not biblical at all. It was an animistic shamanism typical of the Tibeto-Burmese hill people of southeast Asia. Its small number of biblical features came from the *mi lui* in the north. These were most pronounced among the Hmar and Kukis tribes, who had the greater contact with the *mi lui*; less so among the Mizo; and least among the Burma Chin. Had Sailo and Yosi realized their dream of traveling all the way to Arakan, they would have been disappointed.

I faxed Yosi in care of the Aizawl post office immediately after returning to Israel to ask about Lianpuisuaka's will. In reply I received a fax from George Lawma. "Shalom!!" it began. "How are you? How is your Mrs? We got the original copy of the priest Lianpuisuaka's last will. We are sending it by registered mail. As we came to know that under Mr. Samuel Joram's inspiration we were criticized to the Rabbi by Aizawl people, we did not trust him to carry the original copy." George requested that I send him $500 so that he and Yosi could "go at once" to all "the nooks and corners" to gather "many facts about the tribes."

I faxed back that I was not sending any money and was waiting to receive the will. There followed a correspondence in which George wrote me extortionary letters in Yosi's name while seeking to prevent me from contacting Yosi by instructing me, allegedly to circumvent CID surveillance, "When you write to me, write my name, Yosi Hualngo, inside the letter, but outside the envelope please write only:

> To the Manager
> Hotel Zodin
> Electric Veng, Aizawl."

A few rupees slipped to the manager would ensure that any such envelope ended up in George's hands. The man was incorrigible. It therefore came as a surprise when, soon after this, Lianpuisuaka's will arrived by registered mail.

At first glance, it gave the impression of being authentic. It was written, in blue ink that had faded badly in some places and appeared to have been washed away in others, on both sides of a sheet of paper that looked yellowish-brown from age and had been folded as if stored in a space too small for it.

On second glance, I had my doubts. In two places on the front, where the original writing was effaced, the word "Manmansi" [sic] appeared in a different hand and ink. At the bottom of the reverse side, a third hand had printed, in Mizo, "Written by Selchhunga, 14–10–1948." What was most suspicious was that the text of the will in Yosi's notebook had no missing words to correspond to the illegible lacunae in the document I had just received. Yosi had filled these words in on his own. But how could he have known what they were? Clearly, the document was a forgery, copied *from* the notebook rather than into it, and then artificially aged.

But this, too, was a hasty conclusion. The lacunae were at most a few words long. Yosi could have guessed at their contents, especially since they were likely to have been formulaic phrases known to him. And why would a forger change handwriting and ink? Perhaps this indicated that the document *was* genuine and had passed through several hands.

In the end I took it for examination, along with samples of Yosi's and George's handwriting, to a forensic document specialist in Jerusalem. The answer I received was:

Re: Examination of an old document from India.

The document in question was examined for indicators of its reliability.

1. The document was examined both with a microscope and with infrared and ultraviolet optical equipment.
2. In examining the document microscopically, I found that it was originally written with a fountain pen and subsequently worn by dampness, dirt, and having been folded. I also determined that it was written on part of a larger sheet of paper and shows signs of having been cut along one of its vertical edges. Some of the dirt appears to be earth, but I lacked the means to verify this.
3. Although I found no evidence to show that the document has been aged artificially, I was unable to arrive at an absolute conclusion.
4. No traces of bleaching materials such as were introduced from the 1950s on were found in the paper.
5. The corrections and additions in the document were written with a ballpoint pen.
6. The two sample handwritings that I received are not compatible with the handwriting in the document.

The bottom line was that if Lianpuisuaka's will was a forgery, it was the work of a thorough professional who had left no telltale signs. It seemed unlikely that Yosi or George would have looked for, much less found, anyone of that caliber in Aizawl. In the balance, the document had to be given the benefit of the doubt. It was most probably genuine. Yosi had told the truth about it.

Had I been apprised of this before meeting Dr. Khuplam, I would have been thrown for a loop. As it was, Lianpuisuaka's will could be considered one more problematic piece of supporting evidence. It fit my hypothesis well. There was, it so happened, one unusual thing about the Hualngo tribe — namely, that if the tradition cited in Yosi's notebook was correct, its migration route from the Tibetan highlands to the Chin Hills had included a stopover at Moirang, near the shores of Loktak Lake at the southern tip of the Imphal Valley. This put the route well to the west of the routes of other Kuki-Chin-Mizo tribes. It also put the Hualngo, moving from north to south at an earlier date than the south-to-north thrust of the Hmar, in an area inhabited by the *mi lui*. If their priestly traditions had biblical elements that other tribes lacked, these may have come from direct contact with the *mi lui*. The fact that this contact was relatively ancient could explain such biblical names, known to Hualkhaia and Lianpuisuaka but not to Dr. Khuplam, as "Tera," "Apram," "Iaksak," "Muriah," and "Si-nai." The Hualngo priests may have remembered things learned from the *mi lui* that the *mi lui* themselves had forgotten.

Several months later I received a second envelope from Yosi. Having quarreled with George, he wrote, he was using the translation services of Zohminga, the motorcyclist with the Israeli flags. In the envelope were the affidavits of ten people who, like himself, had personally witnessed or heard firsthand reports of the *bawrh keu*, the mock circumcision ceremony. These were mostly Chin Hill Hualngos, of whom five had signed their names and five — Kaikungi, Kapruma, Zawna, Larothanga, and Thathangi — had affixed thumbprints. Yosi had put together a composite account of their testimonies, including details not in his notebook, such as the words chanted by the priest who passed the newborn child through the coiled vine:

(In a loud voice) Do protect, do protect!
(In a whisper) O Rising from Mount Muriah, do protect!
O Rising from Akuptan, do protect!
O Rising from the Big Red Water, do protect!
O Rising from the Marah water that we once drank, do protect!
O Rising from Sai-on, do protect!
(In a loud voice) O he protects, he protects!
(In a whisper) O you whom I worship, Za, Khuavang,
    Khuanuleng, whom our forefathers worshiped, do protect this baby!
Protect him in the place where the sun rises!

Protect him in the place where the moon rises!
Protect him in the eight layers of the earth!
Protect him in the eight layers of the sea!
O do protect!

The priest then rubbed the foreskin of the penis with the blunt side of a knife, cleaned with a quill the baby's forehead and the *bawrh* or smegma from its pubic area, and ordered the evil spirits to leave it. He dripped the blood of a chicken over the forehead, neck, armpits, navel, knees, and penis of the baby; cut flat pieces of yam; held them to the baby's ears; and made a hole in each ear with the quill, pulling thread through it and leaving it there. Hualngo tradition held that this custom went back to a time when the men of the tribe were married to "*tuluk* Chinese women." These women opposed the custom of circumcision and complained about it to the Chinese authorities, who banned it. "Because of the *tuluk* women," Yosi wrote, "the village authorities checked the penis of each newborn baby, so we could not do anything but make holes in our ears." To this day there were Chin Paites who derogatorily called the Hualngos *zangbawt*, or "foreskinless penises." Sometimes, a baby was born with such a penis. Then the priest blessed it, saying, "Holy penis, old penis, made by nature, cut by Khuavang," and performed the rest of the ceremony. Such babies were known as *khuavang serhtan sa a piang*, "born circumcised by Khuavang."

I received other mail from northeast India. Dr. Khuplam sent his greetings. Navi Songtiniam let me know that "a huge stone has been erected at Tuikun village in commemoration of your recognition of us as the Manmasi Tribe." Lalchhanhima Sailo wrote that he hoped to come to Jerusalem "for a face-to-face talk with the Israeli government." Elisabeth Zodingliani informed me of the recent Purim celebration in the new Sephardic Jewish Community of Aizawl. H. Fung Kung blessed me "by the hand of our Almighty Jaweh" and inquired, on stationery belonging to "Ephraim's Seed of Chin National Council," whether I could arrange in Israel "jobs of labour works for ten persons." K. L. Samuel sent me a copy of a memorandum mailed to the Israeli prime minister. V. L. Ngawta wanted to know what progress I had made in marketing his revolutionary gearbox. Nithanthluai apologized for not having returned to the Hungle region. "Most honorable Rabbi," she wrote, "I am very busy in looking after my aged mother, so I could not send your honorable Rabbi the tape-record concerning we being the lost tribe of Israel. Please do pray for me, most honorable Rabbi."

From little Liana there was no word.

࿊

There were, then, indications that circumcision had once been practiced by the Hualngos. Their maintaining that the custom had been suppressed by the Chinese was not to be dismissed out of hand. Chinese armies had made frequent incursions into Burma over the centuries. Although the Chinese were not known to have forbidden circumcision, it was conceivable that a local Chinese commander or governor sought to suppress it on his own. Repellent to most Chinese, "circumcision," in the words of the Chinese historian Gao Wangzhi, "was in direct contravention of the Confucian injunction against 'harming the body bestowed by one's parents.'"

Yet even if the story had an element of truth, infant ear piercing was not invented as a mock circumcision rite. It was widely practiced by other peoples in the region, such as the Lakher of Burma and many Naga tribes. The Nagas of the Rengma Hills, for example, according to the British ethnographer J. P. Mills, considered it to be of "the utmost importance, as a person with unpierced ears would not be recognized or welcomed by relatives in the world of the dead." At most, the custom had been borrowed as a circumcision substitute by a people who had not previously engaged in it.

One had to be careful about such things. Some of the worst gaffes made by Lost Tribe hunters came from anthropological ignorance of their hunting grounds. Although my own overall knowledge of Tibeto-Burmese hill tribe religion was limited to a few books, it was enough to make me realize that I had been lured down more than one false trail. My theory about the Kuki-Chin-Mizo dual priesthood, with its "private" and "public" priests, was an example. Such a division was in fact common to many southeast Asian hill peoples. It stemmed not from an interface between two different religious traditions but from a distinction within the same tradition between shamans who communicated with spirits causing illness and misfortune to individuals and masters of ritual who performed communal ceremonies and sacrifices in homage to the gods, and it corresponded exactly to the difference between the Mizo *bawlpu* and *sadawt* and the Kuki *doipu* and *thempu*.

Or take the resemblance I thought I saw between the double-chicken sacrifice I had witnessed in Lianpui and the biblical practice mentioned in Leviticus. Slaughtering one bird while releasing another was also practiced, it turned out, by the Ao Nagas, who believed the freed rooster took with it the illness that had occasioned the sacrifice. It was not unique to the Kuki-Chin-Mizo.

And there was the frequent repetition of the number seven, which had struck me in Dr. Khuplam's chants; specifically, the image of the "seven folds of heaven" and "seven folds of earth." Not only was seven a semi-sacred number in the Bible, but the heavens were commonly imagined as seven-tiered in the biblical Apocrypha and post-biblical Judaism. Was it not likely that these traditions were connected?

It was not. The notion of heaven and earth having seven, eight (as in Yosi Hualngo's chants), nine, or even thirteen levels was common throughout ancient China and Tibet. The Rengma Nagas held that there were six skies above the visible one, and the Karens prayed to the "Lord of the seven heavens and the seven earths." And for sheer frequency of sevens, you couldn't beat the *Mvuh Hpa Mi Hpa*, the Lahu creation epic.

It could get trickier than that, however. Consider Dr. Khuplam's pair of *themthu* about the creation of man. As far as I could determine, these were unlike other Tibeto-Burmese hill tribe creation myths, which were of two types. One, common among the Kuki-Chin-Mizo and their neighbors, described mankind as emerging from the bowels of the earth. The other, subscribed to by peoples like the Lahus and the Lisus, and by the Karens I'd met in Thailand, traced the human race to a primeval gourd. Neither had a Bible-like earth man into whom a god breathed life.

But wait. Some Austro-Asiatic creation myths were different. The Dusuns of North Borneo, for instance, believed that their creator-god Towadakon first made man from a tree trunk and discarded him because he failed to respond to his creator's commands; next, from a stone, rejected for the same reason; and lastly from earth, which satisfied Towadakon because the earth man obeyed him. This was clearly similar to Dr. Khuplam's "three Adams" *themthu*. Admittedly, Aunt Lhingneng's *thusim* about God breathing life into the red-earth man was closer to the biblical account. Yet if one sought an outside source for this part of the Manmasi tradition, why prefer the ancient Israelites to the Dusuns?

Perhaps there had been both biblical *and* Austro-Asiatic influences at work. This was possible, since Austro-Asiatic tribes like the Khasis had inhabited northeast India before the Tibeto-Burmese invasion and could have interacted with the *mi lui*. The problem was that Dr. Khuplam had made no attempt to separate the native southeast Asian material in his possession from the material that had come from elsewhere. This was because he believed that the entire Kuki-Chin-Mizo people had come from elsewhere. The result was conceptual chaos.

You could see this in his handling of the *chhinlung* story, with its *noikhopi*, or "lower village," within the earth in which all men had lived under the rule of Noimangpa, the "Great One Below," until his son, the heroic Chongthu, led a party into *chungkhopi, the* "upper village" of sun and light.* Despite this clearly being an origin-of-mankind myth too, Dr. Khuplam had refused to recognize it as such, because this would have meant ascribing two such myths to the Kuki-Chin-Mizo, one like and one unlike the Bible's. Instead, he had chosen to interpret it as an account of exile, connecting it with the expulsion of Pu Vanthang's people from Leiduppi-Leithaopi. His description in *The Wonderful Genealogical Tales* of these exiled people "dwelling in caves, holes of rocks, [and] holes of earth" until they reached "the upper city located at the eastern north of the globe" — that is, northeast India — was nothing but a misreading of Chongthu's escape from the underworld.

The same held true for the *thimzin*, the seven-day "great darkness," and for Kholkip-Kholzang, the legendary land where human beings and animals had lived together in peace. Although both were typical southeast Asian myths set at the beginning of time, Dr. Khuplam saw the first as an allegory of spiritual darkness following the exile from Leiduppi-Leithaopi and treated the second as the Manmasi tradition's version of the Garden of Eden. But this caught him in a contradiction, for whereas the biblical Garden of Eden preceded the great flood, Kholkip-Kholzang came after it; it was a refuge from the *tuitobin* or "plugged water." Rather illogically, therefore, *The Wonderful Genealogical Tales*, though patterned on the Bible, treated Eden as postdiluvian.

Dr. Khuplam's flood stories also represented an unwitting mixture of

---

* The Thado word *kho*, "village," could also, depending on the context, have the sense of "city," "region," or even "world," a reflection of the fact that one's village — which under the leadership of a powerful chief might develop into a town of many thousands of people — *was* one's world and the only imaginable form of social life.

traditions. While the Pumtuhpa *thusim* was closely parallel to the biblical tale of Noah, the "plugged water" motif was southeast Asian. A Lakher legend, for example, related that all rivers on earth had once drained into a single outlet, kept from silting up by a giant crab that dredged it with its claws. Eventually these claws became worn and inefficient, whereupon the rivers backed up and caused a deluge that forced all life to flee to the mountains. Then the crab molted and grew new claws, the dredging began again, and the flood receded.

It was curious that none of Dr. Khuplam's oral texts made any allusion to a Tower of Babel story, even though such a legend was known in a pre-Christian form to the Karens and others in the region. The Angami Nagas, for example, told of building a tower so that they could visit the sky goddess Ukenpemptu — who, alarmed by the prospect of having to give them gifts, multiplied their languages, thereby forcing them to abandon the project. The Mikir believed their ancestors had sought to conquer the gods, who turned them back by confounding their speech. Perhaps the Manmasi tradition had once held such a story but lost it. Possibly, people like the Karens and the Nagas had taken biblical motifs from the *mi lui*, whether directly or through intermediaries. If K. L. Samuel could be trusted, the Rongmei Nagas had even, like the Kukis, borrowed the *mi lui*'s "children of Manmasi" identity.

One puzzle that remained unsolved was the matter of Zion. The "Enter, Enter Zion" dance was itself a conundrum, especially since its movements, far from being English, were indigenous to northeast India and had been witnessed by J. H. Hutton among the Angamis in the form of "two lines, which walk in and out of one another, serpentine." But "Sion," or "Sai-on," also turned up in both Yosi Hualngo's chants and Dr. Khuplam's "Song of Hope," which spoke of leaving it behind "in the south" and "going toward the north." If "Sion" was really Zion, which in the Bible could mean only Jerusalem, this was illogical. In the first place, Manasseh was a northern tribe. Even if "leaving the south" were interpreted as being exiled northward to Assyria, how could Jerusalem, a southern city, have been, as this *lapi* called it, "the land of [Manasseh's] sojourning"? Why remember with longing the capital of the southern kingdom of Judah, with which the northern tribes were in a state of rivalry and sometimes war, rather than Samaria, the capital of the north?

There were Kuki-Chin-Mizo historians who sought to identify

"Sion" with the north-central Chinese city of Xian, the capital of the book-burning emperor Shi Huang Ti, first mentioned to me by Zai-thanchhungi in connection with the legendary lost scroll. Some, like C. G. Verghese and R. L. Thanzawma, in their *History of the Mizos*, wove entire historical episodes out of this. According to them, the ancestors of the Kuki-Chin-Mizo inhabited the Tsinling Mountains south of Xian and were forced by Shi Huang Ti to labor on the construction of the Great Wall, which ran just north of the capital. Chafing from their en-slavement and the emperor's destruction of their scroll, they joined his eldest son in revolt. After the rebels' defeat, they fled back to the Tsinling Mountains and took shelter there in caves. Subsequently, they wandered south, until they reached their present homeland in northeast India.

This account, although it was accepted by many Kuki-Chin-Mizo as authoritative, was a castle built on sand. It rested on, in addition to the equation of "Sion" with Xian, two other baseless conjectures: that the Tsinling Mountains could be identified with the *chhinlung* of the creation myth, and the "dogs" who ate the sacred scroll with the Chinese. The rest was pure fantasy. "Sion" could not be Xian, because in Shi Huang Ti's time Xian was called Changan. By accepting myth as history, men like Verghese and Thanzawma made the same mistake that Dr. Khuplam did. They fell victim to the self-esteem of a proud people who, having just emerged from the stage of so-called primitive thought, were ashamed to admit they had ever been in it. "Who could be so stupid as to believe men came from inside the earth?" Yehoshua Thangjom had asked me indignantly during an argument in which he insisted that "Chhinlung" must be a real place. But this merely led to more myths.

The Thangjoms came to Israel that winter to attend the wedding of their daughter Ruth, Yitzhak's sister, in Jerusalem. The afternoon of the ceremony it began to snow, and by the time the first guests arrived at the wedding hall, over a foot had fallen. The groom's family, Israelis of Moroccan background, lived in Kiryat Arba, a town on the outskirts of Hebron, where Yitzhak's parents were also staying. Because the snow blocked the Hebron-Jerusalem road, Mr. Thangjom, the groom's mother, and a large number of others never made it to Ruth's wedding.

Miraculously, it turned out to be a happy affair. Much of the credit went to the rabbi, who refused to yield to the mood of despondency. An infectious dervish of a man, he all but forced even the empty chairs and tables to get up and dance. A defiant joy swept the hall. Mizos, Kukis, and Israelis locked arms and circled with abandon, each moving enough limbs for several missing guests. Before leaving, I went over to Mrs. Thangjom, who was still in shock from her husband's absence, and asked her to give him my warm regards. I would go to Kiryat Arba to see him, I said.

I never did. He died of a sudden heart attack a few days later, and since he had not been rabbinically converted, the religious authorities in Kiryat Arba refused to bury him. After a hurried search, a cemetery in Beersheba agreed to take him.

And so Yehoshua Thangjom was laid to rest in a Jewish grave. Old Zephaniah Haokip would have envied him. Yitzhak said the Kaddish and a cantor sang the *el malei rahamim*, the "Lord Full of Mercy," for the up-lifting of his soul. He had made it home, if that was the meaning of a text found in Dr. Khuplam's diary, dated March 28, 1958. It was meant to be chanted at a funeral:

> Hei, hei, hei, ei, ei, ei, Za!
> Let the ground part!
> Let the ground open up!
> Today the sons of Manmasi
> Are going back to their land
> That is in Leiduppi-Leithaopi.
> Trees and stones,
> Move away!
> The children to their land
> Are going back.

✼ 12 ✼

Across the Sabbath River

Only nine of the questionnaires distributed in Manipur were returned, a disappointing number. But they were informative and helpful. The respondents, all male, were between the ages of fifty and eighty; three were from Imphal, three from Kangpokpi, and three from other villages. Their answers revealed a fragmentary knowledge of many of the names and words in Dr. Khuplam's texts. While one person could identify X but not Y, another knew Y but not X. Few responses showed the influence of the Bible. The overall picture was of an ancient body of lore that had crumbled, leaving different slivers in different hands.

For example, one respondent, asked about "Za," said that it was "God's name." One said, "I only know it is not a human." Seven professed ignorance or gave other answers. Eight had never heard the word "aborizah"; a ninth remembered it from "games played as a child." Four knew that Pumtuhpa was a man saved from the flood. Five had heard of Pu Vanthang, identified by one person as "he from whom mankind came about." One thought he had "saved humankind from a famine." One took him to be Joseph. One knew only that "the chief trusted him," and one had heard of him "in stories from my grandparents." Four of the five knew that Pi Lhangmi was Pu Vanthang's wife. Four respondents also knew the names Gelet, Ulam, and Lamza. One could not recall whom they referred to, two believed them to be the names of ancestors, and one, Tongjam Haokip, replied, "Gelet is the name of one of our forefathers, while Ulamza [sic] is also one of the names. I heard these names in

a chant in a naming ceremony." Thanglam Lhouvum was the sole respondent to mention the lullaby about the *sangah meichol*. He was also the
only person with a specific response to the term Leiduppi-Leithaopi,
which he remembered from the same funeral chant recorded by Dr.
Khuplam. Six of the respondents were familiar with the word "selah" in
the sense of "say it again" or "do it again." One said that it was a word
"from long ago." One knew it from an old *lapi*.*

I too encountered "selah" in an old *lapi*. In July 2000, I made a return
visit to Imphal, accompanied by Yitzhak, for another round of meetings with Dr. Khuplam, who came in from Saikul for the week. He had
invited some *lapi* singers from the village of Gophalbung, the only such
organized group in Manipur. Apart from its director, a hawk-faced man
named Laokhalet Haokip, it was composed of younger people — three
men, four women, and a fat baby in a shoulder cloth. Laokhalet Haokip
was Gophalbung's elected chief and had recently founded the group to
keep the old musical traditions alive. The singers were still getting the
hang of it and were none too sure of themselves. They were performing
only to please their chief, they told me. The old songs were difficult and
they would rather sing modern ones.

Because of its "selah"s, one of the songs was repeated several times.
This led to a discussion of the word in which the village chief recalled a
rhyme from his childhood, repeated at top speed as a jawbreaker:

> *Tanbobulah, tanbobulah,*
> *Tanbokawah, tanbokawah,*
> *Tanbokomah, tanbokomah,*
> *Tangloi selah, tangloi selah*

Dr. Khuplam knew this rhyme. It came from an old *thusim* about a
blind man and a lame man. In order to be healed, the two had to cross

---

* As I was preparing the manuscript for publication, eight more completed questionnaires arrived belatedly from Manipur. Although the answers given by their respondents, who ranged in
age from 61 to an alleged 105, were briefer than those in the first batch, they showed a greater
familiarity with many words and names. All eight men had heard the name "Za," three of them
in priestly chants. Such chants were also remembered by three men as having contained the
word "aborizah." Seven knew of Pu Vanthang. Seven were familiar with the word "selah." All
eight identified *sangah meichol* as a figure used to scare children. Four recognized the names
Gelet, Ulam, and Lamza. The 105-year-old, Mangpithang of Kangpokpi, recalled hearing these
names recited when "my grandfather and father died." Paojagin, age sixty-seven, from the village of Longphailum, said, "When my grandfather and father died, the mourners expressed
their rage [presumably by hacking at the doorposts of the home] and these names were said."

seven mountains, the lame man seated on the blind man's back. After the last mountain, they came to a large tree and a pile of skulls. The blind man's task was to climb the tree's branches and hang all the skulls on them. *"Seling maw?"* he asked at each fork in a branch, which meant, said Dr. Khuplam, "Where am I?" in an unknown language. *"Bulah!"* the lame man called up at the first fork, meaning, "At the beginning." *"Kawah!"* he called up at the second fork, meaning, "At the big branching." *"Komah!"* he called up at the third fork, meaning, "At the little branching." *"Selah!"* he called when the skull was hung, meaning that the blind man should climb down and repeat the climb with another skull. When all the skulls were hanging on the tree, the blind man could see and the lame man could walk.

This *lapi* was followed by the "Song of Hope." It was, the village chief said, usually sung after the drinking of much *zu*. Often this was at a *kut*, or celebration, when drinking bouts went on all day and all night and sometimes for several days running. People drank nonstop. They sat in concentric circles, alternately of men and of women, with a leader in the middle who chose the songs and called the lines. Whoever had to sleep lay down in a special area and resumed singing and dancing upon waking.

The village chief wrapped his head in a cloth turban, threw an embroidered *pon* over his shoulder, and chose a woman singer to dance with him. He danced with small measured steps, his knees bent and his arms flapping slowly. The woman stepped the same way, keeping her hands on her hips. The *lapi* singers drummed and sang. The hawk-faced chief flapped like a great bird, a *mulaopi*. The woman dancer was like a little rabbit looking for cover in the rocks. How the great bird would smother her! How carefully the little rabbit chose a rock! The great bird's wings rose and fell. But how the little rabbit really wanted to be caught! How she craved to fly in the *mulaopi*'s claws! Then Mrs. Khuplam joined the dance. Now there were two rabbits. The great bird wheeled between them, uncertain which to pounce on.

At that moment the three Thangs arrived — Thin Thang, Once A Thang Two Thang, and the Buffalo Herder. But I'd better start from the beginning.

⚶

The original plan was for me to spend the week in Saikul. Although by now I was fairly confident of my *mi lui* theory, I had many questions for

Dr. Khuplam. As this seemed a good opportunity for me to meet other knowledgeable people, I suggested that he invite any he might know.

But Dr. Khuplam did not know many people, and Saikul was considered unsafe for a prolonged stay. The alphabet-soup organizations were more active than ever and the venue was switched to Imphal, where, Mrs. Thangjom having decided to remain in Israel, the Thangjoms' apartment was standing empty. Dr. Khuplam was put up with his wife in a room on the roof, from which he came down each morning and remained through lunch before going back upstairs for a nap and returning for a second session, which lasted until dinner. Other than a security guard he'd brought from Saikul, he had invited only the *lapi* singers and the three Thangs.

These were Thinthang Lenthang, Onzathang Thuthang, and Zankothang Haokip. Zankothang Haokip herded buffalo. He came from the village of Tenkong and was, to the best of Dr. Khuplam's knowledge, the last old-religion priest still active in Manipur. Because he was a *doipu* rather than a *thempu*, however, Dr. Khuplam was not sure how much I would learn from him. Nor was he sure how much Zankothang Haokip would want me to know. *Doi* dealt with evil spirits and was not originally part of the Manmasi tradition. It had been introduced by a renowned hunter named Galgnam. Galgnam had a friend, a *saheim* and great wizard, called Hansei, who was half man and half tiger. One day, while the two of them were hunting, Galgnam noticed that his friend was carrying a small box in which, after shrinking them by *doi*, he kept all the animals he had trapped. While handling the box, Galgnam inadvertently opened it, whereupon the animals escaped and regained their former size. Hansei had to use more *doi* to shrink them again, and this so intrigued Galgnam that he kept releasing them to see how Hansei put them back. Finally Hansei said, "Look, if you want to learn *doi*, why don't you ask me instead of fooling with my animals?" And so he taught Galgnam all he knew.

At first Galgnam kept his new knowledge to himself, using it mostly when hunting. *Doi* would never have spread had he not fallen in love with a famous *doikungpi*, or *doi* mistress. "This *doi* mistress," said Dr. Khuplam, "was just like a human being except that she had a horizontal rather than a vertical vagina." Galgnam courted her by challenging her to a *doi* contest in which each had to duplicate the other's magic. The *doi* mistress accepted the challenge, and they met on the appointed day, each equipped with a *doi buom*, a collection of *doi* objects. The hours went by without a victor. Galgnam and the *doi* mistress each knew the other's tricks. Whatever one could do, the other could do also. Even when the *doi* mistress coaxed Galgnam to lie in her lap so that she could *hlim* him, he soon woke and did the same to her.

To *hlim* someone was to put the person in a trance. While the *doi* mistress was *hlimmed,* Galgnam undid her *pon,* smeared her horizontal vagina with his saliva, and waited for her to awake. "Well," he said when she did, "it looks as if I've won. I made love to you while you slept." Although at first the *doi* mistress did not believe him, she became convinced when she saw what she took to be his sperm on her. "All right," she said, "I'll marry you. But you had better not tell anyone what you did to me, because something very bad will happen if you do."

Galgnam promised to tell no one and went back to his village to await the wedding day. Meanwhile, he went fishing with his friends and used *doi* to haul in a huge catch. "You're some magician!" said his friends, who hadn't netted a single fish. "Pshaw!" said Galgnam. "I can do a lot better than that. I've even made love to the *doi* mistress. You should see her vagina!" He told his fishing friends all about it, and soon everyone knew the *doi* mistress's secret.

The *doi* mistress was furious when she heard of Galgnam's betrayal. Determined to take revenge, she sent for him and said sweetly, "My darling, it's time we chose a wedding day. Come lie in my lap and we'll discuss it." Galgnam lay in her lap and she *hlimmed* him. Then she built a stone wall around him, covered it with a stone roof, and went away.

When Galgnam awoke, he was surrounded by darkness. He groped with his hands and realized he was imprisoned. Not having his *doi buom,* he could make no more than a small magic hole in the wall. Through it, he begged for food and his *doi* objects. Someone heard him and went to tell his wife, who set out at once with the *doi buom.* After a while she reached a river. "Where is Galgnam?" she asked a man standing there. "You're too late," the man said. "Galgnam has starved to death in the *doi* mistress's prison." In her despair, Galgnam's wife threw the *doi buom* into the river.

The *doi buom* floated down the river. "*Kong zai toi, kong zai toi,* I'm floating down, I'm floating down!" sang each of the *doi* objects. At last they came to the country of a Kuki tribe called the Kom. The Kom heard them singing in the water and were afraid, so they sent a blind old man to fish the *doi buom* out, thinking that if anything happened to him, it wouldn't matter. The old man fished the *doi buom* from the water and opened it, and as soon as he did, he grew young and could see again.

And so the *doi buom* was carried back to the Kom village, which was called Sekong. Because of it the place began to prosper. Everyone learned *doi* and used it to meet their needs, even the children. If a child was asked to look after his younger brothers and sisters, he would *hlim* them and go out to play. *Doi* was even used for pranks. This went on, Dr. Khuplam said, until one day some young men from another village came to visit and the young maidens of Sekong caused their penises to crow like roosters. The embarrassed village elders ruled that henceforth the use of *doi* would be restricted to priests.

Shaw had written about the *doi buom*, or *indoi*, as it also was called. It was the Kuki version of the Mizo *pathian bom* or "god box," which Zaithanchhungi, without grasping its true nature, had once told me about. It wasn't really a box; it was a collection of seven sacred objects — usually a pig skull, a pair of goat horns, a gourd, a *dao*, an iron staff, a second gourd with a chicken bone, and a boar's tooth — bound together by a creeper called a *khaopi* and hung from a bamboo rope called a *gopi*. In his sacrificial chant on the lawn of the Kuki Inn, old Zephaniah Haokip had mentioned several of these items while invoking the name of Galgnam. In the past, every house had its *doi buom*, which was honored with an annual sacrifice. The rest of the year the sacred objects hung from the roof beams of the veranda. The old man in Zai's story had not, as Zai mistakenly thought, been hiding his god box in the roof. He had been keeping it where it belonged.

Dr. Khuplam knew another *thusim* about the *doi buom* that apparently originated with the *mi lui*. According to it, the *buom* was an innovation of a priest named Zamneh. One night after the children of Manmasi lost their sacred scroll and their fortunes flagged, Zamneh placed two grains of rice beneath his pillow, as was the custom when requesting a dream augury, and asked Pathen for advice. Pathen appeared to Zamneh in his sleep and gave him instructions for making a *doi buom*. "You will call it 'The Treasure of Your Fathers and Forefathers,'" Pathen said. "I bequeath it to the children of Manmasi as a sign between you and me. Whenever you are in need, sacrifice a chicken and sprinkle its blood on the *doi buom*, and I will answer you." In the morning Zamneh did as he was told. He composed a *themthu* that went:

O *buom* that came from heaven,
Commanded by the God of the sevenfold heaven, the sevenfold earth:
Make it of a *khaopi*, twined seven times and seven measures long!
Make it of a gourd with its seeds intact!
Make it of a horn!
Make it of an iron staff!
Make it of a two-bladed *dao!*
Make it of a gourd with an unbroken rooster thighbone!
Make it of a gourd with seven windings without!
Make it of a goat skull!
Endow not your creatures with fault.
For the flesh of my forefathers, for the flesh of my fathers,
For the good of the eyes and of the teeth,
For the health of the mind and of the body,
We the children of Manmasi
Ask you.
   Aborizah!

"But that's a totally different story from Galgnam's," I observed. "And the traditional *doi buom* had a pig skull, not a goat skull."

Dr. Khuplam had an explanation for the pig skull. It called for yet another *thusim*.

Once upon a time, according to this *thusim*, only goats were used for sacrifice. It was so long ago that the *doi buom* was still called the *Manmasi chate go buom*, "the treasure *buom* of the children of Manmasi." In those days the children of Manmasi worshiped only Pathen and had no dealings with the *thilhas*.

One day the *thilhas* kidnaped a girl named Japhal. Her parents searched for her everywhere. They went to the jungle and performed sacrifices and cried out, "We are the children of Manmasi! Let go of our daughter!" But Japhal was not found, and her parents gave her up for dead.

And then one night a *thilha* appeared to Japhal's father in a dream. "Do not grieve for your daughter," the *thilha* said. "She is alive and well and married to one of our youths. She will soon be giving birth and has no desire to return to the world of humankind. The time has come for us to pay you her bride price. If you wish to receive it, raise a pig. When the pig is big and fat, make a post from a forked tree bough and drive it into the ground. Then sacrifice the pig to us. Drip its blood on the post and stick its head on one of the prongs. In return, we will grant you prosperity."

Japhal's father carried out the *thilha*'s instructions. He bought a piglet and fattened it and sacrificed it and grew rich. His neighbors inquired about this, and Japhal's father told them of his dream. Soon the whole village was raising pigs and sacrificing them to the *thilhas*. The *thilhas*, who loved pork, were delighted and saw to it that everyone prospered.

But the children of Manmasi were a migratory people, and soon the time came for them to abandon their village and move on. As was the custom, each family took down its *buom* from the rafters and packed it. Since the forked post was too big to carry, they removed the pig skull and added it to the *buom*.

"Since then," Dr. Khuplam said, "the *go buom* was called a *doi buom* and had a pig's skull rather than a goat's."

Doi was a serious matter. I realized this when I tried making a joke of it. Hearing that Zankothang Haokip had refused to come to Imphal unless someone could be found to tend his buffalo, I asked, "Why doesn't he shrink them and bring them with him?"

This elicited no laughter. Dr. Khuplam replied that doing such a thing was dangerous. If used for illegitimate purposes, *doi* could have unpredictable consequences.

"It's like this," Yitzhak said. "Think of the laws of physics. Every act of *doi* has its equal and opposite reaction. If the priest were to put his buffalo in a box, something bad might happen somewhere else."

Western, rational-minded Yitzhak!

It was perhaps only vestigial superstition. Yet for the first time in dealing with the old Kuki religion, I felt I had touched on something live. It gave me a start. It was like a rustling in dead leaves. You wondered what might be moving there.

☩

The buffalo herder was sulking. A tall, dark-skinned man, he sat thrusting out a fat lower lip. Perhaps he missed his buffalo. Perhaps he was annoyed that Once A Thang Two Thang was hogging the conversation.

It wasn't clear to me why Once A Thang had been invited, since he was neither a practicing *doi* priest like the buffalo herder nor a retired one like Thin Thang. He was a nudnik, the kind of man who asks "How are you?" and spends the next hour telling you how he is. He kicked off his shoes, folded his stockinged feet on his chair as though it were a yoga mat, uttered the obligatory "I have something to say," and launched a tale of how, in 1940, when he was a boy of ten, and there was a lunar eclipse, and he had heard his father shout, "Let go of the moon, we are the children of Manmasi," and he had asked who Manmasi was, he was told that he had lived long ago, in a time when men and jungle spirits could still converse, and that his children had been so powerful that they nearly killed off the spirits, leaving only two of them, who went to Pathien and complained, "Your creatures are destroying us," so that Pathen counseled them to put yeast in the children of Manmasi's water, which they did, only to be told by Pathen when they asked him to destroy the Manmasites completely, "Thus I cannot do as they alone worship me with the white chicken," and then, in 1953, and so on, and so forth, and all this time the buffalo herder's lower lip was swelling as though bitten by a bee.

Since I already knew the story of the *thilhas* and the yeast, I didn't notice at first that Once A Thang's version contained an important new detail. I was more concerned with Zenkothang Haokip, who was firmly clutching in his lap an overnight bag that, for all I knew, was full of shrunken buffalo. Moreover, Thin Thang, a venerable ancient with a grin of merry dotage, was beginning to get a *blimmed* look. Interrupting Once A Thang, I said I'd gladly listen to his stories later but first wanted to talk to the two priests. Shortly after, he rose and left in a huff. The Khuplams went upstairs for their nap, leaving me with Yitzhak, Thin Thang, the buffalo herder, and the village chief, who had remained when his *lapi* singers departed.

My first object was to ascertain whether Thin Thang and the buffalo herder knew any of Dr. Khuplam's *themthu*. They didn't. They were *doipu*, not *thempu*, they said, and did not know *themthu* at all. *Themthu*, said the buffalo herder, who brightened up once Once A Thang left, were for Pathen. You couldn't make a living from them. Pathen was worshiped on only a few occasions. It was hard enough nowadays to make ends meet from the jungle spirits, who went around causing illness every day.

"Suppose," I said, "that the spirits gave me a stomachache. What would you do for it?"

The buffalo herder said that first he would take my pulse, which would indicate whether my complaint came from the village or the jungle.

Since I didn't spend much time in the jungle, I said, it would presumably have come from the village.

Well, then, he said, he would sacrifice a chicken, split it in two, and place one half on either side of my street. Passing between them might cure me. If it didn't, he would slaughter a larger chicken, give it to me to eat, and recite a *doithu*. He would offer the heart and liver to the spirits responsible and say:

> Lelonu, Lelopa,
> Zowminu, Zowmipa,
> Who descended from the great heavens,
> Who descended from the *kungpi* tree.
> Who descended from the *chalpi* tree,
> Who descended to the roots of the *seh* tree,
> Who descended to the bones of the fish,
> Who descended to the legs of the crab —
> You have come into this man's dwelling.
> You have sat upon his hearth.
> You have climbed upon his bed.
> You have afflicted his stomach.
> You have disturbed this man!
> You have upset this man!
> He who is afflicted, let him go!
> You have tasted the heart.
> You have tasted the liver.
> Lelonu, Lelopa,
> Zowminu, Zowmipa,
> Take what you are given and depart!

The buffalo herder thought that would do the trick. If it failed, there were other means. He might build a little statue from the red earth of an anthill and breathe on it — *f-f-fiiiii!* just like Aunt Lhingneng — and recite another *doithu*. This was an excellent remedy.

"A *leisanpa!*"

The buffalo herder knew it by a different name. He called the little statue a *thonbil*.

Thonbil or *leisanpa*, I said, Pathen created the first man from such earth.

The buffalo herder didn't know that story. He said, "Pathen created the children of Manmasi."

I: "How?"

Buffalo herder: "Don't expect me to remember that!"

Village chief: "I've heard we came out of a cave. But if there's a cave like that, why aren't people still coming out of it?"

I: "Perhaps it was only for you."

Village chief: "I'm confused. I've heard we came from a cave and I've heard we came from Manmasi. How are both possible?"

Buffalo herder: "We came from the lower village. Now we're in the upper village."

I: "But who was Manmasi?"

Buffalo herder: "We're his offspring."

Thin Thang: "The whole world is his offspring."

Village chief: "How can it be the whole world? We're the only ones who call ourselves his children."

Thin Thang: "It's the whole world!"

Buffalo herder: "Now I remember. The children of Manmasi are the ones who survived the flood. I heard it from the old people. Some of the animals and people escaped to a mountain. It was called Kholkip-Kholzang."

Village chief: "I heard that, too. The ones who survived were the children of Manmasi."

I: "Who here has heard of Tuisogiet?"

There was no response.

"How about Leiduppi-Leithaopi?"

Village chief: "That was the beginning of everything. That's where they called out the name of God."

Buffalo herder: "Leiduppi-Leithaopi is fertile earth."

I: "Where?"

Buffalo herder (pointing to the floor): "*This* earth."

I: "Manipur?"

Buffalo herder: "Everywhere."

Thin Thang: "The whole world."

Buffalo herder: "In times of sickness, the priest divided the land. He drew a line between the village and the jungle and said, 'This side is for the children of Manmasi in Leiduppi-Leithaopi and this side is for the spirits.'"

Village chief: "That's right. The village is Leiduppi-Leithaopi. That's why it's holy. Everything else belongs to the *thilhas*."

I: "Who knows about Pu Vanthang?"

Buffalo herder: "My parents did. He was an important man."

I: "How about crossing a sea?" (To the village chief): No, not you. You just sang a *lapi* about it."

Buffalo herder: "My grandfather knew that story. It was very hot, and the sea dried up. The children of Manmasi crossed over. The others died from the heat. The trees around the sea died too."

It was all hopelessly confused. If there had ever been a halfway coherent Manmasi tradition, not even the last practicing priest in Manipur knew anything about it. He knew other things, though. He knew that a male child born without a foreskin had once caused people to say, "An ancient one has been born." (The village chief agreed. He remembered the very same expression.) He knew the child's ears were pierced and its family lineage recited at a naming ceremony. He knew the lineage was also recited when a person died, at which time the family rapped on the doorposts with a sword and called out, "A son of Manmasi is coming." (He did not know the names "Gelet" or "Ulam." His rendition of this chant began with the founders of his own Haokip clan.) He knew a *thempu* was not allowed in the house of mourners, which was purified with water on the third day by a *themzong*. He knew of the *doi buom* and the annual sacrifice for it. This was a *hun*, a worshiping of Pathen, which took place in late spring or early summer.

I said, "I thought such a celebration was called a *kut*."

No, said the buffalo herder. A *kut* was more of a purification. For example, the *chol ngol ni nikho*, the day of abstention from yeast — that was a *kut*.

"What day was that?"

All three men — all four, since Once A Thang Two Thang had returned — knew about the *chol ngol ni nikho*. It was a holiday on which a special unleavened rice bread was prepared and eaten at a communal village feast.

I glanced at Dr. Khuplam, who had come back down from his nap. "Did you know about this?" I asked.

"Of course," he said.

"Then why didn't you tell me?"

"I didn't think it was important."

Two peoples in the world had a holiday on which a special unleavened bread was eaten, and he didn't think it was important!

⚶

Was it? It wouldn't have been if not for everything else. If an obscure people in a little-known corner of southeast Asia had a holiday reminiscent of the biblical Passover and that was all, you could put it down to the great seducer, Coincidence.

But you couldn't get away with it that easily. And one reason you couldn't was that, like other southeast Asians and unlike the biblical Israelites, the Kuki-Chin-Mizo were not bread eaters. Bread was simply not part of their diet. They used yeast, but for other purposes. The main one was for preparing *zu*. This was done by wetting and pounding rice into a mash packed in layers of leaves at the bottom of a jar, to which a solution of yeast water was added to hasten fermentation. Yeast was also used for making rice cakes, a festive food not eaten every day. Everyday food was rice. Yet here was a day, said Zankothang Haokip, on which "the whole village sat down together to a meal with bread. It was the only time all year that we ate it. You *had* to eat it. You ate it whether you wanted to or not." And it had to be bread without yeast. The holiday was named for that.

I asked each of the men for his memories of the *chol nghol ni nikho*, the day of abstention from yeast. Dr. Khuplam, who sat listening silently, added his later. Then I pieced them together.

The holiday took place right before spring sowing. The date was set by the village chief and the village priest for the night of the next full moon. First came a three-day period of "purification," during which all work was prohibited. On the eve of the first day the priest made the rounds of the village, going from door to door and announcing, "It's time to prepare your rice and dough!" The women of each household then pounded rice into flour, prepared dough, wrapped it in banana leaves, and boiled it. The boiled bread, called *changha*, came in two shapes, either flat or sausage-like and tied at the ends. Onzathang Thuthang re-membered his excitement as a child at the thought of eating it. On the first of the three days, the *changha* was eaten at home, and no rice was consumed. On the second day, the *changha* was not eaten. The three Thangs and the village chief recalled that *zu* was drunk on all three days. Dr. Khuplam said that in Haflung *zu* was forbidden.

On the third day of the *kut*, the day of the feast, the bread was brought by each household to the home of the village chief and given there to the priest. After that, according to Dr. Khuplam, all the villagers filed past the priest, who blessed them one by one and gave each a piece of *changha* to eat. Toward evening he announced, "Tonight, at sunset, the purifica-tion is over. You are free to return to your work, your rice, and your *zu*." As soon as the sun went down the villagers gathered at the chief's house for the feast, accompanied by the usual *zu* drinking, singing, and dancing.

The other men remembered it differently. They agreed with Thinthang Lenthang that the unleavened bread, while delivered to the priest early on the third day, was blessed, and eaten only in the evening. The priest handed it out, saying,

> *Kho athang tai.*
> *Kum athang tai.*
> *Nehmo a aumta pai,*
> *Chahmo a aumta pai.*

> The village is pure.
> The year is pure.
> There is nothing forbidden.
> You may eat all.

Naming each recipient of the *changha*, the priest then said,

> From So-and-So are removed
> All restrictions on food,
> All restrictions on work.
> All is pure.

After everyone had eaten the bread and been blessed, the partying be-gan and went on all night. On the next day, known as *chavang kut*, the merrymaking continued. The young men of the village competed in wrestling, stone-putting, javelin-throwing, and high-jumping, the bar to be cleared being the back of a *siel*, Thado for a mythun. There was also a tug-of-war between the young men and young women. If the men beat the women, the year would bring good hunting. If the women beat the men, it would bring good crops.

"I should think," I said, "that good crops would have depended on the men being badly hung over."

"They often were," said Dr. Khuplam.

The *chol nghol ni nikho* had been observed in places in Manipur as recently as ten or twenty years ago. The buffalo herder was trying to keep the custom alive in Tenkong. It was both a spring festival and a new year's day, on which the annual cycle was renewed with a clean slate.

Curiously, the same had once been true of Passover, the biblical Feast of Unleavened Bread that commemorated the exodus of Egypt. In the time of the Bible, the Jewish new year began not in the autumn, to which it was subsequently moved, but in the spring month of Nisan, on the full moon of which Passover fell.

Spring sowing followed the end of winter. If the *chol nghol ni nikho* was a *mi lui* holiday that had spread to some Kukis, could the Hmar winter festival at which the red sea song was sung have been influenced by it too? Had the red sea song originally been part of the children of Manmasi's observance of the day of abstention from yeast? My first inkling that Manmasi might indeed be Manasseh had begun with this song. Now I had circled back to it.

⚜

My next-to-last day in Imphal was set aside for a trip to Saikul. The Khuplams were looking forward to it. They had prepared a gala welcome for me there, with singing and dancing, an exhibit of old artifacts, including a *doi buom*, a demonstration of *zu* making, a native archery contest, and more. It was their chance to make up for not hosting me for the week.

The night before, Yitzhak returned to the apartment looking worried. He had just spoken to several people, he said, all of whom had advised against my going. The situation around Saikul had deteriorated. There was fighting between the Kuki Liberation Army and the Meitei Liberation Front, and other armed gangs were roaming in the area. The gala welcome was public knowledge. It would be a good idea to cancel it.

That was what we did. The Khuplams took it hard. They had spent weeks planning the event. Yet tilting the balance against them was their own security guard, an ex–Assam Rifles top sergeant hired because of threats made on Dr. Khuplam's life and work. (Some, it appeared, by none other than the Reverend T. Lumkin, concerned about the Lost Tribe belief's effects on Christian faith.) A burly fellow who had been decorated for gallantry, the top sergeant agreed that a visit to Saikul was unwise. Too many people had been inquiring about it, he said.

It was arranged for Shlomo Gangte to take the van and drive the staff of the National Research Laboratory to Imphal, where a modest ceremony would be held at the Thangjoms' apartment. But the Khuplams remained dejected, and the pall was thickened further by one of the city's frequent blackouts, which left the apartment in the dark. By the time the lights came on again, we had all gone to bed. Not everyone could sleep. The next day Yitzhak told me that, getting up in the middle of the night for a drink of water, he had found Dr. Khuplam in front of the television in the living room, watching an American western.

⚜

By morning, which he and I spent taping *lapi* and *themthu*, Dr. Khuplam's depression had passed. All things were from God. His faith was as broad as it was deep. On coming downstairs for his breakfast, I noticed, he first kissed the Thangjoms' mezuzah and then crossed himself.

The group from Saikul arrived in the afternoon. Shlomo Gangte had squeezed fifteen people into the van, a feat worthy of Hansei. They trooped in quietly, finding places on the floor when all the chairs were taken. Chairs went to H. H. Mate, the National Research Laboratory's "Chief Secretary"; to Victor John Letkam Hawkip, its "Chief Organizer"; and to Songkhosat Dimngel, its "Director of Art and Culture." Shlomo Gangte stayed on, the gallant top sergeant joined us, and Elitsur Haokip dropped in too, so it was a full house.

Dr. Khuplam had something to say. It was a great pleasure for him to present me to all his staff. By the grace of God I had come to Manipur to help in our common task. He prayed to God to bless me and strengthen me in my endeavors. Had it been God's will that I travel to Saikul today, I would have seen many old traditions. But there was one tradition that I would now be shown in Imphal. I would be *chonned*.

In the old days, Dr. Khuplam explained, being *chonned* was like being knighted. A real *chonning* was a complicated affair. Everything was carried out in sevens. Seven *siel* were slaughtered, seven altars were constructed for each *siel,* seven chants were recited at each altar, and every chant was repeated seven times. And at the death of the person who had been so honored, everything was done again in sevens. The funeral rites took so long that the body was smoked to avoid decomposition before interment. "So!" Dr. Khuplam said. To avoid having to smoke me someday, my *chonning* would be merely symbolic.

He produced a large black *pon* with an embroidered design and enjoined me:

> Hei, hei, hei, Za, creator of the world!
> He who remained faithful
> To the ancestry in Tuisogiet,
> To Leiduppi-Leithaopi,
> Step forward!

I took a step forward. The *pon* was draped around me. This was my *chon* cloak. Dr. Khuplam declared:

> You are glorified!
> Upon Chungkhopi, the place built,
> You are glorified!
> Among your peers, you are glorified!
> Like the seeds sowed, you are glorified!
> For the well-being of the inheritance of your forefathers,
> For the well-being of your father and your mother,
> For the well-being of your offspring,
> Hei, hei, hei, Za!

Then I was given a glass of *zu.* I drained it with the remark that, given the merely symbolic nature of the occasion, I would waive my right to six more glasses. Now *I* had something to say. If the results of my investigations had surpassed anything I had expected, this was solely due to Dr. Khuplam and his work. I wished to thank him for sharing it with me. And I wished to present him and Mrs. Khuplam with a gift, an album of photographs from Israel with a three-dimensional viewer. Finally, I wished us to honor the memory of Yehoshua Thangjom, in whose house we were meeting. A true son of Manmasi, he had died in his land.

I handed Dr. Khuplam the album. The viewer, which had one blue and one brownish-red lens, reminded me of Mr. Thangjom. Soon both were circulating among the guests.

Now H. H. Mate had something to say. Yitzhak translated. "Sir! When you were in Saikul last autumn, you told us you were 90 percent certain that we were the Lost Tribe of Manasseh. How certain are you now?"

"In percentages," I answered, "107."

Their laughter, I thought, came more from relief than from my attempt at humor. So! I had not let them down at the last moment.

"But what makes you so certain?" asked Songkhosat Dimngel.

They were certain. They were just not certain of their certainty. They could not be until it was accredited by the world I represented. They were waiting for me to put on it the stamp of international approval.

"It's a long story," I said. "It goes back three thousand years. If you have the time, I'll tell you what I know."

They had all afternoon.

Where the twelve tribes of Israel came from, I began, was a matter of scholarly debate. Some thought they had invaded ancient Palestine from the outside, as the Lusheis and Kukis had done in Manipur and Mizoram. Others believed they had crystallized from groups already living in the country. Their own legends, as collected in the Bible, which told of nomadic patriarchs and a period of enslavement in Egypt, endorsed the invasion account. In any case, by 1000 B.C.E. they were living in territories that stretched east and west of the Jordan River from today's Israeli Negev in the south to the Golan Heights and Mount Hermon in the north. One of the largest of these territories belonged to the tribe of Menashe, or Manasseh, descended, according to the Bible, from Joseph's eldest son. It ran across central Palestine from the Mediterranean to the mountains of Transjordan, making the Manassites the only tribe to have settled on both sides of the river. The biblical explanation was that when, after a period of wandering following the exodus from Egypt, the Israelite tribes crossed the Jordan from east to west, half of Manasseh joined the tribes of Gad and Reuben in remaining on the east bank.

"So!" someone from Saikul said. "We don't know which side of the Jordan we came from."

"But you do," I answered. "You know because the names of two of your Manassite ancestors, Gelet, or Gilead, and Ulam, have come down to us in your chants. Chapter 7 of the first Book of Chronicles tells us that Manasseh's son Machir was Gilead's father and that Gilead's half-brother Peresh, Machir's son by a woman named Ma'achah, was Ulam's father. But in the Bible, Gilead is also a geographical term, referring to the hill country of what is now the northern part of the kingdom of Jordan. And the Ma'achites were a Manassite clan living even farther north, at the foot of Mount Hermon, near the biblical town of Abel-beth-Ma'achah. Which came first — the names of ancestors later given to clans and geographical regions, or geographical and clan names later personified as ancestors — doesn't matter. The important thing is that Ulam and Gilead are connected with the country east and north of the Jordan. That's where you're from."

I took a framed map of Israel from the Thangjoms' wall and pointed to the hills of Gilead and the Golan Heights, reaching to Mount Hermon. There was a murmur of satisfaction. Returning to Leiduppi-Leithaopi, the children of Manmasi would know where to stake their claim.

The Manassite genealogies in I Chronicles 7 explained something else of importance. "One thing that has troubled me," I said, "is a song known to all of you. It begins, 'I am leaving the south / Sion was the land of my sojourning.' You believe this to be a song of farewell to Jerusalem, and many of your *lapi* are called 'Zion songs' because of it. I never understood how this could be so." I explained the problem in identifying Sion with Zion. Then I pointed out the equal difficulty in equating it with Chinese Xian, and said, "I think I now know the answer.

"It's like this. Chronicles tells us that Ma'achah, Ulam's grandmother, had two brothers with the funny-sounding names of Huppim and Shuppim. We already know those names, because they occur earlier in the same chapter in the genealogies of the southern tribe of Benjamin. And in the Book of Genesis the same two brothers, now called Huppim and Muppim, are listed as Benjamin's sons. Moreover, Chapter 8 of I Chronicles mentions a Ma'achah living in Gibeon, a village in Benjaminite territory. This passage continues: 'And the sons of Ulam were mighty men of valor, archers, and had many sons and sons' sons, a hundred and fifty. All these are of the sons of Benjamin.' It would appear, then, that Ulam, the founder of a clan of warriors, was the grandson of a marriage joining the tribes of Benjamin and Manasseh. Both tribes claimed him as their own."

They liked the idea of having descended from warriors. You could see it by the gleam in their eyes.

I continued, "Such marriage alliances may explain the special ties between Benjamin and Manasseh that we read of in the Bible. For example, we're told in Judges of a great war between Benjamin and all the other tribes that one group alone refused to participate in — the Manassite inhabitants of Yavesh-Gilead across the Jordan. And when the Benjaminites were decimated in that war, four hundred Manassite brides were given them to help repopulate their ranks.

"What does all this have to do with your 'Zion song'? Well, Zion or Jerusalem was in the territory of Benjamin. Nowadays suburban Jerusalem extends all the way to Gibeon. It would have been natural for Benjaminites migrating northward in order to join their new Manassite in-laws to have composed a song about leaving the south. But it wasn't a song about exile. It was about starting a new life. Maybe that's why it was called the 'Song of Hope.' It may seem strange to think of it's having survived for thousands of years, but it's no stranger than other things we're looking at."

There was, Sangkhosat Dimngel declared, a Zion dance as well.

"I know," I said. "I saw it performed last year at the Kuki Inn. I don't believe it's as old as the *lapi*. Other peoples in southeast Asia had similar dances. Your ancestors probably learned it from them and danced it to a song of their own. But I agree it had nothing to do with the missionaries. They're not the ones who introduced it.

"Let's get back to the Bible, though. About 1000 B.C.E. the tribes of Israel changed their form of government from a tribal confederation to a monarchy. According to the Book of Kings, all twelve tribes were united for a brief period under David and Solomon. Some historians and archeologists doubt this, but in any event, by 900 any such union had split into two kingdoms, Judah and Benjamin in the south and the other tribes in the north. The northern kingdom, with its capital in Samaria, was the wealthier and more developed of the two. It reached a peak of prosperity in the middle of the eighth century but went into decline as the Assyrians encroached on it from the east. The Assyrians can be compared with the British in India. They were superbly organized administrators with an unstoppable military machine and experience in running an empire."

I described the Assyrian system of population transfer and its application in Tiglath-Pileser's campaign of 734 to 732 in Transjordan and the Galilee, by the end of which — a decade before Shalmaneser laid siege to Samaria — 13,500 Israelites had been sent into exile. This number would have included Manassites from east and north of the Jordan, since Gilead and the Golan were among the conquered areas. Hence, I observed, after explaining why I believed the *sangah meichol* of Kuki lore to be a garbled memory of Shalmaneser, there seemed to be a new difficulty. If it was Shalmaneser's father, Tiglath-Pileser, who exiled these Manassites, why was Shalmaneser the one remembered by their descendants? "But that's easily answered," I told those assembled in the Thangjoms' living room. "The Assyrian king Tiglath-Pileser, even though credited with his army's triumphs, may not have been its battlefield commander. He may have spent much of the time conducting affairs from his capital of Nineveh. Others would have led his troops, especially the son who succeeded him on the throne in 727. There's evidence that the Aramean capital of Damascus was in fact taken by a subordinate, probably by Shalmaneser himself, in the same campaign of 734 to 732 or shortly after. And if it was Shalmaneser who was the commanding officer in this war — Shalmaneser who at the fighting's end chose thousands of Israelites for exile — Shalmaneser who marched the deported families off on the roads leading back to Assyria — then it was Shalmaneser who would have remained through the ages a byword for cruelty, until, by a quirk of language, he was turned into a wildcat with which naughty children were threatened and little babies sung to sleep.

"And so the Manassites went into exile, though we don't know what proportion of the 13,500 they were. Even if it was a high one, that wouldn't have meant a very large number. And the Assyrians would have divided the exiles into smaller groups and sent them to different places. We have no idea where these were. As opposed to the exiles of 720, whose specific destinations are given in the Bible, all we are told about the exiles of 732 is that they were 'carried captive to Assyria.'

"Maybe the clan of Ulam was allowed to remain intact. If its men were still warriors, they would most likely have been inducted as a unit into the Assyrian army and sent to fight on the empire's borders, which stretched, at its height, to the Mediterranean in the west, Egypt in the south, the mountains of the Caucasus in the north, and western Persia in the east. Presumably, at least some of Ulam's descendants were sent to the east, because that's where we next find them.

"Apart from that, we know nothing about them in the centuries that followed: where they were, how they subsisted, what peoples they lived among, or what languages they spoke. They could have lived in any of innumerable places. They could have been sedentary or nomadic, warlike or pacific, townspeople, farmers, herders, or traders, open to contact with others or keeping clannishly to themselves. We can assume that they maintained some of their old beliefs and traditions even while adopting new ones from their surroundings. Wherever they were, they preserved a memory of having come from elsewhere, from a faraway land of rich soil and abundant oil, a land they had the curious ability to long for without remembering where it was. In time, they lost all sense of belonging to a people called Israel. They became simply 'the children of Menashe,' and, eventually, of Manmasi. They no longer knew there had been eleven other tribes. They didn't think they were lost or that anyone was looking for them. They had no idea there were legends about them."

I related some of these legends. I told my listeners about the Mountains of Darkness and the Sambatyon, the Sabbath River, beyond which the Lost Tribes were said to dwell. I described the waterless flow of this river, all rock and sand, its noise like that of a great storm at sea. I said, "The centuries passed. The Assyrian empire fell to the Babylonians, the Babylonians were swallowed by the Persians, and the Persians were conquered by Alexander the Great, whose army reached the frontiers of India in 326 B.C.E. It soon withdrew, leaving behind a large force in a land the Greeks called Bactria, which was situated in northern Afghanistan. The kingdom established by the soldiers of this force, who intermarried with the local population to create a Greek-speaking ruling class, survived until 130 B.C.E. In its eastern corner, in the shadow of the Pamir and Hindu-Kush mountain ranges, was the ancient town of Kabul — and here, if we can rely on a *themthu* of Dr. Khuplam's, we see again the children of Manmasi. There's an external reason to rely on this *themthu*, although it is a bit iffy. It has to do with a document you're not familiar with."

I told them about Yosi Hualngo's notebook and Lianpuisuaka's will. "I can't swear the will is genuine," I said. "But it seems to be — and if it is, one of the strange things about it is that, right before mention of *sen tuipui* or the Red Sea and *sin-ai tlang* or Mount Sinai, it has the word *akuptan*. This can only be the Greek name for Egypt, Aegyptos. How, you ask, did a Greek place name get into the children of Manmasi's chants? The only place I can think of in which your ancestors may have had prolonged contact with Greek is Bactria. It was probably there that 'Aegyptos' replaced whatever word they had used for Egypt until then.

"So, not less than two thousand years ago, the children of Manmasi were in Kabul, though for how long, it's impossible to say. It could have been months or generations. And after that? The same *themthu* mentions another place that can be identified — Khotan, now Hotien in far north-western China. Khotan was on the Silk Road, the ancient network of trade routes connecting China with central Asia. It wasn't very far from Kabul, about three hundred miles as the crow flies — if crows fly that high. The direct route to it crossed the Pamirs, which rise to 25,000 feet. The passes lower down, though hazardous, were used by travelers who wanted to avoid a long detour. The Manassites could have used them too. But I'd feel more certain about the Khotan of the *themthu* if we had something to back it up with, as we have *akuptan* for Kabul."

Dr. Khuplam spoke to Yitzhak, who said, "We do have something. There's a second *themthu* that refers to Khotan. It belongs to a *siel* sacrifice."

Dr. Khuplam recited the first lines of it; Yitzhak put them into English:

> O *siel*, I call you with salt and harness rope
> From the water hole beneath Khotan.

The stir in the room told me that I looked startled. I knew that wild oxen loved salt; back in the days when they were raised as semidomesticated animals, they had been allowed to roam the jungle freely because they always came home to their salt licks. But what did Dr. Khuplam know about Khotan?

"Nothing," Yitzhak answered after asking. "He only knows where it is on the map."

I said, "You know, that is rather remarkable. Khotan was an oasis town at the southern edge of the Takla Makan desert. The high Tibetan plateau was at its back. There was no rainfall to speak of in the Takla Makan, and caravan stops were in those places where large quantities of snow-melt ran down from the plateau. Khotan was on a hillside. The streams, ponds, and canals on the desert floor beneath it formed one big water hole. It's just as the *themthu* says."

So the children of Manmasi had been at Khotan, drawn by trade or adventure. Perhaps the Pamirs were the "great mountains" of the chant remembered by Navi Songtiniam, the one that went:

> Manmasi who crossed the small and great water,
> The small and great mountains, you crossed them.

In the first centuries of the Christian era, Khotan was a prosperous and cosmopolitan town. Large caravans came and went. The majority of its inhabitants were Sogdians, Indo-European speakers of an Iranian lan-guage, but its streets were filled with Chinese, Turks, Tibetans, Mongols, Bactrians, and Indians. Religions mixed there, too. Before it came to be dominated by Islam in the Middle Ages, Khotan was home to Buddhists, Zoroastrians, Nestorian Christians, Manichaeans, and shamanists, and it was an important center for the translation of religious texts. Although we know of no Jewish community in it or along the Silk Road, Jews must have passed through on their way to northern China, where Marco Polo and others encountered them. Would they and the children of Manmasi have recognized an ancient kinship had they met? Probably not. No known Jewish traveler, at any rate, reported seeing or hearing of the tribe of Manasseh in central Asia. The rumors of the Lost Tribes that began to circulate in the Jewish world toward the end of the first millennium C.E. put the Manassites elsewhere. Eldad Ha-Dani thought they were beyond the Caucasus and in Arabia, which was where Benjamin of Tudela also placed them. The Dutch colonial governor of Cochin, on the Malabar Coast, from 1670 to 1677, Hendrick Adrian van Reedhe, reported meet-ing Jews there who claimed descent from Manasseh. Yet no such tradi-tion is known to have existed among the Cochin Jews, and by then the children of Manmasi had long been in southeast Asia.

How did they get there? This time, too, there would have been a short way and a long way. The short way went up the steep mountain trails leading from Khotan to the Tibetan plateau, crossed the latter from northwest to southeast, and descended through the Himalayas on its other side, perhaps passing through Thimpu in Bhutan. The place name

"Thimphut" was found with Kabul and Khotan in the same *themthu* and this was certainly a feasible route. Tibet's contacts with the southern Silk Road were close; indeed, it even ruled Khotan in the second half of the seventh century, after wresting it temporarily from the Chinese. Not, I said, that I'd put much stock in Yosi Hualngo's cousin Laltaithuama's account of finding local memories of the children of Manmasi in Tibet. Yet you never knew. Sometimes there was a grain of truth in such things.

The long way from Khotan would have been to follow the Silk Road to its eastern end in China, where it emerged from the desert near Lanchou. From there, the Manmasites might have turned south, skipping Dr. Khuplam's great loop through Mongolia, and journeying fifteen hundred miles to Manipur, through densely populated Shensi, Szechwan, and Yunnan provinces and upper Burma. This struck me as less likely. Nomadism was a common way of life in central Asia and Tibet, but not in heavily agricultural China, where a small, wandering group would have been more likely to settle down and blend with local inhabitants. "But all we can know for sure," I said, "is that when the first Old Kuki tribes arrived in the Manipur hills in the fifteenth century, they found the children of Manmasi already there and called them 'the old people.'"

I explained my *mi lui* theory, supplementing the Thado legends cited by Shaw and Hutton with my new knowledge of the tradition, passed down by Onzathang Thouthang's father, that white rooster worship of Pathen — Lenthang's ritual means of bringing back the sun — had once distinguished the children of Manmasi. I was apprehensive about this. So far I had said nothing to contradict my listeners' belief that they were biologically descended from a biblical tribe. Now I was suggesting otherwise.

I said, "Since we don't know exactly when the Manmasites settled in this region, we also don't know who else was here at the time. Their being called 'the old people' by the Kukis suggests they may have preceded the Nagas and the Meitei as well." There were indications that before the invasion of the area by Tibeto-Burmese hill tribes, the population was Austro-Asiatic. Hutton, who was convinced of this, pointed to a number of features in Kuki life and religion that he thought were borrowed from Austro-Asiatic sources, such as the *zawlbuk* and the *doi buom*. Certainly the legend of Galgnam's *buom* floating down a river to the Kom, an Old Kuki tribe affiliated with the Hmar, seemed a way of saying that it was acquired locally. The *mi lui* version of the story, in which the *buom* was given by Pathen to the priest Zamneh, implied the same thing.

I continued, "Pathen, of course, wasn't the original name of the children of Manmasi's god. They took that from the Kukis. Their own god was called Ya, a name retained from biblical times. It wasn't the only biblical feature preserved by them when the Kukis encountered them. They still knew some biblical stories. They practiced circumcision. They observed the holiday of Passover. There's evidence of their shunning pork." I recounted the tale of the kidnaping of Japhal, in which the *thilhas* persuade Japhal's father to raise pigs. "In all of these stories," I said, "the *thilhas* stand for the southeast Asian religion that the children of Manmasi initially resisted. The story of the Manmasites' war with the *thilhas*, at first waged successfully but lost in the end, tells us how the old faith in Ya was gradually undermined by a belief in the jungle spirits. It even tells us how this happened."

The visitors from Saikul had been staring at me for some time as though I might be a *thilha* myself. A stranger who had spent only a few weeks among them, who didn't know their language, and had only a superficial knowledge of their culture, I was now expounding their own past to them. It was chutzpah, no doubt of it, though they deferred to me too much to think of it that way — to think of it as anything other than some mysterious power I must have. But there was no mystery. What I had was a Western education that enabled me to think about textual and historical problems in a way they were unaccustomed to.

I said, "It's a strange story when you think of it. The *thilhas* are on the verge of extinction and beg for mercy from Pathen, who tells them to put yeast in the water of the children of Manmasi, thus darkening the Manmasites' eyes and making the *thilhas* invisible. Why yeast? Why light or dark eyes? You know, I studied literature in college. I learned that there are stories that have to be read for their symbols. It's like interpreting a dream. And I'll hazard the guess that our story, read as a dream, means this. As long as the children of Manmasi remained faithful to their old customs, they maintained their religious vision and saw the *thilhas* for what they were, forces conquerable by the religion of Ya. Yet after a while these customs began to weaken. One of the most important of them was the abstention from yeast — *all* yeast — on an annual holiday of unleavened bread. Maybe one spring when the holiday came around, someone said, 'Oh, well! A little yeast in the *zu* water can't possibly do any harm.

After all, what's a celebration without *zu?*' And so that year the children of Manmasi drank *zu* on the day of abstention from yeast, and after a while they began to eat pork, and then they adopted *doi*, and next they gave up circumcision, and one thing led to another until they were marrying the Kukis and practicing all the Kuki ways. What happens when people with Semitic or semi-Semitic features intermarry with Asians? Their eyes, until then brown, blue, green, or gray, become uniformly dark brown. This is a story about how the children of Manmasi became, in appearance and religion, like southeast Asians. They came to fear and sacrifice to the *thilhas* until they were indistinguishable from the Kuki-Chin-Mizo. Today, you are children of Manmasi *and* Kuki-Chin-Mizo."

The visitors from Saikul looked at one another. They didn't know whether I had spoken fish or fowl. They waited for a reaction from Dr. Khuplam. But Dr. Khuplam was sitting with his eyes shut, as if meditating deeply on something. And so H. H. Mate nodded to Songkhosat Dimngel, who poked Victor John Letkam Haokip, who said, "So! Sir! If we now form the Manmasi Zionist International Liberation Organization as the only apex body of all social and political organizations of the Children of Manmasi-Kuki-Chin-Mizo people, will the government of Israel recognize us through the cooperation of your good self?"

What has been accomplished — the rabbinic saying goes — *by all the promulgations of the sages?*

I tried explaining, once again, that the Kuki-Chin-Mizo people need not worry about recognition by anyone. "All that matters," I said, "is who you are and want to be. You're not Jews. But you do go back, in one branch of your family, to the Israelites of the Bible. That's amazing. What you do with it is up to you."

"But, sir," H. H. Mate appealed, "does not this make you and us the same people?"

"No," I answered. The word had rarely sounded so gross to me. "Some of our ancestors were the same people. That was a long time ago."

It was the best I could do. I told them how extraordinary it was, after centuries of the globe's being combed in vain for traces of the Lost Tribes of Israel, for a fragment of one to be found. I explained the great historical significance of the Israelite branch of their family. It demonstrated the tenacity of group identity and tradition over vast stretches of time and space, and told us that other Lost Tribe stories must be taken seriously. It had implications for biblical studies, too. These went beyond specifics like knowing what "selah" meant. For years now, a war had been raging between the biblical traditionalists and the revisionists, who held that the Bible was a late document composed in Persian and Hellenistic times, when many of its stories and customs were invented. If a group of Manassite tribesman, permanently separated from their fellow Israelites in the eighth century B.C.E., had known some of these stories and practiced some of these customs, it might be possible to refine the terms of the debate. More research was needed. Ethnographers, historians, Bible scholars should join in it. And linguists, who might know where words like *seling maw* and *hitu* came from. But we had made a good start.

They listened without enthusiasm. They wanted fish or fowl, good Kuki grub. I had given them cake.

Dr. Khuplam and his wife took a broader view. They stayed on at the Thangjoms' when Shlomo Gangte drove the Saikul group home. Yitzhak and Elitsur Haokip remained, too. We broke out the *zu* again and talked.

"I'm sorry I couldn't tell your people they're all full-blooded Israelites," I apologized. "I know that would have made them happier."

Dr. Khuplam shrugged. "I'm a Lenthang, and I'm not a full-blooded Israelite either," he said.

"No, you're not," I agreed. "Neither am I. I don't know if there is such a thing. There are plenty of us half-bloods, though. There's been a lot of recent research on the subject. A Jewish genetic profile exists, even if it's not all that different from those of other eastern Mediterranean peoples. It's surfaced in some very odd places." I told the Khuplams about Tudor Parfitt's findings with the Lemba, which showed this black Bantu group to have Y chromosomes indicative of Jewish origins. "The Lemba aren't a lost biblical tribe," I said. "Some of them descend from Jewish merchants from Yemen. But they illustrate the superficiality of skin color and facial features. When typed for Jewish *kohen*ite or priestly Y chromosomes, which have characteristics of their own, they scored higher than any Jews in the world. The fact that you look typically southeast Asian doesn't necessarily mean your genes are."

"But what happens," Yitzhak asked, "if we test the Lenthangs and the Chensongs for Jewish genes and don't find them?"

"You mean would I give up my theory? No, I don't think so. It has too much in its favor. I'd look for another explanation. Perhaps the original group of exiles was so small, and mingled with so many other groups, that its genes no longer show up in the samples. Perhaps the *mi lui* weren't biologically descended from the Manassites but came in contact with a people who were, just as the Kukis came in contact with them. Why worry about that now?"

"There'll be testing," Yitzhak said. "It's inevitable."

I said, "I suppose it is. Genetic studies will be done all over. They may turn up other Lost Tribes."

"But we'll always have been the first," said Mrs. Khuplam. She was preparing to remember it that way, as a woman prepares to remember being a man's first love even before they have parted.

"Oh, definitely," I said. "Absolutely. The first to cross the Sabbath River."

We finished the rice beer. The gallant top sergeant saluted and took his leave. Elitsur Haokip, the dandy of Manipur, went out and returned with some *zu kha* or "bitter *zu*," a distilled, colorless liquid that was more like a whiskey. It came in a transparent plastic bag that resembled an intravenous infusion. He emptied into a bowl some spicy dried peas he had bought, and we drank *zu kha* and munched peas while the servant boys set the table for dinner. I was still draped in my *chon*. Mrs. Khuplam picked up the album from Israel and put on the red-and-blue glasses. She looked like a birthday girl after the party has ended. Elitsur began to sing something familiar.

"It's Samakai Range," Yitzhak said. "You heard it that night at the Kuki Inn."

> O my clansmen, that we have been torn
> Upon the big Samakai range.
> My sadness spreads from north to south.
> Like the water that is flowing, I move on.

We talked and drank. The food grew cold on the dinner table. The servants emerged from the kitchen at intervals to regard it worriedly. Mrs. Khuplam asked when I was planning to return to Manipur.

"I don't know," I told Yitzhak. I had no plans.

"She hopes it will be soon. She's already nostalgic for this week."

And it wasn't even over. The bitter *zu* flowed sweetly in our veins.

GUIDE TO PRONUNCIATION

Both Mizo and Thado use the Latin alphabet, introduced by the British and adapted to local phonetic rules. Although Mizo and Thado names look strange, their words are spelled phonetically. The main difficulty for speakers of English is the aspirated consonants, such as *th* and *ph*. These are not pronounced as in "thin" or "phone," but, rather, as a *t* or *p* accompanied by a puff of breath. Mizo and Thado speakers, like many southeast Asians, differentiate between aspirated consonants and unaspirated ones. If you put your hand in front of your mouth, you should feel the puff only when you say the former. In the transliteration of Thai and Burmese words and names, the *h* indicating aspiration is often placed before the consonant, not after it; *ht* or *hp* are, then, like Mizo or Thado *th* or *ph*. This practice is also followed in some Mizo-Thado words like "Hmar," pronounced with an aspirated *m*.

Apart from aspirated consonants, there are other Mizo and Thado characters pronounced differently from the way they are in English.

Ch sounds like the *ts* in English "cats." (*Chh* is an aspirated *ch*.)

Kh in Mizo is an aspirated *k*. In Thado it is a *ch*, as in "Bach."

Ng is a single sound, as in English "song." At the beginning of a word or syllable, it is weaker, more like a nasal pronunciation of the vowel following it. *Ngo*, for example, can be approximated by uttering *o* through your nose as well as your mouth.

R is pronounced with a tap of the tongue, as in Spanish.

J in Thado is pronounced like a *z*. The letter is not used in Mizo.
The vowels sounds are:

A as in "father."

Ai as in "my."

Aw as in "law."

Awi as in "boy."

E as in "get."

Ei as in "say."

I as in "in."

O as in "only."

U as in "foot."

Eu as in French "*deux.*"

Finally, in my transliteration of Hebrew words, *ch* is like the *ch* in
"Bach." Rabbi Avichail's name is pronounced Ah-vee-CHA-yil.

GLOSSARY

Akiva: A prominent sage (c. 50–132 c.e.) of early rabbinic Judaism.

The *ashrei*, the *barkhu*, the *shema:* Different parts of the morning prayer, which ends with the *aleinu*.

Avraham Yitzhak Hacohen Kook: Well-known theologian (1865–1935) and chief rabbi (1921–1935) of Palestine. Kook's mystical interpretation of secular Zionism had a great influence on the thought of religious Zionism. His son, Tsvi Yehuda Kook (1890–1982), continued his line of thought.

Bawlpu: The "private" priest in the old Kuki-Chin-Mizo religion, as opposed to the *sadawt*, the "public" priest.

Blessed be He and blessed be His name: In Jewish prayer, the many formulaic blessings that begin with the words "Blessed art Thou O Lord" call for two responses. At the end of them, the listener says "Amen." After "O Lord," he says, "Blessed be He and blessed be His name."

Blessings of the Morn: The opening section of the morning prayer.

Challah: The twisted bread traditionally eaten by Jews on the Sabbath.

Changha: The unleavened rice bread eaten on the "day without yeast."

Chavang kut: The festive day following the evening feast of *chol nghol ni nkho*, "the day of abstention from yeast."

Chhinlung: Literally, the "covering rock," the great stone that, in Kuki-Chin-Mizo legend, blocks the passage from the underworld to earth.

Chhinlung chhuak: The "covering rock exiters," the primeval ancestors who emerged from the underworld. In some circles, *chhinlung chhuak* has become an epithet for the Kuki-Chin-Mizo people.

Chibai: Hello.

Chol ngol ni nikho: "The day of abstension from yeast."

Chon: A ceremony honoring someone for his deeds or achievements; also, to perform such a ceremony.

Chongthu: The mythical ancestor and first man to emerge from the underworld.

Chungkhopi: The "Upper City" or "Upper Village," human habitation on earth after the emergence of ancient man from the underworld.

Chungkhuanulang: "One Who Dwells Above," an epithet for Pathian (see entry).

"Come, my love, to meet the bride": A hymn sung by the congregation in the Sabbath eve service. There are a number of melodies for it.

Dao: A long knife with a machete-like blade.

Doi: Roughly translatable as "magic," *doi* is a general word for the various sacrifices and procedures used to control and manipulate the harmful spirits.

Doi buom: A "doi box" or *"doi* basket," the assemblage of seven sacred objects traditionally kept during the year in the roofbeams of each family's house and believed to protect the household.

Doikungpa: A *"doi* master," someone proficient at the practice of *doi.*

Doipu: A priest who practices *doi.*

Doithu: A sacrificial chant recited by a *doipu.*

Eighteen Benedictions: A lengthy prayer, said standing and in silence. It is called that because of the eighteen "Blessed art Thou O Lord" formulations in it.

Eliezer: A prominent first-century C.E. rabbi and contemporary of Akiva.

Exilarch: The state-recognized head of the Jewish community of Babylonia from roughly the third through the tenth century C.E. As the Babylonian community was the largest and most influential in the Jewish world during this period, the exilarch was recognized as a religious authority by Jews in many other places as well.

Falang: Foreigner, especially a European.

Galgnam: A legendary Kuki hero and introducer of *doi* (see entry) into Kuki life.

The Gaon of Vilna: "The Luminary of Vilna," the common epithet for Elijah ben Solomon Zalman (1720–1797), the leading Talmudic authority of his age.

Go buom: Literally, "treasure basket," another name for the *doi buom* (see entry).

Gophipan: A bamboo rope, also known as a *gopi,* from which the objects of the *doi buom* (see entry) were hung.

Gunram: A sacrifice to appease a jungle spirit causing illness.

Ha-Rav: "The rabbi" (or, in direct address, "Rabbi") in Hebrew.

Hashem: Literally, "the Name" in Hebrew, the most common of the many epithets for God used by Orthodox Jews, who may utter the actual words for God, *elohim* or *adonai*, only in prayer.

Hlim: A trance, or to put someone into a trance.

Huai: Mizo for jungle spirit.

Hualhimtu: "Guardian," an epithet for Pathian (see entry).

Hun: A special day of worship.

Jhum: A field cultivated by slash-and-burn agriculture; also, to cultivate in such a manner.

Kaddish: The mourner's prayer, a prayer for the soul of the deceased recited daily by his or her next-of-kin in the year following death and once a year thereafter on the anniversary of the death.

Kapu: Mister, sir.

Karaites: A Jewish sect, originating in the eighth century, that rejected the authority of rabbinic law and claimed to practice a "pure," biblical Judaism.

Kawnglai: A doorpost sacrifice.

Kelkhal: A family thanksgiving sacrifice.

Kenesiyah: Hebrew for "church."

Khaopi: A creeping vine used to bind together the sacred objects in the *doi buom.*

Kholkip-Kholzang: Literally, "the flat, broad place," a legendary place where, in primeval times, men and animals dwelled peacefully together.

Khua: A friendly spirit or deity.

Khuanu: A Mizo name for the chief deity in its feminine aspect, or, in the old religion, one of the goddesses. A *khua* is a friendly spirit.

Khuapa: The supreme deity in its masculine aspect (see *Khuanu*).

Khuavang: See *Khuanu.* Literally, "a guardian *khua*," considered by some to be a name for the supreme deity in the old religion.

Kochhiar: The secretary of a chief or leader.

Kut: Holiday, festival.

Langlap: A six-pointed, red-white-and-black design hung over the altar during a sacrifice.

Lapi: A traditional song, usually sung on festive occasions or during *zu-*drinking sessions.

Leiduppi-Leithaopi: Literally, "Land of good earth, land of oil," a mythical land of fertility.

Leisanpa: The first man; literally, "red-earth man."

Lungdaw: The ceremonial stone around which the Sikpui festival was held.

Lungzai: See *Nungzai.*

Ma'ariv: The evening prayer, the last of the three daily Jewish services.

Maheim: A human being in Kholkip-Kholzang (see entry).

Manasa: In Mizoram, the name of an ancient ancestor whose supposed descendants call themselves "children of Manasa." The name also occurs as Manasia. Among the Hualngo and Hmar tribes, and in Manipur, its common form is Manmasi.

Manmasi: See *Manasa.*

Menashe: The Hebrew name of the biblical tribe of Manasseh.

Menorah: A seven-branched candelabrum such as that which stood in the Temple in antiquity and is currently the symbol of the state of Israel.

Messiah son of David: According to medieval Jewish tradition, there will be two messianic redeemers. The first, "the messiah son of Joseph," will fall in battle against Israel's enemies. The second, "the messiah son of David," will complete the redemption.

Mezuzah: A small container holding a parchment scroll with verses from Deuteronomy. It is attached to the front door jamb of a Jewish home, and, in Orthodox homes, to the doorway of every room.

Midrash: A rabbinic parable or narrative, often in the form of a commentary on a verse in the Bible.

Mi hlim: Literally, "happy people," a self-referential term used in Mizoram by members of the United Pentecostal Church.

Mi lui: Literally, "old people," a term in Manipur for the Lenthangs, Chensongs, and Lumkins, the clans that are believed to be descendants of the pre-Kuki-Chin-Mizo inhabitants of the area.

Mim kut: A harvest festival in the old Kuki-Chin-Mizo religion, held in late autumn.

Minchah: In Judaism, the daily afternoon prayer.

Mountbatten's Chindits: Lord Louis Mountbatten, the last British viceroy of India, was commander of the China-Burma-India Theater during World War II. The native forces enlisted by him to fight alongside British troops against the Japanese, many of them Kuki-Chin-Mizo, were known as Chindits. The deepest Japanese advance into India was stopped by British and Chindit troops near Imphal in 1943.

Mythun: The Asian wild ox, *Bibos frontalis gaurus,* also known as a gaur, gayal, or *siel,* once widely raised by the Kuki-Chin-Mizo as a semidomesticated beast both for its meat and for its use in major public sacrifices.

New Moon: In Jewish ritual, a special prayer is said each month upon the first sighting of the new moon.

Nirleng: A species of cicada.

Noikhopi: The "Lower City" or "Lower Village," the habitation of ancient man in the underworld before he emerged on the earth (see *Chungkhopi*).

Noimangpa: "The Great One Below," the god who was lord of the underworld.

Nungzai: A deity widely worshiped in *doi* practice, also known as Ningzai or Lungzei.

Pathian: The Mizo name for God as the supreme deity. The Chin form of the name is Pasien; the Kuki form, Pathen.

Pathian bom: See *Doi buom*.

Pon: The wraparound cloth that was the daily costume in the old Kuki-Chin-Mizo culture.

P'sukei de'zimra: Literally, "the verses of song," the part of the morning service following "the Blessings of the Morn."

Pu: Mizo and Thado for "Mister."

Ram Huai: The king or ruler of the jungle spirits.

Sabbat salom: The Hebrew *shabbat shalom*, "Sabbath peace," the customary Sabbath greeting.

Sadawt: A "public" priest. See *Bawlpu*.

Saheim: A mythical half-man, half-tiger in Kholkip-Kholzang.

Sangah Meichol: "The long-tailed wildcat," a coyote-like animal with a malevolent reputation in Kuki legend.

Seven commandments of the sons of Noah: According to rabbinic law, the seven prohibitions incumbent upon all mankind, as opposed to the 613 commandments given only to the Jews. These are prohibitions against idol worship, incest, murder, theft, sacrilege, immoral behavior, and the eating of live flesh.

Shalom: "Hello" in Hebrew. The word also means "peace."

She: A kind of tree.

Shekhinah: In Jewish belief, the indwelling presence of God in the world, often depicted as feminine.

Shi Huang Ti: The first emperor of a united China (d. 210 B.C.E.). He built large parts of the Great Wall, and, in 213 B.C.E., ordered the burning of all books not officially recognized as contributing to the welfare of the state.

Siel: See *Mythun*.

Sikpui: The "great winter" festival of the Hmar tribe.

Sumtawng: A sacrifice for the health of animals and crops.

Targum of Yonatan ben Uziel: A "targum" was a translation of the Hebrew Bible into Aramaic, the language spoken by most Jews in the early centuries of the Common Era. The targum ascribed to Yonatan ben Uziel of the first century C.E. was in fact a translation and commentary together, in which many exegeses were interpolated into the biblical text.

Thempu: The Thado equivalent of the Mizo *bawlpu,* or "public" priest.

Themthu: A sacrificial chant recited by a *thempu* (see entry).

Themzong: A Thado priest whose function was limited to performing funerals.

Thilha: Thado for a jungle spirit, the equivalent of the Mizo *huai.*

Thimzin: The "great darkness," the mythical time, believed to have lasted "seven days and seven nights," in which nearly all mankind perished.

Thlaropa: Literally, "owner of our souls," an epithet for Pathian.

Thombil: A mound of enemy skulls, traditionally made by returning warriors after a successful raid.

Thusim: A traditional story or folktale.

Tlangrawi thawi: A goat sacrifice.

Tlawmngaihna: A Mizo word best translated as "virtue," the quality of public-spiritedness and sacrifice for the common good traditionally expected from a member of Mizo society.

Tsvi Yehuda Kook: See Avraham Yitzhak Hacohen Kook.

Tuisogiet: Literally, "the eight flowing waters," a Thado word generally referring to the ocean.

Tuitobin: Literally, "plugged water," the great Flood that, according to Kuki-Chin-Mizo legend, took place in antiquity.

Tulpi pa: A high priest.

Tuluk: Mizo for "dog."

Vanleng: "Heaven Dweller," an epithet for the supreme deity or one of his subordinates.

Veng: A neighborhood or quarter.

Western Wall: The Hebrew and Jewish term for the Wailing Wall, the massive Herodian retaining wall on the western side of the Temple Mount in Jerusalem that is the only remaining structure from the Temple.

Ya ribon olam: "O God, Master of the Universe," a popular hymn sung at the Sabbath eve table.

Zawlbuk: The bachelors' house in a traditional Kuki-Chin-Mizo village in which all unmarried young men lived.

Zel: A trance vision.

Zu: Rice beer.

Zu kha: "Bitter *zu,*" a distilled *zu* with a high alcoholic content.

NOTES

7 after World War One: Torrance's dates in China were 1918–1934. His first publication on the Chiang, "The History, Customs and Religion of the Ch'iang, an Aboriginal People of West China," in which he already made Israelite claims for them, appeared in the *Shanghai Mercury* in 1920. His views are most fully presented in *China's First Missionaries: Ancient Israelites* (London, Thynne & Co., 1937).

10 an article in English: Cammann's article appeared in *Monographs of the Jewish Historical Society of Hong Kong*, vol. III (1990).

David Crockett Graham: Graham's research on the Chiang is summarized in *The Customs and Religion of the Ch'iang* (Washington, Smithsonian Institution, 1958).

30 *The Karen People of Burma: A Study in Anthropology and Ethnology:* Marshall's study first appeared in *The Ohio State University Bulletin*, vol. 26, no. 13. His remarks on Old Testament parallels in Karen folklore are concentrated in Chapters II, XXI, and XXV.

31 Francis Mason: According to Marshall, Mason first stated this belief in a communication to *Missionary Magazine* in 1833. Like Marshall, nearly one hundred years later, he was struck by the lack of parallels between Karen folklore and New Testament stories. This convinced him that Old Testament material could not have come from a Christian source. According to his wife, E. H. B. Mason, in *Civilizing Mountain Men, or Sketches of Mission Work Among the Karens* (London, 1862), Mason did not necessarily believe the Karens were a "lost" Israelite tribe. He tended rather toward the theory that they descended from, or were influenced by, Jews living in China before the Christian era. Mrs. Mason, curiously, on the basis of "a paper read at the meeting of the British Association in Oxford in 1860" by one "Dr. Margowan," located this community in "the city of Chintu, the capital of the province of Szechuan" — i.e., in Chengdu! Avichail would have rejoiced in this "confirmation" of his theory that the Karen and the Chiang were linked religiously, not only ethnically, as thought by Marshall. Yet Karen and Chiang are far from closely related

languages, as might be expected if an ethnic link existed, and there does not appear to be, *pace* Dr. Margowan (whose paper I have not seen), any evidence of an ancient Jewish community in Chengdu.

43   "Mrs. Mason of Burmah": It was under this name that she published *Civilizing Mountain Men*. Her discussion of a possible Hebraic or Judaic past for the Karens is found in pp. 365–384. She quoted there a Karen poem that includes the stanzas:

> The Karen was the elderly brother
> And obtained all the words of God.
> God formerly loved the Karens above all others,
> But because of their transgressions, He cursed them,
> And now they have no book.
> Yet He will again have mercy on them
> And love them above all others.
> Alas! Where is God?
> Our ancestors said that when our younger brothers came back,
> The white foreigners who were able to keep company with God,
> The Karen will be happy.

It is interesting that Marshall (p. 10) cited a letter written by Francis Mason to the Baptist Missionary Society in 1832, a year before he first ascribed to the Karens an ancient Hebrew past, proposing a more pedestrian — or, more precisely, aquatic — explanation for the Karens' Old Testament–like stories and belief in the return of the "white foreigner." Several decades before his arrival in Burma, Mason wrote to the society, a "foreign merchant," presumably European, was marooned in Burma after a boat wreck on the Tenasserim River. Besides disseminating Bible stories, Mason conjectured, this merchant must have assured the local population that one day "white men" would come and "teach them about God." Perhaps Mason later discounted the relevance of this, because the Tenasserim, which flows through the Kra isthmus at the northern end of the Malay Peninsula, is far south of Karen territory.

52   a devil figure in Karen lore: Marshall says of this figure, who, in the guise of a tempter, often assumes a female form:

"He is said to have been a servant of 'Y'wa' at first, but to have been cast out of his lord's presence for offering him a gross insult. The other servants of 'Y'wa' have ever since cherished the desire to destroy 'Mu kaw li' but have never accomplished their purpose. Hence, he continues to roam about, deceiving mankind and spreading death among them, until he shall finally be put out of the way by 'Y'wa' himself. . . . It was through his malicious instructions that the people learned to make sacrifices to the demons" (op. cit., p. 213).

53   if Mrs. Mason was to be believed: She quoted the lines:

> Our ancestors charged us thus:
> If the thing [the ancient book] come by land — weep.
> If by water — laugh.
>
> . . .
>
> Hence the Karen longed for those
> Who were to come by water.

It is odd that she did not seem to have associated this belief with her husband's story of the European traveler who came down the Tenasserim.

54   descended from the biblical tribe of Dan: The rabbinate's ruling was based on the medieval story of "Eldad the Danite" and its acceptance by the rabbinic authorities of Eldad's time. See my account of this story in Chapter Four, pp. 102–105.

98   This happened in the reign of Israel's king Pekah ben-Remalyahu. . . : I Kings 16 tells us that Pekah and "Rezin king of Aram . . . came up to Jerusalem to war," and that the Judean king Ahaz, then ruling in Jerusalem, "sent messengers to Tiglath-Pileser, king of Assyria, saying, 'I am thy servant and thy son. Come up and save me out of the hand of the king of Aram and out of the hand of the king of Israel." The history behind this verse is Rezin's attempt to assemble from his capital in Damascus an anti-Assyrian coalition that Pekah joined; attacked by the two kings when he refused to go along with them, Ahaz appealed to the Assyrians, who came to his aid. Tiglath-Pileser's 734–732 campaign was thus aimed against both Damascus and its Israelite ally. For a comprehensive account of its political and military aspects, see Stuart A. Irvine, *Isaiah, Ahaz, and the Syro-Ephraimitic Crisis* (Scholars Press, Atlanta, 1990).

101   the disagreement cited by Avichail: The dispute between Eliezer and Akiva is in the tractate of Sanhedrin, 110b.

in the Babylonian Talmud: Yebamot, 16b.

by the Jerusalem Talmud: Sanhedrin, 10:6.

102   Josephus Flavius: The passage occurs in *The Jewish War*, Book VII, Chapter 5.

Pliny: *Historia Naturalis*, 31:18.

the Book of Elijah: This short work was composed in 613 under the influence of the Persian King Khosrau II's military campaign against Christian Byzantium, which it dislodged from Jerusalem and Palestine, stirring Jewish messianic expectations. There is no English translation of the Hebrew text, which appears in Yehuda Even-Shmuel, "Legends of Redemption" (Hebrew, Mosad Bialik, Jerusalem, 1954), pp. 41–48.

103   "land of Havilah": Eldad took this name from the biblical story of the Garden of Eden, through which, according to the Book of Genesis, ran four rivers. One of these, the Pishon, "compasseth the whole land of Havilah, where there is gold." Rabbinic tradition identified the Pishon as the Nile.

Eldad's story exists in several medieval Hebrew versions. There is an English version in Elkan Adler's *Jewish Travellers* (London, 1930). The only book-length study of Eldad available in English, dated but still valuable, is Max Schloessinger's *The Ritual of Eldad ha-Dani, Reconstructed and edited from manuscripts and a Genizah fragment, with notes, an introduction and an appendix on the Eldad legends* (Leipzig and New York, 1908). A good up-to-date survey of Eldad scholarship can be found in David J. Wasserstein's "Eldad ha-Dani and Prester John" in *Prester John, the Mongols and the Ten Lost Tribes*, ed. Charles F. Buckingham and Bernard Hamilton (Variorum, Brookfield, Vt., 1995).

104   known to him from other sources: What these sources were is not clear. Although Tsemach Ga'on professed to be familiar with a tradition that, during the last years of the northern kingdom, "the Danites, seeing that the king of Assyria was going to get dominion over Israel, went to Cush," no rabbinic legends to this effect are known. The text of the exilarch's response to the Jews of Kairouan appears in Adolf

Neubauer's monograph "Where Are the Ten Tribes?" (*Jewish Quarterly Review*, Vol. I, 1888–1889).

104   the Falashas: Although the origins of the Falashas are murky, current scholarly opinion is that they first arose as a Judaizing Christian sect no earlier than the fourteenth century. The case for a medieval genesis for them is made both by Steven Kaplan in *The Beta Israel (Falashas) in Ethiopia from Earliest Times to the Twentieth Century* (New York University Press, 1992) and James Quirin in *The Evolution of the Ethiopian Jews* (University of Pennsylvania Press, Philadelphia, 1992). See also Louis Rapoport, *The Lost Jews: Last of the Ethiopian Falashas* (Stein and Day, New York, 1980).

105   Khaibar Jews: A useful summary of what is known about the Jews of the Arabian Peninsula can be found in the chapter on them in Itzchak Ben-Tsvi's *The Exiled and the Redeemed* (Jewish Publication Society of America, Philadelphia, 1961). The presence of Jewish tribes in Arabia is documented as far back as the fourth century C.E. and is no doubt older. Although attempts have been made to trace these Jews to southern Israelite tribes from the biblical period, such as the tribe of Simon in the Negev and the tribe of Reuben in southern Transjordan, there is no tangible evidence for this. Jews reached Yemen, at the southern tip of the peninsula, by the third century C.E. and multiplied there, largely through proselytization, to the point that a short-lived Jewish kingdom arose in Himyar, near Hadhramaut, in the late fifth and early sixth centuries. The kingdom was destroyed when its ruler, Dhu Nawwas, was defeated in battle by an Ethiopian Christian army. A sizable Jewish community continued to exist in Yemen until its near total emigration to Israel in the late 1940s. For the history of the Jews of Yemen, see Reuben Ahroni, *Yemenite Jewry: Origins, Culture, and Literature* (Indiana University Press, Bloomington, 1968.)

the kingdom of Khazaria: The standard work on this kingdom remains D. M. Dunlop's *The History of the Jewish Khazars* (Princeton University Press, 1954). See also, Kevin Alan Brook, *The Jews of Khazaria* (Jason Aaronson, Northvale, N.J., 1999) and Arthur Koestler, *The Thirteenth Tribe* (Random House, New York, 1976). The Khazars were a Turkic people who first appeared on the stage of history in the late sixth or early seventh century C.E., when they settled in an area along the lower Volga River north of the Caspian Sea. The conversion of their royal family to Judaism took place in the middle of the eighth century, and an independent Jewish Khazar state existed until the late tenth century, when it was destroyed by Slavic armies. How much of the population of this state converted to Judaism is a matter of scholarly dispute. So is the question of whether, after Khazaria's downfall, some of its population may have migrated westward into European Russia and joined Jews migrating northward and eastward from Central Europe to form the original kernel of Eastern-European Jewry.

the Cochin and Bene Israel Jews of India: Accounts of Indian Jewry can be found in J. B. Segal, *A History of the Jews of Cochin* (Vallentine Mitchell, 1993) and Moses Ezekiel, *History and Culture of the Bene Israel of India* (Bombay, 1948). A good French summary is Monique Zetlaoui's *Shalom India: Histoire des communauté's juives en Inde* (Imago, Paris, 2000). Most signs point to the Jewish communities of India's western coast having their roots in Yemen, a country whose trade relations with India in medieval times were close. While it is impossible to pinpoint the exact period of the founding of these communities, it was most likely not before the fifth century C.E.

The Travels of Benjamin of Tudela: A superbly annotated edition of Benjamin's text was published by Marcus Nathan Adler in 1907 under the title *The Itinerary of Benjamin of Tudela* and has been reprinted by Philip Feldheim of New York.

108   Saadia Gaon and . . . Moses ibn Ezra: See Neubauer, op. cit., p. 184.

Prester John: There is a large literature on Prester John in English. Buckingham and Hamilton, op. cit., has a full bibliography.

110   Jacqueline Pirenne: Her argument is set forth in *La Légende du Prêtre Jean* (Presses Universitaire de Strasbourg, 1992).

111   missives went forth . . . : See Neubauer, op. cit., pp. 195–196.

112   in a Hebrew journal that he kept: Ha-Re'uveni's journal has never been published in English, in which no serious study of him exists. The Hebrew text, accompanied by a thorough scholarly analysis, can be found in A. Z. Eshkoli's *Sippur David ha-Re'uveni* (Mosad Bialik, Jerusalem, 1940).

116   a Christian pamphlet: See H. Orlansky's preface to the 1974 edition (Ktav Publishing House, New York) of Alan Godbey's *The Lost Tribes: A Myth* (Duke University Press, Durham, 1930).

reports of them began to multiply . . . Baruch Gad: For a digest of these stories, including Baruch Gad's, see Neubauer, op. cit., pp. 408–416.

117   *Spes Israelis:* Walls's 1652 translation is republished in Lynn Glaser's *Indians or Jews? An Introduction to a Reprint of Menasseh Ben Israel's The Hope of Israel* (Roy V. Boswell, Gilroy, Calif., 1973).

118   Shabbetai Tsvi: The standard work on this fascinating figure in Jewish history is Gershom Scholem's two-volume *Sabbetai Sevi: The Mystical Messiah, 1626–1676* (Princeton University Press, 1973). An account of the Lost Tribes enthusiasm that accompanied Shabbetai Tsvi's manifestation appears in Vol. I, Chapter Four, Section 2.

120   . . . to look for the Lost Tribes across the Atlantic: Summaries of the many far-reaching and far-fetched claims made on behalf of an Israelite origin for some or all of the Amerindians can be found in Glaser, op. cit., and in essays by Cyrus Gordon ("The Ten Lost Tribes"), Richard Popkin ("The Rise and Fall of the Jewish Indian Theory"), and Grant Underwood ("The Hope of Israel in Early Modern Ethnography and Eschatology") in *Hebrew and the Bible in America: The First Two Centuries* (ed. Shalom Goldman, Brandeis University Press, Waltham, 1993).

123   Joseph Smith: Several biographies of Smith exist. I have used Fawn M. Brodie's *No Man Knows My History: The Life of Joseph Smith, The Mormon Prophet* (Alfred A. Knopf, New York, 1945).

125   The British Israelites: A history of the movement is given by Michael Friedman in *Origins of the British Israelites* (San Francisco, 1993).

Richard Brothers: Brothers's story was told by the Jewish historian Cecil Roth in *Nephew of the Almighty* (London, 1933).

126   a statement of principles: See Friedman, op. cit., Appendix A.

127   Abraham Firkowitsch: On Firkowitsch's forgery, see Neubauer, op. cit., pp. 26–30.

Chinese Jews of Kaifeng: The best introduction to this subject is *Jews in Old China: Studies by Chinese Scholars*, ed. Sidney Shapiro (Hippocrene Books, New York, 1984). Still existing in the nineteenth century, the Jewish community of Kaifeng, located about 300 miles south of Beijing, was the only one of its kind in China to have survived into modern times. It was probably founded in the late eleventh or early twelfth century by Jewish merchants from Persia who traveled overland by the Silk

Road. Medieval travelers to China like Marco Polo, Giovanni di Monte Corvino, and Ibn Batuta also reported encountering Jews in Beijing, Hangzhou, and other places. These, too, were medieval merchants or their descendants who came by land from central Asia or by sea from India and points west.

127 Asahel Grant: Grant was an American Protestant minister who traveled in Kurdistan and Iraq in the late 1830s and wrote of his experiences in *The Nestorians, or the Lost Tribes.*

Joseph Israel Benjamin: A Rumanian Jew, Benjamin published *Eight Years in Asia And Africa, From 1846 to 1855* in several languages. An English edition appeared in Hanover in 1859. Compared by some to Benjamin of Tudela, he was widely known in the Jewish world as "Benjamin the Second."

Inquiry into the Ethnography of Afghanistan: Bellew's monograph was republished in 1977 by Indus Publications, Karachi. See especially pp. 20–21 and 190–196.

127 The few serious scholars . . . : For Neubauer's study and Godbey's, see notes to p. 104 and p. 116.

128 Lazar . . . Kasdai: Neither of these books has been translated.

129 another book-length investigation of the subject . . . : Parfitt's *The Lost Tribes of Israel*, on which he was working as I was writing this book, was due to be published by Weidenfeld-Nicholson of London in August 2002.

Bustenay Oded: *Mass Deportations and Deportees in the Neo-Assyrian Empire* (Dr. Ludwig Reichert Verlag, Wiesbaden, 1979).

Bob Becking: *The Fall of Samaria: A Historical and Archaeological Study* (E. J. Brill, Leiden, 1992).

more recently discovered Assyrian texts . . . : These inscriptions, most of them unearthed in the 1950s by British archaeologists at Nimrud, are extremely fragmentary and difficult to decipher. Conjectured reconstructions of them can be found in H. Tadmor, *The Inscriptions of Tiglath-Pileser III, King of Assyria* (Jerusalem, Israel Academy of Sciences and Humanities, 1994). There are extensive analyses of those bearing on the fall of the Israelite kingdom by Irvine, op. cit., pp. 23–72, and K. Lawson Younger in "The Deportation of the Israelites" (*Journal of Biblical Literature*, 117/2, 1998), pp. 201–227.

131 We know of ancient peoples: See Lester L. Grabbe, "The Exile under the Theodolite: History as Triangulation," in *Leading Captivity Captive: "The Exile" as History and Ideology* (Sheffield Academic Press, Sheffield, 1998), pp. 82–83.

133 the Lemba: See Tudor Parfitt, *Journey to the Vanished City* (Vintage Press, New York, 2000, first printing 1993).

browsing in Herodotus . . . : *Herodotus, the Histories* (Penguin Book Edition, London, 1954), Book II, p. 89. Although in a note to this passage (p. 561), the editor, Aubrey de Delincourt, wrote that the term "Red Sea" refers to the Indian Ocean, to which the "long narrow gulf" that is our Red Sea is connected, the remarks by Herodotus do not bear this out. He wrote: "Now it is my belief that . . . there were two gulfs, that is, one running from the Mediterranean southwards toward Ethiopia, and the other northwards from the Indian Ocean towards Syria, and the two almost met at their extreme ends, leaving only a small stretch of country between them. Suppose, now, that the Nile should change its course and flow into this gulf — the Red Sea — what is to prevent it from being silted up by the stream within, say, twenty thousand years?" If the "gulf . . . running from the Mediterranean southwards toward Ethiopia" is the Bitter Lakes and the Gulf of Suez, i.e., the course of today's Suez Canal, then the gulf running "northwards from the Indian Ocean toward Syria" must be either our Red Sea or the Gulf of Aqaba. It certainly cannot be the Indian Ocean itself. Of course, it should be kept in mind that Herodotus never visited this region and was trying his best to make geographical sense of reports that reached him. Moreover, different travelers may have used the term "Red Sea" to denote different bodies of water; elsewhere, Herodotus seemed to apply it to the Persian Gulf. It is probable that the original Red Sea was the Gulf of Aqaba, or "Sea of Edom," and that gradually, as often happens with geographical terms, the name shifted location. The Greeks themselves, as they sailed farther and farther from the Mediterranean, would have encountered the Gulf of Aqaba first, then the Red Sea, and only later the Indian Ocean and Persian Gulf. The term "Red Sea," originally acquired by them from Hebrews or Edomites, may have been progressively extended in the same way.

Needless to say, the Israelites of the exodus, who inhabited the Egyptian delta, did not cross either the Gulf of Aqaba or the Red Sea. (A vast literature of scholarly speculation exists on what body of water they may have crossed.) But at an early stage in their own history, the *yam suf* or "sea of reeds" in Exodus appears to have become confused with the identically named *yam suf,* which is the Gulf of Aqaba, in Kings, a work probably written no later than the mid-sixth century B.C.E. — that is, less than two hundred years after the exile of the northern tribes. It is thus conceivable that the confusion already existed before the exile and that a tradition was known to these tribes associating the exodus with the "Sea of Edom" or "red sea."

134   a Hebrew daily: The article ran in *Yedi'ot Aharonot* on June 5, 1955. "Over the centuries," it reported, "the tribesmen have forgotten their Jewish ancestry, intermarried with their neighbors, and been assimilated in many ways. Yet by virtue of the religious customs and practices observed by them since arriving in Burma, they have managed to preserve their ethnic uniqueness." Most unusual was said to be their matriarchal society, which, besides requiring husbands to leave home at the age of forty while bequeathing the management of their worldly goods to their wives, provided for their being bought on the open market. "A young man's price," *Yedi'ot* reported, "depends on his looks and lineage. The youth in question, however, has a right to object to the transaction if the woman choosing him does not please him."

No such customs existed among the Kuki-Chin-Mizo, whose traditional social structure, while relatively liberal sexually and toward women, was patriarchal. Perhaps the *Yedi'ot* article was concocted from fanciful rumors that circulated in the Jewish community of Calcutta following its first contact with adherents of the Israel movement in Mizoram and Manipur, areas it confused with Burma. (For an account of these contacts, see Chapter Six.) The *Yedi'ot* article was timed to appear in conjunction with a state visit to Israel by the Burmese prime minister U Nu.

Myer Samra: Samra's paper, entitled "Judaism in Manipur and Mizoram — A By-Product of the Christian Missions," was published in *Aizawl Seminar Papers* (Aizawl, 1992).

145   Captain T. H. Lewin: Lewin's observations of various Indian hill tribes are described in *Wild Races of South-Eastern India* (Wm. H. Allen, London, 1870, reprinted by the Tribal Research Institute, Aizawl, 1978). The two reminiscences cited by me are on pp. 131–132 and 140–141. The female captives taken by the "Lhoosai" (as Lewis called them) were marched to their captors' village while bound together by a cord passed through their ear lobes.

173 Vumson: In actual fact, Vumson, who was not a Hmar, cited Rochunga Pudaihte, who was one, as his authority for this claim in *Zo History* (Aizawl, 1984, p. 73). Pudaihte wrote in *The Education of the Hmar People* (Calcutta, 1963, p. 63): "The first Hmar man is called Manmasi. He had three sons, Miachal, Niachal, and Nelachal. Melachal is a great warrior and a commander. Niachal is a great farmer. Nelachal is a great hunter. Accordingly the Hmar people are divided into three classes: warrior, farmer and hunter."

the word *hmar* meant northerners: Originally, however, the Hmar were known to the Lushai as *khawtlang*, "westerners," since their first migration away from the other Lushai tribes was westward, into present-day Mizoram. See Pudaihte, op. cit., p. 26.

179 . . . Colonel J. Shakespear observed . . . : J. Shakespear, *The Lushei Kuki Clans* (London, Macmillan & Co., 1912, reprinted by the Tribal Research Institute, Aizawl, 1988), p. 20. The same point was made by N. E. Parry, British superintendant of the Lushai Hills in the 1920s. Comparing the Lushais with the Lakher, a tribal people of Arakan, he remarked, "Unlike the Lusheis, who think nothing of moving to a new village for the most trivial reasons, the Lakher regard migration as rather disgraceful." (N. E. Parry, *The Lakhers*, Shillong, Assam Govt. Press, 1928, reprinted by the Tribal Research Institute, Aizawl, 1976, p. 259).

189 As far back as 1945 . . . : Myer Samra speaks of a number of earlier Mizo Lost Tribe claims made by Chaltuakhuma (1926) and Kapa and Saichhuma (1936), giving as his source personal communications from Zaithanchhungi and L. Benjamin. Although I did not come across these men's names in my investigations in Mizoram, which included several long conversations with Zai and a brief one with Benjamin, this does not necessarily mean that Samra's information is wrong. What is clear in any case is that Lost Tribe interest was "in the air" among the Mizos well before Darnghaka and Chala's catalyzing visions, which Samra misdates to 1946.

193 This happened in Kelkang: See Major Anthony Gilchrist McCall, *Lushei Chrysalis* (Luzac & Co., London, 1949), pp. 220–223.

J. Meirion Lloyd: A good account of the revival movements, and of early missionary work in Mizoram, can be found in Lloyd's *On Every High Hill* (Aizawl, Synod Publication Board, 1984). For the incident of Darphawka — who, like Darnghaka, fell into a trance for three days — see p. 41. For the old-religion counterrevival of 1908, see p. 55.

195 Edwin Rolands: See Lloyd, ibid., p. 45.

196 Small groups living or claiming to live as Jews: There is literature on some of these groups. Accounts of the Abayudaya and the B'nei Avraham can be found in Chapters One and Two of James R. Ross's *Fragile Branches: Travels Through the Jewish Diaspora* (Riverhead Books, New York, 2000). Ariel Segal's *Jews of the Amazon* is an excellent study of Judaizing groups in Peru (The Jewish Publication Society, Philadelphia, 1999).

221 a chapter on the sikpui dance verses: *Mizo Zaite* (Aizawl, Exodus Press, 1994), pp. 31–32.

222 Lalbiakliana's line-by-line analysis: Below are the thirteen lines of the red sea song, consisting of the six and a half distichs appearing in *Mizo Zaite*. Each line is given first in Triac; then in Lalbiakliana and Shmuel's word-by-word translation; and then in the English rendering arrived at by Shmuel and me. The asterisked translations are transcribed from my field notes.

Line 1a:
Sikpui inthang kan ur laia.
sikpui = big winter
inthang = famous
kan = we
ur = prepare for
laia = while

Line translation: "While we prepare for the famous big winter feast."

Line 1b:
Chang tui pui aw sen ma hrili kang in tan.
chang = lurking
*tui pui = big water
aw = an emphatic syllable like English "O!"
sen = red
ma = I
hrili = tell
**kang = cut
in tan = parted, split.

Line translation: "I tell, O! of the parting of the lurking big red water."

*HKR says *tui pui* does not necessarily mean either a river or a sea, each of which is denoted by other Triac words. It could apply to any sizable body of water.

**Kang* can also mean "a place where a spring runs dry," in which case "parting" would be better translated as "drying up."

Line 2a:
Tera lawna ka leido aw.
*tera = Tera
**lawna = from
ka = my
leido = enemy
aw = O!

Line translation: "My enemies from the time of Tera, O!"

*HKR thinks this is a proper name, although not a known Kuki-Chin-Mizo one. It is certainly not an identifiable Triac or Hmar word. One younger informant gave it as *kera*, but HKR is quite sure that *tera* is the correct form.

** *Lawna*, "from," most likely has the temporal sense here of "from the time of." Asked whether it could have a spatial interpretation, so that the line could mean, "My enemies from [a place called] Tera," HKR was doubtful whether this was grammatically possible.

Line 2b:
Sunah surn ang, zana meilawn in vak ie.
sunah = in the daytime
surn = cloud

ang = like
zanah = in the night
**meilawn* = moving fire
in vak ie = going

Line translation: "Like clouds in the daytime, like a fire that goes by night."

* *Mei* means "fire" and *lawn* "to ascend." HKR says this could refer to something like a shooting star or to what is known in Mizo as a chawifa — a phenomenon defined by Shakespear as "a kind of meteor which flies through a village blazing brightly."

Line 3a:
An tur a sa thlu a ruol aw.
an = their
tur a sa = extreme cruelty
thlu = very much, great
a ruol = coming to fight
aw = O!

Line translation: "O how great and determined was their cruelty in coming to fight!"

Line 3b:
In phawsiel le in ralfeite zuong thaw ro.
in = your
phawsiel = shield of mythun hide
le = and
ralfeite = weapons
zuong thaw ro = you have come

Line translation: "You have come with your mythun shields and weapons."

Line 4a:
Sumra zula ka leido aw.
**sumra* = ?
zula = like
ka = my
leido = enemy
aw = O!

Line translation: "? Like my enemy, O!"

*HKR does not know the meaning of this word and could find no surviving Triac speaker who did. It is either a garbling of something or a forgotten archaism.

Line 4b:
Tera lawna mei sum ang hawn in vak ie
tera = Tera
lawna = from

mei = fire
sum = cloud
ang = like
hawn = come back
in vak ie = going

Line translation: "From the time of Tera, fire that came and went like a cloud."

Line 5a:
Sumra zula ka leido aw

Line translation: "? like my enemy, O!" [The same as line 4a]

Line 5b:
Laimi sa ang chang tuipui lem zo va.
laimi = human, mortal
sa = beast
ang = like
chang = lurking
tuipui = big water
lem = swallow
zo va = them all

Line translation: "All the mortals were swallowed by the lurking big water as though devoured by beasts."

Line 6a:
Ava ruol aw, la ta che.
*ava = bird
ruol aw = you all
la ta che = you take it

Line translation: "All of you, take the birds."
   *Although *ava*, Triac for "bird" (*sava* in standard Mizo), can also mean "river," it only has the latter sense when appended to a proper name, as in the Mat(a)va River in Mizoram.

Line 6b:
Suonglung chunga tui zuong put kha la ta che.
suonglung = big rock
chunga = on
tui = water
zuong put = gush out
kha = this, that
la ta che = you take it

Line translation: "Take the water that gushes out on the big rock."

Line 7a:
An tur asa buon rolong aw.
an = they, their

tur = determination
asa buon rolong = how frightening to see
aw = O!

Line translation: "O how frightening to see their determination!"

257   long controlled by a Hindu dynasty: Hinduism came to Manipur in 1704, when a local king, Rongba, adopted the Vaishnavist practices of the Bhakti sect. Because the terrain of the Imphal Valley made possible a degree of centralization and military control unachievable by chiefs in the hill country, a continuous kingdom had existed there — subject to periodic Indian, Burmese, and Chinese incursions — since the first century C.E. Its people, known as the Meiteis, were of Tibeto-Burmese stock, like the Nagas and the Kukis, and were closely related culturally and linguistically to both; until their conversion to Hinduism, they were typical southeast Asian animists. Hinduization was spurred by Rongba's son Pamheiba, who adopted the Indian name Garib Nawaz and made Vaishnavism the official religion of the kingdom. In 1763 the Manipuri royal house signed a treaty with England, by virtue of which it maintained its independence until the 1890s, when the British assumed direct control of the Imphal Valley. In 1919 they set the administrative boundaries of present-day Manipur. These were adopted by India in 1947. See Vumson, op. cit., pp. 302–310, and T. S. Gangte, *The Kukis of Manipur: A Historical Analysis* (New Delhi, Gyan Publishing House, 1993), pp. 29–30.

the greater aggressiveness of their culture: William Shaw, for example, in *The Thadou Kukis* (introduction by J. H. Hutton, 1929; reprinted by the Cultural Publishing House, New Delhi, 1983), observed that "I have often seen Thadous and Nagas pass each other on the paths and in nearly every instance the Thadou has kept the path while the Naga moves aside to let him pass. In Naga villages, where some dancing is on and there happen to be some Thadous present, they will almost always push aside the Naga lookers-on and get in front so as to have the best position without the slightest compunction" (p. 22.). It was this aggressiveness, Shaw observed, that caused the British to prefer the Thados as local law-enforcement troops, so that "for long years they composed the levies of the Manipur State and were allowed to do very much as they pleased with all among whom they took up their abode."

258   the early Baptist missions: The first Christian missionary in Manipur, William Pettigrew, arrived in Imphal in 1894. Two years later he was required by the British authorities to move to Ukhrul, in the hills forty miles to the northeast. Pettigrew founded a Baptist church there that had thirty members by 1901. The first missionary in southern Manipur was the Presbyterian Watkin Roberts, who entered the area from Aizawl in 1910. See Gangte, op. cit., pp. 36–40.

265   In *The Thadou Kukis:* Shaw, op. cit., p. 22.

285   The Joseph of Genesis: Although angels descend from heaven in the Bible, there is no "man from heaven." Such a man does exist in one ancient, post-biblical book, however — and curiously, this is the apocryphal *Joseph and Asenath*, which tells the story of Joseph's marriage to the daughter of the Egyptian priest Pentephres, the Potiphera of Genesis. At one point in this story, Asenath, who loves Joseph but fears she will not be accepted by the God of Israel, fasts and prays for divine guidance. Suddenly, "A man came to her from heaven and stood by Asenath's head. . . . And Asenath raised her head and saw, and behold, there was a man in every respect similar to Jo-

seph, by the robe and the crown and the royal staff, except that his face was like lightning, and his eyes like sunshine, and the hairs of his head like a flame of fire of a burning torch, and hands and feet like iron shining forth from a fire, and sparks shot forth
from his hands and feet." This man from heaven assures Asenath that God will accept
her, and she converts to Judaism and is wed to Joseph. (See *Joseph and Asenath* in *The
New Testament Pseudoepigrapha* (ed. James H. Charlesworth, Doubleday & Company,
Vol. 2, New York, 1985, pp. 224–25.)

Joseph and Asenath, a book most likely written in Hellenistic Egypt, dates, at the
very earliest, to the second century B.C.E. (See the discussion of its date and prove-
nance in Charlesworth, pp. 187–88.) One can hardly assume, therefore, that any of its
motifs were known to biblical Israelites six or more centuries before then. And yet it
is intriguing that its man from heaven is Joseph's double. Can this be a late version of
an old legend of Joseph's heavenly origin, originating in the tribes believing themselves to be descended from him, that is also reflected in the name Pu Vanthang? Although not, perhaps, highly likely, such a possibility cannot be ruled out.

299   exactly of what, however, nobody knew: The meaning of the Hebrew word
selah was lost to Jewish tradition in an early period, presumably when the Psalms
ceased being performed musically. The Psalms scholar Nahum Sarna, writing in the
Hebrew "World of the Bible Encyclopedia" (*Entsiklopedya Olam ha-Tanach, Tehillim*,
Vol. I, Davidson-Iti, Tel Aviv, 1995, p. 17), summed up the interpretative history of
the word:

"*Selah* occurs seventy-one times in thirty-nine different Psalms. . . . It is found
usually at the end of a verse and on four occasions at the end of a Psalm. . . . The biblical translators of antiquity and the medieval commentators disagreed over its meaning and function. . . . Its etymology is unknown. Moreover, as the meaning of *selah* is
unclear in the original Hebrew, so it is in the [earliest] Greek translations of it. The
rendering of the Greek term for it [*diapsalma*] in the [third-century B.C.E.] Septuagint
and the [second-century C.E.] translation of Symmachus as 'pause' or 'sign for pause'
is questionable. The Aramaic translations of Onkelos and Aquila, as well as Jerome's
Vulgate, assumed that *selah* belonged grammatically to the verse preceding it and
translated it as 'forever' or 'eternally' . . . [The medieval Jewish scholars] Saadia
Ga'on, Jonah Ibn Najah, and Rashi agreed with this. David Kimhi in his 'Book of
Roots' differs with them: connecting *selah* with the Hebrew verb *salal* in the sense of
'to raise,' he takes it to be an instruction to sing or play louder. Abraham Ibn Ezra
thought *selah* was the liturgical response of the Psalms' listeners to what they had
heard. A number of modern Bible scholars have sought to link *selah* with the Hebrew
word *sal* [basket], their theory being that a basket-shaped drum of that name was struck
at certain junctures. Others consider the word to have been an acrostic. None of these
explanations solves the riddle of this inexplicable term" (p. 17.). The King James Bible
simply transliterates *selah* into our alphabet with no attempt at interpretation.

300   a fight with two men: Although this detail does not belong to the Joseph
story in the Book of Genesis, it does echo a story in the Book of Exodus about a confrontation between Moses and two quarreling Hebrews whom he attempts to separate. It would appear then that, whether in ancient or modern times, this fragment of
the Moses narrative found its way into the Pu Vanthang *thusim*.

309   Good biblical Hebrew: The word *borey*, "creator," without the definite article *ha-*, is applied to God, and only to God, thirteen times in the Hebrew Bible. Its

earliest written occurrence with the definite article is in the Mishnaic period (first to third centuries C.E.). In medieval Hebrew, *ha-borey*, "the Creator," is a common epithet for God. Its use in biblical times would have been perfectly natural, whether by itself or in tandem with the name Yah.

314 This was a custom that was accompanied . . . : Shaw (op. cit., p. 53) mentioned this custom, though not the chanting of the deceased's lineage as part of it. He wrote, "When the person breathes his last the men shout out, 'Where is the *Thilha* who has taken you away? Let it show itself and we will kill it,' and words to that effect. They usually snatch up a *dao* and hack near posts to show their temper and determination of what they would do to the *Thilha*."

317 a small, nineteenth-century Jewish presence in Calcutta . . . : Calcutta, previously the village of Kalikata, developed into a sizable town only in the eighteenth century, when it became an outpost of the British East India Company. Its first Jewish settler arrived in 1797. See Zetlaoui, op. cit., pp. 315–319.

Manasseh himself . . . : Surah 12 of the Koran, known to Moslems as "the Joseph Surah," retells the biblical story of Joseph but stops with his revealing himself to his brothers when they come to buy food in Egypt. There is no mention of his marriage, let alone of his children, and no way of knowing about Manasseh from Islamic tradition. Similarly, Surah 7, "The Heights Surah," tells of the Ten Plagues visited upon the Egyptians and relates: "Therefore We took retribution from them; therefore We drowned them in the sea . . . And We brought the children of Israel across the sea." None of the details from the biblical story of the exodus that occur in the red sea song are found in this surah or anywhere else in the Koran.

319 William Shaw . . . J. H. Hutton: Shaw, op. cit., p. 24. Hutton's comments appear in a note on the same page.

320 . . . whether "Manmasi" was a proper name or a word: Ibid., p. 131, n.4.

321 But Shaw also knew a Thado folktale: Ibid, pp. 129–136.

322 The story of Pathen's daughter: The contention is not that this story itself was originally a Manmasite one. On the contrary, it contains elements of folklore known to many peoples, including others in northeast India. The Mikir, for example, told a tale about a hero named Harata Kunwar who spies the "six daughters of the King of the Great Palace" — that is, of God — bathing in a river. Falling in love with one of them, he asks his grandmother what to do. She counsels him to make a flute and play on it the next time God's daughters come to bathe. This he does, and when the six are entranced by his music, he steals his beloved's petticoat, seizes her when she runs after him, and marries her. Subsequently, she flies back to heaven and is about to be married off there to the "King of the Wind" when Harata Kunwar, with the aid of a magic gold ring, shows up in the nick of time to win her back. (See *The Mikirs, from the Papers of Edward Stack, edited and arranged by Sir Charles Lyell*, Gauhati, no date, p. 59.)

All three versions of this story — the Mikir, the Thado, and the Manmasite — are similar and all pivot on the use at a crucial moment or moments of a magical device. What is significant is that, in the Manmasite version, this device is the word "aboriza."

324 a forensic document specialist in Jerusalem: This was Mr. Amnon Betsaleli, of 9 Nof Harim Street, a handwriting and documents expert who has worked widely with the Israeli police and courts.

325   the *bawrh keu* . . . ceremony: Shakespear (op. cit., pp. 81–82) mentioned this ceremony, but not as a mock-circumcision. He wrote, "For seven days after a child's birth its spirit is supposed not to be quite at home in the little body and to spend some of its time perched like a bird on the parents' bodies and clothes, and therefore, for fear of injuring it, the parents keep as quiet as possible for those seven days. If either of the parents works during these seven days and a red rash appears on the child, the illness is called *borh*, and the cure, which is called *borh keu*, is as follows: — A certain creeper called *vawmhrui* is brought and coiled round and round, forming a cylinder, and into this the child is dipped three times. This is done at night after the fire is out, and no fire can be lit again till morning."

Several of my informants also knew of such a ceremony, whose name, *bawrh keu*, which means "opening" or "cleaning" the smegma, fits Shakespear's account. *Bawrh keu* itself, therefore, was probably an old Kuki-Chin-Mizo practice that was not related to circumcision. But the Hualngos may very well have introduced a mock circumcision rite into it. Ear piercing of infants, certainly, though not mentioned by Shakespear as part of the *bawrh keu*, was widely practiced among the Kukis and Mizos. Many of my informants were aware of it.

327   Gao Wangzhi: *Jews in Old China*, op. cit., p. 122. Gao commented on the fact that the Jews of Kaifeng deliberately neglected to mention circumcision in three different synagogue inscriptions detailing their beliefs and rituals, because, as he put it, "It would have been unwise to publicly proclaim" such an offensive custom.

It was widely practiced by other peoples . . . : Parry, for example (op. cit., p. 384), observed that among the Lakhers ears were pierced on the fourth day after birth with a porcupine quill or lemon thorn.

J. P. Mills: See *The Rengma Nagas* (1937, reprinted Gauhati, 1980), pp. 201–203).

. . . such a division was in fact common . . . : See, for instance, Jon Boyes and S. Piraban, *A Life Apart: Viewed from the Hills* (Silkworm Books, Bangkok, 1989), a study of the Yao, Akha, Lahu, Hmong, Lisu, and Karen people in northern Thailand. "Most tribes have two types of religious specialists, the village priest, who takes charge of the ritual life of the village, and the shaman, who has special powers to communicate with the spirit world" (p. 6).

328   the Ao Nagas . . . : See Panger Imchen, *Ancient Ao Naga Religion and Culture* (New Delhi, 1993), pp. 63–64. If the freed rooster ran away immediately, the Ao Nagas assumed that the illness went with him.

. . . common throughout ancient China and Tibet: See R. A. Stein, *Tibetan Civilization* (Stanford University Press, 1972), p. 211.

the Rengma Nagas: Mills, op. cit., p. 243. The Angami Nagas, too, believed that the underworld had "seven spheres, one below the other," through which the soul passed after death (Hutton, op. cit., p. 184).

the Karens prayed: Marshall, op. cit., p. 370.

the Lahu creation epic: See Anthony R. Walker, *Mvuh Hpa Mi Hpa: Creating Heaven, Creating Earth* (Silkworm Books, Bangkok, 1995). The stock trope of "seven days and seven nights" in the sense of "a long time," found in many of Dr. Khuplam's *themthu*, occurs frequently in the *Mvuh Hpa Mi Hpa*.

. . . common among the Kuki-Chin-Mizo and their neighbors: The Lakher, for example, believed that "all men came out of a hole beneath the earth . . . A similar story is current among the Khyeng" (Parry, op. cit., p. 4). The Angami Nagas, according to J. H. Hutton, believed that they sprang "from ancestors who emerged from the bowels of the earth" (*The Angami Nagas*, 1922, reprinted Oxford, 1969, p. 6).

328 subscribed to by peoples like the Lahus and the Lisus: See Walker, op. cit, pp. 44–57. A parallel Lisu myth holds that an Adam-and-Eve brother and sister, themselves born from a water gourd, produced by their union another such gourd containing one hundred couples, from each of which came a different ethnic group. (See Jonathan Boyes, *Tiger-Men and Tofu Dolls: Tribal Spirits in Northern Thailand*, Silkworm Books, Bangkok, 1997, p. 81).

the Dusuns of North Borneo: See Penelope Farmer, *Creation Myths of the World* (Atheneum, New York, 1979), p. 31.

329 the *thimzin*: The Lakhers told of a great primeval darkness, called the *khazangra*, that fell upon the earth in ancient times. It lasted for seven days and seven nights and was survived by a single brother and sister, who repopulated the earth (Parry, op. cit, p. 5). The Rengmas called the great darkness *tsang kuzong* (Mills, op. cit., p. 270).

a Lakher legend: Parry, op. cit., p. 490.

330 the Angami Nagas: Hutton, op. cit., p. 265.

the Mikir: "They [the ancestors of the Mikir] were a mighty race of men, and in the course of time, becoming dissatisfied with the mastery of the earth, they determined to conquer heaven and began to build a tower to reach up to the skies. Higher and higher rose the building, till at last the gods and demons feared lest these giants becomes the masters of the heaven . . . so they confounded their speech and scattered them to the four corners of the earth" (*Stack*, op. cit., p. 71).

. . . and had been witnessed by J. H. Hutton: Hutton, op. cit, p. 196.

331 *History of the Mizos:* (Vikas Publishing House, New Delhi, 1997), pp. 55–57. Other native writers have been more skeptical. T. S. Gangte, for example (op. cit., p. 17), while observing that "it is generally believed" by the Kuki-Chin-Mizo that "they came out of the Great Wall of China in about 225 B.C. during the reign of Shi Hungti" {sic}, called for taking such "highly subjective and conjectural" theories "with a pinch of salt." Yet he too failed to note that these "theories" are simple reifications of nonhistorical myths.

Changan: See *The Times Concise Atlas of World History* (Times Books Ltd., Hammond, N.J., 1982), pp. 29, 50.

335 When all the skulls were hanging on the tree: The practice of hanging enemy skulls in a tree was common in the warrior culture of the northeast Indian hill tribes. Parry (op. cit., p. 215) wrote: "After a successful raid on another village by the Lakhers, the heads [taken] were hung up on a *pakhai* tree or on a *pazi* tree in the jungle outside the village and were left there till they fell off and got lost. . . . The word *pazi* in Lakher means to follow, so it was believed that if the head was hung on a *pazi* tree, the spirit of the slain would undoubtedly follow the spirit of his slayer as his slave after the slayer in his turn went to the abode of the dead." The Sabeu, Parry wrote, hung the skull of a dog on a branch above the human skull, so that the dead man's spirit, which feared the dog, would not harm the man who killed him (ibid.). The blind man and lame man in Dr. Khuplam's story were thus entrusted with a vital task that had been neglected by the warriors themselves.

338 Shaw had written about the *doi buom:* Shaw, op. cit., p. 73. Hutton, in a note to Shaw's description of the *doi buom*, remarked that while it is unique in northeast

India and Burma to the Kuki-Chin-Mizos, it has "a very close parallel to the *siap aioh* of the Kenyahs in Borneo."

345 Two peoples in the world had a holiday . . . : There are two monumental studies of worldwide parallels to Old Testament rituals and customs: Sir James G. Frazer's three-volume *Folklore in the Old Testament* (Macmillan & Company, London, 1918) and Theodor H. Gaster's *Myth, Legend, and Custom in the Old Testament: A comparative study with chapters from Sir James G. Frazer's Folklore in the Old Testament* (Harper & Row, New York, 1969). Neither mentions the ceremonial eating of unleavened bread by any people other than ancient Israel.

347 the Hmar winter festival: An interesting description of this ceremony can be found in Dr. Lal Dena's *Hmar Folk Tales* (Scholar Publishing House, New Delhi, 1995, pp. 216–217). In a tale about two star-crossed Hmar lovers, Neilal and Tuoni, we read:

"As time passed by, each and every household of [the village of] Sawrtrui was ready for the Sikpui dance and the *zu* of each household had also become matured and sweet. As a prelude to the dance, the young lads were singing the song of Buontlaw:

> "The famous hero who had heads
> From east and west
> Also took ten heads from the south.
> The famous thick village remained unchallengeable;
> Never will it be destroyed

"The villagers were then starting the Sikpui dance with the *khuongpu* or drummer and the *khuongpuzailak* or chanter sitting in the middle on a flat stone especially erected for the occasion and the dancers making two rows — old men against old women, married men against married women, young men against young women, small boys and small girls, and then children in the last. Neilal and Touzo [a girl Neilal is friendly with] were facing each other and the song of the Sikpui dance was started thus:

> "While we are preparing for the Sikpui feast,
> The big red sea becomes divided.
> As we are marching forward fighting our foes,
> We are being led by a cloud during day,
> And by a pillar of fire during night.
> Our enemies, Ye folk, are thick with fury,
> Come out with your shields and spears.
> Fighting our foes all day,
> We march along as cloud — fire goes afore.
> The enemies we fight all day,
> The big sea swallowed them like a beast.
> Collect the quails,
> And fetch the water that springs out of the rock.

"After having celebrated the Sikpui festival for seven days happily, they arranged a big community feast on the eighth day. After the feast, they parted from one another with tears in their eyes."

Dena appended two notes to this passage. On "the song of Buontlaw," he wrote,

Notes 387

"This is a folk song sung by young children as a prelude to the Sikpui dance." And on the word *sikpui* itself he observed that, for the Hmar, it had two meanings: "First, it means community sharing of rice-beer and meat collected from each household; secondly, it also means winter, and since this festival falls in winter, it is also called winter festival."

In his introduction to this volume (pp. viii–ix), Dena also wrote:

"The story of Tuoni and Neilal refers to the Sikpui festival, which was usually celebrated during the winter season by the Hmars from time immemorial. In one of the songs of this festival, there is a vivid reference to the Israelites at the time of their liberation from Egyptian bondage under the leadership of Moses and [to] the events that followed after they crossed the Red Sea. On the significance of the song, L. Keivom comments: 'This popular song occupies such a sacred place that the Sikpui festival can start only after they [the participants] sing it with rapt attention. This fact may, therefore, suggest that the incident referred to in the song might have been an unusual happening of great consequence in the pages of their national history. Otherwise they would not have attached such importance [to it].' Now one theory emerging out of this folk song is that the Hmars might perhaps be one of the lost tribes of Israelites (Manasseh). The earliest known ancestor of the Hmar was Manmasi. Could this Manmasi be a corrupted form of Manasseh?"

Manmasi, as we have seen, was not an actual Hmar ancestor but one borrowed from the *mi lui*. And if the red sea song had such resonance after having been borrowed too, its significance for the *mi lui* must have been great. Dena's remark that the Sikpui involved "community sharing of rice-beer and meat collected from each household" is noteworthy. If one substitutes "unleavened bread" for "rice-beer," this is a description of the *chol nghol ni nikho*. Normally, village feasts among the Kuki-Chin-Mizo were not of this nature. They were generally sponsored by a single individual or family, often in conjunction with a sacrifice.

It is significant too that of all the versions of the red sea song known to me, Dena's is the closest to Lialbiakliana's. Apart from the omission in his version of the unclear line about "Tera" (which may have been done for literary purposes), the two texts are — allowing for their different renditions into English — practically identical.

352   the special ties between Benjamin and Manasseh: It should also be pointed out that Ulam is listed in I Chronicles 7:16 as having a brother named Rekem, an uncommon name that appears elsewhere in Joshua 18:27 as that of a town in the territory of Benjamin. Noteworthy also is the close relationship between King Saul, a Benjaminite, and the Manassite town of Yavesh-Gilead (see I Samuel 11 and 31:8–13 and II Samuel 2:4–7), as well as the verse in Obadiah 1:19 that prophesies: "And they of the south shall possess the mount of Esau; and they of the plain, the Philistines; and they shall possess the fields of Ephraim and the fields of Samaria; and Benjamin shall possess Gilead." Since Obadiah is describing a future in which different Israelite groups will reclaim territories rightfully theirs, his assigning of the mountains of Gilead (in his day under the suzerainty of the Ammonites) to Benjamin rather than Manasseh is another indication of the kinship between the two tribes. See the discussion of Manassite genealogies in the "World of the Bible Encyclopedia" (op. cit., *Divrei ha-Yamim, I*), pp. 116–117.

353   the Aramean capital of Damascus was in fact taken . . . : See Becking, op. cit, p. 14, n. 75.

356   Hendrick Adrian van Reedhe: Van Reedhe later published a memoir of his tenure in India, which I have not been able to obtain. It contained a chapter on the Jews of Cochin (see Zetlaoui, op. cit., p. 125). That van Reedhe knew of a tradition of Manassite descent among these Jews was reported by Alexander Hamilton, a Scottish ship captain, trader, and adventurer who sailed widely in the Indian Ocean and South China Sea and wrote about it in *A New Account of the East Indies*, published in England in 1727. According to Hamilton, this knowledge came from "[the Cochin Jews'] records, engraved on copper plates in Hebrew characters . . . [which] show their history from the reign of Nebuchadnezzar to the present time." He continued: "Myn Heer Van Reedhe, about the year 1695, had an Abstract of their History translated from the Hebrew into low Dutch. They declared themselves to be of the Tribe of Manasseh, a Part whereof was, by Order of that haughty conqueror Nebuchadnezzar, carried to the easternmost Province of his large Empire, which, it seems, reacht as far as Cape Cormerin, which Journey 20,000 of them traveled in three years from their setting out of Babylon."

Not only, however, did Nebuchadnezzar's empire never reach Cape Cormerin; it never came anywhere near India. And although the "copper plates" referred to by Hamilton did exist, they were not in Hebrew but in Tamil, and contained not a history but a charter of privileges granted the Cochin Jews by local rulers. The text has been dated by scholars to anywhere between 450 and 1020 C.E. The tribe of Manasseh is certainly not mentioned there. Possibly van Reedhe was told by Cochin Jews that they were descended from the tribe of Manasseh and Hamilton heard a garbled report of this; possibly, he garbled what he heard. In any case, no such tradition has survived. Even had it existed, it would have almost certainly been groundless, as the Jews of Cochin observed many features of rabbinic Judaism and could not have descended from a biblical tribe detached from its coreligionists at the time of the Assyrian exile.

357   Hutton, who was convinced of this: "Many Thado customs," Hutton wrote, "are suggestive of the Khasis and of the Hos [a Munda people of northern India], both of Indonesian affinity . . . There are many points of Kuki culture which are vividly suggestive of the culture of the pagan Malays of the Indian Archipelago and the Philippines" (Shaw, op. cit, p. 5).

358   they took that from the Kukis: Although the precise relation of the different spiritual powers in the old Kuki-Chin-Mizo religion is unknown, the concept of Pathian as a supreme deity is old and predates Christian monotheism. As part of what is probably the earliest Western description of the Kuki-Chin-Mizo on record, J. Rennel, the English chief engineer of Bengal, wrote in 1800: "[They] give to the Creator of the world the name of patyen, or Putchien. They believe that in every tree resides a deity, that the sun and moon are gods, and that the worship rendered by them to those deities of secondary importance is agreeable to Patyen, the Great Creator" (Lewin, op. cit., p. 144). The "deities of secondary importance," of course, were largely the *huais* and *thilhas*.

BIBLIOGRAPHY

Adler, Elkan, *Jewish Travellers* (London, 1930).

Adler, Marcus Nathan (ed.), *The Itinerary of Benjamin of Tudela* (Philip Feldheim, New York, first printing 1907).

Ahroni, Reuben, *Yemenite Jewry: Origins, Culture, and Literature* (Indiana University Press, Bloomington, 1968).

Avichail, Eliyahu, *The Tribes of Israel: The Lost and the Dispersed* (Amishav, Jerusalem, 1990).

Becking, Bob, *The Fall of Samaria: An Historical and Archaeological Study* (E. J. Brill, Leiden-New York-Koeln, 1992).

Beckingham, Charles F., and Hamilton, Bernard (ed.), *Prester John, the Mongols and the Ten Lost Tribes* (Ashgate Publishing, Brookfield, Vt., 1996).

Bellew, H. W., *An Inquiry into the Ethnography of Afghanistan* (Indus Publications, Karachi, 1977, first printing 1891).

Benjamin, J. J., *Eight Years in Asia and Africa, From 1846 to 1855* (Hanover, 1859).

Ben-Tsvi, Itschak, *The Exiled and the Redeemed* (The Jewish Publication Society of America, Philadelphia, 1961).

Boyes, Jonathan, and Piraban S., *A Life Apart: Viewed from the Hills* (Silkworm Books, Bangkok, 1992).

Boyes, Jonathan, *Tiger-Men and Tofu Dolls: Tribal Spirits in Northern Thailand* (Silkworm Books, Bangkok, 1997).

Bradley, David, *Thai Hill Tribes* (Lonely Planet, Berkeley, 1991).

Brodie, Fawn M., *No Man Knows My History: The Life of Joseph Smith, the Mormon Prophet* (Alfred A. Knopf, New York, 1945).

Brook, Kevin Alan, *The Jews of Khazaria* (Jason Aronson, Northvale, N.J., 1999).

Cammann, Schuyler V. R., "The Chiang People of Western Szechuan: The Miscalled 'West China Jews'" (*Monographs of the Jewish Historical Society of Hong Kong*, Vol. III, 1990).

Charlesworth, James (ed.), *The Old Testament Pseudepigrapha*, Vol. II (Doubleday, New York, 1985).

Cogan, Mordechai, and Eph'al Israel (ed.), *Ah, Assyria* (Studies in Assyrian History, Vol. XXXIII, The Magnes Press, Jerusalem, 1991).

Chatterji, N., *Monoliths & Landmarks of Mizoram* (Tribal Research Institute, Aizawl, 1979).

Delincourt, Aubrey de (ed.), *Herodotus, The Histories* (Penguin Book Edition, London, 1954).

Dena, Lal, *Christian Missions and Colonialism: A Study of the Missionary Movement in Northeast India with Particular Reference to Manipur and the Lushai Hills, 1894–1947* (Vendrame Institute, Shillong, 1988).

Dena, Lal, *Hmar Folk Tales* (Scholar Publishing House, New Delhi, 1995).

Dunlop, D. M., *The History of the Jewish Khazars* (Princeton University Press, 1954).

Epstein, Abraham (Hebrew), "Eldad Ha-Dani: His Stories and Ritual Laws in Variant Manuscripts and Old Books" (Pressburg, 1891).

Eshkoli, A. Z. (Hebrew), "The Story of David Ha-Re'uveni" (Mosad Bialik, Jerusalem, 1940).

Even-Shmuel, Yehuda (Hebrew), "Legends of Redemption" (Mosad Bialik, Jerusalem, 1954).

Ezekiel, Moses, *History and Culture of the Bene Israel of India* (Bombay, 1948).

Farmer, Penelope, *Creation Myths of the World* (Atheneum, New York, 1979).

Foltz, Richard C., *Religions of the Silk Road* (St. Martin's Press, New York, 1999).

Frazer, Sir James G., *Folklore in the Old Testament* (3 vols., Macmillan, London, 1918).

Friedman, Michael, *Origins of the British Israelites* (San Francisco, 1993).

Frye, Richard N., *The Heritage of Central Asia: From Antiquity to the Turkish Expansion* (Markus Wiener, Princeton, 1996).

Gangte, T. S., *The Kukis of Manipur: A Historical Analysis* (Gyan Publishing House, New Delhi, 1993).

Gaster, Theodor H., *Myth, Legend, and Custom in the Old Testament* (Harper and Row, New York, 1969).

Glaser, Lynn, *Indians or Jews? An Introduction to a Reprint of Manasseh Ben Israel's* The Hope of Israel (Roy V. Boswell, Gilroy, Calif., 1973).

Godbey, Alan, *The Lost Tribes: A Myth* (Duke University Press, Durham, N.C., 1930).

Goldman, Shalom (ed.), *Hebrew and the Bible in America: The First Two Centuries* (Brandeis University Press, Waltham, Mass., 1993).

Goudge, H. L., *The British Israel Theory* (London, 1933).

Grabbe, Lester L. (ed.), *Leading Captivity Captive: "The Exile" as History and Ideology* (Sheffield Academic Press, Sheffield, 1998).

Graham, David Crockett, *The Customs and Religion of the Ch'iang* (Smithsonian Institution, Washington, D.C., 1958).

Grant, Asahel, *The Nestorians, or the Lost Tribes* (Harper, New York, 1841).

Grinhut, Elazar Halevi (ed., Hebrew), "The Travels of Petahiah of Regensburg" (Jerusalem, 1905).

Hamilton Alexander, *A New Account of the East Indies* (1727).

Harel-Hoshen, Sarah (ed.), *Beyond the Sambatyon: The Myth of the Ten Lost Tribes* (The Museum of the Jewish Diaspora, Tel Aviv, 1991).

Hayes, John H., and Irvine, Stuart A., *Isaiah: The Eighth-century Prophet* (Abingdon Press, Nashville, 1987).

Hluna, John Vanlal, *Church & Political Upheaval in Mizoram* (Mizo History Association, Aizawl, 1985).

Hopkirk, Peter, *Foreign Devils on the Silk Road* (University of Massachusetts Press, Amherst, 1980).

Hutton, J. H., *The Angami Nagas* (Oxford, 1969, first printing 1922).

Imchen, Panger, *Ancient Ao Naga Religion and Culture* (New Delhi, 1993).

Irvine, Stuart A., *Isaiah, Ahaz, and the Syro-Ephraimitic Crisis* (Scholars Press, Atlanta, 1990).

Kaplan, Steven, *The Beta Israel (Falashas) in Ethiopia from Earliest Times to the Twentieth Century* (New York University Press, 1992).

Kasdai, Tsvi (Hebrew), "The Tribes of Israel and the Preserved of Jacob" (Haifa, 1928).

Khiangte, Laltuangliana, *Folktales of Mizoram* (United Publishers, Guwahati, 1997).

Koestler, Arthur, *The Thirteenth Tribe* (Random House, New York, 1976).

Kyndiah, P. R., *Mizo Freedom Fighters* (Sanchar Publishing House, New Delhi, 1994).

Laitanga, C., *Paite in Mizoram* (Tribal Research Institute, Aizawl).

Lalbiakliana, H.K.R., *Mizo Zaite* (Vol. I, Exodus Press, Aizawl, 1995).

Lazar, Shimon Menachem (Hebrew), "The Ten Tribes and Their Solution" (Drohobycz, 1908).

Lewin, T. H., *Wild Races of South-Eastern India* (Tribal Research Institute, Aizawl, 1978, first printing 1870).

Lloyd, J. Meirion, *On Every High Hill* (Synod Publication Board, Aizawl, 1984).

Marco Polo, *The Travels*, tr. Ronald Latham (Penguin Books, London, 1958).

Marshall, Harry Ignatius, *The Karen People of Burma: A Study in Anthropology and Ethnology* (Ohio University Bulletin, Columbus, 1922).

Mason, E.H.B., *Civilizing Mountain Men, or Sketches of Mission Work Among the Karens* (London, 1862).

Mate, Langsun D., *The Mate Tribe* (Mate Anthropological Society, Manipur, 1997).

McCall, Anthony Gilchrist, *Lushai Chrysalis* (Luzac & Co., London, 1949).

Mendus, E. Lewis, *The Diary of a Jungle Missionary* (Mission Press, Liverpool, 1956).

Mills, J. P., *The Rengma Nagas* (Guwahati, 1980, first printing 1937).

Na'aman, Nadav, "Population Changes in Palestine Following Assyrian Deportations" (*Tel Aviv*, Vol. 20, 1993, pp. 104–124).

Neubauer, Adolph, "Where Are the Ten Tribes?" (*Jewish Quarterly Review*, Vol. I, 1888–89).

Newton, Arthur Percival, *Travel and Travellers of the Middle Ages* (Routledge & Kegan Paul, London, 1926).

Oded, Bustenay, *Mass Deportations and Deportees in the Neo-Assyrian Empire* (Dr. Ludwig Reichert Verlag, Wiesbaden, 1979).

Ostling, Richard N., and Joan K., *Mormon America: The Power and the Promise* (HarperCollins, San Francisco, 1999).

Parfitt, Tudor, *Journey to the Vanished City: The Search for a Lost Tribe of Israel* (Vintage Books, New York, 2000).

——, *The Lost Tribes of Israel* (Weidenfeld and Nicholson, London, 2002).

——, *The Thirteenth Gate: Travels Among the Lost Tribes of Israel* (Weidenfeld and Nicolson, London, 1987).

Parry, N. E., *The Lakhers* (Tribal Research Institute, Aizawl, 1976, first printing 1928).

Parry, N. E., *A Monograph on Lushai Custom and Ceremonies* (Tribal Research Institute, Aizawl, 1988, first printing 1928).

Pirenne, Jacqueline, *La Légende du Prêtre Jean* (Presse Universitaire de Strasbourg, 1992).

Pudaite, Rochunga, *The Education of the Hmar People* (Navana Printing Works, Calcutta, 1963).

Quirin, James, *The Evolution of the Ethiopian Jews: A History of the Beta Israel (Falasha) to 1920* (University of Pennsylvania Press, Philadelphia, 1992).

Rapoport, Louis, *The Lost Jews: Last of the Ethiopian Falashas* (Stein & Day, New York, 1980).

Ross, James R., *Fragile Branches: Travels Through the Jewish Diaspora* (Riverhead Books, New York, 2000).

Roth, Cecil, *Nephew of the Almighty* (London, 1933).

Salamon, Hagar, *The Hyena People: Ethiopian Jews in Christian Ethiopia* (University of California Press, Berkeley, 1999).

Samra, Myer, "Judaism in Manipur and Mizoram — a By-Product of the Christian Missions," (Aizawl Seminar Papers, Aizawl, 1992).

Scholem, Gershom, *Sabbetai Sevi: The Mystical Messiah, 1626–1676* (Princeton University Press, 1973).

Segal, Ariel, *Jews of the Amazon: Self-Exile in Paradise* (The Jewish Publication Society, Philadelphia, 1999).

Segal, J. B., *An History of the Jews of Cochin* (Vallentine Mitchell, London, 1993).

Sen, Sipra, *Tribes of Mizoram: Description, Ethnology, and Bibliography* (Gyan Publishing House, New Delhi, 1992).

Shakespear, J., *The Lushei Kuki Clans* (Tribal Research Institute, Aizawl, 1988, first printing 1912).

Shapiro, Sidney, *Jews in Old China: Studies by Chinese Scholars* (Hippocrene Books, New York, 1984).

Shaw, William, *The Thadou Kukis* (Cultural Publishing House, New Delhi, 1983, first printing 1929).

Shtull-Trauring, Simcha (ed.), *Letters from Beyond the Sambatyon: The Myth of the Ten Lost Tribes* (Maxima Press, Israel, 1995).

Stack, Edward, *The Mikirs* (ed. Sir Charles Lyell, Guwahati).

Stein, R. A., *Tibetan Civilization* (Stanford University Press, Palo Alto, 1972).

Tadmor, H., *The Inscriptions of Tiglath-Pileser III, King of Assyria* (Israel Academy of Sciences and Humanities, Jerusalem, 1994).

Torrance, Thomas, "The History, Customs, and Religion of the Ch'iang, An Aboriginal People of West China" (*Shanghai Mercury*, 1920).

———, *China's First Missionaries: Ancient Israelites* (Thynne & Co., London, 1937).

Vaynshtok, Moshe Ya'ir (Hebrew), "The Twelve Tribes of Israel" (Metivta Torat Hesed, Jerusalem, 1956).

Verghese C. G., and Thanzawna, R. L., *A History of the Mizos* (2 vols, Vikas Publishing House, New Delhi, 1997).

Vumson, *Zo History* (Aizawl, 1984).

Walker, Anthony, *Mvuh Hpa Mi Hpa, Creating Heaven, Creating Earth: An Epic Myth of the Yahu People in Yunnan* (Silkworm Books, Bangkok, 1995).

Wolff, Joseph, *Narrative of a Mission to Bokhara* (London, 1845).

Woodthorpe, R. G., *The Lushai Expedition, 1871–1872* (Tribal Research Institute, Aizawl, 1978, first printing 1873).

World of the Bible Encyclopedia (Hebrew, Davidson-Iti, Tel Aviv).

Yehoshua-Raz, Benzion (Hebrew), "From the Lost Tribes in Afghanistan to the Mashhad Jewish Converts of Iran" (The Bialik Institute, Jerusalem, 1992).

Younger, K. Lawson, "The Deportations of the Israelites" (*Journal of Biblical Literature*, Vol. 117/2, 1998, pp. 201–227).

Zaithanchhungi, *Israel-Mizo Identity* (Aizawl, 1990).

Zetlaoui, Monique, *Shalom India: Histoire des communautés juives en Inde* (Imago, Paris, 2000).